ISBN 978-90-819840-9-6

Published by R&P, The Netherlands

Edition III.TC1. First Printing. This is the Hardcover Print Edition.

ISBN PDF: 978-90-819840-8-9
ISBN hardcover: 978-90-819840-9-6
Contact info: info@masteringarchimate.com

Mastering ArchiMate

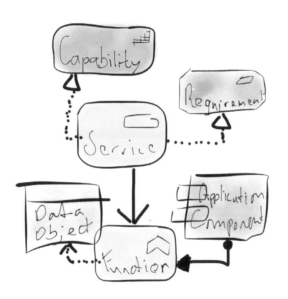

Edition III.TC1

Praise

Forewords

In the 15 years since its inception, the ArchiMate language for enterprise architecture modeling has come a long way. I have had the privilege of being part of its development from the start, first as project manager of the R&D project that developed the language, a collaboration of the Dutch Telematica Instituut and its partners, and later, after it was transferred to The Open Group in 2008, by leading the team that further developed and extended the standard.

Over the years, the popularity of ArchiMate has grown tremendously, supported by an increasing number of useful resources. Gerben's book has been one such resource and is of great value to anyone who wants to use ArchiMate in practice. The book gives an in-depth analysis and explanation of the language, complemented by many useful examples, modeling patterns and working practices. It goes beyond a mere explanation of ArchiMate, but also provides excellent insights in more general considerations of architecture and design.

The discipline of Enterprise Architecture is evolving, and ArchiMate has evolved with it. Since version 1, we have added concepts for expressing the rationale behind architectures, for describing how their implementation is planned and executed, for relating architectures to business strategy, and for modeling the physical world (something often overlooked by architects with an IT background). This has also served to align ArchiMate with other architecture approaches such as TOGAF and BIZBOK.

Now this book of course offers Gerben's personal perspective on ArchiMate, and we don't always agree. But the ArchiMate community is a big tent and the language can be used for many more things than it was designed for. As a self-confessed 'ArchiMate fanboy', he is nonetheless critical of what he sees as weaknesses in the language, and rightly so. Several of his past suggestions for improvement have been included in the current version of the language.

Next to the team who originally developed ArchiMate, Gerben is probably the most knowledgeable expert on the language, and the book you are now reading condenses much of this expertise. Where the *ArchiMate Specification* contains the formal definition of the language and the book *Enterprise Architecture at Work* describes the background of its design, *Mastering ArchiMate* provides you with the perspective of what I would call a 'rigorous practitioner'. All self-respecting enterprise architects should have these three next to each other on their bookshelves.

Marc Lankhorst

Managing Consultant & Chief Technology Evangelist
BiZZdesign
Enschede, The Netherlands, August 2017

I discovered ArchiMate in mid 2011 while trying to find a standard notation for architecture that would go beyond UML. I decided to read the official standard, which (in my opinion) is much easier to digest than the UML one. Despite being easy to understand, the ArchiMate standard itself wasn't of any help to start practicing (it contains descriptions of elements and relationships but it doesn't provide guidance). So I started a quest for information and examples…

I must admit that the small number of articles or blog posts about ArchiMate worried me. But, one day, I discovered Gerben's blog and my quest ended. In a short amount of time, thanks to Gerben's insightful posts, I was able to really understand key concepts, and I finally had examples of real ArchiMate use. Almost a year after having discovered ArchiMate, I was finally able to understand and use ArchiMate, just in time for a big and exciting company project for which architecture description was a key success factor.

Then the first edition of this book was published. Based on my experience with the blog, I expected much from it, and I was not disappointed: the book was presenting ArchiMate the right way, allowing people without any prior knowledge to understand it in a few days. It enabled me to quickly train my colleagues. Plenty of examples were already included, helping me and my team to quickly provide value, thanks to ArchiMate.

The title — *Mastering* ArchiMate — sounds exaggerated. How many books are there that promise you to 'master' something, while at the end you've barely learnt anything? But in this case it is real.

Together with *Enterprise Architecture at Work* by Marc Lankhorst, *Mastering ArchiMate* is the book that any serious Enterprise Architect should possess, to learn ArchiMate fast. This clearly is the kind of book that changes your practice as it also provides insightful comments about the standard itself, its limitations and how to overcome them. In this third edition, *Mastering ArchiMate* covers all new concepts and domains of ArchiMate 3. It also provides numerous new or improved examples that will certainly echo several of your needs (virtualization, DevOps…).

This is the book that has had the largest influence on my career. Without it I would not have learnt ArchiMate the right way, and I certainly would not have joined The Open Group ArchiMate Forum. I recommend it to everyone that joins an ArchiMate training: a training helps you for a week, but this book helps you for years.

Jean-Baptiste Sarrodie

Vice-Chair of the ArchiMate Forum
Enterprise Architect at Arismore, part of Accenture
Paris, France, August 2017

Table of Contents

Table of Contents

Introduction

Introduction

1. Why This Book?

This book grew out of the desire to share the things I learned over the course of several years with respect to seriously employing the ArchiMate® Enterprise Architecture Modeling language. As Lead Enterprise Architect, working for the Asset Management unit of one of the largest Fiduciary Managers in the world, I introduced the use of ArchiMate in 2010, because it seemed to me — for a variety of reasons — the only reasonable choice for our modeling in the line of our Enterprise Architecture work. The choice was based on an estimate of the practicality of the language, and I grew very satisfied with how it worked in daily practice. This practice included — next to models for projects and target architectures — the maintenance of a single very large (tens of thousands of objects and relations) 'current state' model of our enterprise, built along strict guidelines and used for analysis, reporting and as source for other systems, as well as use for future state and project architectures. The scope and detail of our modeling taught us very valuable lessons about ArchiMate modeling, which I have shared in the various editions of this book: Edition I in 2012 (ArchiMate 1) and Edition II in 2014 (ArchiMate 2). Now that ArchiMate 3.0.1 (a bug-fix release for version 3.0) has been released, it is time for a new Edition, which is based on ArchiMate 3.

When we started using ArchiMate, I decided to stick almost religiously to the official definitions and not think or talk about diverging until we had a reasonable body of experience. After all, only when you have enough experience are you capable of really estimating the effect of the choices you have when changing the language. We still stay very close to what ArchiMate prescribes to this day, even if the depth of our experience has led me to some criticism and improvement proposals (see Chapter "Discussing ArchiMate" on page 207).

This book also grew out of the desire to provide a better introduction than what was available at the time. What was available was often pretty limited in scope and in my opinion sometimes even damaging in its explanations, as it would not teach the things to become a *good* modeler in ArchiMate. At best they would teach you some random patterns without for instance learning the pitfalls of those patterns. No introduction I had seen explained the language well enough and I did not see introductions that actually prepared you for sizable modeling work. This was certainly true also of the official certifying courses and training, which generally taught you only to reproduce the standard.

This book intends to do three things:

- Give a decent initial introduction in the concepts and relations that make up the language;

- Present a number of patterns and uses that may be useful when modeling in the language;

- Give enough content so you can develop a feel for the language.

The latter means that you will find some pretty deep and arcane discussions and examples in this book, here and there. These are not meant as practical examples to follow, but they are there because thinking about at the 'edges of practicality' improves your choice and understanding of practical solutions.

In the end, understanding is about being able to *apply* what you know. Understanding is know *how*, not know *what*. If you master the use of something, you understand something. Hence: *Mastering* ArchiMate.

1.1 Uncle Ludwig

Here and there, partly for fun, you will find references to an 'Uncle Ludwig'. Uncle Ludwig stands for the twentieth century philosopher Ludwig Wittgenstein, whom some characterize as the most important analytic philosopher (as opposed to, say, moral philosopher) to date. Wittgenstein in his entire philosophical life concentrated on 'meaning'. His result came in two parts. The first part in his youth, where he tried to build meaning on top of logic. The results were limited (but sadly had the most influence in the computer science discipline of all of his work). Later in life he tried to answer what meaning then was for all the rest of what we say, where logic does not give you the definitive answer. He came up with the solution 'meaning lies hidden in correct use'. Given that ArchiMate is in part a service- (and thus use-) oriented language, this maxim is useful here and there. Actually, I find the maxim extremely useful for work even beyond modeling, e.g. wondering about the actual use of documents sheds light about their meaning.

If you want to know more about Wittgenstein, I suggest "Wittgenstein's Place in 20th Century Analytical Philosophy" by P.M.S. Hacker. Wittgenstein has been misinterpreted by many (e.g. when people misinterpret him as having stated that "meaning is *equivalent* to use"). Hacker not only understands Wittgenstein (he has written extensive and insightful analyses) but he also can explain it rather well. Wittgenstein often sounds daunting to people, but in my experience it can be pretty practical.

2. Enterprise Architecture

So you're working in an organization. The organization consists of many people, organized in organizational structure, in groups, departments and sections, and — if large enough— business units or even separate companies. If you look at what these people do, you look at business functions — say, 'after-sales' — or business processes — say 'handling a warranty claim from a customer'. These business functions and processes are a way to look at the behavior of your organization.

Now, these days, you have computers to support your work. You might not look at them anymore as computers (e.g. the iPhone or iPad you are reading a book on), but they are. And if your work is not shoe repair, plumbing, building, etc., your work will involve handling information. And even if it *is* shoe repair, the informational aspects of your work (planning, billing, accounting, etc.) are supported by IT. You *use* IT in the line of your work. The IT that supports people also has structure and behavior, just like the business itself. You use *applications*, and these 'running' applications have *functions* (i.e. behavior) and deliver *services* (support) to the business process. The applications themselves need an IT infrastructure to 'run', maybe large servers, maybe just your laptop or iPhone (where the applications are called 'Apps'), and there have to be all kinds of networks so all these systems can communicate with each other.

And not only is there IT that supports people, some of it operates *independently*. Software that runs robots in a factory. Web sites that completely handle the customer's interactions.

For about half a century now, the information revolution has moved most data from paper and other non-electronic media to IT systems, even the data that eventually is printed on paper. Not a multimedia, but a *unimedia* revolution has taken place: from all kinds of different storage and transport media, the information has been digitized and been moved to being small electrically charged or magnetized spots, each of these spots representing a single yes/no choice: a bit. We hardly think about that level, but we all know what a *file* is these days, and generally we do not think of the paper original that the term originally stood for.

And next to much of the *stuff* of business, the *behavior* of business has also become more and more digitized. And even our physical products have sometimes felt the result. Mass customization (the fact that you can have both scale and variation in production) is possible because we have computers handling all the diversity.

In large organizations, all these applications and files that support (or even are) the business have become an almost impossible to control, complex landscape, where many things can and do go wrong and where change is fraught with peril. Because changing something here will crash something somewhere else over there, in a landscape that is one big web of dependencies of business and IT. And even if that was not the case, translating business strategy and requirements to the right IT-support, or using IT-innovations to improve your business are difficult. Because, contrary to popular belief and partly as a result of that inertia-building web of dependencies, IT does *not* change fast. Mostly because its rigid logic lacks the flexibility of human compensating behavior. Building a new office is generally a process that takes less time than implementing (let alone building and/or implementing) a new core IT system.

This web of objects (physical and virtual products, bank accounts, bills, roles and actors, applications, data, servers, files, networks, etc.) and relations between them is what Enterprise Architecture is about. It is about the design of your business and the IT that supports it. It is about having the right business organization, having the right IT for your business and letting the business innovate, now and in the future. Especially, it is meant to lead to better IT choices, because, as stated above, (the complex landscape made possible by) IT is often more difficult to change than the stuff humans do. Humans are flexible. Digital computers have enabled a landscape full of brittle dependencies that shows many forms of inertia: resistance to change. But change is what we want and need.

The appearance of Enterprise Architects in this field is relatively recent. Not too long ago, if you would try to find that role you would end up looking at an organizations management. 'The' Architect of an 'enterprise' is its manager. He or she finally decides on how the business is organized, how it is run and what IT is implemented. But the field has become complex enough that a special function has appeared: the (Enterprise) Architect. The management has in fact outsourced the (rough) design of its solutions to a specialized function, whose task it is to handle all that complexity. Here at least is already one important point: Enterprise Architecture should be the responsibility of (organizational *management* of) the business, not of the IT provider. It is meant to help management make fundamental decisions, not leave them to someone else with some requirements and then say "make it so".

Now, the Enterprise Architecture function has proliferated and also fragmented. There are now business architects, security architects, application architects, data architects, information architects, integration architects, enterprise architects, infrastructure architects, domain architects, IT architects, solution architects, integration architects, the list seems endless. And to make matters worse: the same job name may mean quite something different depending on whom and where you ask for the definition. What one company calls a business architect, the other company calls an enterprise architect or a lead architect and what one company calls an enterprise architect another may call information architect, etc.

So, I am going to lay out my own definition and fragmentation of Enterprise Architecture. First, in line with the Enterprise Architecture modeling language ArchiMate, I divide Enterprise Architecture into the following (ad hoc) practical *perspectives*:

- Business Perspective (processes, roles, abstract business objects such as 'account', etc.)
- IT ('virtual') Perspective (IT systems, data, programs, IT integration, data transport, etc.)
- Physical Perspective (physical goods, tools, transport, hardware, etc.)

These perspectives are tightly linked.

Enterprise Architecture for me has nothing to do with the organizational unit (department, business unit, project) that the architect has as his *domain*, but everything with the fact that he or she is architect on all *perspectives*: business, information, application, data, physical, infrastructure. *Enterprise Architecture is about the coherent design and modeling of all perspectives*. For me, a Solution Architecture is also Enterprise Architecture, because the subject is also a domain, and thus an 'enterprise' in itself.

Today, these perspective are often called layers, as if the business layer sits on top of an application layer which sits on top of a physical world. This BDAT stack has long permeated Enterprise Architecture thinking, because Enterprise Architecture was born from the problem of managing the complexity of many IT systems getting interconnected, and at that time, the stack was real enough: people used applications, applications used 'hardware'. Those simple days have gone.

I do recognize specialization of architects from a perspective: a Business Architect is concerned with the business perspective and an Infrastructure Architect with the IT-infrastructure perspective. Some call these layers 'domains' as well, but I find that confusing. I reserve domains for recognizable divisions of the organization, such as departments, business functions or projects. So, for me, a Domain Architect is an Enterprise Architect within a certain domain.

If enterprise in 'Enterprise Architect' does not denote organizational level, how do we then call the chief enterprise architect of the organization? My favorite job name for such a function is 'Lead Enterprise Architect' (and he or she should fulfill (amongst other things) a role comparable to that of the 'Lead Legal Counsel').

You can forget all of this, except for one thing: in the context of ArchiMate, 'Enterprise Architecture' says nothing about being in the top of the organization, but about the fact that an 'enterprise' is a coherent landscape that can be divided in business, application and technology layers (or very roughly: people, software and hardware) and Enterprise Architecture is about *all* of them.

A second division, is often made in our field: a division between 'architects' and 'designers'. For me, there is no fundamental difference between the two: both are forms of design and the only difference is the level of detail they are concerned with. Leaving out details is not to be taken lightly, though. It is one of the most difficult aspects of Enterprise Architecture. In my view, an Enterprise Architect is concerned with all details, but sparingly goes into those details. Architecture is (in part) "the art of leaving out *irrelevant* details". Leaving out details, sadly, often derails into religiously ignoring details. The key word, however, is 'irrelevant': as the Chinese proverb says: people stumble over molehills, not over mountains. An architect consciously leaves out details that he or she has decided are irrelevant to the decisions to be made.

In the early 90's, I had to follow a basic course on safety when working as a contractor for Shell. Here I learned a very valuable lesson: working safely is not about *avoiding* risks, it is about *consciously taking acceptable* risks. There is no such thing as *not* taking risks. For me, the same applies for abstraction in design. *Abstraction* is not about *ignoring* detail, it is about *consciously leaving out* detail. And luckily, as we will see later, ArchiMate is equipped for that, as it has a mechanism that supports having coherent detailed and non-detailed views of the same model.

There is a third division one can make in Enterprise Architecture. Basically, an organization can use architecture in the following three settings:

The Current-State (or As-Is or IST) architecture. This is a descriptive model of how the current landscape of business and IT is. It can be used for reporting (e.g. to regulators) and analysis;

The Future-State (or To-Be or SOLL) architecture. This is a (rough) prescription on how the future landscape should be. It generally consists of both high level models and guidelines or requirements for the more detailed work done in the line of moving towards the intended state;

Change architectures. These are the descriptions of what Change initiatives like projects will produce. A common form is a Project (Start) Architecture or a Solution Architecture (this is also true when working in an Agile methodology, both 'up-front design' and 'agile' require (a good documentation of) a good architecture). Like the Future-State, these are a combination of models and requirements, but the detail should generally be comparable to the Current-State as the Change initiative actually results in a very specific change of that Current-State.

Enterprise Architecture is in the end about:

- Making good *choices* in the light of the strategic goals and positions of your enterprise;
- Making coherent *choices* across your enterprise
- Making good *choices* in themselves (e.g. in sense of total cost of ownership, etc.)

In all of these, modeling your existing state and your choices in ArchiMate can be really helpful.

2.1 Where are the principles and guidelines?

You might wonder, with all this talk about modeling: where are my architecture principles and guidelines that architecture is all about and that guide development for instance? I can say this about it here:

There are many definitions of what Enterprise Architecture is. The widely quoted ISO/IEC/IEEE 42010 standard, for instance, defines (system) architecture as

> *fundamental concepts or properties of a system in its environment embodied in its elements, relationships, and in the principles of its design and evolution*

There are two aspects: the *design itself* (elements, relationships) and the *principles of design*. This book is about the first aspect. I know many Enterprise Architects who are of the opinion that it is all about the second aspect. I could not agree less, and hence my approach to Enterprise Architecture is above all about the *actual* Business-IT landscape decisions that have to be made and the design of the next step in the perpetual change. Whether the use of principles and guidelines is a good way to come to such decisions is a question that is outside the scope of this book. It is one of the subjects of my other book: Chess and the Art of Enterprise Architecture.

2.2 The Why, the How and the What

There is another issue that needs clarification, related to the previous ones. As remarked above, many Enterprise Architects are of the opinion that Enterprise Architecture is all about the *why* of choices (strategy, translated to what and how), or in other words: about *intentions*. Now, I consider the why important, but for me — though the context of a design is very important — it is not part of that design, and the idea that it makes sense to model the why is questionable. Modeling your strategy and intentions (in ArchiMate called motivation) may be useful, but it is also naive: the complex, contradictory almost quantum-like nature of our intentions cannot practically be caught in a couple of simple models with a few boxes and arrows depicting influences. That is not to say that it cannot be useful to create a couple of visualizations that support a certain message.

Still, this book is mostly about using ArchiMate to model the actual enterprise, not its intentions, though some attention is paid to that subject and the basics are explained. As thus it is about using ArchiMate for Solution Architecture and Enterprise Architecture, and the discussion about what is the difference will be left to the audience.

And importantly: if at any point while reading this book you get the feeling "why am I looking at diagrams of arcane (technological) details of some sort of deployment or some sort of business?", remember: the book is not about teaching you those (maybe for you irrelevant) details, it is about teaching you ArchiMate (even if in the course of that it might also need to address context, such as explaining blockchain before showing diagrams about Bitcoin (Section 27.7)).

2.3 Disclaimer

I have to warn you: in case you did not know: you almost can't learn anything from a book (the exception being do-books like Bobby Fisher's *Chess Lessons*). The only way to learn something is by *doing* it (which is why Bobby Fisher's book is an exception as it centers around doing all the time). Knowledge is about 'know how' not about 'know what'. It's funny that — while being convinced of this — I have written a *book* to teach ArchiMate. But anyway, *you won't really learn ArchiMate from this book*, you need to seriously *use* the language to really learn it. But if you do that, this book is meant to help you out and speed you up. Writing the book, by the way, is almost (but not quite) as much fun as teaching a class (and educational in itself).

3. Gratitude

I am very grateful for the assistance of the following people:

- First and foremost: Jos Knoops, colleague at APG, who has been an invaluable sparring partner from 2010 to 2014 when discussing how we would be using ArchiMate, e.g. patterns;
- Former APG colleagues Joost Melsen, Floris Hack, and APG colleague Paul Hamers for more real world pattern discussions between 2011 and 2014;
- Leon Joosten, former colleague at APG and my then-time manager, who supported me at APG when I wanted to introduce ArchiMate to the organization in 2009.

Without that opportunity I would not have been able to gather the experience to be able to fill this book;

- Peter Spiers of Adobe Forums, who helped me get started with Adobe InDesign and helped me solve serious issues in my first attempts at the document in 2012 and later in 2014, and without whose help, I would not have had a tool to produce this book at all;
- Marc Lankorst, the 'father of ArchiMate' and Jean-Baptiste Sarrodie, the Vice-Chair of the ArchiMate Forum, for their blush-inducing forewords on page 5.

- Steven Bradley for providing me with around a thousand linguistic fixes, improvements and suggestions.

- And of course, last, but certainly not least: my family, who — while I was writing — have carried the burden of the fact that I was writing and thus had less time to do my chores and be a sunny, active part of family life.

4. License & Legal

This book comes in four different versions:

- A hardcover version distributed via normal channels for printed books (ISBN 978-90-819840-9-6);

- A full electronic version (PDF) that is restricted (printing not allowed) and stamped (ISBN 978-90-819840-8-9);

- An syntax excerpt electronic version (PDF) containing only the basic introduction to the language.

You can contact me at the following e-mail address:

info@masteringarchimate.com

Heerlen, The Netherlands,
Gerben Wierda

5. Release Notes for Edition III.TC1

August 2017:

-  In a few places I've used Donald Knuth's 'dangerous bend' image from The T$_E$X Book (here shown on the left) to warn you that it gets a bit complicated. It's a way to show my respect for Knuth's work and to express my deep felt wish[*] it would have been feasible to do this book in T$_E$X (if only because in my experience InDesign is slow and corrupts documents easily, i.e. has been poorly engineered).

- ArchiMate 3 was released in June 2016. It has taken more than a year to update Edition II to Edition III.TC1. There were some personal reasons (this is done in my spare time, of which I had little); I write from actual experience, and I needed to build that experience; and ArchiMate 3.0 was seriously broken (mostly the formally allowed relations table was broken and it was often unclear which relations were allowed and which not). I wrote about that in January 2017 on my blog and I had to wait until ArchiMate 3.0.1 (Technical Corrigendum 1, or TC1[†]) was released before I was certain my book would be correct.

- The numbering of diagrams is imperfect. Often higher numbers appear before lower ones. I have not found a way to do this properly in InDesign.

- Section 30 "A Possible Linking of BPMN and Archi-Mate" on page 164 is partly still based on ArchiMate 2 limitations, as my tool has stopped supporting the BPMN-ArchiMate linkage that was developed in it. The parts that could be different in ArchiMate 3 are colored in magenta.

- In several places I have left the term 'infrastructure' for the IT part of what is since ArchiMate 3 called the technology layer (and which supports physical technology next to digital technology) in place (though all elements are named properly). This is intentional, as infrastructure is a common term for that part of IT.

- Given that I have some room to spare: this book could not have been produced in the time that took without the music via/of King Crimson, (early) Gentle Giant, Camille Saint-Saëns, Edvard Grieg, Reinhard Mey, Jethro Tull, Studio Brussel, Pjotr Ilitsch Tschaikovsky, Georg Friedrich Händel, Simeon Ten Holt, Braak, (early) Allan Parsons Project, Pink Floyd, Alquin, Count Basie Orchestra, Philip Glass, (later) The Beatles, (early) DeWolff, ELP, Frank Zappa, Jean-Michel Jarre, Joe Satriani, Johann Sebastian Bach, Mike Oldfield, Muse, Sergei Prokofiev, The Police, Red Hot Chili Peppers, Renato Carrosone, Stromae, Alfred Brendel, several soul songs, and many/much more...

---

[*]   And not just because I received a TUG Award once. I truly love T$_E$X's output quality, stability (boy, do I miss that), and logical writing through a macro package

[†]   Hence "Mastering ArchiMate Edition III.TC1"

ArchiMate Basics

6. An ArchiMate Map

ArchiMate has over the years become a rich environment that covers many aspects of modeling in Enterprise Architecture. It started out as a simple language to model information-heavy enterprises, focused on modeling the relation between 'the Business' and 'IT'. In version 3 it covers a lot more. From modeling the strategy of an enterprise to the modeling of physical processes. The old core of ArchiMate 1 is still there, and it is appropriately called the 'core language'. It is what you use to model an actual enterprise: its processes, roles, actors, IT, physical equipment and facilities and so forth. This part of ArchiMate is about modeling *the enterprise itself*, as it is, as it should be, as it could be, whatever you need to express in your model.

As of version 3 of the language, ArchiMate now also has a part that is meant to model *the strategy of the enterprise*. It contains elements such as capability and resource. The language sees strategy as something that can be realized by 'the enterprise itself', it is thus seen as some sort of abstraction. We will get to the finer points about thinking about abstraction (and recursion) later.

As of version 2 of the language, ArchiMate has a part that is about modeling *the change of the enterprise*. Here we find elements to express (project) work packages, (architectural) plateaus, identified gaps that need to be filled, deliverables (of projects) and so forth. Though meant to model change of 'the enterprise itself', it can easily also be used to model changes of the 'strategy of the enterprise', e.g. we might model a deliverable that realizes a Capability.

Finally, also as of version 2, ArchiMate has a part that is about *intentions* which consists of elements such as requirement, goal, driver, stakeholder, et cetera. Though originally meant as a part that is used to model the intentions of the *architecture* of 'the enterprise itself', it can as easily be used to model intentions of 'the enterprise itself' or the intentions of 'the strategy of the enterprise' or the intentions of the 'change of the enterprise'. In fact, Mastering ArchiMate Edition II, the previous version of this book, only used them to model risk & security in relation to 'the enterprise itself'. All of these parts are shown in View 1.

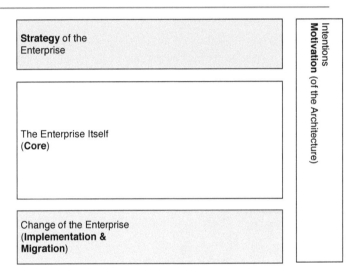

View 1. *The ArchiMate Map — Rough*

This book focuses on the ArchiMate Core, *the enterprise itself*. The main reason for this is that it is there that we encounter the complexities that make modeling actually very useful. Another reason is that I have my doubts that modeling intentions and strategy are actually very useful. Modeling strategy cannot be much more than illustrative for what in reality is a narrative that has many aspects that practically can't be modeled at all in the same way that intelligent behavior cannot be caught in rules. Both intentions and strategy are domains that are far from logical in the real world and trying to map them onto a logical structure (which is what we do when modeling in ArchiMate) will have serious limitations, limitations which turn into 'bewitching ourselves' when we ignore them. Both also tend to invoke with me doubts that stem from being a bit acquainted with analytic philosophy. For the 'change of the enterprise' part of ArchiMate, I doubt if simply adding these to a model is usable and scalable and, again, their practical use might be only illustrative. Here, in my estimate, the main problem is that we do not have tooling yet that is capable of actually using this in a scalable way. For all three parts, small toy-size examples, such as used by consultancy, tool and training providers can be easily created. But having these used in a large-scale complex setup in a way that is actually useful (and thus meaningful) is quite something else. I will pay attention to these parts, enough to give you a good introduction, but I will mainly focus on using ArchiMate to model 'the enterprise itself', using the other parts to strengthen that goal.

7. Main Core Elements and Relations

When modeling Enterprise Architecture, we need a language that knows about the concepts of 'the enterprise itself', and ArchiMate does a good job. To start with, you need to know that almost all of ArchiMate is built from three types of *elements*:

- elements that act: active (structural) elements
- elements that represent the behavior of those 'elements that act': behavioral elements
- elements that cannot act and which are acted upon by that behavior: passive (structural) elements

The three element types, connected by *relations*, can form sentences of sorts. A pickpocket (the application) steals (the application function) a wallet (the data). This is what makes ArchiMate a grammar, although people generally call it a language. The structure of the ArchiMate grammar is partly based on the subject-verb-object pattern from natural language.

Your model is therefore a story of sorts. It tells the reader the basic structure of the story: who acts on what.

Going back to our rough ArchiMate Map, we might add this internal structure as seen in View 3:

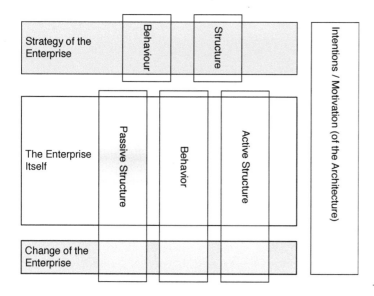

View 3. *The ArchiMate Map - With Aspects*

As you see, there is a slight anomaly here. The *Strategy* part of ArchiMate doesn't have active and passive structure, it just has structure (and only one element in that: Resource (but we'll get to that later).

We're not entirely done yet with mapping ArchiMate. The core of ArchiMate, the part about modeling 'the enterprise itself' has the classic (some would say 'orthodox') B(D)AT

layering common to most enterprise architecture approaches. There are layers, from *Business* (processes, actors, roles and so forth) 'down' to *Application* (application components, application functions, etc.) and *Technology* (computing and other physical infrastructure and objects). So, a complete map would look like this:

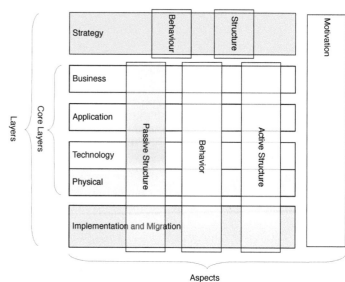

View 4. *The ArchiMate Map — Complete*

The *Motivation* and *Implementation & Migrations* parts were extensions to the Core that first appeared in ArchiMate version 2. With respect to version 2 of ArchiMate, ArchiMate 3 has gotten an extension of the technology layer to model the physical side of the enterprise. This is why I (and others) prefer not to show the physical side as a wholly separate layer.

With all that said, we will now begin to start explaining the elements and relations in all these parts. We will start somewhere in the middle of 'the enterprise itself', specifically at the application & data perspective of classic IT-oriented Enterprise Architecture.

7.1 Application and Business

An application is fully modeled in ArchiMate as seen in View 2.

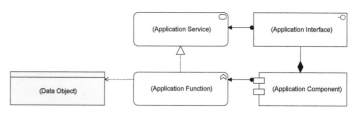

View 2. *The Basic Application Pattern*

This is possibly the first snippet of ArchiMate you have ever encountered, and it already has five element types and four relation types, so we are going to take our time to describe it.

Roughly, the two yellow and two blue elements in the image together make up the 'application' and the green element is the data the application operates on; i.e. think of it as the blue and yellow elements representing the word processing application and the green element representing the document being edited*. The lower three elements represent the *internals* of the application (blue & yellow) and the data (green). The two upper elements represent how the application can be used by and is visible for (exposed to) a 'user', the *externals*.

One of the most essential aspects of ArchiMate is that modeling the behavior is separated from modeling the structure. The blue elements in the figure represent the active structure ('who') and the yellow elements represent the behavioral aspects of the 'who' elements — they are two sides of the same coin: in a certain sense one can't exist without the other.

It seems rather excessive that you need four elements to model a single application. We will later see that you can simplify this, even to a single one of these elements, but for the moment it is very important to understand what the underlying structure looks like. Actually, the lack of addressing this in documents and courses I have seen, has been a major reason for writing this book. An understanding of the foundation is required to model *well* in ArchiMate.

Having said that, here is a short explanation of the 5 element types in View 2:

This is an Application Component. It stands for the 'actor' that an application in your Enterprise Architecture landscape actually is. It is one side of the coin of which the Application Function (its behavior) is the other.

This is an Application Function. It stands for the behavior of the Application Component, how the application can act. It is one side of the coin of which Application Component is the other.

Application Component and its behavior are, in a way, inseparable. You cannot have an actor that does not act unless the actor is dead, and in that case it should not appear in your architecture. And without magic, you cannot have an act without an actor. Again, later we will see how to leave things out of our views and models, but for now we stick to the details.

This is a Data Object. It is what the Application Function acts upon. The Application Function might create, read, write, update or delete the Data Object. Conceivably, the Data Object

might not be needed; you can imagine behavior that does not access a passive element. You can also imagine that you do not model Data Objects that only exist *inside* your application. Not every variable in the application code is modeled. But as soon as the Data Object is visible to other parts of your landscape, or when it is persistent, it could be there. Generally, that means we generally only model (semi-)persistent Data Objects. Note: this is not the file or the database itself — those are represented on a lower level: the Technology level. We are still one abstraction level up. To illustrate the difference: an RTF file (technology) can be both an MS Word Data Object or an Apple TextEdit.app Data Object, depending on which application is used to access it.

Two elements in the image have not been explained yet. They have to do with how the application is used/seen (by the business or by other applications):

This is an Application Interface. It stands for the route via which the application offers itself to the business or to other applications. Note: both separate concepts (used by people and used by other applications) are supported by this one element. One example would be a Graphical User Interface (GUI), but it can as well be an Application Programming Interface (API), a Web Service or one of the many other ways an application offers itself to other 'actors' in your landscape. Given that difference in use (and thus, as Uncle Ludwig would say, meaning), it is unlikely that the same interface will be used by both a human or another application. But it can be; e.g., in the case of a Command Line Interface (CLI) used by a scheduler system. Application Interface is a 'handle' of the 'actor' that is the Application Component. It is one side of a coin of which Application Service is the other.

This is an Application Service. It stands for the 'visible' behavior of the Application, how the Application Interface can act *for a user*. It is one side of the coin of which Application Interface is the other side. Here again, the service may be 'technical' in that it is offered by one application to other applications or it may be part of your Business-IT integration: services offered to business processes (behavior of humans). The same type of element is used for both. This, by the way is a common first hurdle for architects coming from the engineering side, where it is common to define 'application service' as 'service provided by an application and *used by another application*' and define 'business service' as a 'service provided by an application that is *used by the business*'. In ArchiMate, a business service is something else, which we will see below.

---

* ArchiMate is color-neutral. Color has no grammatical meaning. Most tooling use a 'layered' default color setup. I use a matrix based on the original ArchiMate 1 default coloring which stresses the difference between active/passive structure and behavior. See Section 14.4 "Using color" on page 60. I've found this choice to be easier for communication (and thus education, i.e. this book) but your mileage may vary.

Now, apart from the elements, there are relations between the elements. There are four in the initial image:

⇐⋯⋯⋯⋯ This is the Access relation. The access relation always depicts a behavioral element accessing a passive element. Here it depicts the behavior of the application (the Application Function) accessing a passive data element (the Data Object — something that in the end generally resides in a file or a database). An arrowhead (on either side) is optional and it may depict read access or write access (e.g. two for read/write).

◆━━━ This is the Composition relation. It means that the element at the end with the diamond is the *parent* of the element on the other end and that the child *cannot exist independently* from the parent. The relation depicts the composition of larger wholes out of smaller parts, but it does not mean the set of children modeled must be necessarily complete in your model: there may be parts that are not modeled. This relation could also for instance be used to show that an Application Component has various subcomponents.

⋯⋯⋯▷ This is the Realization relation. This has two types of use in ArchiMate. Here it means that the element at the end without the arrowhead is the element that 'creates' the element at the end with an arrowhead: the application's internal functionality realizes a service, which is the externally usable functionality of the application.

◀━━● This is the Assignment relation. This also has more than one meaning in ArchiMate. Here, it means that the side with the dot (the active element) *performs* the behavior that is the behavioral element on the side with the arrow head.

Important and possibly initially confusing aspects of ArchiMate are thus that — while we have multiple elements (structural and behavioral) representing what is in the mind of many a single thing (an application or an application interface) — we also have single elements (and as we will later see, relations) that can be used with multiple meanings. When you get the hang of it, everything becomes pretty natural just like it is with natural language, but if you are looking for a strictly disjunct (made of independent concepts) approach to a modeling language (e.g., like a programming language or like UML), it might be confusing in the beginning.

Having modeled an application, we can turn to modeling the way this application is used by the business. And before that, we need to look at the way the business & information layer of Enterprise Architecture is modeled in ArchiMate. Luckily, it looks a lot like what we saw in the application

layer so it is easy to understand now and it can be seen in View 6.

I have left out the actual human actor — the one that fulfills the Business Role — for now to stress the equality between this pattern and the one about the application in View 2 on page 18. It looks quite the same and that is not a coincidence. The relations are the same as with the application image above. The new element types are:

This is the Business Role. The Business Role is an 'actor' in ArchiMate, but it is slightly more complicated than that, because it is an abstract sort of actor based on 'being responsible for certain behavior'. The real actors are people and departments and such. ArchiMate has an element type for those as well, but we leave that for later. Business Roles can perform Business Processes, just like Application Components can perform Application Functions.

This is the Business Process. It stands for a set of causally-related activities that together realize services or create something. Roles can be assigned to a Business Process, they perform the process, just as the Application Component performs the Application Function. Just as in the application layer, a Business Process cannot exist without a Business Role (which does not mean you must model both, I am talking about the reality you are modeling), they are two sides of the same coin. We also have Business Function, but we leave that for later.

This is the Business Object: the (generally) abstract element that is created or used by a Business Process. Think of objects like 'a payment' or 'a bank account' or 'a bill'. Though it is named Business *Object*, it is more like a *Concept*. It may represent non-informational objects as well, e.g. if your company produces steel beams, you may have a 'Steel Beam' Business Object representing the beam itself and not information about the beam.

Again, just as with the application, these elements can make sentences of sorts. The proverbial 'second hand car sales' role performs the 'sell second hand car' process, which

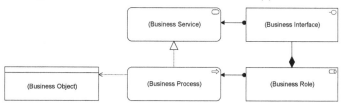

View 6. *Basic Business Process Pattern*

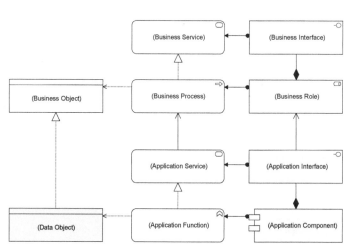

View 5. *Basic Application is used by Basic Business Pattern*

creates a 'bill'. Criminal, crime and — in this case, possibly — proof of crime.

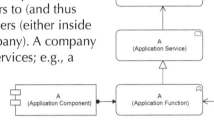 This is the Business Interface: the way the role interacts with others. You can think of it as a 'channel'; e.g., phone, mail, meeting, etc. The interface is the visible manifestation of a role. E.g. if the role is 'help desk agent' the interface might be 'telephone', 'Twitter' or 'web site chat'.

And this is the Business Service: more or less what it is always about in an organization. This is the reason for the existence of the process. This is the service it offers to (and thus can be used by) others (either inside or outside the company). A company might offer many services; e.g., a bank offers at the most abstract level a 'savings' service or a 'loan' service.

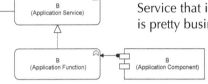

Having set up a couple of basic elements and relations, we can now fill in the missing links. Because on one hand we have the business that offers services to others, on the other hand we may have IT that offers supporting services to the business. Together they look like View 5 on page 20.

The application level is connected to the business level by three relations. On the left we see the already familiar Realization relation (········▷). Here it means that the Data Object realizes the Business Object. In a concrete example: the 'bank account' Business Object may be data (a Data Object) of an accounting application; it is the same item's representation in a different architectural 'layer'. Note: we will get back to 'concrete versus abstract' modeling later.

In the middle and on the right we see a new relation:

◄——— This is the Serving relation. It means that the element at the end without the arrowhead *serves* the element at the end with the arrow head. In previous versions of ArchiMate this relation was called Used By and you will still see this name in many places. The Application Service, for instance, Serves (is used by) the Business Process. The Application Interface (e.g. the Graphical User Interface) Serves the Business Role.

The fact that an Application Interface can serve a Business Role is the 'other side of the coin' of the same Serving relation between Application Service and Business Process. They are twins. Both illustrate the 'service oriented' way that ArchiMate relates one layer to the next as far as actors and their behavior goes.

With what has been explained so far, you can already do much of the modeling you need in terms of Business-IT focused 'Current State' or 'Change/Project' Enterprise Architecture. There are two more things that need to be explained before the basic setup is complete: applications using other applications, and business processes/roles using other business processes/roles. Here again, what happens at business

level and application level is identical, so we are going to illustrate only one.

7.2 The double use of the Serving relation

So far, our example has only shown Serving as a relation *between* levels in your architecture. But the same relation type can also be used *within* a level. The business may use an application, but an application can also be used by another application.

In View 7 you see the same Serving relation (◄———) twice. Once between the 'A' Application Service and the Business Process that uses the 'A' application, and once between the 'B' Application Service and the 'A' Application Function. This means that the 'A' application makes use of the 'B' application. Though the relation is Serving in both cases, it has quite a different role to play. Often, the definition of an Application Service that is used by the Business is pretty business-like in its description, something you discuss with a senior user or a process owner. But the relation between applications is more of a technical nature and you discuss it with application architects. The difference generally shows itself clearly in the types of names and descriptions of the service. It is hard to truly imagine an Application Service that is both used by another application and a Business Process. After all, both uses will be pretty different, unless we are talking about a fully automated business process, which we will handle later.

View 7. An Application Using Another Application

It is good to mention here that 'serving' (or 'used-by' as it was called before) is not unambiguous. If Application A calls a service (API, web service, etc.) of Application B, but it does this to deliver information that Application B needs, who serves whom? Arguments can be made for either direction. We'll get back to this in Section 25.2 "Who is Serving Whom Anyway?" on page 128 when we will discuss the choice of pattern in some more depth. For most of our patterns we will not need a deep discussion.

7.3 Function versus Process

So far, we have modeled business behavior as a Business *Process* and application behavior as an Application *Function*. But ArchiMate actually has two main work horses for behavior in all layers: process *and* function. In terms of the grammar, they are completely identical. They allow for exactly the same relations with other elements. In fact, you could see them as 'convenience types' for a generic 'behavior' element in each layer. For now, as we are doing the superficial introduction, it is best to use the following guidelines:

- You use a process if you are thinking of a causally-related set of behaviors ('activities') that in the end *produce* something, normally a service or an object. Business

Process is thus an outside-in way of dividing up business behavior, based on what the behavior actually *produces*.

- You use a function if you are thinking of a grouping of related behavior based on — for instance — same tools, same skills or same role that performs it. Business Function can thus be seen as an inside-out way of dividing up business behavior, based on what it *is capable of*.

In section 18 "Business Function and Business Process" on page 91 we will look into the difference in the business layer in more depth and see that there is a nice way of combining them both when modeling your business layer.

Business Function looks like this:

And Application Process, as you might expect, looks like this:

We will get into the use of colors later, but as you can see I use colors to separate the aspects (structure, behavior) and intensity to separate the layers (business, application). It suffices to repeat the earlier footnote on page 19 here that ArchiMate is officially colorless. I use these colors because in my experience they really work well.

7.4 Business Actor

Earlier we encountered the Business Role. The Business Role is an abstract sort of actor. But in a business architecture there are of course *real* actors: people, departments, or even business units or companies or maybe regulators. ArchiMate has an element for that: the Business Actor, as seen in context in View 8.

View 8. *Business Actor in Context*

On the left we see the already familiar Business Process to which a Business Role is Assigned. The Business Role *performs* the Business Process. On the right we see the new element type Business Actor, which is Assigned-To the Business Role. This must be read as the Business Actor *fulfills* the (responsibilities of the) Business Role. ArchiMate was designed to be economical with relation types, so it re-uses the relation for a slightly different meaning.

7.5 Adding Technical Infrastructure to the Mix

Just as the Business Process in our current scenario needs the Application Service to be able to be performed, the Application Function needs (IT) infrastructure to run. If we add the infrastructure to the application layer, we get View 9.

There are no new types of relations here, but there are new element types:

 This is the Node. This is a slightly complicated concept in ArchiMate and more details follow later. For now, think of it as a generic piece of IT infrastructure: hardware combined with its system software, where files are stored or applications can run. We'll see the details later.

 This is the Technology Function. Just as with the Application Function and the Application Component, the Technology Function stands for the behavior of the Node. They are two sides of the same coin. As you might guess, there also is a Technology Process, which is the same, just with an 'arrow' icon in its standard visualization.

 This is the Technology Service, the visible behavior of the Node. In many ways, this is what the infrastructure is all about, what it can do for the applications, its reason for existence. This is what the applications need to function. Typical examples of Technology Services are for instance a 'file share' or 'application execution' or a 'database service'. The latter may cause confusion, because you might wonder why that is a *Technology* Service and not for instance something at the *application* level. We'll discuss that in Section 12.7 "Why two types of software?" on page 52, but for now, it is enough to say that the Node comprises both the hardware and the system software. A database system is generally modeled as 'system software' and the database as an Artifact (see below).

This is the Technology Interface. This is not that easy to explain. For Application Interface, one can easily dream up an easy example: the (graphical) user interface. But for the Technology interface, ArchiMate is not very clear; it says it might be best thought of as a kind of contract that the 'user' (the application) has to fulfill. An example would be a protocol, like the SMB or NFS protocol for file sharing and the TCP/IP or UDP/IP ports where the service is offered. Unless you are a dedicated infrastructure architect, you can generally do without this one. I am just mentioning it here to be complete and because leaving

View 9. *Basic Application uses Basic Infrastructure*

it out here would introduce the concept of 'pattern' before it is wise to do so.

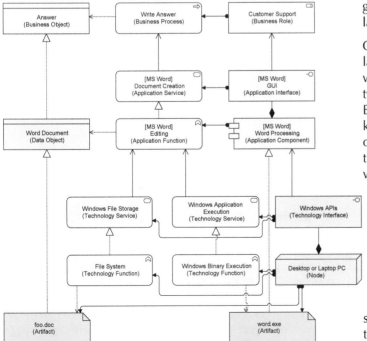

The last new element (for now) is the Artifact. This one is pretty simple. The best example is a file. Another often-used example is the actual database where your application's data resides. Another example is the actual 'executable' (file) also known as 'the binary': what your application is when you look at the 'byte' level. The 'data bytes' Artifact in the model above is the one that realizes the Data Object that is accessed by the Application Function. The 'executable bytes' Artifact forms the bytes (a file, or a set of files often called a 'software distribution') that the system can read and interpret as a program. On the infrastructure level, 'a byte is a byte' in the sense that both passive (Data) elements and active (Application) elements are in the end nothing but a collection of bytes. Deep down, we get to the basic level of zeros and ones (as we should).

The relations are mostly pretty straightforward. The Assignment relations (◄────●) between Node and Artifacts stand for the fact that the Artifacts *resides* on the Node. In other words, it depicts where in your infrastructure you can find a file. Also pretty simple are the Serving (◄──────) relations between Technology Service and Application Function and between Technology Interface and Application Component. If an Application Function needs access to a file that resides on a file system, the file system is a Technology Service that Serves the Application Function. And its mirror is the Serving relation from Technology Interface to Application Component. This mirroring is depicted by the Assignment relation (◄──────●) between Technology Interface and Technology Service, exactly as happens in the levels above between the 'interface' and the 'service'.

And lastly, there are the Realization relations (┈┈┈┈▷) between an Artifact and both Data Object and between Artifact and Application Component. This one is also pretty simple and easiest to explain by example. Suppose your application is Microsoft Word, then the file you are editing could be called "foo.doc". And if the application is MS Word, the Artifact realizing the Application Component could be "word.exe".

Note: we are still in an IT-focused scenario. The Technology Layer of ArchiMate's Core has (since version 3) elements to model the physical side of an enterprise, e.g. a physical production process. We will get to that below. For those that are already acquainted with earlier versions of ArchiMate: the name of the 'bottom' layer of ArchiMate has changed from (IT) 'Infrastructure' to the more generic name of 'Technology' so it better fits the non-IT oriented use.

I have a detailed example model for you in View 10 to see everything in a single context. The model shows someone writing a letter to a customer that contains an answer, supposedly to a question the customer has asked. Two infrastructural services are needed for this to work. The application should run and the document must be stored. In this example, everything happens on a standalone PC.

If you are an 'enterprise' architect you may think that all this detail is irrelevant and that the language looks like a language for detailed design only. Don't worry: using ArchiMate does not mean you absolutely must model all these details, the language can handle both: a roughly sketched Business Operating Model down to the nitty-gritty details you have to confront when you are in a project. I am simply using an example everybody knows, to illustrate how it works in ArchiMate. And even in View 10, I have left some things out, and I have combined the Technology Interfaces into one element. I could also have combined the Technology Services into one element. I will address handling details later when I am discussing 'modeling patterns'.

One more comment, before we go on with the rest of the language. As you might have noticed, the initial example with infrastructure in View 9 had no Access relation between the Technology Function and the 'executable' Artifact. But the 'write answer' example of View 10 does have that kind of a relation (shown in red). Here an explicit Technology Function for application execution was modeled and that function needs access to the 'executable' artifact. So which one is correct? The answer is: whatever your brief is and what you want to show. ArchiMate is a grammar, so it is *your* choice what you want to put in that grammar and how you put it. You have considerable freedom and you will certainly develop your own style. You can certainly model incorrectly in ArchiMate, just as you can write false statements or make grammatical errors in any language. So, yes, there are wrong models, but I will be unable to show you a way to model 'the right way'. The syntax of the ArchiMate language does not by definition lead to correct statements, but there are also many ways to say the same thing, just as with other languages. Later, we will

View 10. *Write Answer Process, supported by MS Word and a Standalone PC* address choosing your style and patterns, the latter being like 'common phrases in the language'.

7.6 System Software and Device

Our first use of IT infrastructure elements was pretty limited. We added the Technology Function, the Technology Service, the Node, the Technology Interface and the Artifact. Archi-Mate adds two useful active structure concepts to model the actual infrastructure level of your IT architecture: Device and System Software. The best way to explain them is by giving an example of how they can be used.

In View 11 we see a model of a database server in our landscape. The name of the server is 'srv001' and that could be the name it carries in a CMDB for instance.

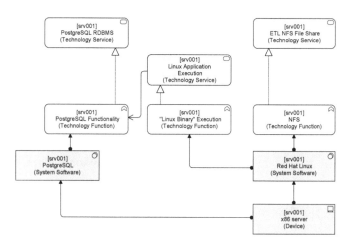

View 11. *Device and System Software*

The new element types are:

This is the Device, the actual hardware, the 'iron', the equipment of our infrastructure. In this example, two elements of the type System Software have been deployed on it (Assigned-To it). The little logo of the element is an image of a keyboard/screen.

This is the System Software element. It stands for software that we consider to be part of our Technology layer and not our application layer. Common uses are operating systems or database systems, but also runtime environments are generally modeled as System Software (the name of which is a bit quaint, given its wider use). In our example both are available: the Red Hat Linux operating system and the PostgreSQL database system. Modeled too is that the PostgreSQL software uses the Red Hat software. (If we have our existing landscape modeled in such detail, we could by analysis find all PostgreSQL databases that run on Red Hat, handy if we are planning an update and there is something about PostgreSQL running on Red Hat that merits extra attention).

What really sets System Software apart from Application Component is that System Software is often a sort of *platform*. It is an environment where other software can run. So,

for instance, Java on your computer is System Software. It can read and execute JAR files which contain Java instructions. See also section 12.7 "Why two types of software?" on page 52.

7.7 Composition and Aggregation

We already met the Composition relation (◆——) earlier. The composition represents a whole-part relation. It is best to look at the ArchiMate version of this common relation as the relation between a tree (a real one from your garden, not the computational concept) and its branches. A branch is a branch of a single tree and cannot be a branch of multiple trees. If the tree is destroyed, all of its branches are destroyed as well.

Generally, you may always create a Composition relation between two elements *of the same type*. View 12 contains an example.

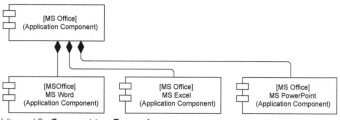

View 12. *Composition Example*

The Aggregation relation (◇——) is a variation on the theme. It looks like View 13.

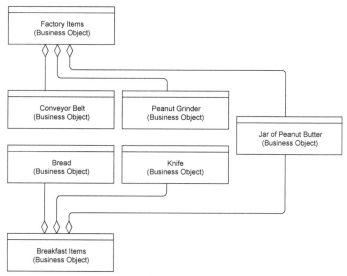

View 13. *Aggregation Example*

It is best to look at the Aggregation relation as a kind of grouping (note: in Section 7.13 "Grouping" on page 28 we will see an official way to 'group' various elements of *different* types). The 'parent' (on the end with the diamond) represents a 'collection' of the children. But unlike Composition, the children may be a member of multiple Aggregations as you can also see in View 13: The 'Jar of Peanut Butter' is both part of the 'Factory Items' of the peanut butter factory and the 'Breakfast Items' of a consumer's home. It's like the number 4 being both part of the collection of squares of integers and the collection of even numbers. Composition versus Aggregation is sometimes described as 'has-a' versus 'part-of', the difference being not directly clear from the terms. Also, composition is sometimes referred to 'strong ownership', whereas aggregation is sometimes referred to as 'weak ownership', again somewhat problematic as the aggregation does not 'own' the child at all.

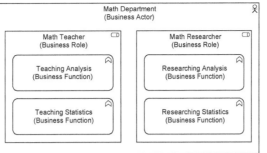

View 17. *Assignment Nesting, Two Levels Deep*

7.8 Nesting

There are four relation types that may be drawn by nesting an element inside another element: Composition, Aggregation, Assignment and Realization. These are the so-called *structural relationships*. Note: tooling often allows more than the language does, especially if you use tooling that is nothing more than a good model-drawing application such as Visio for Windows or OmniGraffle for Mac OS. Anyway, let's take the 'Factory Items' from View 13 as an example. Nested, it looks like View 15, which looks a lot cleaner and

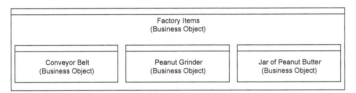

View 15. *Nested Aggregation*

that is why many modelers like it. But we can already see a disadvantage: you no longer see anymore what the relation is between parts and whole: Composition? Aggregation?

It gets worse, when you want to model both Aggregations from View 13 in Nested form in one view as in View 16.

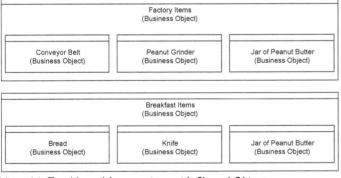

View 16. *Two Nested Aggregations with Shared Object*

Not only are you unable to see the actual relations, it has now become necessary to include the 'Jar of Peanut Butter' element twice. And though the name is the same, there is nothing that will tell you if behind-the-scenes it is the same element. You can have two different elements with the same name in ArchiMate, after all, the label has no meaning inside the language (as the language' is in fact a *grammar*) even if it has a meaning in the world of an architect. Besides, even if your modeling guidelines force different names for different elements, think of a very large view with the

same element twice. Are you going to spot that the same element occurs twice? Probably not. So are you going to see the dependencies in full? Again: probably not.

View 17 contains another Assignment example of Nesting, now two levels deep.

In summary: Nesting makes for nice views on your model, views that are easy on the eye. But don't think about them too lightly, because constructing your model this way comes with risks. And even bigger risks than you think, because some tools will let you create nestings without actually creating a relation between the nested elements (which is in conflict with the ArchiMate standard), or they may create a default relation which was not the relation you were thinking of. I've seen one tool that was unable to produce View 16 unless the shared object was not shared at all, but created twice in the model; because nesting was used to show model structure.

7.9 Using a Node to encapsulate infrastructure

Now that we have seen Composition and Nesting, we can look at View 11 on page 24 that introduced System Software and Device and show in View 14 and View 22 on page 26 how it might be modeled.

In this example, the System Software and Device elements are children (Composition) of an abstract Node element (the Composition relations are not explicitly shown here, but instead modeled as Nesting). This is kind of a nice grouping of an infrastructure element as the composition's children have no independent existence or use. We can also go further: in View 22 on page 26, everything has been Nested.

In this introductory section, we only look at the element types and how they relate to each other. Later, we will look into finding a sweet spot for using a Node for encapsulating infrastructure details when we discuss patterns. E.g. in Section 15.2 "A Basic TI Pattern: A Database" on page 63,

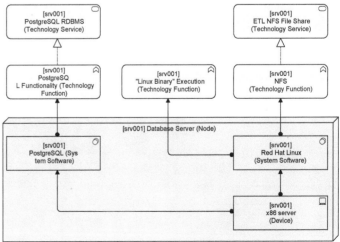

View 14. *Device and System Software Nested in a Node*

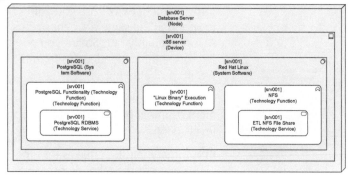

View 22. *A maximally Nested Node*

we will see that it might be handy to restrict ourselves here, to make analysis of the model easier. You have the choice of course wether you want to model these details (and you can go as far and deep as you like). You can Nest or not. It all depends on the use you want to make of your model (in other words: Uncle Ludwig always wins).

7.10 Event, Trigger and Flow

So far, we have handled the structure of and dependencies in your architecture, and all relations so far were so-called 'structural' and 'dependency' relations (explained below). ArchiMate is not big on the dynamics of an architecture, but it does have two 'dynamic relations': Trigger and Flow.

In View 18 we find Trigger (———▶) and Flow (----▶) relations in a business layer example. We see three Business Functions here from the asset management world: 'Portfolio Management' is taking investment decisions, which result in orders for the 'Trading' function. So, 'Trading' starts trading when it receives an order from 'Portfolio Management'. Triggering means there is a causal relation between the two functions. The flow between 'Portfolio Management' and 'Trading' says information flows from one to the other. In this case it is the 'Order'.

View 18. *Trigger and Flow*

But the Trading function also regularly receives a list of allowed counterparties, countries and currencies from the 'Risk Controlling' function. This information Flows from one to the other, but it does not Trigger a trade. A Flow relation between two Business Functions could also be modeled as Business Objects written (Accessed) by one function and read (Accessed) by another. If we add those, it looks like View 19.

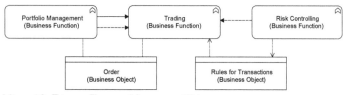

View 19. *Trigger, Flow and Access to Objects*

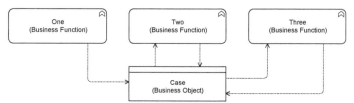

View 20. *Business Functions sharing Access to a Business Object, without Flows*

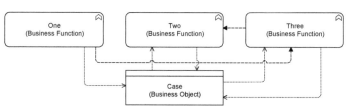

View 21. *Business Functions sharing Access to a Business Object, with Flows*

So, how useful is the Flow relation if you can also use the Business Objects and the Access relation? Well, it has a few advantages:

- You can make simpler views by leaving the Business Objects out and for instance label the Flow relations. The problem, though, is that such a label generally cannot be used to analyze what goes on your landscape, I'll say it already here: watch out for relying too much on labels and properties of elements, as they often live outside the 'analyzable' structure of your model.

- Technically, both Access relations do not guarantee a Flow. After all, if two functions access a warehouse, can you say that which one has put in the other takes out?

- But, most importantly, your dependencies can become clearer with a Flow. Take, for instance, the example of a 'Case' flowing though your business from Business Function to Business Function. Having read/write relations from these Business Functions to that single Business Object tells you nothing about how information flows. Take the example in View 20.

This does not tell you how the 'Case' Flows through your organization. What do you think? Look at View 21 and it becomes clear what the flow of information is.

Without the Flow relations, would you have known? Could you have drawn the wrong conclusion? Certainly. Is that a bad thing? After all they all depend on that Business Object. Well, take this example: without the Flow relation, you might think that the roles behind function One, Two and Three may have to agree concurrently on all the contents of the Case Business Object. But, in reality, you might only need to set up talks between One and Two on the one hand and Three and Two on the other and depending on the issues at hand, that might be simpler.

The above discussion of Flow is valid for ArchiMate 2 and earlier (I have left this in to make the book not entirely useless for those still using ArchiMate 2 as well as for didactic reasons). ArchiMate 3 has bridged the gap between Flow and Access, however, by allowing relations to relations, which is specifically useful for Flow.

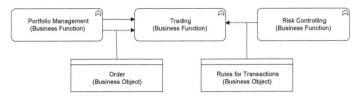

View 24. *Flow with Payload*

This is shown in View 24. ArchiMate allows us to draw relations to relations. A main reason for this is this construction. Here we have used an Association relation (simple line) between a Business Object and a Flow relation, thus signifying that the Business Object is the payload of the Flow.

Trigger and Flow relations may generally be drawn between behavioral elements within a layer; e.g., from Application Function to Application Function or from Business Process to Business Process.

ArchiMate also has a special element in each layer that depicts an event, 'something that happens' or a 'state'. Business Events can trigger business behavior and they can be 'raised' by business behavior, which is also depicted with a Trigger relation. An example can be seen in View 23. Application Event and Technology Event are likewise available in the other core layers.

View 23. *Business Event Triggers Business Process*

ArchiMate does not fully support detailed process modeling, it only has a limited support for the dynamics of behavior. In section 30 "A Possible Linking of BPMN and ArchiMate" on page 164, I will present a method to use ArchiMate for EA while using BPMN for process modeling.

7.11 Modeling the Physical

As of version 3, ArchiMate has special elements to model physical aspects of the enterprise. This is a major improvement as it was until this version an enterprise architecture language that was rather narrowly information/IT-focused. But enterprises are not just about information, even if enterprise architecture as a discipline was invented (and still mostly needed) because of the complexity of the overall landscape of information systems.

In View 25 a small example of the use of ArchiMate's elements for modeling the physical is shown. What we see here is a Factory that contains an assembly line that builds Daleks

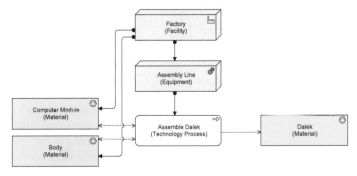

View 25. *Modeling the Physical — Assembling Daleks*

(evil cyborgs from the Dr. Who TV series) based on the pre-assembled parts body and brain. Several new element types are introduced here.

This is a Facility. It is meant to model places where you can deploy technology. Mostly, they will be used for physical production facilities, e.g. a factory. But if, for instance, your process is growing a specific fungus that can be added to raw sheep milk cheese and you need a specific kind of cave for that, such a cave would also be a facility. A facility is something that in the end houses a physical process of sorts.

This is Equipment. Equipment is meant as an active element that can perform a physical process. In this case, we have an assembly line, that is housed in the facility which, we assume, provides power, security, etc., etc.

As you can see, the behavior of the Equipment is modeled as a (generic) Technology Process, which is an element we already encountered before. This means that there is in ArchiMate a separation between physical and computational *structural* elements (subjects and objects in our 'sentences') in the Technology layer, but the behavior (the verbs in our sentences) is not so separated. This and the way these active structural elements are positioned in the language have some interesting effects on modeling, which we will see later. Note: much can be said about the choices that the ArchiMate designers have made. At the end of the book I will discuss these and I will concentrate my criticism there. In this chapter I will — apart from a remark here and there — just report how the language is set up.

This is Material. Material is the physical sibling of the computational passive element Artifact. It is meant to model any physical material. But unlike Artifact, which can realize active software elements (the Artifact foo.exe realizes the 'foo' System Software for instance), it cannot Realize a physical active element, e.g. it cannot Realize Equipment or Facility (which I think is an oversight, but I will keep my discussion of and critique on the language largely to chapter "Discussing ArchiMate" on page 207).

The Access relations from Technology Process to the Material elements show that the process takes the parts and creates the whole. To model the fact that the assembly process 'destroys' the parts, I've chosen to model those Access relations as read/write. Here we encounter a bit of pure-IT-origin of ArchiMate, because in IT of course, reading is not the same as exhausting something, whereas in physical processes generally the input disappears when the output is created. For those new to ArchiMate (including those that will get exposed to your views without having learned the language), seeing those Access relations pointing both ways might raise questions.

The Assignment relations from Facility to Material represent that the Material is deployed at the Facility. We could of course also have Assigned them to (deploy them on) the Equipment. Here we encounter already an important modeling issue: is one approach better that the other? The grammar itself is neutral on the issue and while learning the grammar (and for instance getting certified in it) is a good thing, it doesn't teach you how to model *well*, how to model for the purpose you are modeling *for*. This, then, is of course the main subject of the other chapters of this book.

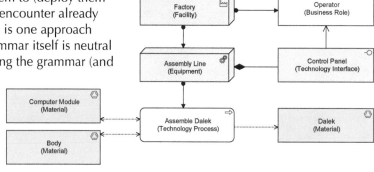

View 30. *Assembly Line with Interface and Operator*

In View 30 I have added the operator and the interface he or she uses to operate the Equipment. I've modeled the operator as a Business Role and the control panel as a Technology Interface. Here too, we see that both the informational/computational and the physical infrastructure use the same element for their interface: Technology Interface. So, here too, the separation between physical and informational/computational does not exist. In section 8.5 on page 35 we will see how everything in the technology layer hangs together.

One final remark: the Technology layer can Serve the Business layer directly. No need for an intermediate application.

7.12 Junctions

ArchiMate 3's Junction (a 'relationship connector') has been greatly improved with respect to previous versions of ArchiMate. Up to and including ArchiMate 2, it was restricted to connecting Flows and Triggers. Now, it can also be used to logically combine Assignment, Realization, Association, Influence (see page 44), Access, and Serving (all relation types to a Junction must be the same type, though), and it comes standard in two forms: AND and OR. Note that in ArchiMate the OR must be understood as XOR, the exclusive OR, meaning that only one of the possible connections is valid at the same time. An example is shown in View 28.

Shown here is an asset management organization's rule that if a system failure happens in times of market volatility, the *combination* of these events trigger the initiation of the crisis mode processes. An example of the (X)OR Junction can be seen in View 29. Shown here is an insurance firm's rule that a claim is evaluated, after which it *either* goes to the payment

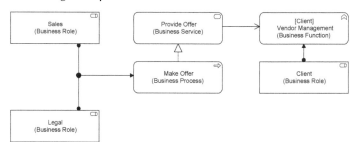

View 28. *AND Junction*

View 29. *(X)OR Junction*

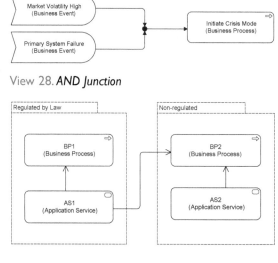

View 27. *A Grouping*

process, *or* the 'deny claim' process, *or* evaluation is extended with a 'visit claimant' process.

One practical use of Junction is to model collaborations. As we will see below, ArchiMate has special elements for this, but using a Junction is possible since ArchiMate 3 and this makes modeling collaboration a lot simpler. Have a look at View 26. Here we see modeled that Sales and Legal (both Business Roles) *together* perform the 'make order' Business Process

View 26. *Collaboration through the use of Junction.*

that Realizes the Provide Offer Business Service which is used by the Client's vendor management Business Function. Note also: ArchiMate 3 allows the arrow heads at the end points of relations that attach to a Junction not to show.

7.13 Grouping

Another element of ArchiMate that has been greatly improved in ArchiMate 3 is Grouping. For those already acquainted with earlier versions of ArchiMate: it *was* just a graphical construct (misnamed as a relation), it now *is* a true element that can Aggregate everything else. And it shows as a grouping because you normally present it as a Nesting (see section 7.8 on page 25). An example is shown in View 27. Here we see two Business Processes that each use an Application service. BP1 and AS1 are regulated (e.g. by the government) and BP2 and AS2 are not. What really is in the model if we un-Nest is shown in View 33 on page 29 Note specifically that not just the elements are (can be) Aggregated by a Grouping, relations can also be Aggregated.

Just to be precise (so you won't fail an exam on my account on this subject): Grouping is not formally a part of the official ArchiMate Core Framework, it is part of a separate domain

'Composite Elements' which was not shown in the overview in View 4 "The ArchiMate Map — Complete" on page 18,

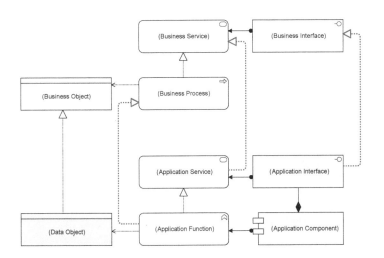

View 32. *Assembling Daleks — with Communication and Distribution*

or the two diagrams before it. In my defense of not showing them there: neither does the standard...

7.14 Automated Processes

So far, our landscape was based on a business process performed by people (actors fulfilling a role). But what if a process is fully automated? ArchiMate has the following solution: If a process is run by people, a Business Role is Assigned-To the Business Process and a Business Interface is Assigned-To a Business Service. The Business Role *performs* the Business Process. If a Business Process is *performed* by an application, ArchiMate allows us to use the Realization relation to say that the Business layer elements are abstractions of the application (or technology) layer elements. View 31 shows them (in red, only application to business layer).

View 31. *Automated Process*

This way, we can model an application that by itself performs a process that realizes a service*.

7.15 Distribution of data and matter (Path and Network)

We have already seen that distribution of information between behavioral elements can be modeled with Flow and/or with Access to passive elements. ArchiMate supports three concepts to model the infrastructure that is required for distribution to happen. One of these is Path, a more abstract element type that can be used to logically model any sort of distribution. The other two are Communication Network and Distribution Network, Extending the example from View 25 on page 27 to View 32, we can show all three.

This is a Path. A Path is a kind of abstract element that stands for any form of distribution, physical, information or both. In the example it is used to model the distribution of parts and information about the parts from the warehouse to the production facility. The (logical) Path is Realized by two networks:

This is a Distribution Network. A Distribution Network stands for any setup to handle *physical* transport. It could be a fleet of trucks, a railway setup on the organization's premises, people running around as couriers with packages, and so forth. In this case, the warehouse-factory complex has a fleet of small autonomous trucks that automatically drive between warehouse and factory delivering the parts from which a Dalek will be assembled.

This is a Communication Network. A Communication Network stands for any setup to handle *communication* transport. Most commonly this will be a digital data network, According to the standard, it represents 'the physical communication infrastructure' (with Path being the element that represents the 'logical' (communication) infrastructure. There is some vagueness here, because what is 'physical'? Communication networking is in reality a stack of technologies,

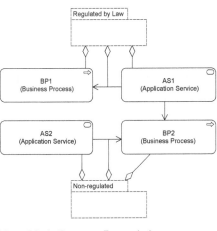

View 33. *A Grouping Expanded*

* This is fundamentally different from the way it was done in previous versions of ArchiMate, which allowed direct Assignments of Application Components to business behavior. These are no longer allowed.

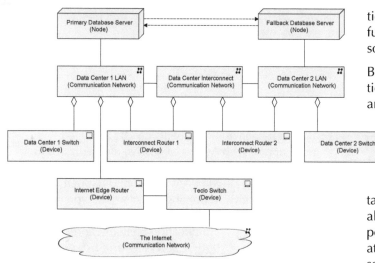

View 34. *Using Aggregations to Model Networking Devices*

with physical cabling (or the ether) as the only really physical part, in network engineering terms 'layer 1'. Your organization's LAN will generally have on top of that (switched) ethernet (layer 2), (routed) Internet Protocol (layer 3), and more.

One new relation is shown, that is the Association relation — a simple line — about which we will say more below. Here, it is used to associate Facilities with Paths, and Networks with passive elements that are transported by them. Another use (not shown) is associating a Device or System Software with a Communication Network.

Networking components may have two types of relations with their environment. As mentioned above, Association is used to show which elements *make use of* the network, and Aggregation is used to model the elements that *create* the network. An example is shown in View 34. Here, two database servers in two data centers form a cluster of sorts, but only Data Center 1 is connected to the Internet. The example is rather old-fashioned, as these days we might see multiple data centers configured as one large 'stretched fabric' (not routed at all, but switched).

As an aside: the example also shows something else: I've changed the graphic shape of the 'Internet' Communications Network. ArchiMate doesn't forbid that, I can do graphically what I want, the visual forms are just 'practice' or 'default', it is the *model* structure that counts.

Anyway, I seldom saw these networking concepts used before ArchiMate 3. For the new elements, this is no surprise, obviously. A reason for the lack of use of the Path/Network elements that have been in ArchiMate from the start, I think, is the following: For the application people, it's all just 'networking', or 'infrastructure', but for the networking people there are a lot of software systems involved to make all that transport happen. The elements are thus not very usable in the reality of this part of the business. For the infrastructure people, the actual devices and systems that make up networking (and the management of said networks) are more useful to model. So, the language may position 'networking' as 'technology/infrastructure' and not 'business' or 'applica-

tion' (for the business), the infrastructure people will rightfully disagree. The Networking element itself then becomes some sort of abstraction/decoupling point in a model.

Behind this discussion are views on the way we should practice enterprise architecture. Are we focused on the business and is 'technology/infrastructure' an unimportant low-level aspect of it? Or does enterprise architecture extend all the way down into all the complexities that make up a modern enterprise? Are we making simple abstractions for strategic business purposes, ignoring all (possibly devastating) detail? Or are we using the modeling language to grapple with all the complex dependencies in a modern enterprise? My personal perspective is the latter and that of course permeates this book. This handling of different perspectives/uses is something that requires attention when we model, because modeling an enterprise from just the 'primary business' perspective is something that is in my view too simplistic for the goals of enterprise architecture. We will get back to this aspect of modeling enterprises in Section 19 "Secondary and Tertiary Architecture" on page 104.

I do expect, though, that — thanks to the changes in ArchiMate 3, such as the physical, the big influence of innovations in IT infrastructure and the rise of the 'Internet of Things' — the Network and Path elements might start to play a role in ArchiMate modeling, though it is a question wether they are actually needed to model networking at all. After all, we could model any network as a Technology Service/Interface used by other elements of the physical or communications infrastructure. This will be shown in Section 28.1 "Networking" on page 150.

7.16 Who is in Charge?

So far, ArchiMate looks like a very orthodox IT-oriented enterprise architecture modeling language. It can show how the business is supported by applications which are supported by infrastructure. Physical processes and materials have been added to 'infrastructure' (which has been renamed to 'technology') but we still are in effect talking about a classic BAT-stack (Business–Application–Technology). From ArchiMate 3 on however, this strict layering has been loosened in an important way. This is an important improvement, because it was always a rather difficult puzzle to model complex stacks, because of the strict one-way layering.

I've illustrated this in View 35 on page 31. On the right hand side, we see our classic BAT-stack. There is a Business Process performed by a Business Role, the process and the role are supported by an Application Service and Application Interface which are the visible parts of the application. The application itself is supported by a Technology Service and Interface (runtime environment, file shares, database, etc.). Everything is as we already saw in View 5 on page 20, View 9 on page 22, and View 10 on page 23 but, in View 35, something is added on the left hand side.

Here, two things have been added. First, there is a Business Process that checks the infrastructure every day and that restarts the server if certain criteria are met. The scenario here is that we do not want to restart if we can avoid it but sometimes we have to. This is done by an infrastructure engineer. Now, instead of modeling that the infrastructure engineer also uses the infrastructure, we have modeled that the infrastructure depends on the engineer's process directly (to perform well). This is shown in red. Let's stress this: instead of a human — the infrastructure engineer — using the infrastructure, it has been modeled as the infrastructure using the engineer to remain operational. If the engineer would have been some automated infrastructure (automated infrastructure will return in Section 28.2 "DevOps Ready Data Center (DRDC)" on page 151), we would have modeled the dependency likewise. Since ArchiMate 3, we can now express that same sort of dependency regardless of the layers.

Second, I have also modeled in View 35 that the engineer uses an application to manage the infrastructure. The engineer's application is used by (is Serving) the infrastructure (in blue).

In View 36, you see the blue route from View 35, and it illustrates that the stack in ArchiMate 3 is not only BAT, but also TAB (it is also TBA, TA, BT, BATABAT, etc.). And it nicely shows how, via applications and technology) the primary business process depends on the infrastructure maintenance process. While *technically* it all may depend in a different direction (the IT interface is Serving the human), *logically*, the human is Serving the IT. ArchiMate can do both, what is modeled is *your* choice depending on *your* needs.

7.17 Abstractions

Abstraction is a favorite tool in the enterprise architect's tool chest. ArchiMate employs and enables abstraction in several ways and for several purposes. Here we will describe some ways ArchiMate 3 supports abstraction.

The first abstraction we already encountered in the first sections and it was shown in View 10 on page 23. It is the abstraction in the 'passive aspect' of ArchiMate's Core. A file (Artifact, e.g. 'answer.doc') may Realize a Data Object (MS Word data) which Realizes a Business Object (e.g. 'Answer Letter'). All three elements stand for the same thing, but at different abstraction levels (which come from data modeling).

Related to this is the abstraction that goes from Artifact to Application Component (or System Software). The Artifact stands for the *deployment* of software, the bits and bytes, the Application Component (or System Software) for its role as active element in the landscape. This was illustrated in View 9 on page 22 and View 10 on page 23.

The third abstraction is one we encountered previously in section 7.14 on page 29 (View 31): modeling that our business is (partly) automated. There might be something we would like to call a Business Service, but in fact it is provided by automation. A good example is for instance internet banking. At the business level, the bank provides an 'internet banking' Business Service via a 'web' Business Interface, but in fact all this is IT: applications and infrastructure. ArchiMate 3 allows us to model this by modeling both the application (or technology) elements (such as Application Services or Technology Interfaces) as well as the business layer elements (such as Business Service or Business Interface) and use Realization relations to let the IT elements realize the business elements, thus turning the business layer elements into abstract representations of the IT layer elements.

A fourth abstraction runs from the Tech-

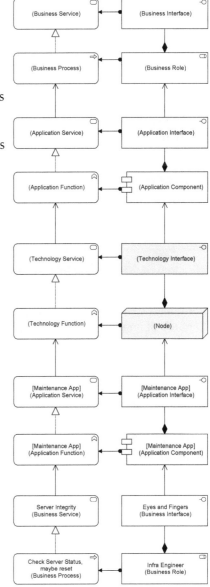

View 35. *Technology uses Application and Business*

View 36. *Who is in Charge?*

nology layer to the Application layer. It is possible to create Realization relations from Technology Function/Process to Application Function/Process, from Technology Service to Application Service, and from Technology Interface to Application Interface. Sadly, though, the standard does not really explain what is meant by these abstractions.

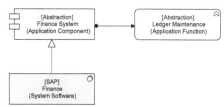

View 38. *Abstraction Generic-Specific: Application abstracted from Technology*

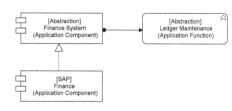

View 39. *Abstraction Generic-Specific: á la TOGAF*

An abstraction that is often employed in enterprise architecture modeling is that of generic versus specific IT. E.g. you can have a generic application, such as "the accounting system", but in the real world of your enterprise this is a real application, say the "MainAccount" application from the firm "Pro-IT". ArchiMate 3 supports several ways you could model this*:

- Using the application layer for the 'generic' application while using the technology layer for the specific application. An example is shown in View 38. This might be the intended use of the fourth abstraction;

- Using a Realization relation from respectively Application Component to Application Component or Node to Node. This has been put in at the behest of the TOGAF people (ArchiMate is after all owned by TOG), but apparently The ArchiMate people don't like it enough to fully document it. In TOGAF, by the way, this is confusingly called 'physical versus logical' applications (or technology). 'Actual' (or 'real') versus 'logical' (or 'conceptual') would have been better, I

think. Anyway, an example is shown in View 39. Note true 'physical' versus logical is in ArchiMate supported by the deployment scenario from Artifact above.

- Using Specialization within a layer. We will describe this below, when describing the Specialization relation.

The first one should be avoided, I think. Though the relation is allowed in ArchiMate you should not use it this way, as it means quite something different from what we have in mind now. It is an example of an ArchiMate pitfall which we will discuss later. The latter two have advantages and disadvantages, which we will see later in the book when we are discussing modeling patterns.

The standard also says that an active element (e.g. Application Component) being assigned-to behavior (e.g. Application Function) might be seen as an abstraction, as — in this example — the Application Component is 'implementation' and the Application Function is 'implementation independent'. I think (again) that this is questionable, and we'll discuss this in chapter "Discussing ArchiMate" on page 207.

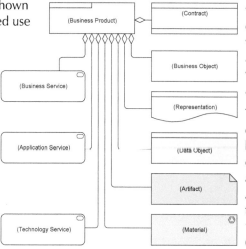

View 37. *Product, Contract, Value and a Product's Constituents*

8. Other Core Elements and Relations

With the elements and relations of the previous section (21 of ArchiMate Core's 40 element types), you can probably do much of an enterprise architect's work, if that work is focused on 'Current State' and 'Change/Project' Architectures. Here is the rest of the Core:

8.1 Product and Contract

If you want to model the offerings of your organization to the outside world (anyone who uses what you produce, be it clients or regulators), a handy element is Product. A Product is a simple enough concept. It is an Aggregation of one or more services and/or passive elements, and (also optionally) a Contract. It is often Associated with a Value. It looks like View 37.

As you can see, the Product element breaks the active-passive-behavior pattern. It Aggregates behavioral elements (the actions themselves) *and* a passive element. It also is a business-layer element, but it may Aggregate an applica-

tion-layer or technology-layer element. This is because it is a *Composite Element*. ArchiMate 3 has introduced this category, and it consists of Grouping (see section 7.13), Product, Location (section 8.7), and Plateau (section 10.2). The new element types are:

This is the Contract. It represents the formal or informal agreement that covers the delivery of the service provided. This might be a specific Service Level Agreement or General Terms & Conditions.

This is the Product. It is what you offer to the outside world. For a department of your organization, the Product may be something offered 'internally'. It can be handy to make the link between your Enterprise Architecture and how management looks at the organization.

---

* One is reminded by Andrew Tanenbaum's remark that "the nice thing about standards is that there are so many to choose from".

8.2 (Formal) Collaboration and Interaction

Suppose you have two Business Roles in your organization that need to work together to get some specific work done. For instance, the 'sales' and the 'legal' Business Roles need to work together to create the offer for the prospective client. Within ArchiMate there are generally two ways of modeling this.

Using the elements and relations we already described, you can put one of them in the lead and let the second provide a service. In our example: 'sales' produces the offer, but it uses the (internal) services realized by (the processes of) 'legal' in its processes (see View 40).

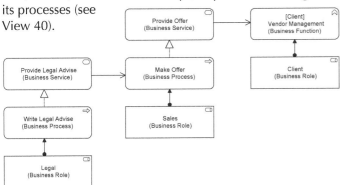

View 40. *Collaboration: Sales Uses Legal on Order Creation*

In this set-up, it is clear who is in charge. 'Sales' decides to send the offer out, not legal. 'Legal' must provide something (and for instance withholding approval means 'sales' cannot proceed), but the service to the client is realized by the process of 'Sales'.

ArchiMate offers a second way to model such collaborations and their behavior explicitly as elements. You can create a Business Collaboration element that consists of (Aggregates) the Business Roles that are part of that collaboration. You can then assign a Business Interaction to that collaboration, the interaction being the behavior of that collaboration. It looks like View 41.

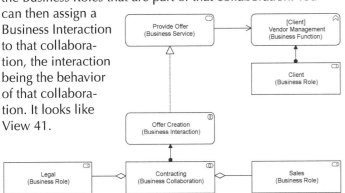

View 41. *Collaboration: Sales and Legal Collaborate on Order Creation*

The whole 'offer creation' 'process' is now modeled not as *one* of the parties 'owning' it, but *both*. There are a few new elements:

 This is the Business Collaboration. It is a special kind of Business Role that Aggregates multiple other Business Roles (or Business Collaborations, of course, as these are also types of roles, see Section 8.5 "The Specialization Relation in an Actual Model" on page 35). It is the

concept that defines multiple roles forming a (specific) single 'collective' role to do something together.

This is the Business Interaction. It is the behavior of that Business Collaboration, the activities they do together. Note that, while the Business Collaboration Aggregates two or more Business Roles, the Business Interaction does *not* Aggregate Business Functions or Business Processes. What is not clear in ArchiMate is whether we must see a Business Interaction as functional or process-like. Given that it generally produces a result, it is probably best to see this as process-like.

One consequence of using a Collaboration is that it is not clear who is in charge. This might be more acceptable to the organization in terms of sensitivities, but sometimes it is just true: nobody really is in charge. In Section 18.2 "Business Function or Business Process?" on page 92, I will present a 'modeling pattern' of the business that uses Collaboration to show the loosely coupled nature of some of the organization's 'end-to-end' processes.

Both methods (using a service and using an interaction) are correct; it is a matter of style what you want to use and both approaches have some consequences. If you think about it, you could even model the sales-client interaction as a collaboration, after all the transaction requires decisions of both sides. For this introduction, it suffices that you have seen this.

Let's not forget we already saw collaboration in the enterprise modeled in View 26 on page 28. Here we used the Junction to let two Business Roles perform some behavior together. That way, we also showed that the 'Make Offer' process is assigned to two roles, in fact forming a 'de facto' collaboration.

There is of course a still simpler way. We could just Assign two Business Roles to a single Business Process or Function. This is shown in View 42. There are issues, though. Why is this a *collaboration*? Maybe *either* of the two performs

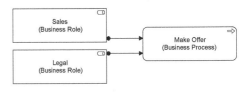

View 42. *Informal Collaboration*

it. The standard generally (but not everywhere) says that it is preferable to look at parallel relations to an element as that either one is 'enough'. But it does not demand this. In chapter "Style & Patterns", when we are discussing modeling patterns, we will discuss this more thoroughly.

In the application layer (and in the technology layer), something similar exists in ArchiMate, as is shown in View 43 on page 34 for the application layer.

The Application Collaboration stands for the collaboration of two Application Components. The behavior of that collaboration is the Application Interaction and such a behavior may realize an Application Service. Here too, it is not clear who is in charge, though as we saw in section 7.2 on page 21, the Serving-pattern is also ambiguous. This is all a matter of patterns and style, and we'll get back to that later in the book. The Technology Collaboration and Technology Interaction are similar, but in the Technology layer.

Certainly in the Application and Technology layers, ArchiMate's Collaboration and Interaction elements are generally abstractions of what is technical reality. See Section 16.1 "Application Collaboration is an Anthropomorphism" on page 84).

8.3 The Association Relation

The weakest relation, the 'catch-all' relation of ArchiMate, is the Association relation which is depicted as a simple line (———). It has a couple of formal roles in ArchiMate, but it also has the role of 'relation of last resort'. If you want to model the relation between two elements, if you know they are related somehow but you cannot model how, you can use Association. It is, therefore, often a sign of lack of knowledge or effort, so it is a matter of style if you want to use it (we'll talk about style later). For now, know that it exists and that it has a few official uses, such as we saw in the relations between Nodes and Paths or Distribution Networks and Material or between 'payload' and Flow.

8.4 Specialization in the *Meta*-model

I have to warn you up front: this part of ArchiMate is not only complex, it is a bit of a mess. I'm going to explain this, but you should not give up if this part initially gets too convoluted or complex. In the end, the actual use becomes not that difficult and the language remains of practical use.

The Specialization relation (◁———) is probably the most complicated (some would say, 'confused') relation in ArchiMate, because it is used in two fundamentally different ways that influence each other.

Before going on, let me first clearly describe the difference between an ArchiMate *model* and ArchiMate's *meta*-model. A *model* is what you create using ArchiMate, e.g. a model of your organization's current landscape, or a model that describes the outcome of a transformation such as a project. The ArchiMate *meta*-model is a model of how the different element types and relations together form the (grammar of) the ArchiMate language *itself*. This book (this chapter above all) explains the *meta*-model so you can use it to make *actual* models.

Returning to Specialization, Specialization first plays a role inside the ArchiMate *meta*-model:

- In the *meta*-model Contract is a Specialization of Business Object (in an *actual* model, Contract plays an independent role);

- In the *meta*-model Business Collaboration is a Specialization of Business Role (and in an *actual* model *Aggregates* Business Roles)

- In the *meta*-model Application Collaboration is a Specialization of Application Component (and in an *actual* model *Aggregates* Application Components)

- In the *meta*-model Technology Collaboration is a Specialization of Node (and in an *actual* model *Aggregates* Nodes)

- In the *meta*-model Device, System Software, Equipment, and Facility are all Specializations of Node (in an *actual* model, *this* Specialization is not modeled; Composition or Aggregation are often used between a Node and the 'IT subtypes').

These Specializations in the *meta*-model have consequences for what can be modeled in *actual* models. It means that the child concept *in the meta-model* inherits all the relations of its parent *in the meta-model*. To illustrate this, have a look at View 44 where the place of Contract in the meta-model is illustrated. The blue relations are in the meta-model. Because an Access relation

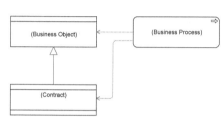

View 44. *Specialization of Contract in the Meta-model*

exists between Business Process and Business Object, and because Contract is a meta-model Specialization of Business Object, there also exists an Access relation between Business Process and Contract. It also means, for instance, that *any* Business Collaboration in an actual model can have *exactly* the same relations to other types of elements that a Business Role can, e.g. being Assigned-To a Business Process. Note that the opposite is not true. A Contract may be Aggregated by a Product in an actual model (as we saw above), but from that we may not conclude that it is true the other way around. Actually, we may model a Business Object as part of a Contract in an actual model, but the reason for that is different and will be discussed later.

One important secondary effect comes from Composition and Aggregation. As *any* element type can Compose or Aggregate itself and because *any* child type is also a parent, the parent type can Compose or Aggregate each child type. We already employed this earlier when, since Device is a subtype of Node, we modeled a Device as Composite part of a Node (as in Section 7.9 "Using a Node to encapsulate infrastructure" on page 25.

View 45. *Silly Composition*

But as any child type is *also* a parent type, any child type can Aggregate or Compose *any* member in the whole 'family tree', the parent type and all its children, grand-children and so forth. This leads to weird consequences such as: (non-physical) System Software may Compose (physical) Facility, as shown in View 45. Grammatically,

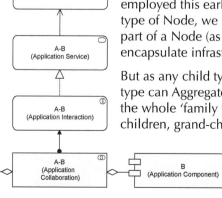

View 43. *Application Collaboration*

you are allowed to do this in ArchiMate. There is no constraint but it is probably unwise to do it.

Another *seemingly* weird effect of this also takes place in the Technology Layer. In View 47 all the child types of Node, both physical and computational/informational are shown. I have outlined the physical elements in red, the informational/computational ones in orange and the neutral ones in violet. Look at the right hand side first. Here you see that performing behavior by active technology elements has been made possible by the Assignment between Node and Technology Process. The same is true for the interface. Technology Interface is defined as a Composite child of Node. The result of the Assignment between Node and Technology Process is that *any* child type of Node may be modeled to perform *any* Technology Process. This in itself is not problematic: it is after all *up to us* not to model apparently crazy things such as "System Software saws wood". If we take the left hand side into account, there is an additional effect. On that side I had to show a 'hidden' element, one from ArchiMate's meta-meta-model, an abstract one (one that never gets actually used in a real model).

In the meta-model, Material can reside on (Assignment) Equipment and Artifact can reside on (Assignment) System Software. But through Technology Process, System Software can Access Material. So, the language does not stop us to model (informational) System Software or Device *accessing* (physical) Material while it does stop us from (physical) Material being *deployed* on a computational/informational system (below we will see it actually doesn't, but for this stage of the explanation it is true enough). This is not so weird as it may look. Suppose the tool for sawing is not a simple hand saw, but an automated 'sawing machine'. Is it that strange to say that its software 'performs' the sawing, together with the rest of the equipment? If not, then "software saws a tree into planks" is also not that strange after all, it is a modern day equivalent of "human saws a tree into planks", which also is rather impractical without the actual saw. The standard, by the way, says all of this is very useful for 'the Internet of Things', but we don't need 'the Internet of Things' at all for this to be useful: a lot of our 'things', from factory robots to

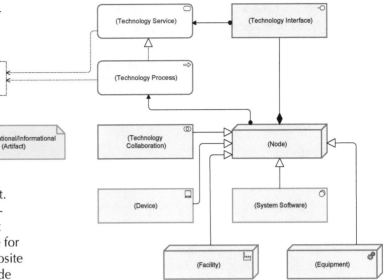

View 47. *How the Node ties informational and physical together in the meta-model*

washing machines have become automated and depend on software, regardless of internet connections.

Summary: the Specialization relation *in the* meta-*model* is like a 'class-relation', which are well known from software engineering. The Specialization relation *in the* meta-*model* says that an element *type* is a kind of another element *type* and an instantiation of it can do whatever an instantiation of its parent can.

8.5 The Specialization Relation in an *Actual* Model

When you use Specialization yourself, you will be using it in actual models. In an actual model, Specialization can also be used with a sort of 'inheritance' in mind. For instance, a 'car insurance' and a 'travel insurance' are both a kind of 'insurance'. Or a 'stock' and a 'bond' are both a kind of 'liquid asset'. An example is shown in View 46.

Here, we say that 'Cash' is a kind of 'Liquid Asset' (a liquid asset is an asset that you can easily trade) and another kind is 'Security' which again can be specialized into 'Stock' (a deed to a partial ownership of a company) and 'Bond' (a loan to an organization or country). If an element is a specialization of another element, whatever relations are true for the 'parent' (the element at the arrowhead) must be true for the child. If a Business Process handles 'Liquid Asset' (e.g., a reporting process), it must be able to handle both 'Cash' and 'Security'. On the other hand, if a business process handles 'Security', it must be able to handle both 'Stock' and 'Bond' but it does not need to be able to handle 'Cash'. Importantly, this interpretation, is *not* forced upon us by ArchiMate itself.

In Object-Oriented (OO) design, the specialization is sometimes called the 'Is-A' relation. Its counterparts are the 'Has-A' relation, which in ArchiMate is Composition (◆——) and the 'Refers-To' relation, which in ArchiMate is Aggregation (◇——). Generally, what you can do with an

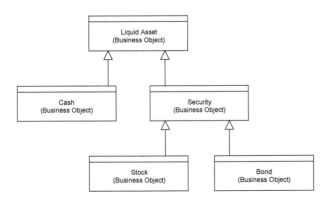

View 46. *Specialization Example: Investment Types*

'Is-A' Sub-classing (which is what you do with the Specialization relation in the meta-model), can have complex consequences. Take for instance 'Cash' from the current example. Suppose our company says we may only use cash as collateral for securities we lend (and thus not (other) securities). We would have a new Business Object in our landscape called 'Collateral' and 'Cash' could be a kind of 'Collateral'. It looks like the example in View 48.

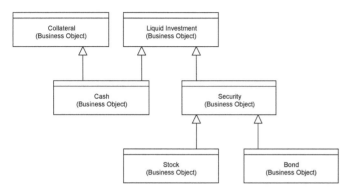

View 48. *Specialization Example: Multiple Inheritance*

What we have here is called in OO-terms 'multiple inheritance': Cash is both a kind of collateral and a kind of security. Most OO languages do not support true multiple inheritance (C++ does, more modern Objective-C, Java and C# do not) and for a reason: it tends to become messy because the 'parents' may have conflicting rules of behavior for the 'child' to inherit (a bit like parenting in real life, true, but maybe not the best paradigm for software engineering or business architecture modeling).

But ArchiMate's Specialization relation *as used in actual models* is not like that. If we have a Business Process that Accesses 'Liquid Asset', we may formally *not* conclude from the model that it Accesses 'Cash' or 'Security'. That relation we must explicitly model ourselves. Nobody does this in practice, but technically we should.

That Specialization in *actual* models is different, is driven home by the fact that it is a relation that is allowed between 'instances of the same type'. We already saw this. In View 46 on page 35 and View 48, we saw Business Objects Specialized into Business Objects. This *model*-Specialization' is inherited by child types via '*meta-model*-Specialization'.

This is best illustrated with a simple example. Have a look at View 50. Here we see a model-Specialization of a Business Object that is a Specialization of a Contract, which is the reverse of what the meta-model-Specialization is between both concepts. Modeled here is a Business Object that is an anonymized version of a Contract so it can be used for analytics. To illustrate that, both

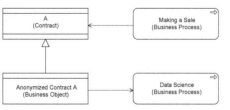

View 50. *Model-Specialization (versus Meta-model-Specialization)*

Business Processes are shown. From a software engineering perspective this Specialization is problematic, for instance, it does not adhere to the 'Liskov substitution principle' (the child type can always replace the parent type in a specific situation where the parent type plays a role). In this case: we cannot use an 'Anonymized Contract' as object for the 'Making a Sale' process.

This way of modeling is possible because:

- Any element type can model-Specialize itself;

- Hence: Business Object can model-Specialize Business Object

- This model-Specialization is inherited by Contract through: Contract is a *meta-model*-Specialization of Business Object;

- Hence: Contract (is a Business Object and thus) can Specialize a Business Object.

The result of this is that ArchiMate allows us to model more freely than it would if the model-Specialization relation was more 'software engineering'-like (or more meta-model-Specialization-like). It allows us to model things, like the almost certainly silly model-Specialization in View 49. This is allowed because any Node can model-Specialize itself and because System Software and Facility are both meta-model-Specializations of Node.

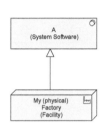

View 49. *Silly Specialization*

None of this is properly documented in the standard (e.g. when the model-Specialization relation is defined), though it can be implicitly concluded from the way ArchiMate omits a role for any kind of Specialization in the model-'derivation' of relations (derived relations will be explained in Section 9 "Derived Relations" on page 39). Truly, this is not ArchiMate's clearest and most elegant part.

There is another aspect to the use of model-Specialization in ArchiMate models. ArchiMate as a language is completely agnostic with respect to 'class versus instance' modeling in actual models. You can make concrete models, where you model real elements, such as how the 'Pro-Fin' financial application supports certain business processes and depends on certain infrastructure.

But you can also make abstract models, where you use elements that represent a 'type' or 'class', e.g.:

- A model valid for any finance application of which there are supposed to be several in your landscape. Or a model where you don't model every single desktop in your organization, but just a generic 'Desktop PC' or "Tablet" element. Or more specifically a "Windows Desktop" or "Apple iPad" end user device. You could of course also use Aggregation here to connect the 'class' to its 'instances').

- A model where your parent doesn't necessarily represent a collection, but where you are modeling 'conceptual' versus 'actual' elements in your landscape, as in section 7.17 "Abstractions" on page 31.

An example of the latter is shown in View 53. Here, the same generic-specific relation is shown as in View 38 and View 39 on page 32. I've added something extra: the element

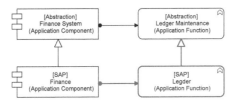

View 53. *Abstraction Generic-Specific via the Specialization relation*

and relations (outlined) in red. Here is a question for you: would you add them or not? Some say you shouldn't, as the function itself is an abstraction of the implementation (in this case the Application Component). In fact, the ArchiMate standard's text suggests as much. Others would argue that the real behavior of the real system is not an abstraction at all, but more an aspect of the system. There are, after all, no two systems in the world that behave exactly the same, and ignoring that can be perilous. We're back in 'modeling pattern' territory here, and such discussions are for the rest of the book.

8.6 Representation

Earlier we encountered the Business Object, the work horse of passive structure in your business layer architecture. We saw how this business-level element could be Realized by an application layer Data Object. Take for instance the 'Answer' Business Object that was Realized by the 'Word Document' Data Object in View 10 on page 23. ArchiMate also has another way to Realize a Business Object, it can be realized by a Rep-

resentation. A good example would be a print of the answer letter you are sending to your customer. The relation between a Business Object and its direct surroundings looks like View 51.

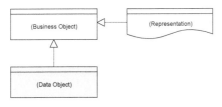

View 51. *Representation and Data Object Realizing a Business Object*

The new element types are:

This is the Representation. While the Data Object is the element in our application layer that represents the Business Object, the Representation is another way of representing the Business Object and it stands for a representation that can be shared with others, e.g. a print, a PDF file you send as attachment in a mail message, or a web-page.

Representation was sometimes a useful link to the physical world in pre-version-3 ArchiMate (e.g. for the actual real Steel Beam we mentioned in 7.1 "Application and Business" on page 18), but as far as I'm concerned it is a strange leftover of days where the IT/application-centric ArchiMate,

designed with administrative systems in mind, needed an element to model information on paper. It has no relation to the physical domain in ArchiMate 3 and its description has always overlapped with Artifact (PDF *'file'* after all).

8.7 Location

The final Core ArchiMate element to explain is Location. This was introduced in ArchiMate 2 and an example is given in View 52 (note the informal 'collaboration').

This is the Location element. This element stands for a geographical location where something resides. You can use the Aggregation relation to link it to several other element types to model where they are located.

Again, for reasons of correctness: Location is not part of the ArchiMate Core Framework, but — together with Grouping — part of the 'Composite Elements' category, the category of elements that can Aggregate many element or relation types.

8.8 The Complete Core

Without taking the rest into account, ArchiMate's Core is already rich. There are 42 element types (including the Composite Elements) and 10 relation types in Version 3.0.1.

In View 54 on page 38 you'll find an overall picture of a selection of ArchiMate's Core element types and their relations. This is often referred to as the ArchiMate meta-model. Note:

- Business Process, Business Function and Business Interaction take the same place and are represented by the Business Process icon in this view of the meta-model;

- The red relations are those that are used to model automated business layer elements. E.g. the Business Service 'web site' that is technically in reality an Application Service provided by IT. See section 7.14 "Automated Processes" on page 29.

- The orange relations are those that are used to model generic/specific abstractions, such as the generic 'finance application' versus a specific system that is actually used. See section 7.17 "Abstractions" on page 31. For a third way, see section 8.5 "The Specialization Relation in an Actual Model" on page 35.

- The green Specializations are *meta*-model relations. They show that the children are also parents (a Device is also a Node, just like a ball is also a toy). These are not modeled in actual enterprise architecture models, they are shown because you need them to interpret the meta-model correctly. See section 8.4 "Specialization in the Meta-model" on page 34.

- View 54 is repeated (somewhat larger) on page 239. During the rest of the book, you might want to look back at the meta-model to check for things. If you keep

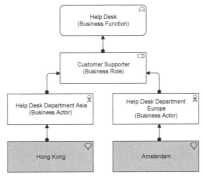

View 52. *Example use of Location object*

your finger between that page and the one before it, the core of the meta-model is always readily available (no such ease for the PDF users, I'm afraid).

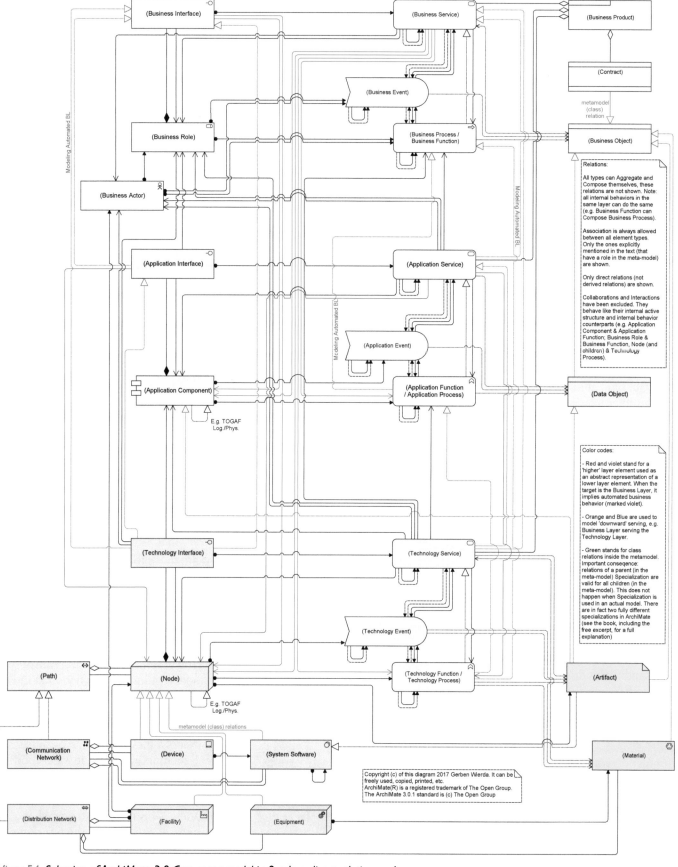

View 54. *Selection of ArchiMate 3.0 Core meta-model in 9 colors, direct relations only*

9. Derived Relations

9.1 Derived Structural and Dependency Relations*

So far we have included every concept, every element type and all connecting relations of the Core. ArchiMate however, offers a mechanism to create 'shortcuts'. The researchers, business users and students that created ArchiMate even offered a mathematical proof that their definition of the shortcuts are 'correct', in the sense that there is not a runaway one which in the end creates the situation that everything can be related to everything else using every kind of relation. Adding these shortcuts to the model was originally seen as extending 'ArchiMate proper' to a sort of 'ArchiMate+', but these shortcuts are so handy and useful that most practitioners (or teachers) do not really distinguish between the direct and shortcut relations anymore (which is a bad thing, as we will see). Add to that, tools generally do not support the actual difference (well) and it is easy to understand that the shortcuts are probably one of the most (implicitly) used but least (explicitly) understood aspects of ArchiMate. It did not help that for a long time (and because the text was full of omissions and ambiguities), the ArchiMate people stated that the real definition of the language was in the appendix of the standard where all possible relations are given and that 'all relations mentioned there were equal'. ArchiMate 3.0.1 has gone a long way in strengthening the standard on this point and is the first version to be adequate on this point.

Officially, ArchiMate calls these 'shortcuts' *derived relations* and I generally explain them by saying that the derived relations are a summary of a 'dependency route' that lies between two elements in a model. All tools have to allow you to model such a 'summary' without modeling the underlying 'true' route of elements and relations, but in the end each summary relation implicitly assumes that such a route with real elements and relations is there, even if you have not (or need not have) created them in your model.

As of ArchiMate 3, the relations are divided into the following categories:

- Structural Relations (Composition, Aggregation, Assignment, Realization)
- Dependency Relations (Serving, Access, Influence — which we haven't seen yet, but we will later on)
- Dynamic Relations (Trigger, Flow)
- Other Relations (Specialization, Association).
- A Junction is not a relation but a relationship *connector*.

The best way to illustrate the derivation rules is by using an already familiar example, the earlier used 'write answer' example. It is shown again in View 55 for easy reference (ignore the redness of one relation this time).

Given this example, the questions we may want to ask are:

a. What is the relation between the 'Desktop or Laptop PC' Node and the 'Write Answer' Business Process?

b. What is the relation between the 'word.exe' Artifact and the 'Document Creation' Application Service?

c. What is the relation between the 'Desktop or Laptop PC' Node and the 'Answer' Business Object?

For this, ArchiMate comes with the following procedure for routes that are made up from structural and dependency relations:

- Find a route from one element in the model to another following the *structural* and *dependency* relations between them. There is a additional requirement: a route is only valid if all relations followed are followed in the *same direction*. All structural and dependency relations have a direction.

- Every structural and dependency relation has a *strength*. If you have a valid route, the derived relation between both ends of the route is the *weakest* relation found on the route, much like the weakest link in a chain. The strengths are (from weak to strong):

1. Influence

2. Access (direction: from behavioral element to passive structural element, *independent* from arrow which depicts read or write. Note very well: that the direction may be opposite to the arrow is a pitfall when starting with ArchiMate.)

3. Serving

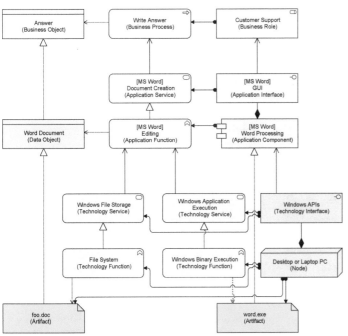

View 55. *Write Answer Process, supported by MS Word and a Stand-alone PC*

---

* Note: this section is about derivation in a *model*. ArchiMate sets out additional rules for the use of derivation in the *meta*-model. Derivation in the meta-model is used to calculate all the allowed relations from the direct relations and the rules. See appendix B of the standard

4. Realization

5. Assignment

6. Aggregation (direction: from parent to child)

7. Composition (direction: from parent to child)

Using this procedure, we can answer the questions above:

a. From the 'Desktop or Laptop PC' Node, via Assignment (strength: 5) to 'Windows Binary Execution' Technology Function, via Realization (strength: 4) to 'Windows Application Execution' Technology Service then via Serving (strength: 3) to the 'Editing' Application Function then via Realization (strength: 4) to the 'Document Creation' Application Service then via Serving (strength: 3) to the 'Write Answer' Business Process. The weakest relation encountered is Serving, which is the (derived) relation between the PC and the Business Process: *the PC Serves the Business Process*, which makes good sense.

b. The 'word.exe' Artifact Realizes (4) the 'Word Processing' Application Component, which is Assigned-To (5) the 'Editing' Application Function, which Realizes (4) the 'Document Creation' Application Service. The weakest is Realization, so *the 'word.exe' Artifact Realizes the 'Document Creation' Application Service*. A conclusion which also makes sense.

c. If we take the route from (a) we need just one extra step: from the 'Write Answer' via Access (strength: 2) to the 'Answer' Business Object. The weakest of that route is now Access, so *the PC Accesses the 'Answer' Business Object*.

Assignment was bidirectional before ArchiMate 2. The Open Group's ArchiMate Forum's decision to make Assignment unidirectional in ArchiMate 2 solved the problem that quite a few nonsense derivations were possible. In ArchiMate 1 it would for instance enable the route from the 'foo.doc' Artifact via the PC Node to the 'Windows File Storage' Technology Service with Realization as the resulting relation, or in other words: 'foo.doc' Realizes Windows File Storage. Hmm, I think not. In ArchiMate 3, Assignment's directionality is also shown in the visualization of the relation (from dot to arrowhead).

Anyway, sometimes multiple shortcuts do still exist. For instance, there is an alternative answer to question (c): From the PC Node via Assignment (strength: 5) to the 'foo.doc' Artifact, then via Realization (strength: 4) to the 'Word Document' Data Object and via another Realization to the 'Answer' Business Object. The result is: the PC *Realizes* the 'Answer' Business Object.

In other words: the PC *Accesses* the 'Answer' Business Object and it also *Realizes* that same 'Answer' Business Object. Here it is clear that we are looking at two aspects of this PC, it both executes the application and it stores the data. If the data were to reside on another server, we would not have both routes. So, the two routes are in fact a true aspect of

the situation: the PC does both and so both relations dutifully appear. No problem.

So, all is well? It gets a little more complicated. Have a look at the Basic Application pattern, repeated in View 56.

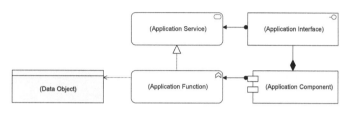

View 56. *The Basic Application Pattern*

If you go from Application Component to Application Service, you can follow two routes. The first route (via the Application Interface) leads to Assigned-To as the (weakest) derived 'summary' relation. But the one via the Application Function leads to Realization as the (weakest) derived 'summary' relation. ArchiMate does not tell you which one to take if two possible routes exist. That is OK, as we saw in the previous example, when two routes stand for two different aspects. But in this case, either derived relation says something about how you view the concept of Application Component. If you choose Assigned-To, you keep to the separation of active component and its behavior. If you choose Realization, you look at the Application Component from a more behavioral point of view. We get back to this confusing issue when we discuss the language and look at possible improvements in Chapter "Discussing ArchiMate" on page 207.

What all of this so far implies is that derived relations are useful to make summary views or abstract representations of a complex landscape, but there are risks involved in using them without (or mixed with) the underlying reality. The risks we have seen so far are still benign. But there are some pitfalls we will see later.

Finally, returning to View 11 on page 24 in System Software and Devices, if we add a couple of Technology Interfaces to that view we get View 57.

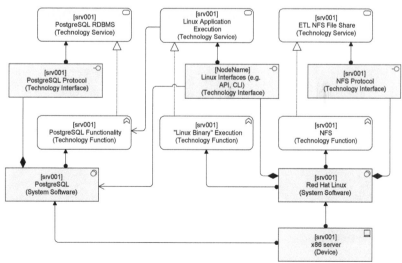

View 57. *System Software and Device with Interfaces*

You might understand why I did not show this in View 11: very complicated for something as simple as a server that provides a file share and a database. But using derived rela-

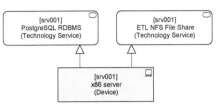

View 59. *Simplified/derived version of View 57*

tions, you can conclude that View 59 is a correct representation of the same. So, if you want to keep it simple: you can just model these. Keeping it simple and using abstractions make your models and views easier for the reader, but there are some caveats. We'll encounter several of those later in the book.

9.2 Derived Dynamic Relations

Since ArchiMate 2 there is also the possibility to create derived relations from *dynamic* relations. The procedure has changed in ArchiMate 3 and now is: you may move the start or endpoint of a Flow relation at an element to the start of a *structural* relation (Composition, Aggregation, Assignment, Realization) that ends at that element.

Take a look at the example in View 58 which uses Flow. If we start with Flow A (red) and we move the endpoint of that Flow to the start of Realization relation 2 (purple), we get Flow B (blue). We can also move the start of A to the element at the start of Realization 1 (violet) and get Flow C (green). We can do both in either order and get Flow D (orange). And so forth to produce all the other Flows in the diagram.

For Trigger the procedure is almost the same. There is a constraint: Instead of all 'moving an endpoint up' the dependency of all structural relations you may *only* move it up for Assignment.

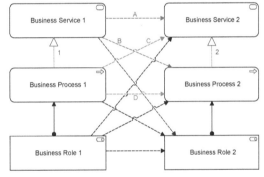

View 58. *Derived Dynamic Relations*

The Trigger relation is also transitive: if *a* Triggers *b* and *b* Triggers *c*, then *a* Triggers *c*. This is a conclusion that is not always valid of course. The fact that the Legal Business Function Triggers the Sales Business Function (e.g. when there is an update in the service agreement text for customers), combined with the fact that the Sales Business Function Triggers the Finance Business Function (e.g. when an invoice needs to be sent) does not mean that the Legal Business Function Triggers the Finance Business Function. The logical nature of a rule-based grammar is never able to cover all the possible meanings in real world scenarios.

9.3 Are derived relations real relations?

The ArchiMate 3.0.1 standard contains a table (appendix B) with all allowed relations between element types. This table is calculated from the direct relations in the meta-model and 'meta-meta-model'* and the derivation rules. It contains all the possible direct and derived relations in ArchiMate and tools must support these to be ArchiMate compliant. All of these are, according to ArchiMate, to be seen as valid relations. Note that the table† in version 3.0 of the standard was horribly broken and this was fixed more than a year later in 3.0.1.

Most practitioners will use the relations in the table as if they are all 'independently real' in a way, that is, not bothering about a relation being indirect and what that means.

Derived relations have subtly changed over the years. The original (seductive, but naive) idea seems to have been that it should be possible to 'calculate' valid summary views from complicated models, thus providing both the designers and the business with a preferred way of looking at the landscape *automatically*, while being sure that both were just different views of the same model and thus coherent‡. Of course, this changed when in reality people started to model using derived relations without bothering about the underlying (implicit) details. As a result, the difference between derived and direct has all but disappeared in ArchiMate modeling circles and the main function for derivation today is to calculate the relationship table from the meta-model and meta-meta model. But some derived relations can only have a meaning if understood through an underlying route of direct relations. For instance, many business processes depend on the local network (The LAN); if the network goes down all hell breaks loose. But no business process uses the network directly, they use applications and these applications use infrastructure. If you draw a Serving relation from a Router to a Business Process (an approach that neglects ArchiMate's official but rather limited Networking elements to model networking, see 28.1 "Networking" on page 150), it is certainly true, but in reality it implies that the intermediary elements are there, even if they have not been modeled. The situation is even more complex because even what could be a direct relation may be derived. If Application Service A Serves Application Function C, it is still possible that in between sits Application B (and potentially many others as well).

---

* There are underlying abstract elements in the standard, such as 'Composite Element', 'Core Element' that are used in the description of the standard. The meta-model is what we actually use when modeling and what is described and used in this book.

† There were also many problems with the text and figures in the rest of the standard. And while not everything has been fixed, I strongly advise against relying on ArchiMate 3.0 and not updating to ArchiMate 3.0.1.

‡ The name ArchiMate stems from a contraction of the words 'Architecture' and 'Animate'. The original research idea was that it should be possible to animate architecture views (probably based on that idea of derived 'shortcuts/summaries' and other ways of providing different users with different viewpoints *automatically*).

9.4 How useful are derived relations?

As a syntactical procedure that creates useful inferences from a detailed model, derived relations are of limited use. They will not allow all meaningful conclusions and allow for many false ones because deriving valid inferences requires more than what a syntactical/logical procedure can deliver. (We could have known given Uncle Ludwig's analysis of more than half a century ago). The derivation mechanism, in other words, is insufficiently reliable in the real world.

I tend to use them above all as a guide during the development of modeling patterns. For analysis in models, I allow more freedom than ArchiMate's derived relations allow. Every modeled relation is fair game from which to draw conclusions (across the entire model).

10. Non-Core ArchiMate domains

10.1 Strategy

As mentioned in section 6 "An ArchiMate Map", ArchiMate sees Strategy (in part) as some sort of abstraction which is Realized by the 'enterprise itself' (the Core). It is easiest to present a small example first. One is shown in View 60.

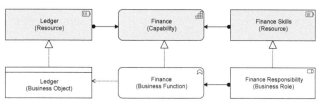

View 60. *Capability and Resource are abstractions of the 'enterprise itself'*

Here we see that the enterprise's Finance Capability is Realized by the Finance Business Function, which, you will recall, generally is the behavior performed by a Business Role, in this case the Finance Responsibility Business Role. At the Strategy level, this role represents a Resource, which I have named Finance Skills. This Resource is then Assigned to the Capability. On the left hand side, something that looks like it happens: we have a Ledger Business Object that Realizes the Ledger Resource in the Strategy domain. As you will recall, the Finance Business Function is behavior, which can Access Business Objects, in this case the Ledger Business Object. Note that there is a difference between the layers: where Business Function *Accesses* the Business Object, the Resource is *Assigned-To* the Capability.

According to ArchiMate, Strategy is about 'long-term or generic plans'. Strategy, thus, cannot be easily made up from elements of 'the enterprise itself' (which, I might stress here, is a term I have coined, it does not come from the standard). Being a more reality-oriented architect, I tend to disagree. All this abstraction makes the things we use less easy to use (and thus with a less practical meaning). In other words: I think the capability of deploying a fighting force of such and such size, with such and such equipment, and such and such skills is made up of real elements of 'the enterprise itself' (in this case: an army). However, this section of this book is devoted to describing ArchiMate as it is, so let's describe the first two new element types:

This is Capability. This is meant to model the high-level representation of the abilities of an organization (either existing

or desired). Capability in ArchiMate is a 'behavioral' element, which means that it needs structure that can 'make that behavior happen'. Those are the Resources:

This is Resource. A Resource is an asset that an organization controls/owns. These can be tangible (facilities, equipment, cash) or intangible (rights, skills). Resources are needed for a Capability to exist, which is modeled by Assigning them to the Capability.

As mentioned before (see View 3 on page 18), the Strategy domain doesn't fully reproduce ArchiMate's standard active-behavior-passive aspect split. It is useful to quote the standard's exact definition here:

"A capability represents an ability that an active structure element, such as an organization, person, or system, possesses. "

However, as you can see in the example, Capability is not positioned as 'possessed' by 'actual' active structure, only indirectly: It is positioned as an *abstraction* of the behavior (of active structure). Here (as in many other places), by the way, we encounter the fact that natural language and our human concepts are often impossible to define strictly in exact terms (Uncle Ludwig again). While active structure 'performs' behavior, we — as humans — often say some agent 'has' behavior and we mean the same thing. Along the linguistic route of 'has' comes the term 'possess', while along the term 'performs' comes the use of the term 'assignment'. In the Strategy domain, Assigned-To means 'needs' or 'requires'. It is best not to dwell on such 'imperfections' stemming from the essential conflict of non-logical natural language and logical modeling and just accept what the standard gives you as a 'tool'.

To illustrate that the ArchiMate layers are not really layers (in terms of being stacked in a single order), a variation on View 60 is shown in View 61. Here, the Strategy-domain elements are Realized by application-layer elements.

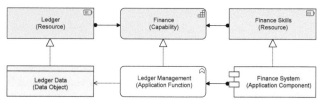

View 61. *Capability and Resource can be Realized by any 'layer' of the ArchiMate Core*

Now, strategy is of course about defining what you are going to do. Hence, the Strategy domain of ArchiMate comes with an element that can be used to model this (high-level, long term of course).

 This is Course of Action. It is meant to model what the enterprise has decided to do (strategically of course). Now, as almost always, an example will explain its use best.

In View 62, a simple example is shown. We have a dinosaur company that is being eaten alive by nimble small start-ups using big data analytics. To survive, the company has devised the strategy that it will acquire these startups and merge them with its own operations. For this, it has devised the "Resistance is futile, you will be assimilated" strategy. The Strategy has as its main Course of Action "Acquire Big Data Startups", which consists of two parts: merging the startup's operations with its own and merging the startup's employees with its own. Shown in the view is how this plays out in the company's *actual* Capabilities, which consist of indoctrinating new employees so they'll fit the existing company culture perfectly and burying IT innovation in non-productive setups. Also shown here: the use of Grouping to aggregate a set of arbitrary concepts, in this case the Strategy concepts and their relations.

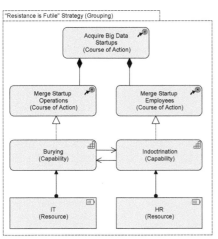

View 62. *Simple Strategy Example: "Resistance is futile, you will be assimilated"*

Strategy is a brand new domain in ArchiMate. This means that — as I am writing this — there is little experience and — just as with most other changes in ArchiMate with respect to the previous version(s) — some kinks will still have to be ironed out. To give a simple example: suppose a Course of Action requires us to build a new Capability? Should not a Course of Action be able to create one in some way?

To complete this explanation, View 63 contains an overview of the Strategy domain's meta-model and its relation to the rest (the stacked elements are not perfectly ArchiMate) and how it is related to the rest of ArchiMate (with the exception of the Motivation aspect, which will follow below). In section 12.11 "The Use of the Non-core Domains" on page 54, we will shortly discuss the use of this domain in enterprise architecture modeling, but I can already say here that the rest of the book will not pay extensive attention to this domain. Not that it is needed: it's simple enough.

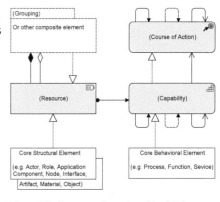

View 63. *Strategy domain of ArchiMate*

10.2 Implementation & Migration

The Implementation & Migration domain has been part of ArchiMate since ArchiMate 2. The domain is meant to model everything related to change. This means it can be used to model plateaus (enterprise architecture lingo, see below), 'gaps' between plateaus, and the work needed to realize enterprise changes (go from one plateau to another) in projects programs. It can again best been explained by an example.

In View 64, we see the Program that has come out of the strategy of the previous section. This Program consists of a couple of Work Packages that Realize Deliverables. These Deliverables Realize Plateaus, which Aggregate 'real' elements of our landscape. There is an initial Plateau that stands for the situation at the start of the Program.

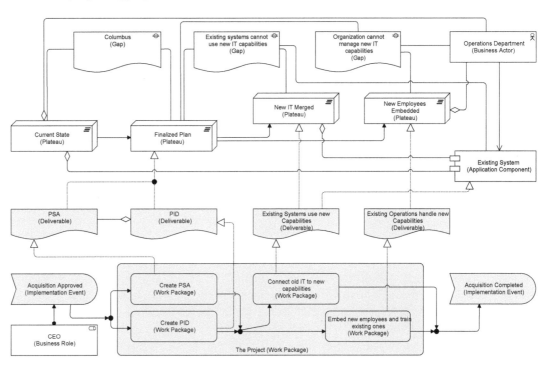

View 64. *Example of the Implementation and Migration domain with a bit of context*

A few possible relations with Core ArchiMate elements are shown. The CEO is Assigned-To the approval to signify his importance for this event. Some Plateaus Aggregate the Existing System an the Operations Department, as these are objects of the changes. They are also related to some of the identified Gaps. Let's describe the various elements.

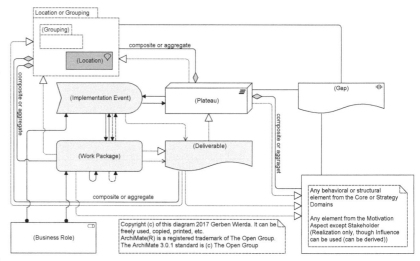

View 65. *Implementation and Migration domain of ArchiMate — meta-model overview*

 This is the Plateau. It generally stands for 'a state the enterprise 'landscape' can be in', mostly used to describe intermediate states in a larger transformation of the enterprise's landscape), but — as you can see in the example — it can also be used to model phases in a program or project. In the example, the startup phase of the project delivers a Project Initiation Document (from the Prince2 method) and a Project Start Architecture (from the DYA framework).

 This is the Gap. It stands for a difference between Plateaus. It will generally be the product of a gap-analysis, so it is an assessment of sorts. It can be Associated with Plateaus or with elements from the Core (the 'enterprise itself'). In the example, the Columbus Gap (Columbus Management — as I read it originally from Jan Hoogervorst — is: "When we left, we did not know where we were going, when we arrived we did not know where we were, and everything was paid for by other people's money") is Associated with the state at the start of the project and the moment the plans are finished. We know where we are, what we are going to do, and where we will end. Or at least we have that illusion.

 This is the Work Package. It stands for an amount of work to be done in a project-like setting. So, actions intended to achieve a well-defined result, within time and resource constraints.

 This is the Deliverable. It stands for anything well-defined that comes out of a Work Package. In most project management methods, these need to be signed-off on by for instance a project executive, or by customers, end users, and so forth.

And finally, this is the Implementation Event. It plays the same role in the Implementation and Migration domain as the other events do in the Core language: a marker to signify the start, status or end of behavior.

In View 65, the full Implementation and Migration part of the meta-model (including all the allowed direct relations, with the exception of the general rule that any type may Compose or Aggregate itself and Association is always allowed) is shown, including how it connects to the rest of ArchiMate (the gray diamonds represent that these relations can be either Composition or Aggregation).

In section 12.11 "The Use of the Non-core Domains" on page 54 we'll shortly discuss the use of this domain in enterprise architecture modeling, but I can already say here that the rest of the book will not pay extensive attention to this domain.

10.3 Motivation

As mentioned in section 6 "An ArchiMate Map", ArchiMate has a whole part intended to model the 'why'. It contains several concepts. It is easiest to illustrate (most of) them in an example as can be seen in View 66 on page 45.

The new elements and relations are:

 This is a Goal, which is an end state that a Stakeholder wants to achieve, or a direction a Stakeholder wants to move in. In the example, the Business wants to achieve 24/7 operations and the IT Run wants to lower IT cost.

 This is an Outcome. This is like Goal, but where Goal is about a *desire*, the Outcome is an actualy *achieved* result. In the example. the 24/7 Outcome Realizes the 24/7 Goal (this organization has been successful).

 This is a Requirement, which is a obligatory aspect of what a system or process Realizes. In the example, there is a Requirement to use only standard operating systems in your infrastructure, to have high-available infrastructure and to have a certain business process fully automated.

 This is a Driver, which is something that drives the organization to set goals and implement changes. These may be external (e.g. market forces, regulation) but also internal (e.g. the mission or vision of an organization). In the example, there is one driver: 'Increased World-Wide Competition'.

 This is an Assessment, which is the outcome of an analysis of a Driver. E.g. if a driver is "customer satisfaction", a poll might result in an assessment. In the example, there are two Assessments: a new competitor has arrived on the scene and we win/lose 10% of our customers each year (because they come to/from the competition)

This is a Stakeholder, which is a role that is interested in achieving a Goal. In our example, there are two Stakeholder roles: Business and IT Run (the responsibility for keeping the systems operational). Note that Stakeholder is not related (or equivalent) to the Business Role element in the Core.

There also is a new relation:

This is the Influence relationship. It is used to model the way Driver, Assessment, Goal, Principle, Requirement and Constraint can influence each other. Normally, a label on the relationship is used to denote the type of influence. In the example, the Requirement to use standardized operating systems in the infrastructure influences positively the 'Low IT Cost' Goal, but the 'High Available IT Infrastructure' influences that same Goal in a negative way. The 'High Available IT Infrastructure' Requirement positively influences the '24/7 Operations' Goal and the 'Fully Automated Business Process A' influences '24/7 Operations' positively but 'Low It Cost' negatively.

The full Motivation domain of ArchiMate is shown in View 67. It shows the allowed direct relations, excluding the always allowed Composition and Aggregation of an element type by itself. Also not shown in that diagram is that — except for Stakeholder — *any* Motivational element type may Influence *any* other Motivational element type. Stakeholder is the exception: the Stakeholder element type may *only* Influence itself.

Which leaves us at explaining the remaining Motivational element types:

View 67. *Motivation domain of the meta-model — most Influence relations not shown*

This is a Constraint (a Specialization of Requirement), represents is a forbidden aspect. Examples are budgetary or time constraints for a project (Work Package), technology constraints for a system (allowed technology), or legal constraints for processes or services. We could say that Constraint is a 'convenience' type, any role it performs in a model could have been fulfilled by a Requirement.

This is a Principle, which is a sort-of Goal that is a generalized Requirement, specifically for the *architecture* of the enterprise. There is no Principle modeled in the example, but — like Constraint — it behaves more like a Requirement than a Goal, though, even if it is not a Specialization of a Requirement.

This is Meaning. In earlier versions of ArchiMate, which lacked the Motivation aspect, it used to be part of the business layer. It represents an interpretation of something (e.g. a core element) by someone (e.g. a Stakeholder). If used in Association with passive structure, it is generally used for the intention of that element.

This is Value. In those earlier versions of ArchiMate, this also used to be part of the business layer. It stands for the value of either an element from the Core or from Outcome. But you can of course Associate it to anything, as Association is the catch-all. As far as I have seen modeling with the use of valuation, it is generally done differently, with valuation as (financial) numbers in the properties of elements. In other words: I've hardly ever seen this (or Meaning, which is evermore suspect from Uncle Ludwig's perspective) used in a useful (meaningful) way.

The Motivation aspect of ArchiMate shows its origin: the designers wanted to catch the intentions for the *architecture* of the enterprise (which was modeled with the Core elements) in their modeling language. Hence, the use of

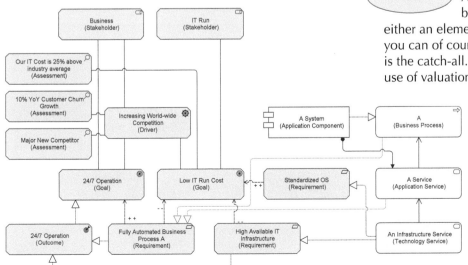

View 66. *ArchiMate Motivation aspect example*

the concept of Principle (which is a popular — though toxic (see my other book *Chess and the Art of Enterprise Architecture*) — concept in enterprise architecture circles), next to Requirement and Goal.

The concepts of the Motivation domain are clearly not exactly, discretely separated. It is sometimes a matter of taste if something is seen as a Goal or a Driver. Having a certain strategic Goal as an organization may count as a Driver, it seems to me. The divide between a requirement and a principle is not very clear either. It seems it is a Requirement that has been promoted to a Goal in a certain context. These overlaps and indistinctnesses are not really a problem (there are more issues like this in ArchiMate), it then comes down to creating your own good patterns to use them. Just don't rely on the standard to be a good guide here.

What this part of ArchiMate also shows is how different the world of human intentions and motivations is from the logical world of IT and how difficult it is to map one onto the other ("I have one negative influence and one positive. Now what?").

The relations between the elements are generally Influences or Associations. The exceptions are that Realization is used to:

- let a Requirement or Constraint (potentially via Principle) Realize a Goal, via Outcome;

- let any ArchiMate concept from other domains Realize a Requirement. In the example, a Technology Service, an Application Service and a Business Process all Realize a Requirement. An interesting question is if you have — as is the case in the example — a Requirement like 'Fully automated Business Process'. Is it the Business Process that Realizes this Requirement (in red) or the Application Service (in blue) or both? There is quite a bit of freedom in choosing your patterns.

In section 12.11 "The Use of the Non-core Domains" on page 54 we'll shortly discuss the use of this domain in enterprise architecture modeling, but I can already say here that the rest of the book will not pay extensive attention to this domain with respect to its original goal: modeling the intentions of the *architecture* (principles and all).

Nothing stops us from using this for other practical uses, that is modeling intentions of the *enterprise*, however. As shown in section 20 "Modeling Risk & Security with Motivation Elements" on page 111, the Motivation domain offers us a basic mechanism to model Risks, Control Objectives (including those from Security) and Control Measures and in that way link ArchiMate models to the world of Risk and Security.

Closing Remarks on ArchiMate

ArchiMate has improved and matured over the years, but there are still remnants that will make you wonder. If you get the feeling that ArchiMate is not 100% clean, I cannot fault you. But even with these issues (which we will visit later) I must stress that in my experience, ArchiMate is *extremely* usable, and even more so in version 3 than in previous versions. Creating Project Start Architectures based on detailed ArchiMate models has, in my experience, substantially reduced delays and unforeseen issues — having a detailed 'Current-State' model has seriously improved control over and reporting on our landscape to regulators.

When we started to use ArchiMate, we initially had many doubts about how the ArchiMate designers had set up the language. But, we did follow the rule that we would strictly stick to the meta-model and not change or adapt it in any way (even though our tool supported that). We did this for two reasons:

- Any future tool update might break our models or require a lot of work;

- Understanding something comes only after a lot of experience. Though we did sometimes dislike what we saw, we decided to distrust our (beginner) skills more than the skills of the language designers. This was wise: when our experience grew, we learned to appreciate most of the choices the designers had made.

If you focus on finding faults (something that comes naturally for architects as they are always for the lookout of something that may break) you will. But in my experience, that does not affect the usability much. ArchiMate is very, very usable.

11. Some Beginners' Pitfalls

11.1 Pitfalls of Derived Relations

I once encountered the snippet in View 68.

The modeler intended to model a file that was accessed by an application. He used an Artifact for the file (which makes sense), but his tool did not allow him to draw an Access relation from Application Service X to the Artifact.

Having an Access relation from Application Service to Artifact is not in the

View 68. *Artifact 'Used-By' Application Service?*

core meta-model. Having an Access relation from Application Service to Artifact as a derived relation was not possible at the time (ArchiMate 2) as it required traveling a route with relations in opposite directions (Realization from Artifact to Data Object and Access from Application Service to Data Object). In ArchiMate 3 it is possible, because the layering has become less strictly bottom-up (see 7.16 "Who is in Charge?" on page 30).

His tool suggested though, that the Serving relation was possible. At the time, that relation was still called Used-By, and from a human language point of view, it made sense: "the file is 'used by' the application service'. If you say this to a fellow human being, he or she will know what you mean. So, he assumed that all was well and — driven by an understandable desire to be productive — carried on.

But in ArchiMate, this is not what it means because ArchiMate's Serving (formerly 'Used-By') relation is not equivalent to natural language's 'used by'. Since this Serving relation is not a core relation, it is some sort of a derived relation. So, the question is, what route lies behind this derivate? What hidden assumptions are there that make this relation possible? View 69 shows a possible expansion of what his derived Serving relation means (his original relation in red).

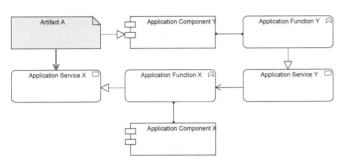

View 69. *Artifact 'Used-By' a Business Service: the hidden objects*

As you can see, the Serving relation from Artifact A to Application Service X was possible, because an application can use *another* application (and not so much data), and that *other* application is then Realized by our Artifact A. He thought he modeled the use of data but he actually modeled the use of another (hidden) application.

So, even if the language allows the relation, it is not certain that the relation actually means what you think. That shortcut leaves intermediate structure out, and sometimes (as shown here) that structure in ArchiMate will be something that is not what you intended to show.

> Pitfall 1. Derived relations may not mean what you think.

This is one reason why I generally say that it is best to keep as close as possible to the core relations in the meta-model, and only use derived relations when they are part of patterns. We will discuss many patterns in the rest of the book.

11.2 Don't trust the language or the tool blindly: know what you are doing

A tool sometimes offers to create you a 'default relation' between two elements. If you draw a relation between an Application Component and a Business Process, it may prefer the core relation Assigned-To over the derived relation

'Serving'. I have seen quite a few beginner models in ArchiMate 1 & 2 that had Assigned-To relations between Application Components and Business Processes that was *not* an automated business process. (This was the way automated business was modeled in previous versions of ArchiMate. You might still encounter diagrams that use this, so I keep this information in). They meant to write that an Application Component was Serving a Business Process (a derived relation and also what they meant to model) but ended up drawing an Assignment and thus effectively writing (in ArchiMate 1 & 2) that the application automatically performed the Business Process.

Another beginner modeled View 70 (in the ArchiMate 1.0 days).

View 70. *This was possible in ArchiMate 1.0*

For this one, I could not find a derived route at all. Here, it turned out, the ArchiMate 1.0 specification did allow it (it was in the table that has all the possible relations and derived relations). This was a leftover of earlier versions before ArchiMate became a standard of The Open Group. It was never removed from the table and dutifully implemented by the tool builder. Sadly though, it was an error in ArchiMate 1.0. The error, by the way, has been fixed since ArchiMate 2.0, so decent tools in recent versions will not allow you to draw this relation anymore. But there are always errors. ArchiMate 3.0 as released in June 2016 for instance, omitted relations from the 'all relations table' that were subsequently often not implemented by a tool. A tool may often support relations that are not allowed or omit relations that are.

> Pitfall 2. Not checking/knowing if your relation makes sense in the meta-model.

And finally, I once modeled an Interaction and a Collaboration. To my surprise, the tool allowed an Aggregation from Interaction to Function, but not the other way around as I wanted. It can be seen in View 71. Now, this is not exactly how ArchiMate defines the Interaction elements (Interaction elements are not defined as an Aggregate of functions/processes, they are just the behavior of a Collaboration, which is an Aggregation (of roles or application components, recall Section 8.2 "(Formal) Collaboration and Interaction" on page 33).

Whatever I did, I could not get the Aggregation relations on the left the way they are on the right, the way they make sense when you want to model this detail. It turned out, the tool makers had forgotten to implement the allowed relation between Interaction and its constituent Functions and when you tried to create it, the tool found another relation that was possible because of *meta-model*-Specialization: since Interaction and Function were both implemented as Specializations of an underlying implicit behavioral element in the meta-model that was more or less a left over from pre-ArchiMate-1 (remember: this was still ArchiMate 2, ArchiMate 3 has a better foundation), and

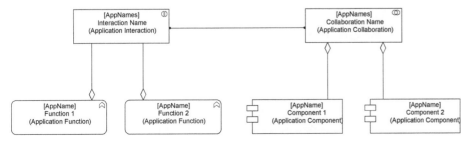

View 71. *Not quite what ArchiMate intended,*

because any type of element can Aggregate its own kind, it was possible to Aggregate an Interaction under a Function.

Pitfall 3. Trusting your tool blindly.

Lastly, ArchiMate (and several tools) support 'viewpoints'. In ArchiMate 3, Viewpoints have become optional, which is a good thing in many ways (for one: if you want to certify, you don't need to be able to reproduce them all). Viewpoints are in fact subsets of the ArchiMate meta-model (the subset may include derived relations). A viewpoint may restrict which types of elements you may model and what relations are allowed between them. They are a sort of patterns, but not quite, as they do not so much prescribe *how* to model but only offer constraints in *what* you can show.

I use 'view templates' for modeling (see Section 31 "Construction & Use Views" on page 189). A tool will constrain your use of elements and relations in an ArchiMate Viewpoint and not being able to create a relation may not be because it is not allowed, but because it is not allowed in the active Viewpoint.

Pitfall 4. Using a viewpoint without knowing that you are.

11.3 Misunderstanding the standard meta-model diagram

I have seen beginners often just copy the relations they see between element types in the basic meta-model (View 54 on page 38). This is generally fine, but there are some snags.

A common snag is the way the standard meta-model shows the relation(s) between a function/process and a service. This looks like View 73.

What the view illustrates is that 'a' function can realize 'a' service and that 'a' service can be used by 'a' function. But

in real modeling, we model generally not 'a' service or function. We model specific (even if they are abstract) services and functions.

So, when a beginner models something like View 73 as the relations between a specific function and the service that it provides, he actually says the function also uses the service it provides: it uses itself. Now, as a way of modeling recursion, this could be OK, but that is probably not what is meant (we generally do not model this kind of technical details in Enterprise Architecture). In short: the *meta-model* pattern of View 73 should most likely *not* appear in our models.

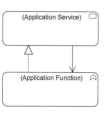

View 73. *How Function and Service are displayed in the Meta-model*

What the above snippet illustrates is that *an* element of the *type* Application Function can Realize *an* element of the *type* Application Service, and that *an(other)* element of the *type* Application Function can use *an element* of the *type* Application Service as illustrated in View 72.

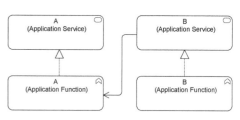

View 72. *How the function/service relations in the meta-model are intended.*

The Realize and Serving relations are between the same *types* of element, but not between the same *elements*. And of course, the same is true at the Business and Technology levels.

Pitfall 5. Copying relations in the meta-model to your model blindly.

12. Some Noteworthy Aspects of ArchiMate

12.1 Licensing

Though being the property of The *Open* Group, it is debatable wether ArchiMate is an *open* standard. Most definitions of 'open standard' require the standard to be royalty-free and maintained by a not-for-profit organization. ArchiMate meets neither requirement. There are definitions of 'open standard' without these requirements, such as industry standards in a commercial domain, e.g. telecom standards (which are generally based on patents). These are licensed against FRAND (Fair, Reasonable, And Non-Discriminatory) terms. Whatever your interpretation of 'open', the short story is (Spring 2017):

- Writing about ArchiMate (blogs, books) is royalty-free;
- ArchiMate is royalty-free for academia;
- ArchiMate is royalty-free for internal use by organizations;
- ArchiMate is royalty-free for internal use by organizations that use it to do consultancy for others, mainly as

long as you do not advertise that you sell 'ArchiMate consultancy';

- Selling ArchiMate tools & training requires (in practice, possibly not legally) a commercial license from TOG, especially if you want to use the ArchiMate® Registered Trademark in commercial traffic. Prices start at US$ 2500/year. Think twice before you start building a tool with a plan to sell for $10 in the App Store.

There is a more extensive treatment of the (rather toxic) legal issues on the underpinnenechess.com web site. The legal reality is much more complex than the bullets above and there is no warranty that the above stands up in court. You need to read the actual licensing conditions of ArchiMate's material and the use of the ArchiMate® Registered Trademark and consult a good IPR lawyer if you do not want to pay unnecessary fees when exploiting ArchiMate commercially (or pay up, which is probably cheaper). Besides, these may change in the future while this book will not necessarily follow. I personally do not consider ArchiMate an *open* standard (but a *commercially exploited consortium* standard), but as I'm not religious about using only open standards. I do not mind.

12.2 ArchiMate, the modeling language

ArchiMate started out as a public Dutch research institute project, supported by a couple of large administrative organizations, both public and private. Its initial version was finalized in 2004. In 2009 it was published as a standard by The Open Group.

Enterprise Architecture is not new and quite a bit of modeling has been done, most of it not in ArchiMate.

People create models for projects, often just as a set of images in an 'architecture' document. Sometimes, some modeling for projects is done in UML, but most of the time, you will look at some non- or semi-standardized use of boxes, arrows, dotted lines, nesting, etc., generally some sort of free-format graphical tooling will be used like Microsoft Visio for Windows or OmniGraffle for Mac or worse: Microsoft PowerPoint. One of the 'nice' aspects of such modeling is that it is often ambiguous enough for all stakeholders to see their own preferred reality in it. A more vague and ambiguous approach enables this often 'politically' expedient modeling. Everybody is happy, that is, until it turns out there is a problem somewhere during a later phase of a project. In my experience, people do not understand detailed Visio images either, but they seldom have to understand them anyway, so everybody is happy. When ArchiMate arrives, suddenly people are confronted with views that they have to agree on as a definition of sorts, and suddenly they have to understand what the image says. And the result is that some of them will fight adoption of the language. They want to stick to the old simpler way. Other resistance comes from people who see some of ArchiMate's weaknesses (especially software architects are often in this group, as ArchiMate's 'looseness' is in conflict with their need for solid foundations).

It gets even worse with the modeling of your current state. Once every few years, the lack of insight into the existing landscape will cause an effort to create an overview. People work for months at unearthing the situation and generally in the end you will have a few large posters with boxes and lines (and a legend to explain what every box type, arrow type and color signifies). The model is never maintained and after a year, it becomes so outdated that it becomes pretty useless for anything but a general introduction. Now, with ArchiMate, this can of course also happen if you just draw your visuals in ArchiMate without the support of tooling that can keep thousands of elements and relations in a single coherent model.

The fact that a single coherent model is useful is of course clear to many. So sometimes modeling is done in Enterprise Architecture tooling. These tools often have their own internal proprietary language or meta-model: a meta-model that also comes with a certain philosophy on what Enterprise Architecture is. These days, some of these tools will have ArchiMate as an option, often (more or less successfully) grafted on top of something like UML or their own proprietary language. I'll say a bit more about tooling in Chapter "Tooling" on page 219.

Modeling in ArchiMate brings the advantage of a fixed syntax of your models with reasonably clearly defined element and relation types. Modeling with a tool brings you the possibility of having those different views on what you are modeling to be actually related 'under the hood' and it brings more possibilities of actually maintaining and using your models. Modeling in ArchiMate also brings modeling that is independent of your modeling tool. If you ever decide to migrate to another tool that supports ArchiMate, it is possible. In the worst case the migration cannot be automated and migration is a lot of hand work, but it is possible without translation to another meta-model (which in a practical sense can be considered impossible: you will largely have to redo all your work).

In Chapter "Discussing ArchiMate" on page 207, I will discuss some of the areas where I think ArchiMate could be improved. In this chapter I'll say a few things about its strengths and some other weaknesses. But, although I have had my criticisms in the past and still have some to this day, *my overall conclusion remains that the language is very practical in actual use*. I would not have written a book about it if I were not convinced that ArchiMate can be extremely useful for Enterprise Architecture work. And the most important argument is this: there is currently no better practical alternative.

In the final document of the original research project, the authors write:

> *During the initial design of the ArchiMate language no explicit attention was paid to any desired formal properties of the metamodel itself. Emphasis was put on the applicability of the language.*

And this is also what resulted: a very *usable* language, which is not perfectly logical. As mentioned above, this sometimes offends architects who desire a formal, certain language which can be used without interpretation (or so some architects think). ArchiMate offers a 'rational' way of looking at Enterprise Architecture, but it does not offer a 'perfectly logical' way. Later versions of ArchiMate have improved and extended (where every aspect of the latter is not by definition an expression of the former) the language and some original choices leading to severe problems. The derivation mechanism could still be improved (though we know it can never be perfect). But it still remains noticeable here and there that the language never was based on a formal model. This remains true, even if ArchiMate 3 comes with a meta-meta-model, giving the language (the meta-model) an improved foundation.

12.3 Separation of 'actor' and 'behavior'

At the business level, separating process (behavior) from role (actor) is common practice in modeling. There is some confusion with respect to a business function (as will be discussed in Section 18.2 "Business Function or Business Process?" on page 92).

Some approaches see a function as behavior embedded in some sort of actor-like element, you can recognize it in the language used: a function *is* behavior (as in ArchiMate) versus a function *does* something (function *performs* behavior, it thus seems to be an actor of sorts). ArchiMate is a language where the separation is more fundamental and the separation has been replicated in all layers. This clarity in the meta-model really helps to make good models, but it is important to stress that at every layer, the 'actor' and its behavior are fundamentally inseparable. You can choose not to *model* one (and use derived relations to pass them by), but they are implied to exist even if they are not explicitly modeled.

The split often is confusing for those coming from ways of thinking that do not have that split, e.g. Process Modelers who seldom use the function concept at all (for more depth, see: 18.4 "The 'End-to-end' Business Process" on page 95) or Software Architects where (like in mathematics) a function is both structure and behavior in one.

There is another misinterpretation I've come across. If you say 'passive element' to people, they sometimes interpret that as 'not taking *initiative*', as 'reacting only'. This I encountered for instance when a colleague first was told about the interface concepts in ArchiMate. He found it illogical to say that an interface is an active element. Because an interface does nothing by itself, it needs to be used before it does something. In his use of the words active and passive it meant an interface is passive. But ArchiMate does not mean '*reactive*' by the word 'passive' and it does not mean 'taking initiative' by the word 'active'. In ArchiMate terms:

- Active means *capable* of performing behavior (either acting or reacting);
- Passive means *incapable* of *performing* behavior (or sometimes just the aspect of being incapable, e.g. an executable file of a program ("foo.exe") is passive. It's just a file; but it can Realize an Application Component, an abstraction that stands for the executable file being executed and becoming an active element in your landscape).

Behavior is what links active to passive elements: Active elements are Assigned-To behavior and behavioral elements Access passive elements. The passive ArchiMate elements are philosophically speaking 'objects' and the active ArchiMate objects are philosophically speaking 'subjects'. What the colleague said was not wrong, it is just not how ArchiMate defines the terms 'active' and 'passive'. For completeness, here quotes from ArchiMate's official underlying core definitions of active and passive:

Active structure elements are the subjects that can perform behavior.

A passive structure element is a structural element that cannot perform behavior.

Active structure elements can perform behavior on passive structure elements.

And service and interface are defined as:

[...] a service [...] represents an explicitly defined exposed behavior.

[...] an interface [..] represents a point of access where one or more services are provided to the environment.

12.4 One View Type

One of the beautiful aspects of ArchiMate is that it is a true Enterprise Architecture language. ArchiMate has been designed to model the interrelations and dependencies across *all* 'layers' in your Enterprise Architecture: from Business via Applications down to Infrastructure/Technology and vice versa. Though tooling often offers you all kinds of different view types (many of which are suggested optionally in the standard), ArchiMate in effect has only one single view type: the entire Enterprise Architecture. Those optional ArchiMate *Viewpoints* (which I do not use) only restrict what is in an ArchiMate view, but it is not a fundamentally different view.

At the software level, UML with all its different kind of views on the same objects and classes might be more precise. But to model the whole shebang, ArchiMate does a very good job.

12.5 On the direction of structural relations under the assumption of 'worst case'

In ArchiMate 3.0 the structural (Composition, Aggregation, Assignment, and Realization) and dependency (Serving, Access, Influence) relations all have a single direction. This direction plays an important role in calculating the derived

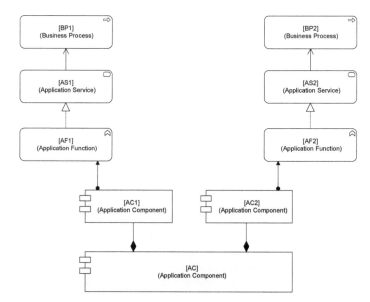

View 74. *Example used for discussing 'worst case' versus 'happy flow' assumptions about dependencies*

relations between elements that are indirectly related in a model.

The idea behind it seems logical. Take the example in View 74 on page 50. If you look at it, having a derivation mechanism that makes Business Process BP1 independent from Application (sub)Component AC2 is logical. After all, Business Process BP1 uses only Application Function AF1 and not Application Function AF2. But the question is, what do we mean exactly by dependency? Business Process BP1 is clearly not *meant* to depend on Application Function AF2, but does that mean it is *in*dependent? Suppose Application Function AF2 has a fault and it breaks the Application Function of Application Component AC and *as a consequence* Application Function AF1? In that case, there *is* a relation between Application Service AS1 and Application Function AF2, even if the relation is not *meant to* play a role and even if the relation from Application Component AC2 to Application Component AC has the opposite direction as the one from Application Component AC1 to Application Function AF1.

Or that interesting example of a Technology Service that does not depend on what Application Function or Technology Function uses it, except of course when the Application Function or Technology Function overwhelms the resources of the Technology Function which for instance happens when a Denial-of-Service attack hits your web servers, but it can also happen in normal cases. Suddenly, in that 'worst case' there *is* a dependency from 'served' to 'server'.

How you interpret 'dependence' has to do with the scenarios you take into account. Look at 'happy flow' only, and it makes sense that, for instance, Composition and Aggregation have a direction. But look at 'worst case' (a natural way of looking from an architectural point of view) and the Composition and Aggregation relations will create dependencies in the opposite direction too.

Or: if you look at 'worst case' instead of 'happy flow', all structural relations become bidirectional. Going back to the example above: there seems no way Business Process BP1, Application Service AS1, Application Function AF1 and Application Component AC1 can depend on Business Process BP2, because whatever breaks in Business Process BP2 cannot influence Application Service AS2. But if BP2 overwhelms AS2, AS1, AC1 and thus AC, BP1 will be affected. BP1 then depends on BP2.

Maybe in a well-designed model, one could give properties to the relations about their influence strength in both directions and then calculate the degree of dependence across a model (but now I am dreaming and it is probably not feasible either).

12.6 On the limitations of derived relations

Structural and dependency relations in ArchiMate have a direction and this direction plays a role when creating valid derived relations.

The directionality of relations was required during the development of ArchiMate because of the way derived relations

were set up. In that set up, bidirectional relations (Assignment and Association — then a structural relation, but the setup has changed with ArchiMate 3) were (for the sake of analysis) replaced by two unidirectional relations.

In ArchiMate 2.0, the bi-directionality of the Assignment relation was replaced by a unidirectionality. This was a good thing and it removed quite a few nonsense derived relations. The ones that made sense (like a Business Service Serving an Actor) were added explicitly as 'core set' relations to the meta-model (which is why my version in View 54 on page 38 has these explicitly added, often these are forgotten in views of the meta-model as they were not necessary in ArchiMate 1.0). The new meta-meta-model and the improved foundation of the full relationship table of version 3.0.1 has meant that even more relations that were no longer derivable have been added as direct relations (e.g. the dynamic relations between services and events).

If I look at the relations and their direction and I want to have some sort of criterium to be able to decide on making summaries and which combinations should and should not be allowed, I end up choosing the concept of 'dependence'

(Note: I originally wrote this for ArchiMate 1 and 2. The generic use of the term 'dependency' now overlaps with ArchiMate 3's use of the term for the differentiation between structural and dependency relations, and there is little I can do about it. There is a sort of dependency in all of ArchiMate's relations, so the choice in ArchiMate has been unfortunate.).

If element A depends via relation R on element B, but B does not via the same relation depend on A, then the relation from B to A is unidirectional. The clearest example is the Serving relation: if a Technology Service X Serves an Application Function Y, Y depends on X, but not the other way around. For the Technology Service X it is totally irrelevant if whether is actually used or not: it does not depend on being used (but as we saw above: this is not quite true, as real-world Denial-of-Service attacks prove). But — in a simplified design-sense — for Application Function Y, life stops when Technology Service X is not available and not the other way around.

Take also, for instance, the Access relation. It has a direction that runs from the behavioral element to the passive element. Now, I can understand that in part: a Data Object that is created or deleted by an Application Function depends for its existence on the work done by the Application Function. It also fits with the subject-verb-object like structure of ArchiMate. But a Data Object that is read by an Application Function does not depend on it at all, it is the other way around: if the Data Object is not there or it is broken, the Application Function may fail. The object may influence the subject, as in "The broken tile caused him to fall". In natural language, objects without behavior may be used as causes (become active). In ArchiMate, passive elements are not like that.

ArchiMate 3.0 has fixed some of these limitations by allowing 'top-down' dependencies (e.g. Technology being Served by the Business Layer as described in Section 7.16 "Who is in Charge?" on page 30). E.g. think of a Business Process that requires access to a certain document. The document is a Data Object that is Realized by a file Artifact and that itself Realizes a Business Object (e.g. a letter). The file Artifact resides on a server (Node). When you look at such a situation, there is nothing weird or 'wrong' with thinking that the Business Process Accesses the Artifact and your business people will probably think that way. They often think in files, not in abstract Business Objects. But the derived relation is *not* allowed along the passive or behavioral column because of the direction of Realization. You can create derived relations from Infrastructure to Process (a few are illustrated in View 75), but *not* the other way around. Thanks to a loosening of the bottom-up layering, we can now model a Business Process Accessing an Artifact (or Material, which in fact makes the Representation element superfluous, but they haven't removed it yet).

One of the things that initially attracted me to ArchiMate was not only the reasonable and holistic meta-model that is its foundation. It was the promise of derived relations. To have a model where you can have all the necessary details for a decent analysis as well as views where you have summarized the complex views in simpler ones for consumption by for instance management. And both views are correct and come from the same underlying structure.

I must admit, the official ArchiMate derived relations have lost much of their initial attraction for me. There are too many problems where you as an architect know that the language does not allow you a (derived) relation, but where you know it makes sense to have one. In my practice, it has turned out that the official derived relations have a very limited use. They are too restricted in many situations. It turns out that, depending on the patterns you use, you develop the need for quite different 'derived' relations.

I also have not seen a tool yet with decent support for derived relations. The original ArchiMate project created them as an extended set of relations on top of what is in the basic meta-model and they provided a mathematical proof (somebody has to get his M.Sc. or Ph.D. after all) that if they were defined as they were defined, the new set of 'basic + derived' relations was again a closed set. The standard now says the derived relations are as proper as the core relations.

It also is being presented as such in most courses and educational material. I haven't seen much material that goes into the limitations of this approach.

Adding derived relations next to the direct ones explicitly to a model creates a lot of new analysis routes in those models. And if you use tooling, the number of possible routes quickly overwhelms your effort to keep your analysis viewpoints (often some sort of algorithmic viewpoint logic) working. This is why I advise to stick as much as possible to the basic meta-model and *only* use derived relations in the creation of your *patterns* (which we will starting from Section 15 "Patterns"). That way you create a stable subset of all the possibilities that makes analysis of your models achievable. I advise against using too many derived relations other than those of your patterns.

Finally, it is often possible to draw false conclusions from derived relations. Have a look at View 76.

We have two Locations where Daleks are being built. These are services provided to some customer, e.g. by two contractors at the same location who perform the processes. Note: the processes with the same name are separate elements in the model. It could very well be that they are slightly different because of different circumstances, regulations, etc. From the original Flow (top) we may derive all the lower ones. But the red ones (marked 'False') are not valid derivations in reality. The materials gathered in London are used in London, not Amsterdam. Another Uncle Ludwig moment: meaning does not follow from grammatical rules. I have to admit that the example is somewhat contrived. Creating an example for unintended derived dynamic relations in ArchiMate 3 was more difficult than in ArchiMate 2. But there are many other examples, and even if the derivation rules are further improved (which I hope), they will still never be reliable.

12.7 Why two types of software?

ArchiMate has two element types for software:

- At the Technology Level (IT infrastructure), there is System Software, which is Assigned-To a Technology Function which Realizes a Technology Service;

- At the Application Level, there is the Application Component, which is Assigned-To an Application Function which Realizes an Application Service.

Now, if you know a bit about computers, you know that this distinction is engineering nonsense. After all, — maybe with the exception of the operating system ('supervisor') or virtualization software ('hypervisor') that directly interfaces with the hardware — software is software, whatever its use. That Relational Database System that you model at the Technology layer (e.g. Oracle, SQL*Server, DB2, PostgreSQL) is technically just another application that runs within the

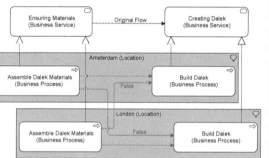
View 75. *From Node to Business Layer*

View 76. *Drawing false conclusions from derived dynamic relations* constraints of the operating system. So, an IT-engineer will probably initially balk at ArchiMate's separation of software in two types, where it is also can be a matter of taste (or confusion) how you model something. Take for instance the spreadsheet: it will be shown in Section 15.3 "Modeling Spreadsheet Applications" on page 65 that it can be modeled in two ways: either at the application layer or at the Technology layer. That seems problematic. Why should there be such confusion possible in the language?

But if you look at the reality of Enterprise Architecture, the discussion about types of software is *not technical*. It is about modeling for the enterprise how business, applications and infrastructure together (should) work. And when you take the *business perspective* and not the technical perspective, it is quite clear that such a mission-critical application that has all that specific business process oriented logic embedded in its code, is quite something different from that generic 'off the shelf' database that is needed to support it. If you look at the separation as 'business-specific' (i.e. containing business logic) versus 'generic', then the separation becomes more useful. Hence, the database is System Software, but the business-specific logic that is written inside it should be modeled as an Application Component, which is realized by that same database which, in fact, acts as an application *platform* in itself. As will be shown in the Application Deployment Patterns in Section 15 "Patterns" on page 62, it can become quite complex to create patterns for modeling modern architectures like three- (or even four-) tier application architectures and more modern inventions like SaaS. On the other hand: you have to invent the patterns only once — or take them from his book ;-) — but you can use them many times.

For sake of argument, we could try to imagine what would happen if we were to try to have only one software type in ArchiMate. The System Software of the Infrastructure would become (the equivalent of) an Application Component. Then, either the Application Function should be able to realize a Technology Service (which kind of makes the Technology Service a clone of Application Service) or the Technology Service realized by Software should become an Application Service (which means you have in fact software service versus hardware service). This leads to all kinds of problems with the business perspective on Enterprise Architecture. We either have application-layer elements in the Technology layer, which is confusing, or we have to limit infrastructure to hardware only. But the latter is also problematic because you can have many infrastructural components that can be Realized by both hardware and software. A couple of examples:

- A virtual hard disk in memory (RAM Disk);

- Software RAID;

- A network filter built from a general purpose computer with two network interfaces and dedicated software.

I think especially this latter problem is what would make a single type of software type in ArchiMate perhaps technically superior, but in terms of a business perspective (and a usable view on Enterprise Architecture) inferior. From a tech-

nical perspective the meaning comes from how it is *implemented* (is it a Device or an Application Component?), but from a business perspective, the meaning comes from its *use* (is it business-specific or generic functionality?). I think for the usability of ArchiMate for Enterprise Architecture modeling, it is a good thing ArchiMate has the (technically flawed) concept of two types of software, though I can imagine other solutions outside the constraints of ArchiMate.

12.8 There is more than one-to-one

An Artifact can Realize an Application Component. It can also Realize a Data Object. One data object can even Realize both. As will be described in more detail in Section 19 "Secondary and Tertiary Architecture" on page 104, realizing both will lead us to more complete thinking about our Enterprise's Architecture. Or the same Artifact can Realize both active and passive elements, as will be shown for instance in 15.3 "Modeling Spreadsheet Applications" on page 65. ArchiMate is very powerful, because of that, but it might take some getting used to.

Sometimes, concepts from the real world you are modeling will end up in quite different ways in your model. This has nothing specifically to do with ArchiMate, but ArchiMate does have support for it. A good example is a customer. That customer is both an Actor in your Enterprise Architecture, but it might *also* be a Business Object. ArchiMate can let you do both and so catch the two quite different aspects of your customer (what he does and how he is represented inside your business) very well.

12.9 Detailed or not?

We architects love abstraction. Abstraction makes the nitty-gritty and complex details disappear. Abstraction makes the unmanageable, manageable.

Our business colleagues also love it when we produce abstractions. It makes our end products easier to digest.

In the ArchiMate language, you can do both, which means that – apart from the precision-like modeling that you do, for instance, when building 'Current State', 'Solution', or 'Project/Change' detailed models – you can use the ArchiMate language in a more 'loose' set-up; e.g. when designing a landscape top-down, even in a rough way with broad strokes.

For instance, when designing, if you have a Business Process that requires the services of an application, you generally start with defining that application service in terms of 'what the process needs' and then you design how this service will be realized by one or more applications.

The ArchiMate language has enough freedom to be used to make models with a lot of abstraction, and as such it also supports an approach to Enterprise Architecture design that sees services as abstractions defined top-down (from the needs of those that use the service). In fact, such thinking was an important aspect of the design process of the ArchiMate language in the first place.

But the ArchiMate language also supports a more specific and precise use that is useful for creating precise 'Current State' or 'Project/Change' models that can be used for documenting or designing your enterprise.

There is much more that can be said about this, but you can rest assured that the power of expression of the ArchiMate language is good for both, even if the concepts have mostly been explained so far in the 'precision approach'. Besides, the ArchiMate language has another important way of simplification: the use of derived relations (with their limitations, as we saw in section 12.6 "On the limitations of derived relations" on page 51).

Together, both ways ('more abstract use of the concepts' and 'derived relations') create a powerful set that enables very high-level/abstract modeling in the ArchiMate language. More of this in Section 34 "Why Model? (And for Whom?)" on page 200 and in other places in this book.

12.10 Layering Ambiguity

ArchiMate 3 has what I would call 'layering ambiguity'. It contains in itself two separate and irreconcilable ideas about layering:

- Service-orientation: Elements from different layers represent *different* items and can Serve each other (Section 7.1). A GUI of an application Serving a (human) Business Role. A Technology (infrastructure) Service such as a File Share Serving an Application Function.

- Abstraction: Elements from different layers represent the *same* item in a different way (Section 7.14). An Artifact Realizing a Business Object, or — since ArchiMate 3 — an Application Service Realizing a Business Service of itself to signal an automated Business Service. Or (see Section 7.17) a Technology Service that Realizes an Application Service representation of itself;

ArchiMate started out as what is now the core, something that mixed the service-oriented structure of 'infrastructure serves application serves humans' in the behavior and active structure aspects while at the same time using the abstraction approach between layers in the passive structure aspect. These days, the abstraction approach is available almost everywhere (just not for internal active structure).

The mix of these two disjunct approaches to layering in the language can be quite confusing. More about this in Chapter "Discussing ArchiMate" on page 207.

12.11 The Use of the Non-core Domains

As illustrated in View 4 on page 18, ArchiMate can be divided into the Core and several other domains. The Core is used to model 'the enterprise itself'. The other domains have other functions. One can wonder what the uses of these other domains are.

What does putting strategy in a model add, really? And is it realistic to assume that we can actually model something complicated as strategy realistically in a set of simple distinct concepts and relations? Doesn't a model become a mess of arguable choices as soon as it becomes more realistic? Modeling the enterprise itself does not suffer from this problem as it is founded on the reality of the enterprise itself. But strategy (and intentions) are much less easy to grasp in discrete elements. So, for strategy at least: modeling will never be more than a rough illustration. I don't expect a board of an organization to use ArchiMate to model the logical structure of their strategy. There is therefore no need to discuss patterns for modeling strategy in the rest of the book. It is all rather basic, superficial, and has little actual practical consequences.

Modeling intentions has the same problem and another one besides: ArchiMate's meta-model for modeling intentions is rich, with 10 different concepts. It is meant to model the 'why' of your *architectural* choices, but it already shows the problems of trying to model human reasoning in rational terms (related to the failed dream of digital AI — and yes, I am aware of big data analytics; and why that is probably not going to change my assessment is not something for this book).

Then there are the overlaps or missing links. The meaning of the Goal concept overlaps with the Course of Action concept, the Driver concept and even with the Requirement and Principle concepts. An Assessment is something that should be 'creatable' by a process, but it isn't a Business Object. Stakeholder and Business Role are separate, without a good reason. See also Chapter "Discussing ArchiMate".

It is not all negative, though. Most of my objections about the potential use of the non-core domains come from having some knowledge about fundamental limitations of approaches like these. But there are practical upsides too. Documenting reasons for choices with the Motivation elements can be useful. The fact that it is a *model* doesn't really add much but documenting is generally a good thing, and modeling (though practiced with restraint here) doesn't cause much harm. Sometimes, the domain can even be used for something really practical from the organization's perspective. For instance, in 20 "Modeling Risk & Security with Motivation Elements" on page 111 I use the Motivation elements to model Risk & Security in a way that allows you to create reports about these from your models (when we started to do this, our regulator immediately upped us a notch in terms of being 'in control' of our landscape).

12.12 Why model?

We will get more into reasons for modeling later in the book and how it influences how you model, but generally there are two reasons:

1. Modeling to explain something visually;

2. Modeling as a tool to work with large complexity.

The former uses the language concepts to improve the clarity of the diagram. Use ArchiMate's Access relation, and it immediately tells you something that a generic arrow from a generic drawing does not. You trust the meaning of the various element and relation *types* to help you convey a message. Of course, this does require that the receiver also understands the language.

The latter uses the fact that the language is a form of structure that enables you to set up a body of knowledge that you can analyze, either by traveling through the model or by setting up automated analyses, such as "which processes depend on this program?". Especially in large models (I know of models with 100,000 elements and relations or more), this is an important reason for modeling.

Ideally, of course, your model can do both. But there is a trade-off: using automated analysis requires a limitation in the patterns you use and a strict discipline. More in Chapter "Reflections" on page 199 and elsewhere in the book.

13. From ArchiMate 2.1 to ArchiMate 3.0.1

The 3.0.1 version of the ArchiMate is a major upgrade. Almost all of ArchiMate 2 is still valid and so is most of ArchiMate 1. My patterns have evolved over the years and most of the patterns in this book are still valid in ArchiMate 2. Working purely from ArchiMate 3, sometimes other (non backwards-compatible) choices could be made. I'll pay some specific attention to these and I have also changed a few fundamental choices since Edition II because ArchiMate 3 allows better solutions.

The most important changes between ArchiMate 2 and ArchiMate 3 are in my view:

- The addition of Physical Elements and the Strategy domain;

- Most (but not all, sadly) of the strict BAT-layering (Business-Application-Technology) has gone:

    * Direct relations between the business and technology layers. There is no explicit or implicit 'application' in between;

    * The possibility to model 'top-down' dependencies, e.g. a Business Service serving a Technology Function etc. This is a very important change as it drops the classic layering straitjacket almost completely and allows for new useful patterns;

- Events in all Core layers;

- The possibility to use Junctions on Access, Serving, Assignment, and Realization relations;

- The removal of the Grouping non-concept and introduction of the Grouping true concept;

- The change in the way 'automated business' can be modeled;

- More possibilities to model abstractions;

- Assignment from System Software to System Software (but missing still: from System Software to Application Component).

Several of these were part of the improvement proposals that were part of Edition II of this book (such as the Grouping concept, automated business, events in all layers, and Capability (though in a different way), so I must be pleased*. And while I am, there remain several problems in my view, which I discuss in Chapter "Discussing ArchiMate" on page 207.

---

* The bad news was that as a result it was a *lot* of work to update Edition II to Edition III.TC1. Not only were different patterns sometimes required but also the workarounds I had created for limitations had to be removed from the patterns.

Style & Patterns

Style & Patterns

14. Aesthetics (Style)

14.1 Why aesthetics matters

If your views are simple, with only a few elements and relations, it will not be difficult for people to read them. But soon you'll find the need to create larger, more encompassing, views. And when you start having several tens of elements and many relations in a view, you'll find that it is hard for people to read them. You might even find it hard yourself when you get back to that view a few months later. It gets worse, when the view is a mess, visually.

Modeling with ArchiMate in that sense is not so different from writing ordinary text. Though in the end it is the conceptual aspect that matters, layout can have a devastating effect on the readability of text. The use of a lot of different fonts, sizes, styles, colors, etc., creates a chaos that overwhelms the senses and makes it difficult to get at the concepts. And that is exactly what style does: when style is good it becomes invisible: at its best it even helps making things clearer. The main task for visual style is — when used to improve readability, that is — to become as little a distraction as possible.

When the Apple Mac ushered in the area of graphical computers in the 80's, and formatting of text became for the first time something everybody could attempt, the first consequence was that the world was confronted with a lot of very ugly documents with disastrous visual styles and layouts. People tended to use every effect that was available in a single document. You often see the same when children start to create their first documents on computers. The same thing happened when the web went graphical in the 90's, you might remember the appalling web sites with a lot of blinking, distracting, banners, and so forth.

In terms of Enterprise Architecture modeling we're — as I'm writing this — at the same 'childish' stage: most views look very ugly, are chaotic in their layout and style, and in the end are much less usable than they could be.

So, in this section, I'm going to give some simple suggestions to improve the readability of your views. Note: archi-tects, especially the ones that tend to create the more complex models, belong to the somewhat smarter demographics and as such also on average somewhat to the more 'lazy' demographics. Laying out your views cleanly takes some energy. Keeping the views well laid out when you change them even more: add one element and you might well up having to rearrange tens more. So be prepared to put some effort into this. In my experience: it repays itself many, many times over.

The basic idea behind a good visual style is that the view should be `easy on the eyes'. That means it should be 'quiet'. And next to that, you need some ways to fight ambiguity and you need some redundancy. To give an example, have a look at View 79 on page 58, it contains a selection from the ArchiMate 2.1 meta-model in an unreadable layout. A readable layout of a selection from the ArchiMate 3 meta-model was View 54 on page 38.

14.2 Arranging relations

So, the first thing to do is:

> Style Guide 1. Make your relations in general go in vertical and horizontal directions only.

Keeping your relations like that immediately makes the view easier to look at. A lot of lines at a variety of angles overwhelms the HVS (Human Visual System). Only very rarely do I use a line segment at an angle. One exception is the Associations between elements and relations. Only when I think it makes the view easier on the eye (which is the general rule here), will I do it. The same goes for you: develop and follow your 'designer' instincts (which I think you should have if you're an architect). Generally, horizontal/vertical lines work best.

You must watch out for overdoing it, though. Many people will make their view even easier on the eye by using overlapping lines. But overlapping lines have a danger of being ambiguous. Have a look at View 80 on page 58.

Can you see which Business Objects are accessed by which Business Processes? You can't. So it might be easier on the eye, but it hides essential information. Therefore, it is normally better to model non-overlapping lines as shown in View 81.

So the next guideline is:

Style Guide 2. Don't let relations overlap.

As you can see in View 81, I have also rearranged the order of the Business Objects to prevent lines from crossing each other. Because:

Style Guide 3. Minimize the number of line crossings.

And finally, in View 81, I have arranged both Access relations beginning at Business Process X to lie close to each other, while having a larger distance to the Access relation

View 80. *Style: Overlapping Lines*

View 81. *Style - Non-overlapping Lines*

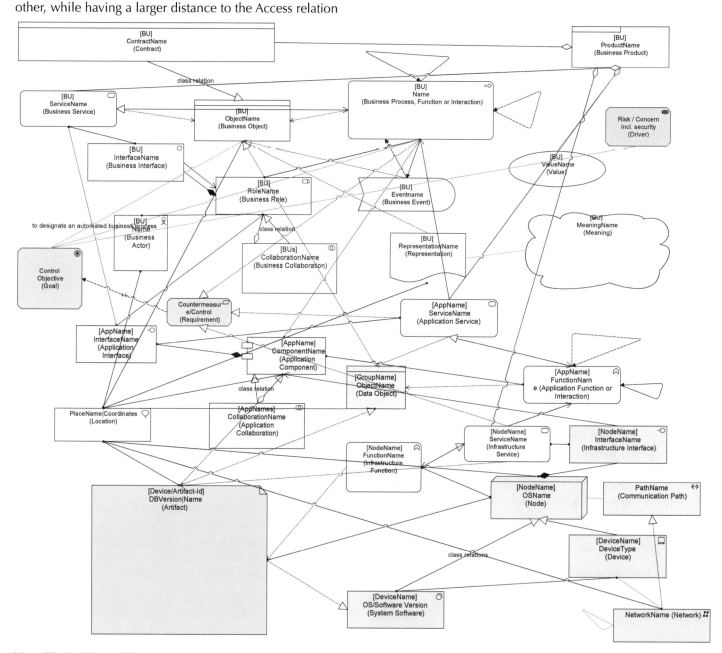

View 79. *ArchiMate 2.1 Metamodel in Bad Layout*

beginning at Business Process Y. I have created some sort of grouping on the first two relations, supporting the fact that they both are attached to Business Process X. Thus:

Style Guide 4. As far as possible: Group relations according to either source or destination.

What also helps is to align relations. Say, you have three elements in a row and two relations (between left and middle, and middle and right), it is easier on the eye the have the relations aligned vertically. Have a look at the example in View 83.

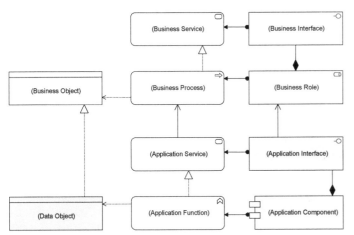

View 83. *Style: Non-aligned Relations*

Now compare with the one in View 82.

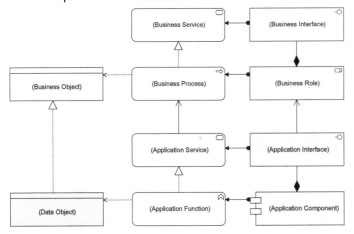

View 82. *Style: Aligned and Equally Sized objects, Aligned Relations*

You can see that — even in this small view — the second one is slightly 'quieter'. The effect is more pronounced the more complex your model becomes. Hence:

Style Guide 5. Align relations, even unrelated ones.

14.3 Sizing and Arranging elements

There are a few simple rules on sizing and arranging your elements that makes the view easier on the eye. So far, the last views above had all the elements created at the same size and laid out in a grid. Have a look at the variation on View 83 in View 84.

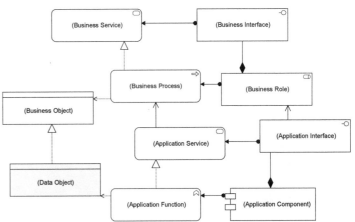

View 84. *Style: Equally-sized, non-aligned objects*

As you can see, removing alignment of the elements makes the view again more cluttered. So the fifth guideline is:

Style Guide 6. Align elements, even unrelated ones.

Then, of course, we can make View 84 noisier still, by varying element sizes as in View 85.

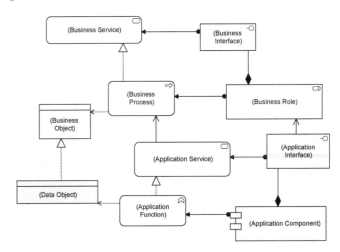

View 85. *Style: Variable-sized, non-aligned objects*

This is again more cluttered, so the next guideline is:

Style Guide 7. Use as few as few different element sizes as possible (analogous to not using too many font sizes in a text document).

Preferably, most of your elements have the same size. Note: you could have different sizes for different types of elements (say, all application services have one size and all application functions have another), but though the extra distinction might make it easier to spot different element types quickly, having multiple sizes quickly makes more chaos and that chaos overwhelms the advantage of the extra clue to separate element types. Besides, there is a better way to help separate element types (see below). So in general, use as few sizes as possible in your view.

We can make matters even worse still as can be seen in View 86 on page 60.

Just by rearranging the elements, I have created a view with 5 unnecessary line crossings. Note: there are no unnecessary

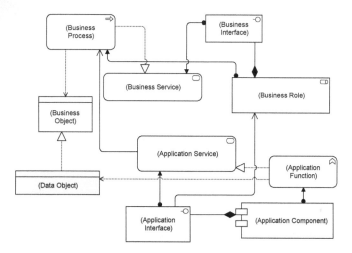

View 86. *Style: Variable-sized, non-aligned and non-ordered objects*

crossings here (under the constraint that I don't go around the outside). Try to imagine what would happen if I would change the order of attachments of relations on the Application Interface in this example. Hence, the next guidelines are:

> Style Guide 8. Align elements and attach relations such that relations are as simple as possible and with the least number of line crossings, preferably straight lines from one element to another.

And:

> Style Guide 9. If you have a nested element or groupings, align the elements that are on the inside as well.

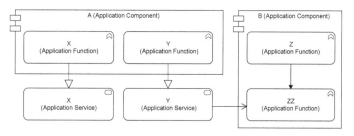

View 87. *Style: Align nested objects*

Note that in the example in View 87, Application Function Z is aligned with Application Functions X and Y and that Application Components A and B are also aligned.

Thus:

> Style Guide 10. Distribute elements evenly within their `group`.

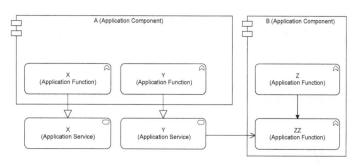

View 88. *Style: Objects not distributed evenly in their 'group'*

With a group, I mean that you might have a couple of related elements, I do not mean just actual ArchiMate Groupings or nestings, though there it applies as well. Such a group in my views will have all elements of the same size, aligned and evenly distributed. An unevenly distributed variation on the previous example can be seen in View 88.

Again, these rules are basic rules. Always, your main goal must be:

> Style Guide 11. *Make a view as easy on the eye, as 'quiet' as possible without losing essential information.*

This is the underlying idea. As we mentioned before, the Human Visual System takes up precious brain power and you want to free up maximum brain power for passing on essential information and a minimum wasted on unnecessary distractions. So sometimes you must break one of the rules to get the 'quietness' you desire. And so be it, unless of course, you will lose information in the process. A good example would be Style Guide 2 on page 58 in a case where there are a great number of relations and overlapping cannot make you draw false inferences. Aesthetics is never a matter of just following rules anyway.

One important final remark on sizing and arranging: the above guidelines lead to views that are rather 'boring'. For technical views for your fellow architects, that should not be a problem. But when you communicate to non-architects, you should allow yourself more freedom to get the message across (technical views do not have a 'message' per se).

Therefore, when I want to communicate with non-architects (e.g. management or users), I will relax the approach above, or, I will use something other than ArchiMate for that specific message. A message is often only valid at a certain moment in time anyway, so doing a one-off is not really a problem.

In fact, the HVS can even be 'underwhelmed'. If there is not enough 'to do', it switches attention off. This is why in my preferred visualization, the Application Component isn't a box with an app-icon, but it is a large 'icon'. This breaks up the monotony just enough. Using slanted Associations for relating payloads with Flows is another example.

14.4 Using color

Color is a powerful tool for communication. And it's easy to start using different colors for different (type of) elements in your view, say, you could color all elements of one business unit blue and of another business unit green. I think most of those uses for color can be done with labels and grouping (see below). I use color to mark certain *types* of elements consistently to improve readability of the *structure* I have created.

The official ArchiMate specification is colorless. The original ArchiMate project of Telin (Telematica Instituut), before the first TOG (The Open Group) standardization, used colors in a consistent way, though they were never a part of the original specification, they were a more something of a custom.

Those original `ArchiMate Colors' were blue, green and yellow. Blue was used for the active elements, like Actor and Role at the business level, Application Component on the application level and Device on the infrastructure level. Yellow was used for behavioral elements, like Business Process and Business Service on the business level, Application Function and Application Service on the application level and Technology Service on the infrastructure level. Green, finally, was used for passive elements, like Business Object at the business level, Data Object at the application level and Artifact on the infrastructure level.

But another way of separation, using the same colors was later introduced as well. This was mainly because there is one 'problem' with the original color scheme, and that is that the `interface', `service' and `data/business object' elements all have the same form/icon and would become indistinguishable (the same is true for 'function' and 'process' elements). Hence, if such an element were to be found in a view, it would not be immediately clear, either from the form or from the color, whether we were looking at a Business Service, an Application Service or a Technology Service. So, some people started to use the yellow/blue/green separation for business layer, application layer and infrastructure layer instead. This way of using colors also became the standard way for some tools.

ArchiMate is color-agnostic, but I have a preference for the original coloring. The reason is that one of the strong points of ArchiMate is the way it focuses on behavior as the link between 'actors' and `acted-upons'. In my modeling work, behavior is actually leading. For instance, when somebody started a discussion on adding the 'owner' of a system to our model, I realized that owner is a *role* and hence the ArchiMate-driven question arises: what is the *behavior* (process/function) of this role? And what does this behavior actually change, what is the `acted-upon' here? This led to what has been described in Section 19 "Secondary and Tertiary Architecture" on page 104.

Using the original color scheme strengthens that basic strong point of ArchiMate because it keeps a focus on the different roles the different elements in the ArchiMate grammar play. I find it especially useful because it supports my preference for modeling with behavior as the central axis around which everything revolves. It also works better in an explanatory setting, such as this book.

Still, it is handy to be able to discern to which layers elements belong. So, I came up with the color scheme I am using in this book too and which can be seen in View 54 "Selection of ArchiMate 3.0 Core meta-model in 9 colors, direct relations only" on page 38. Never mind the color used to signal aspects of certain relations in this image, this is just about the colors of the elements.

As you can see there, I kept the blue-for-actors, yellow-for-behavior, green-for-acted-upon separation of the original ArchiMate coloring, but with a twist. I deepened the colors for the technology level and lightened those of the business level (as the higher you go in the meta-model, the 'softer' reality becomes). Former colleague Joost Melsen told me:

Our usual demarcation is such, that a business process allows for a larger degree of freedom in behavior than an application function, which in turn is 'richer' in behavior than a Technology Function. We will probably never take away too much freedom on the human processing level in favor of IT, because it allows each of us humans to act and decide according to our own values of correctness, and thus be meaningful.

(Unless IT is in charge, of course — see section 7.16 "Who is in Charge?" on page 30). Anyway, if we now create overview views with all levels represented (e.g. for a Project Architecture), it is with this color scheme immediately clear what is business, what is application and what is infrastructure. It is also immediately clear what are actors, what is their behavior and what does this behavior change. It is easy to explain this to business and developers alike. But you will probably need to change the default settings of your tool.

14.5 Visual grouping

ArchiMate has an official 'Grouping' concept (see Section 14.5 "Visual grouping" on page 61) and for three relations (Composition, Aggregation and Assignment), you are also allowed to depict it by Nesting (see Section 7.8 "Nesting" on page 25). Here, I want to say something about 'visual grouping', as a means to keep views easy on the eye. For this, you can of course use the ArchiMate Grouping concept (though it does come with underlying Aggregation relations which you might not want in your model), but you can also do it in a purely visual way. For instance, you can put all the elements from the Business Layer close together, so that you can focus on one part of the view to see the business aspects. Or you can group on the basis of subprocesses in a view. The goal here is to make the layout of your view such that they eyes have to travel a minimum distance, based on what you want to convey. We'll see a few uses later in a few examples in the book.

14.6 About labels

ArchiMate has been labeled an `architecture language'. It certainly has aspects of a language. The combination of actors, behaviors and acted-upon elements resembles subject-verb-object of the grammar of a normal language. And that is intentional: the designers of the language had this in mind. But what makes a language a language?

There are two issues I'd like to discuss here (and yes, they have a practical application in Enterprise Architecture work):

• Redundancy in a language;

• Syntax versus semantics (grammar versus meaning.

To start with the latter: take the following natural language sentence: "The customer drinks a bicycle". Assuming that there is no cocktail called 'the bicycle', this is not a meaningful sentence in the English language. You can't *drink* a bicycle. Grammatically (syntactically), the sentence is correct, but semantically, it is nonsense.

We can do the same in ArchiMate. It is easy to use relations to connect elements in a grammatically correct but meaningless way. E.g. using a word processing application to steer the magnets of the Large Hadron Collider in Geneva. Easy to model in ArchiMate, but meaningless in practice.

So, not only the *form* your sentences take is important, but also the *words* themselves. So, take a good look at ArchiMate: its elements are word-*types*, *not* actual words. Without a label in each element, views become meaningless (incidentally, we use an anonymizing script in our tool before we send models to the tool company's help desk to help prevent the leaking of confidential business information). ArchiMate, therefore, looks more like an architecture-*grammar*, than an architecture-*language*. This means that thinking about the labels becomes important. If you are a language speaker who has perfect control of grammar, you still need to find the right words.

The single most effective choice I made with regard to communicating our views was to keep the *type name* of an element *in the label* of an element. This is of course redundant, as (with the icons and the right color coding) every element type is already visually different from another. But it is very effective. For people who do not read models every day, the addition '(Business Process)' at the end of the label hugely speeds up understanding the model. 'Business Process' immediately triggers the right concept in their mind, while the icon by itself does not. This is even true for experienced architects that use ArchiMate every day. In fact, adding this simple redundancy has in my opinion immensely enhanced the usability of ArchiMate views in our organization. For instance, already early on, specialists expressed an interest to replace their own visualizations (spreadsheets, drawings) with our ArchiMate views. That is something you generally are told is not to be expected. "Don't expect to be able to use large and complex ArchiMate views outside of your core architect group", you are told when you go to your first ArchiMate course. In practice: a little redundancy goes a long way towards readability.

I also use other guidelines for labeling of elements. These have to do with easy use and especially reconciliation and integration with other models that exist in other tools in the organization, e.g. the CMDB, the process- or risk modeling tool, the software design tool and others.

So, is this practical? In my experience yes: forget the nice grammar for a moment: the power of language in the end lies in semantics. And there, redundancy improves communicability. There is nothing new there: nature has done it first: natural language is full of communication-enhancing redundancy (to the great pleasure of code breakers through the ages, by the way).

Architects are normally inclined to simplify, have a single definition, etc., in other words do everything that reduces complexity, to rationalize — to make logical. But Enterprise Architecture relates strongly to the real world, where logic, certainly pure logic, has its limitations and much of it actually may make matters worse.

The pattern I use generally puts three things in a label:

- First line: some grouping information between square brackets. In the infrastructure layer, generally the device name, e.g. '[winsv001]', in the application layer, generally the application name and in the business layer the business unit name.

- Last line: type name between brackets, e.g. '(Application Service)' for the Application Service.

- In between: whatever short labeling you want there, but generally the 'name' of the element.

14.7 Don't Use the 'Children's Visuals'

After having gone into things you can do to improve readability, here is in my view one thing you generally should *not* do: use ArchiMate's 'playful' element forms like the big puppet for Actor or the big PowerPoint-like arrow for Business Process, etc. In my opinion, these forms are for children, not for grown-ups. They are also not visually 'quiet'. Maybe for the absolutely simplest views with only a few elements that are shown to people who never have to look at ArchiMate views again, but in that case I would probably not use ArchiMate at all, but create a funny drawing with Greek columns, jumping dogs, images of police constables, etc. ArchiMate is intended for serious modeling and serious messages and using the 'funny forms' is akin to writing your serious design document in limerick form. Your diagrams are serious business, they should look the part.

15. Patterns

Note: From now on, it might be practical to keep a finger on page 239 so you can easily move there and back.

15.1 The Use of Patterns

Asking "How do you model X?" is probably the most asked question by those starting to use ArchiMate. This chapter intends to offer solutions for many such questions, like "How do you model a spreadsheet?" or "How do you model a Business Rule Engine?". These patterns are certainly not the *only* way to do it (and certainly not advertised as the 'best') and I will even offer some alternatives here and there. In

the end, if you become experienced, you will tend to create your own patterns. Modeling style is after all like writing style. And good modeling is like good writing: a mixture of good content and good style.

But there is more to patterns than just a nice way to model something. If you end up using ArchiMate to model your Current State Architecture, for instance, the model that contains your existing Enterprise Architecture becomes much more usable (and thus following Uncle Ludwig, much more meaningful) because using the same pattern in comparable situations enables you to create (depending on your tool of choice) automated exports and analyses.

Imagine you have that large Current State model and it enables you to do an analysis that can tell you that if a certain Business Process needs a Return To Operations (RTO) of 4 hours, you can easily find all the servers that need to support that requirement. Or if you have an application owner modeled, you can easily find which applications he or she is responsible for. Or you have a server nearing the point where its capabilities are overwhelmed and you can easily identify the business processes responsible. ArchiMate is an *Enterprise Architecture* language, which entails *all* the 'layers' and it is well suited to provide the foundation for such information.

In the coming sections I will present several patterns. I will start with a basic Infrastructural pattern. The reason for that is that this pattern will return in a few guises and also as an underlying pattern for some application patterns. So, without further ado, here is:

15.2 A Basic TI Pattern: A Database

ArchiMate has its three layers and some of what happens in your architecture will be classified as Infrastructure. In ArchiMate, that is more than just hardware. It is also artifacts like files and it is software with its behavior: operating systems, surely, but also other systems like relational databases and so forth. ArchiMate has software on two levels, and though that is useful, it can also be confusing. Because if you have software, how do you model it? As System Software or as Application Component? If you look at it from an IT perspective, the difference is illogical: after all software is software. But from a business perspective it makes kind of sense. For the

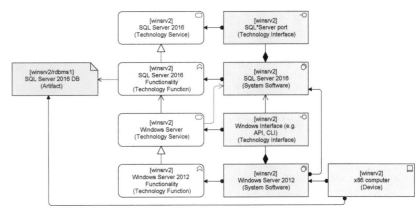

View 90. *Deploying a database, without the hardware details*

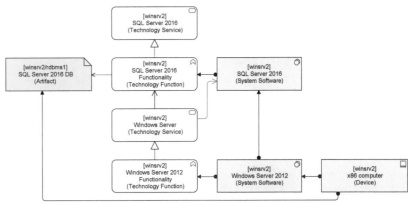

View 91. *Deploying a database, without hardware details and interfaces*

business, its business-critical applications are what count as 'application', the software beneath it like databases are 'infrastructure'.

If you want a fully detailed model for a database at the infrastructure level, you could get something like View 89.

Unless you are an Infrastructure Architect interested in modeling these details (and even then), you will probably never model it like this. But it is the basis from which we are going to simplify to get to the practical pattern we will use.

This is what is modeled in View 89: Bottom-right, there is a Device, the actual computer hardware, in this case an x86 server. This is hardware, thus an *active* element, and thus it has *behavior*: it has functions it performs and services it provides. Running on the Device (the Device is Assigned-To the System Software) is an Operating System. This active element again has behavior: the functionality of the Operating System and the services it can provide. Its functionality requires the use of the hardware services that the *Device's* functionality provides. Deployed on the Operating System (Assigned-To) is the SQL*Server 2016 Relational Database Management System (RDBMS). The SQL*Server 2016 System Software performs (Assigned-To) its behavior (the SQL*Server 2016 Functionality Technology Function), which in turn Realizes a SQL Server 2016 Technology Service, which can be used by Application Functions elsewhere in your model. The SQL*Server 2016 Functionality requires the Operating System's Technology Services to function. On the left, there

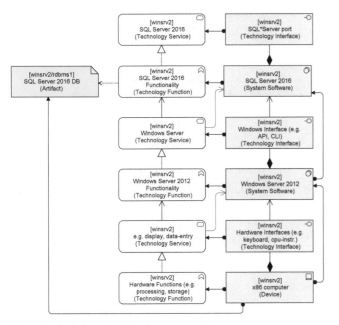

View 89. *Full details of deploying a database*

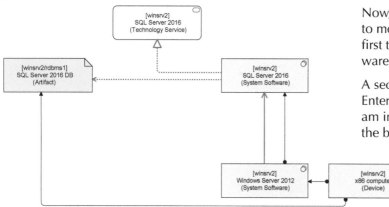

View 92. *Deploying a database, without hardware details, interfaces and internal behavior*

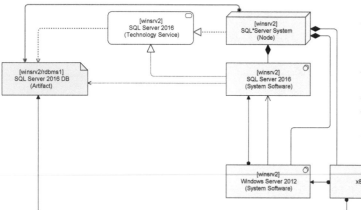

View 93. *Deploying a database: using a Node to make an abstract device*

is the actual database Artifact (in the end: the bits), the Device is Assigned-To this Artifact, signaling the Artifact resides on the Device. The SQL*Server's functionality accesses that database artifact.

Since the Assigned-To relation in ArchiMate 2 & 3 is uni-directional (mainly: from active element to behavior), ArchiMate 3 has a few explicit extra relations to show that all active elements can use services. Normally, with such a detailed view, we would not add these. I have added these in red in View 89, though, because we use them below to simplify.

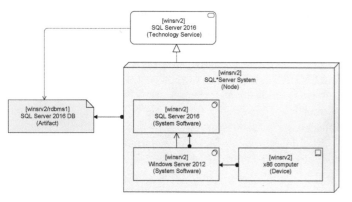

View 94. *Deploying a database: Nesting details in a Node*

Now, for the pattern I want to use, I must decide what I *need* to model for future use, e.g. for analysis or reporting. The first thing I really do not need is all the details of the hardware. Removing those gives me View 90 on page 63.

A second thing I often do not model are interfaces. I look at Enterprise Architecture from the perspective of *behavior*. I am interested how behavior of the applications are used by the business for instance. I am interested in the services the infrastructure must provide for the applications to function. How this is technically done (Technology Services for instance represent infrastructure protocols like HTTP, SMTP or database server protocols) is not something that interests me as an Enterprise Architect, though it might of course interest me as a TI-Architect. A model could of course contain that information, even if I as Enterprise Architect do neither use that for analysis nor show it in the views I use.

Without the interfaces, View 90 turns into View 91 on page 63.

Actually, as an Enterprise Architect I am also not interested in the internal behavior of my infrastructure. I want to know what System Software has been installed on it and what Technology Services and Artifacts they provide for the outside world. So my View 91 can be simplified to View 92.

Now, when I removed the internal behavior elements from View 91, links between active infrastructure elements and the Technology Service and Artifact, that are exposed to the outside world, were lost. These have been replaced by derived relations (in red). For instance: from the Windows Server System Software via Assigned-to the Windows Server Functionality via Realization to the Windows Server Technology Service via Serving to the SQL*Server 2016 System Software (here we need that extra Serving (in red) relation from the previous views.

For infrastructure, I can adopt the use of an intermediate (abstract) Node to encapsulate everything below that which is exposed to the outside world as already suggested in Section 7.9 "Using a Node to encapsulate infrastructure" on page 25. This is shown in View 94. This Node has the internal System Software and Device elements as Composite parts. From the Node, we can create new derived relations from that Node to the Artifact and Technology Service that is exposed to the outside world. These are shown in red in View 93.

When we then use Nesting to get all the Composite parts inside the Node, we get View 94.

I use the Serving relation for behavioral dependencies (without in this case explicitly modeling behavior) and Assignment for deployment. Generally, the Serving relation is implied in the Assignment in this case, so you might want to simplify by only using Assignment. View 96 on page 65 contains an extension on our basic pattern. Ignore the red relations for now. Here it is shown that both the database and the web server are deployed on the operating system, but the web server *uses* the database without being *deployed* on it. In fact, that web server uses the Technology

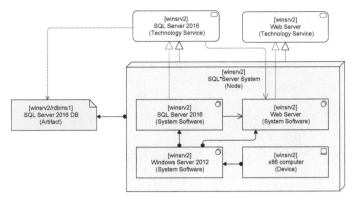

View 96. *Node providing two services*

Service that has been modeled on the outside of the Node. We could also have modeled that the Technology Services are Realized by the System Software on the inside and the database service is used by the web software. These options are shown in red. As in many cases, these variations show that there are many ways to model the same thing and working with ArchiMate in a disciplined manner means choosing your patterns and sticking to them.

This is also a good moment to discuss the Assignment of the Artifact. We started out by modeling the Artifact as deployed on the device. Or do we need to Assign it from the operating system? We might even argue that, while the bits are on the device, the files are accessed by the database via the operating system. Some might even say that in a sense the database *file* is deployed on the database *software*, though that is in my opinion more difficult to defend. Using the Node as an encapsulating element circumvents this difficult discussion about all the different modeling choices that have to be made.

View 96 (without the red relations) is actually the basic pattern I prefer for modeling IT infrastructure items. I do not model all the omitted intermediary elements and internal structures that I used to come to this summary pattern. I used derived relations to get this result. There is no need for the other details in my Project Architectures or Current State Architecture. But even if I model the above, I can still when it suits me present an even simpler view on that pattern as can be seen in View 95.

View 95. *Deploying a database: Collapsing the Node*

Now, this is a pretty simple TI-structure pattern. We have a Node that embeds a single Device to which two System Software elements are Assigned. We Realize the Technology Service directly from the Node, making the Node (and the Technology Service and the Artifact) a sort of cut-off (encapsulation) between Infrastructure use and Infrastructure structure. The Node is used in fact as a sort of object in an object-oriented approach, hiding its internals, exposing its interfaces. Later, we will see a few more complex examples when we look at 'clustered' infrastructure setups. And important: a server can of course Realize multiple Technology

Services, say a RDBMS service *and* a Web Server as we saw above.

15.3 Modeling Spreadsheet Applications

Excel Spreadsheets are IT's (and an Enterprise Architect's) bane. First, there is no way of tracking them, so you may have all kind of mission critical stuff in spreadsheets that have no access control, no logging or auditability, and which are written poorly, etc. But except being a nightmare, they are also a fact of life in any modern organization. And it is worse: Excel is often augmented by all kinds of plug-ins from all kinds of vendors. SaaS-vendors, Data vendors, functionality vendors etc. distribute plug-ins (statistical plug-ins, access to tooling plug-ins, etc.) that become part of the Excel application environment.

So, all that mission critical application behavior that is in Excel is something that gives headaches to Enterprise Architects (and Support Organizations) because it generally is not tractable. In architecture descriptions, people often end up with models that have boxes with the label 'Excel' in them that stand for 'anything that is done in Excel' and that generally means 'we have no idea at all what is happening there'.

Personally, I think most of what is in Excel is not a real problem (except for that access control, auditing and logging and such, if these are required) for Enterprise Architects if looked at properly. First, those little spreadsheets that employees create for their daily job are mostly not that mission critical at all. They tend to improve the efficiency of what they otherwise would have to do by hand (and can do by hand if need be). (Some, however, are not that innocent at all, like the spreadsheet I once saw that had all the information of another application copied into it for easy reference and that was two years out of date). Also, in some organizations you will find literally hundreds of thousands of spreadsheets, that on closer inspection tend to be some sort of smart form. One person enters data, another reads the data. And afterwards the form is never used again. It sits on your servers as an archive copy of something that happened once. It's not an active element, it is an old passive element, which probably never will bother you again.

But, if you look into your organization, you will probably find there are indeed some mission critical applications that are in fact spreadsheets and for which there is no business case to turn them into properly built and maintained applications. Think of the analysis models Asset Management Portfolio Managers use and play around with. Turning these into formal applications with change procedures and lead times of weeks (if not months) defeats their object. You still want these in your models, though, and you don't want them in there as a generic 'Excel' element. So, there is need to decide on how to model a spreadsheet application.

Initially, you might want to start with adding Excel as an Application Component to your landscape as shown in View 97 on page 66.

In this diagram, Excel's application functionality Accesses 'spreadsheet' Data Objects that are Realized by .xls Artifacts.

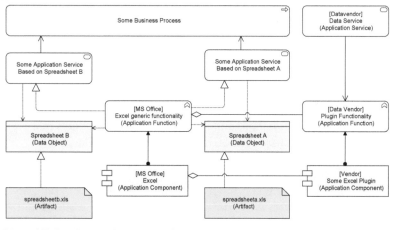

View 97. *Excel as an Application Component*

There are two spreadsheets in this example, one of which depends on a vendor plug-in that connects to an outside data service. Think for instance of a stock market plug-in that delivers live price data for stocks and bonds.

In the example, spreadsheet B is a normal spreadsheet based on Excel's functionality only. Its data is contained in the spreadsheet and so is its logic (macros, programming). The Excel Application Component is Assigned-To the generic Excel Application Function (all of Excel's functionality). This functionality reads the spreadsheet data object and — with the logic contained in the Data Object and based on its internal engine to process that logic — it Realizes the Application Service that is used in a Business Process.

Spreadsheet A requires the use of a vendor plug-in. This is modeled as follows: the plug-in is generally installed as part of the Excel installation. On the infrastructure level we are generally talking about some sort of Windows on-demand loadable library (a DLL) which is loaded by Excel and the plug-in becomes a 'part of' Excel. This has been modeled with an Aggregation. On the functional side, both Application Components have their Application Function, covering everything that the Components can do. The main Excel Application Function is in the lead and it Accesses spreadsheet A and it realizes Application Service A. It is the plug-in's functionality that accesses the outside vendor's Application or Technology Service.

So far so good, but there are a few disadvantages to modeling it this way:

- Because the generic Excel functionality is in charge of Realizing all Application Services, everything is related via that Application Function. Application Service B is made to appear on the plug-in, although it does not need the plug-in. It is in fact not possible to discriminate between Application Service A and B if you want to know who depends on the vendor's data service and plug-in.

- The .xls artifact contains both data and logic, but the logic does not end up in a recognizable Application Function. Application Functions are nice to have when discussing creation and maintenance of IT.

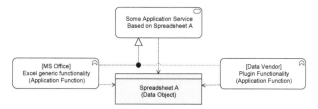

View 99. *Excel as an Application: linking a plugin to the Application Service*

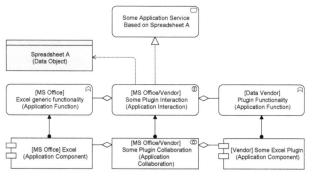

View 98. *Excel and the plugin as an Application Collaboration*

The first disadvantage can be solved by having a relation between the plugin's function and Application Service A (and not B) as seen in View 99.

The Realization (in red) is not true in a technical/real sense of course, because it is Excel that creates the Application Service *using* the plug-in, and not the plug-in directly. But in a more abstract sense, we can say that both functions are required to create the service.

Another way to do this properly in ArchiMate (and possible in ArchiMate 2) is to use Application Collaboration and an Application Interaction as in View 43 on page 34. This is shown in View 98.

This third alternative is not really attractive to me, so on the application level, I would stay with the second solution or (in ArchiMate 2) the first variant. The dependence of spreadsheet B on the plug-in is not really a problem: after all, the functionality of the plug-in could actually still break spreadsheet B, so in that sense the dependency is still real as we noticed in section 12.5 "On the direction of structural relations under the assumption of 'worst case'" on page 50. Making the plugin an Aggregate part of Excel (both Application Component and Application Function) shows this more clearly than the Junction, but the Junction shows the functional dependency more clearly.

The other disadvantage (no visibility of the functionality, the behavior that comes from the logic (macros and such) inside the spreadsheet) remains in all cases. A spreadsheet itself can be a kind of application, people 'program' spreadsheets, but this application shows up nowhere in this approach. That is why I prefer another solution. I consider the .xls as an Artifact that Realizes *both* a (passive) Data Object *and* an (active) Application Component. The spreadsheet itself is an application also, not just data. Excel then becomes the (generic) *platform* on which the application runs, a bit like a Java Virtual Machine being the platform within which the

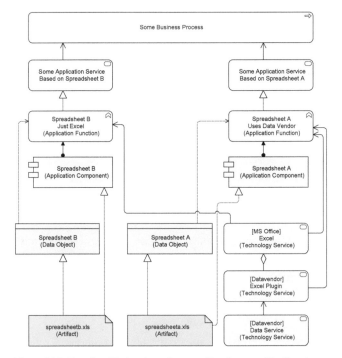

View 100. *Excel as Technology Service (Application Platform)*

Java application (that is Realized by a '.jar' Artifact) runs. This can be seen in View 100.

Here, the spreadsheeta.xls Artifact Realizes not only a Data Object from the data in the spreadsheet, but it *also* Realizes an Application Component from the logic in the spreadsheet. That Application Component is assigned to the Application Function that stands for the *behavior* of the spreadsheet. This behavior has access to the data (in fact, the Excel formulas and Macros have access to the (passive) data that is *also* in the spreadsheet, this happens internally). The behavior then Realizes the Application Service for B that is used by the Business Process. This can be extended to a spreadsheet like A that uses the plug-in to access a vendor's data service. This can be modeled in various ways. Here it is modeled as the plug-in being an aggregate child of the Excel Technology Service so that we still have the link between the plug-in and Excel (if the plug-in breaks, Excel can be affected). But for the rest, the plug-in service is used by the Application Function that represents the behavior of spreadsheet A. Also modeled is a direct Serving relation at both the application layer and the infrastructure layer to show the use of the vendor's data service. Technically, the Serving relation from the data vendor's Technology Service to the plugin's Technology Service is not fully modeled. The data vendor's Technology Service should ArchiMate-technically be modeled as being Serving a Technology Function, which in its turn Realizes the plugin's Technology Service. As it is, the Serving relation is a derived relation.

The biggest advantage of modeling Excel as a Technology Service is not that stuff with the plugins. It is that it so clearly shows that a spreadsheet can be an *application*. Spreadsheets are used as passive *and* active elements. We tend to think of passive elements as 'harmless' (they aren't, of course, wrong data may send behavior completely haywire) but the fact is that all those spreadsheets are the nightmare for IT and Enterprise Architects because they often are not

harmless passive elements at all. They often are (serious) applications and should be treated that way. That Excel-wizard Asset Manager is a programmer (and a bad one at that, often, as asset management is his or her trade, not programming) even if he or she does not think so.

Next in line: another 'application' that is not an application.

15.4 Modeling an Internet Browser

It is illustrative to think about the reality of what happens when you use a web site. You start up your browser and you type in an URL, e.g.:

`https://masteringarchimate.com/wp-admin/post.php?post=99&action=edit&message=10`

The browser connects to the web server and loads a web page that the web server sends. What the web server sends is based on the URL, which is composed of three parts: a protocol identifier (e.g. `https://`), a domain name (e.g. `masteringarchimate.com`) and the request part (the rest of the URL, e.g. `/wp-admin/post.php?post=99&action=edit&message=10`). (ArchiMate buffs will recognize an interface, a service and a passive structural object, the request, in that one URL.)

Now, based on that request part, the web server returns bytes to the browser using the 'https' protocol as requested. That data could theoretically be anything, but in this case, the data conforms to a standard language, HTML, which the browser understands. HTML originally was just a simple description of (passive) markup/layout, but browsers these days are far more powerful. They have functionality that allows them to present *active* components to the user, say buttons, pop-ups and so forth and ways to run almost arbitrary code. This code is normally JavaScript, which is an application platform built into almost every browser. JavaScript, by the way, has nothing to do with the programming environment 'Java'. JavaScript was originally called "Mocha", then "LiveScript" until somebody at Netscape thought it a good idea to change the name so it could profit from the hype surrounding Java at that time. But I digress.

Anyway, what is being sent from web server to web browser is just a 'file', a stream of bytes. In ArchiMate terms, this is an *Artifact*. Now, this Artifact Realizes both passive (the text you read) and active (behavioral) elements like those buttons, clickable maps and so forth. What actually happens is that your browser interprets the 'file' (HTML/JavaScript) and realizes *both* a passive Data Object and an active Application Component. This is just like Excel did in the previous pattern: Excel interprets the spreadsheet and Realizes both passive (Data Object) and active (Application Component) elements.

But there is a difference. With a web browser getting the file from a web server, the file may be just 'in memory' and the whole setup is created 'on the fly'. There is no Artifact on a disk needed. The 'file' may just exist fleetingly in memory of the desktop running the browser. Close the browser and it is gone. The pattern is shown in View 101 on page 68.

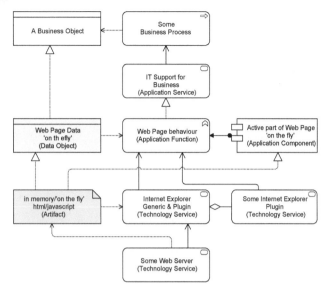

View 101. *The Internet Browser as Technology Service (Application Platform)*

This pattern is useful to make clear where the application is. Sometimes you see models where the web site is modeled as an application. But that muddles the picture because it suggests that the application does not run on your infrastructure. In reality, with browser-based applications, at least a part of the application runs *in the browser platform* which in turn is part of your own infrastructure. It *looks* like everything runs elsewhere, but that is not true. It only *seems* that way because it is downloaded 'on-the-fly' and destroyed as soon as you close the browser window. You have a temporary, downloaded *application* that generally connects back to the same server (or another one) to interact with. The only reason that your security people do not get scared about you downloading and executing applications is because the JavaScript 'runtime' in the browser is a secure 'sand box' that is properly separated from your local infrastructure. But change the JavaScript 'runtime' to some browser plug-in that is used as platform, e.g. Flash or Java, and your security people will become restless because Java and (especially) Flash are plugins that have been known for security breaches.

What we have seen with the spreadsheet and web browser so far is that they are not so much applications per se, they represent a *platform*. Keeping the notion of execution platforms in mind is very useful when modeling.

As hinted above: this is not the entire story. After all, what is sent to us is often just the 'presentation layer' and not the entire functionality. We'll get back to this in 15.12 "Deployment Pattern: Three-Tier Application" on page 73.

15.5 More 'application platforms'

So what are good examples of application platforms of which we now have seen two (spreadsheet and browser)? Here are a few:

- JavaScript (Browser built-in, loads parts of the HTML page, namely the part inside a <script type="text/javascript"> tag. Another script language that can be deliv-

ered inside an HTML Artifact is for instance VBScript (only Microsoft browsers support this);

- Tcl is another scripting language that can be delivered inside an HTML document with a <script> tag. It requires a plug-in;

- Adobe Flash (Browser plug-in). Loads .swf ("shockwave-flash") Artifacts and Realizes Flash applications);

- Microsoft Silverlight (like Flash).

- Canvas (another, but open, graphical language for use in browsers, integral part of HTML5).

The above are browser-based platforms. But there are others:

- Java (Java Virtual Machine that loads .jar Artifacts which Realize Java applications). Sometimes the Artifact is also delivered via a browser, but the downloaded Artifact runs in its own Java sandbox, not in the browser. Citrix used to provide VPN-functionality for working from home that way, for instance;

- Perl, Python, Ruby, Powershell, etc. are languages where a script is read by an application that acts like a platform. This is like the earlier Excel pattern. Perl is not the application, but the Perl script is an Artifact that Realizes an Application Component;

- Unix shell scripts or Windows .bat or .cmd batch files, are examples of Artifacts that are read by platforms and turned into Application Components. The platform here is the operating system;

- Enterprise Service Buses;

- Relational Databases. These generally have programming languages embedded. E.g. In Oracle you can program in PL*SQL: you can see how this would look, expanding on the earlier basic infrastructure pattern which was also explained using a database. As you can see in View 102, the PL*SQL code is an Artifact that is a composite part of the database it resides in. This PL*SQL code Artifact Realizes an Application Component, which uses the Oracle db001 Technology Service, both to be able to run the logic as well as access the data in the database;

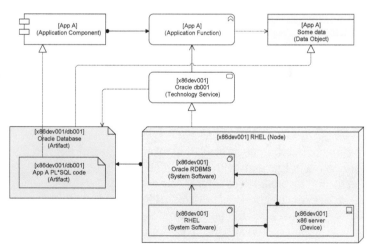

View 102. *Database as an Application Platform*

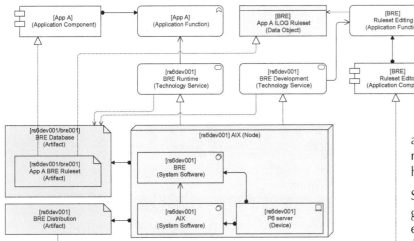

View 103. *BRE as Application Platform*

- Business Rule Engines. This one is illustrated in View 103. This example is a bit more complete as a platform than the previous ones. Here you see that the rule set is modeled as an Artifact that Realizes an Application Component, which uses the BRE runtime environment to function. Next to the runtime, you see that the BRE distribution also contains a development environment to create and edit the rule sets. In this example the development environment runs on the server. In reality, this probably will be some sort of browser based or Java-based environment that has a thin client somewhere and Artifacts will be promoted from development to a runtime, but for simplicity of this example it has been assumed here that development happens on the runtime server. An noteworthy aspect of this example is that the rule-set Artifact Realizes *both* an Application Component and a Data Object. For the developer, the rule-set is *data*. But for the business, the rule-set is an *application* that is used in its business process. That business process is primary to the business; the development of the rule-sets is secondary. That is why I call the direct use of IT by the business Primary Architecture and processes like application management or application development Secondary Architecture. There is also Tertiary Architecture (e.g. The processes of Enterprise Architecture, leading to, for instance, requirements for Primary and Secondary Architecture. We'll get back to that in a section 19 "Secondary and Tertiary Architecture" on page 104.

If you add all these platforms to your landscape, you will begin to appreciate the amount of 'programming' going on in your environment. This is what I would call 'hidden programming'. And because it is hidden, we tend not to see the hidden complexity we have created in our environments. It's not just end-users that do 'end-user computing' (EUC). These days, looking at EUC is on many an organization's radar. But your infrastructure people who write Perl and shell scripts, batch jobs and so forth are not on many radar screens yet. They happily go on creating their landscape of many little applications without attracting much attention, until someone wants to

change something, that is. And that simple off the shelf database might hide application programming as well. When we are done looking at EUC, we might pick up IMC (Infrastructure Management Computing). And after that, we might realize that Business Rule Engines do not remove programming, they just move it from the programmer to that poor business analyst who, just like the sales manager programming his Excel spreadsheet, is a programmer even if he of she does not realize it.

Summarizing: if an environment can be programmed and it provides some kind of run-time environment, you probably are looking at something that can be best modeled using the 'platform' approach. Modeling the applications hidden in these platforms is necessary if you want a complete view of your Enterprise Architecture, because they contain essential business logic.

A suite like MS Office contains both end-user applications (like MS Outlook) and applications that are a mix of platform and application (such as Excel & Access). More on this in section 27.3 "Complex Software Stacks" on page 141).

15.6 Infrastructure 'Building Blocks'

In View 94 on page 64 we encountered a basic TI Pattern. The TI Pattern is that you model the TI as a single Node that hides the internal complexity, then you let that Node Realize Technology Services and the Node is Assigned-To any related Artifact. This makes the Technology Service and the Artifact the linchpins between the infrastructure layer and the application layer.

But in most enterprises, infrastructure is shared between various applications. A file share may be used by many applications, and even databases may be shared by different applications, say, one application that uses the database to store transactions and another separate application that creates management reports on those transactions from the same database. Both use the same database and thus both use the same database Technology Service. The way I prefer to do it is to have the Technology Services clearly named for the Nodes that realize them, whereas an abstract 'aggregate'

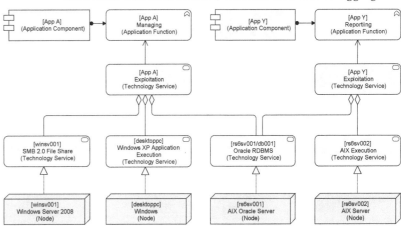

View 104. *TI Building Blocks*

Technology Service aggregates these into the specific set that is needed for each application to function (and hence is Serving the Application Function). This abstract Technology Service is then named the 'Exploitation' Technology Service for that particular application and it is the ideal service for the infrastructure people to provide a Service Level Agreement for running the application. It looks like View 104 on page 69.

In this example, App A (the 'transaction application') runs on a Windows desktop and uses both a file share and a database. App Y (the 'reporting application') runs on a RS6000 server and accesses the same database as App A.

There is a big advantage to this pattern: the application layer of your architecture generally does not change if the deployment changes.

The pattern has a slight 'grammatical' disadvantage: given the direction of the Aggregation relation, you cannot create a (formally) derived Serving relation from either of the Nodes to either of the applications, whereas you know that this relation certainly exists. The abstract 'aggregate' Exploitation Technology Services disable the possibility to derive the relation in ArchiMate terms. In a practical sense, this is not really a problem, because tooling will generally allow analyses that go beyond derived relations, i.e. will allow you to traverse the aggregation relation in the opposite direction. It is a good example of the limitations of the idea of derived relations.

Using Realizations from child building blocks to the 'exploitation' parent is an option, but it does suggest the existence of something in between that is not there, which is why I don't like it.

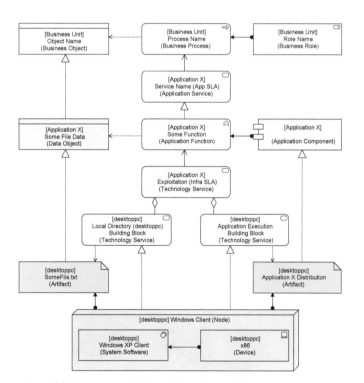

View 105. *Deployment Pattern: Standalone PC*

15.7 Deployment Pattern: Standalone PC Application

We already saw a couple of basic deployment patterns (e.g. the PL*SQL and BRE 'platforms') earlier in this section, Now, we are going to look at a series of examples that are pretty common.

We are going to start with the simplest: an application running on a standalone PC which can be seen in View 105.

Here, a couple of common choices in my example deployment patterns can be seen again:

- I encapsulate TI in a Node like in View 94 on page 64. It is the Node, and not one of its constituents, (which are all composite parts) that Realizes the Technology Service. In reality, it is the Windows System Software on the desktop PC that Realizes the Application Execution Service but we 'hide' those details;

- Any Technology Service and its related Artifacts are coupled with Access relations;

- The Node is named after the embedded Device. In fact, I often use the Domain Name from the DNS system that gives access to the Technology Service;

- The Technology Services are named such that it is clear which Node realizes them;

- As described in 15.6 "Infrastructure 'Building Blocks'", all Technology Services needed to actually run an Application, including its data, are Aggregated into one abstract 'Exploitation' Technology Service which has the name of the application in its label. The actual Technology Services are 'building blocks' and the result is a service which an IT delivery organization could have a Service Level Agreement on;

- The Technology Service Realized by the Node has been split in two: one for the actual running of the application and one for access to the data. In this example, that separation does not make much sense yet, but in more complex situations it becomes useful. So, the simple situation has been modeled slightly more complex than necessary here so it stays in line with the coming patterns.

15.8 Deployment Pattern: Standalone PC Application with File Server based Data

Next is a slight variation on the basic standalone pattern and in fact one which still should be pretty common in most organizations: a standalone desktop application, but with the data stored on a file server. Most organizations do not allow data to be stored on the local disk of a desktop, basically because that makes backing up that data practically impossible. It can be seen in View 106 on page 71.

Not much changes here with respect to the previous pattern. Note:

- It is the Windows Server System Software that actually Realizes the File Share Technology Service, but as in

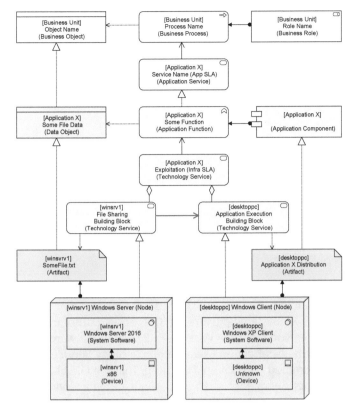

View 106. *Deployment Pattern Standalone PC using a File Share*

the previous example (and all coming examples), our pattern uses the Node as an encapsulation that hides internal structure and behavior;

- It is the Technology Function Assigned-To the System Software on the desktop PC that actually uses the File Share Technology Service, or in other words in this case: the Windows client mounts (in Windows lingo: 'maps') a remote file share under some drive letter. So, if I want to be exact, I need to draw a Serving relation between the File Share and the Windows software on the PC. But as I want the Node to completely hide the internal structure, I have two choices:

  * Let the File Share Technology Service Serve the [desktoppc] Node;

  * Let the File Share Technology Service Serve the Application Execution Technology Service (which is a derived relation of the former one and the fact that the desktop PC Node Realizes the Application Execution Technology Service. My choice is this one for two reasons:

    ° If in a future pattern, the Node Realizes multiple Technology Services. Not all of these may actually use what in this example is the File Share Technology Service. Going via the Node may in the future create dependencies that are not there at all;

    ° I keep the relations between the Technology Services visible even though I do not show the Nodes in a view. Say, for instance, I model the "Internet" Technology Service that my IT Department provides (as some of my systems may

depend on it and I want to be able to take that into account), but I do not model the Nodes such as routers, switches and so forth that are needed to provide those services. The IT Department itself may model them of course. And in my own model, using a division of models in certain fixed 'construction views' makes this choice better, but we get into that in Section 31 "Construction & Use Views" on page 189.

So you see, my patterns do not always follow religiously or fully the world is in core ArchiMate. For a role as Enterprise or Solutions Architect, it is enough to have the relations as chosen now. You may of course choose differently.

15.9 Deployment Pattern: Classic Two-Tier Client-Server Application

The Classic Two-Tier Client-Server application consists of a client application that talks to a database (the server). It can be seen in View 107.

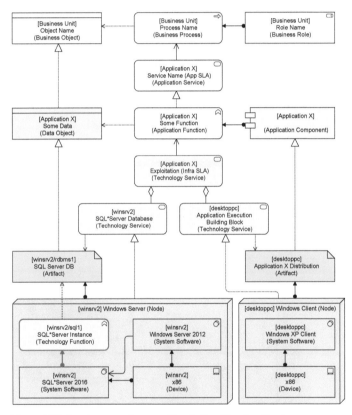

View 107. *Deployment Pattern: Classic Two-Tier Application*

I have modeled a variation in red line/outline. This specific database system consists of independently running 'instances' (in operating system terms: it 'forks' multiple copies of itself). Suppose your large model is input for the CMDB and the infrastructure people need to know quickly what instance of the RDBMS system is at fault when there is a problem with an application. You can then choose to augment your database pattern with this information. In that case, you would have to model the instance inside the Node, while the Artifact is outside the Node. So, this augmentation breaks the basic idea of a Node encapsulating all information. I'll repeat it again: you can create any pattern you want. The most important thing is that you stick to certain patterns if you want the model to be at its most usable.

The next pattern is a variation on the Classic Client-Server.

15.10 Deployment Pattern: Two-Tier Client-Server Application with mounted Client Application and two databases

If the client application in client-server is deployed on a different (file) server, the pattern becomes slightly more complicated, as can be seen in View 108. In this example, I have created two 'instances' of the database software on the server and two databases. This is the variation that I talked about in the previous example.

If you take a look at how the situation is in reality, you know that the *operating system* of the desktop PC mounts/maps the file share on which the application is deployed. Formally, I would have to model a Serving relation between the File Share Technology Service and the Windows XP Client operating system's Technology Function on the desktop. But I try to prevent relations to the inside structure of Nodes as much as possible. So, I create a derived relation in this pattern

between the File Share Technology Service and the Application Execution Technology Service. The big advantage of this choice is that I do not have to show the Nodes (or worse: their internal structure) in a view to see the interdependencies.

Both derived relations I use to shield the inside structure of the Node can be seen in View 109.

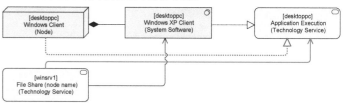

View 109. *Deriving the relations from Technology Service to Technology Service (Serving) & from Node to Technology Service (Realization)*

That the desktoppc Node realizes its Application Execution Technology Service (red) results from the fact that the Windows XP System Software is a Composite part of the desktoppc Node and the Windows XP System Software Realizes the Application Execution Technology Service (via the omitted Technology Function). That the File Share Technology Service is used by the Application Execution Technology Service (blue) is the result of the fact that the File Share Technology Service is Serving the Windows XP System

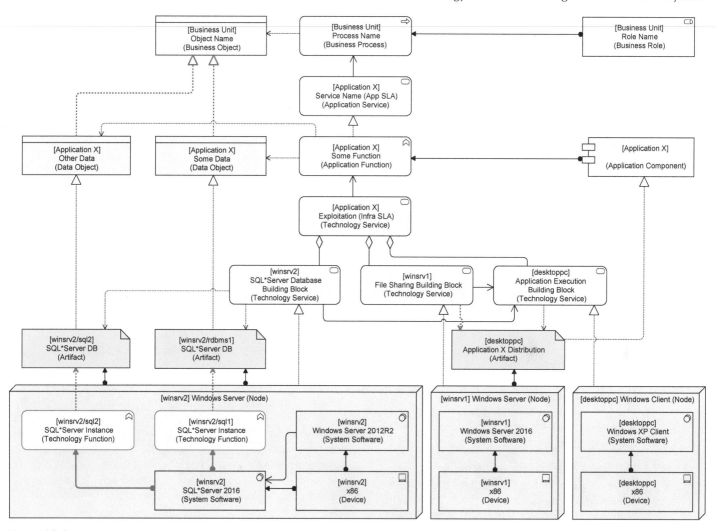

View 108. *Deployment Pattern: Two-Tier Application with mounted client and two databases*

Software and the Windows XP System Software Realizes the Application Execution Technology Service.

Note: the 'Application X Distribution' is Accessed by both the file share and the processing Technology Services. This is correct, but you could leave out the blue one as you already have the dependency via the Serving relation from the file share to processing Technology Service.

15.11 Deployment Pattern: Two-Tier Client-Server with a Remote Server

The pattern in View 110 is another variation on the Classic Two-Tier Client-Server.

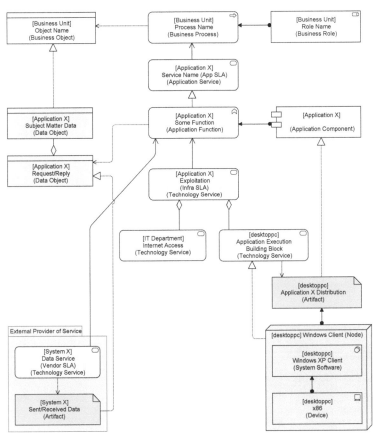

View 110. *Deployment Pattern: Two-Tier Application with remote server*

Here, the server is not your own, but it is provided by an external party. Though the provider provides a Technology Service, we would probably not call this Infrastructure as a Service (IaaS). As often, terms have slightly different meanings in different settings.

This pattern might sound strange, but it actually happens. An example from Asset Management would be Bloomberg's AIM portfolio management and trading application. The Classic two-tier pattern was a client talking a database protocol to some database system. These days, the clients often talk to the server using the world wide web protocols (http or https) and exchange XML- or JSON-formatted objects. But fundamentally, it is still the same. Another example would be Apple's iTunes application.

Note that the external service has not been made part of our Exploitation Technology Service Aggregation.

15.12 Deployment Pattern: Three-Tier Application

A Three-Tier application is an application where a thin client (often not more than a presentation layer without its own data) connects to an 'application server' where an instance of the 'second tier' application is launched specifically for that thin client. The second-tier application contains the actual business logic. This second-tier application itself then connects to the third-tier: the database layer. A first attempt can be seen in View 111 on page 74. The fact that it has three tiers is nicely reflected in the interrelations of the Technology Services (Serving relations between Technology Services). Modeled here is a very basic three-tier, where Tier 1 is an application in itself that is actually deployed on the desktop. These days, the first tier is often browser based; you can combine both patterns.

Now, in the normal Three-Tier case, the first-tier 'thin client' is generally nothing more than a presentation layer and having the actual Application Functions Assigned-To it is stretching it: it is just not true that the presentation layer performs the functionality. The actual business logic is after all in the second tier: the application server. When we looked at the language's 'two types of software' we introduced the notion that if it has business logic, it should be software in the application layer and when it is generic software it should be software in the infrastructure layer. We used that distinction already to set up patterns like the spreadsheet pattern and other 'platform' patterns.

Personally, I like to see all the business logic in software at the application layer. In this case, I would therefore propose another variation on the pattern, which can be seen in View 112 on page 74. The business logic that is deployed on the application server is now visible as an Application Component (the business logic). The thin client is also an Application Component (the presentation layer). Together they make up the system. It is quite a large net we are casting here because we end up creating a composition of Application Components that deep down in the technical IT reality can hardly be seen as one 'program' at all. On the other hand: the entire system's functionality that provides the service for the business is indeed a combination of presentation layer and application layer. I do not think using an Application Collaboration is proper here, as Collaborations are meant for loose collections performing temporary behavior.

Question 1. What Style Guide are we breaking in View 111 and View 112?

Answer 1. The positioning of Application Tier and Database Tier leads to extra line crossings.

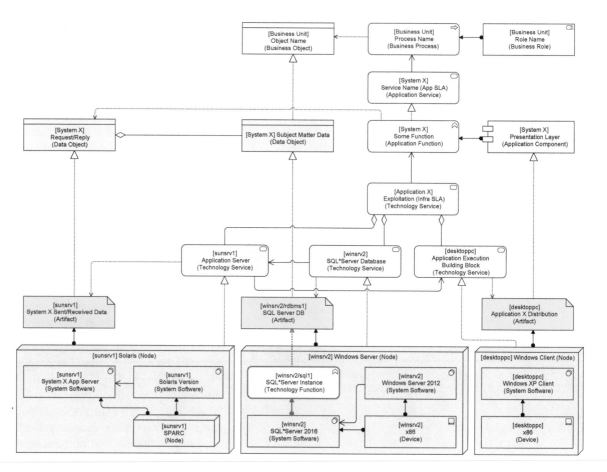

View 111. *Deployment Pattern:Three-tier Application (with missing business logic)*

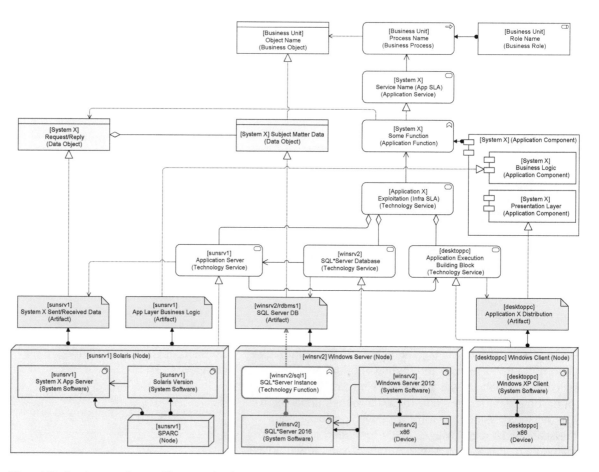

View 112. *Deployment Pattern:Three-tier Application*

15.13 Deployment Pattern: Software as a Service (SaaS)

Another variation is a pattern that is often called 'SaaS' for 'Software as a Service'. It is both a variation on the two-tier pattern and the three-tier pattern. The difference between this pattern and 'Two-Tier Client with a Remote Server' is normally that an internet browser is used as a platform for a very thin client to access the software. As we saw earlier, when we were discussing the browser-based application, the Application Component here is created on the fly from the HTML/JavaScript/etc. Artifact sent by the web server. So, in SaaS, the outside provider provides not only the server, it also provides the (JavaScript) 'presentation' application on-the-fly and we just provide the platform that the application needs to run. In the example in View 113, I made matters a bit more interesting by modeling a SaaS provider that requires from us the installation of a certain plugin for the browser (e.g. Silverlight, Flash or some other proprietary plugin). I have used an Aggregation relation (next to the Serving relation) for the interdependencies of Technology Services, to point out that the relation between the browser and the plugin it *loads* is much stronger

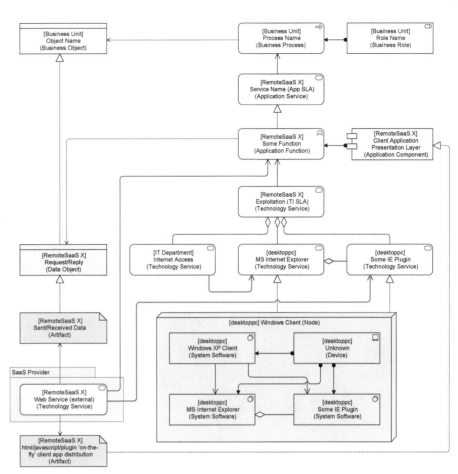

View 113. *Deployment Pattern: Software as a Service (SaaS) - variation 1*

than the relation between the browser and the other services (internet access, remote web server) it *uses*.

This pattern shares with the initial three-tier pattern, however, that the application that runs locally in the browser platform is nothing more than a presentation layer. The business logic runs not locally, but remotely. This has the rather unpleasant consequence that we have to Assign the Application Component representing the *presentation* layer to the Application Function representing the *business logic*.

Therefore, we can better turn our original perspective (our IT provides services to our business) on its head. It is not *our* IT that provides the Application Service to our business, it is *their* IT. It is SaaS after all. *We* just offer *them* Technology Services (a platform for the thin client and an internet connection) so that *they* can offer *us* the Application Service as can be seen in View 114.

This pattern makes it very clear that the external party is providing an Application Service to our business. Our Business Objects that are Accessed in our Business Process do not even have a representation at the application layer as they only exist *outside* our architecture in the 'IT cloud'. Of course, when that same SaaS-provider offers a way for us to get a copy of *our* data, we can model that too in addition to what is shown above. In the real world, SaaS isn't as simple as it seems, if only because all kinds of relations exist between different solutions, SaaS or not-SaaS.

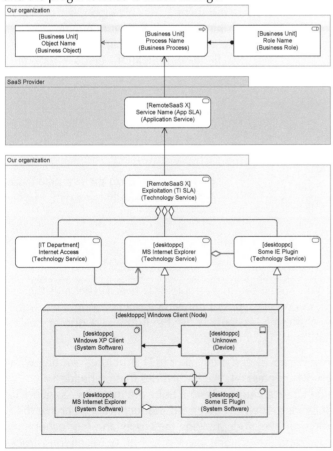

View 114. *Deployment Pattern: SaaS Provider uses our Infrastructure*

15.14 We only model what we can see/'change'

You might wonder why I did not include the Application Functions and Application Components in the SaaS-variant in View 114. The reason is a sort of golden rule: "we only model what we *need*". Modeling the internal structure of how your SaaS provider functions internally (something sometimes found in its documentation) is not only unnecessary, it distracts you from how *you* as an organization

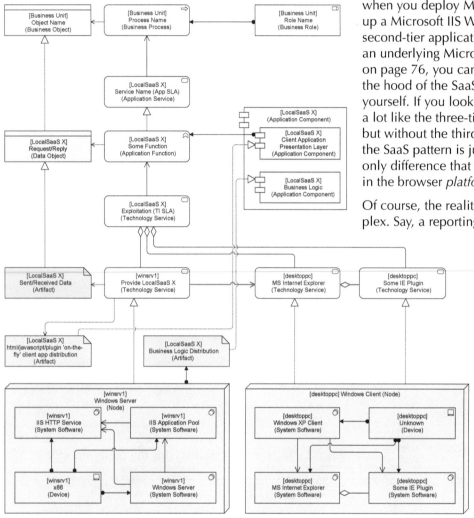

View 115. *Providing your own SaaS/PaaS*

are functioning, which is what your Enterprise Architecture is all about. If your organization has outsourced its IT in a SaaS-manner, modeling data objects and infrastructure of the SaaS-provider gives a false picture of your Enterprise Architecture. It is outside your scope.

So, I suggest to draw the line for modeling at what you actually directly can see from the perspective of your own organization. Everything you model, should be part of what is under the control of your organization (both make and buy). You yourself should be able to check your model against reality to see whether it is correct.

Now, there are reasons why you sometimes need to know more. For instance, regulators may force you to be aware of

the quality or other aspects of your provider. You might have to be able to show to your regulators that you are in 'control' on such aspects as security and compliancy and that may require modeling them as well.

15.15 Deployment Pattern: Providing a local SaaS

A SaaS/PaaS pattern can be used inside your company as well, if you use application servers internally. For instance, when you deploy Microsoft Dynamics, you end up setting up a Microsoft IIS Web Server, upon which you deploy second-tier applications you build, which then again talk to an underlying Microsoft SQL*Server RDBMS. In View 115 on page 76, you can actually see what is going on under the hood of the SaaS pattern because you are providing it to yourself. If you look closely, you'll see that the pattern looks a lot like the three-tier pattern in View 112 on page 74, but without the third tier. This is no coincidence, because the SaaS pattern is just like the three-tier pattern, with the only difference that the presentation layer (the first tier) runs in the browser *platform*.

Of course, the reality of your Local SaaS is far more complex. Say, a reporting server is used to create reports every day and your Local SaaS based solution has to send out mail as well to alert people in certain circumstances. And of course, there is a Third Tier: that data must be stored in a database. Or, if the second tier calls upon the reporting server for some functionality, we actually have sometimes *four* tiers: thin client → application server → reporting server → database server. The extended example can be seen in View 116 on page 77.

Question 2. Which relation is missing in View 116?

Answer 2. The Assignment to the Business Logic Artifact from Node winsrv1.

15.16 The Use of Patterns (reprise)

We will now move to a couple of TI-specific patterns that have to do with types of infrastructure clustering. Infrastructure clustering is generally used to improve performance or reliability.

So far we have seen pretty simple TI-structures, starting with View 94 on page 64. We had Nodes that embedded a single Device and the System Software that was Assigned-To that Device. Then, we Realized the Technology Service directly from the Node, making the Node (and the Technology Service and the Artifact) a sort of cut-off between Infrastructure use and Infrastructure structure. The Node is used in fact

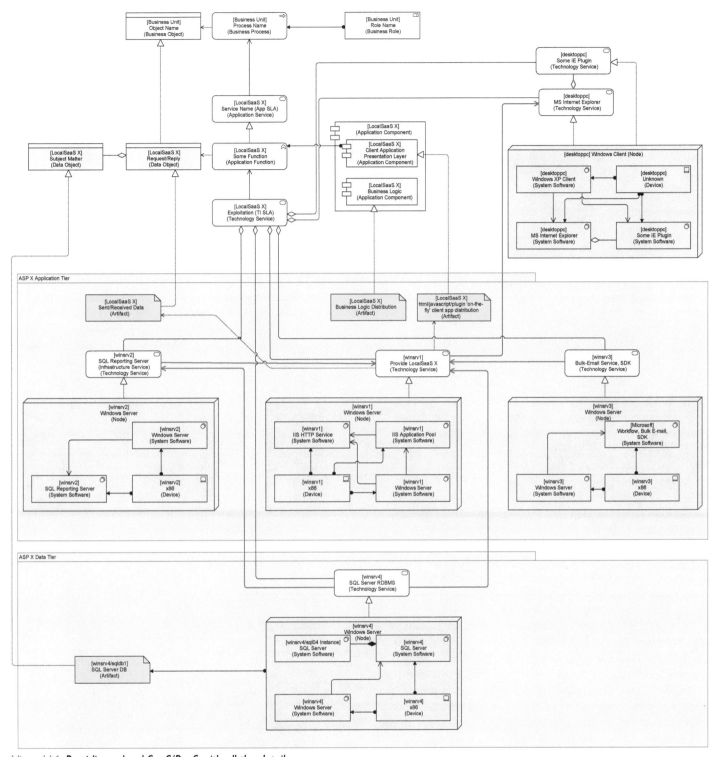

View 116. *Providing a local SaaS/PaaS with all the details*

as a sort of object in an object-oriented approach, encapsulating its internals.

This approach in combination with the Building Blocks approach (View 104 on page 69) creates fixed routes between TI and applications. For instance, if you want to know which Application Function depends on a certain Device, you follow the following route: Device is Composite part of Node, which Realizes Technology Service which is part of an Aggregate 'Exploitation' Technology Service which is Serving an Application Function. This is not a valid route for a formal ArchiMate 'derived relation', but when

you use the patterns consistently, this route will always give you the Application Functions that depend on the device. Such consistent pattern use in your modeling will give you (depending on your modeling tool) all kinds of useful (and more importantly: reliable) automated analyses. The less discipline while modeling, the more variation in your patterns, the more difficult it becomes to define 'standard' dependency routes and use your model effectively. Archi-Mate is not just a language or a grammar, it is a *modeling* grammar, and if you combine a wild selection of modeling styles and patterns, the result becomes less usable. If you do not use patterns at all, you're at the mercy of painstakingly letting a human (probably yourself) analyze the model, something that may overwhelm you if the model becomes large (which it most likely will, if you model your Current State).

However, we will now get into a bit of IT complexity where we might (for sake of aesthetics for instance) decide to introduce alternative patterns. E.g. another level of Node embedding or another level of Technology Service Aggregation. When we do this, it is important to remember the price one pays: for every alternative pattern, you need a second route if you want your standardized (and thus including automated) analyses to be complete.

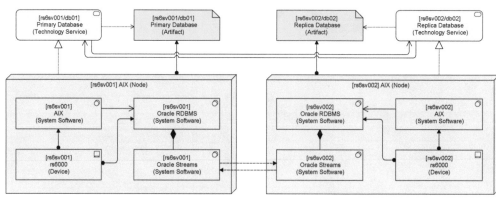

View 117. *Infrastructure Pattern: Database Replication*

15.17 Infrastructure Pattern: Database Replication

The first example of a very lightweight sort of 'cluster' is database replication and it can be seen in View 117. Actually, this is not really a cluster if one defines a cluster as a combination of items that present themselves as a *single* item to the outside world. In database replication, the main database replicates all its actions to a second read-only database. This is above all useful for performance. Suppose you want to run complex management summary reports on your core system's database. Such queries may degrade the performance so much that the actual work being done on them suffers. Maybe you even have queries that take hours of heavy 'data crunching' to complete. You do not want to let those queries bring down the performance for your users. The simplest solution is database replication. Now, replication is not a purely one-way process, even if it sounds like one. As we need to be certain that *both* databases have *exactly* the same data, the primary database needs to be told that the change at the replica succeeded, and if not, it should roll back its own change. Databases generally have some sort of 'persistence' mechanism (in SQL terms a COMMIT) that 'physically' saves whatever data it has written to cells, rows or tables to permanent storage. Now, what replication needs to ascertain is that, should one of the commits fails for whatever reason, the other is rolled back too. Hence, performance wise (though only on COMMIT and ROLLBACK) the primary database will suffer. And since you generally cannot ROLLBACK after a COMMIT has been executed, the 'commit' operation needs another level of 'roll back'. For the rest, both databases can be (except for the replica being read-only) used independently. They turn up as two 'independent' databases in your infrastructure (which is why this is not really a 'cluster'). These tricks have of course been extended to writing in both databases, but for that, better solutions have been created.

In View 117 you see a couple of standard database patterns side by side. Each has its own database. Each Realizes its

own Technology Service. But the 'clustering' has been modeled in two ways:

- As a flow between the replication components of the databases. Note: we break our pattern here that we do not model to the internals of the Node. If you dislike it, you may of course model the flow between the Nodes. I break it however because for complex Nodes it is rather limiting not to know which sub-components actually talk to each other;

- As two Serving relations between the Realized Technology Services. The reason is that, as earlier, we want to be able to see the dependency when we only view the Technology Services 'Building Blocks' (and Artifacts) and not the Nodes. If you offer an 'Exploitation' Technology Service to an application that contains the 'primary' database, you want to be able to see that one of its Building Blocks itself depends on another Technology Service. As the replica database is not really used by the application, the Serving relation is a nice alternative that shows the indirect dependency.

15.18 Infrastructure Pattern: High-Availability Database Cluster

If we create a true cluster from multiple databases, they will behave as a 'single entity' to the outside world. That is, they present a single Technology Service to the outside world and the outside world does not know which actual database is being used. An example is modeled in View 118 on page 79 (have a look at the left (upper when page is turned), ArchiMate 2 compatible variation first). In that example I have modeled a database cluster that provides two databases. I have also put in a little detail about the technical situation. Server rs6sv001 has two databases: rdbms11 and rdbms21 (Assignments in red). Rdbms11 is the rdbms1 database on the first server. Rdbms21 is the rdbms2 database on the first server. In fact only the rdbmsxy databases exist physically, The rest are just aliases in the database system. Rdbms1, for instance, is the alias for either rdbms11 on rs6sv001 or rdbms12 on rs6sv002. The setup in the example uses the second server for the first database as first server for the second database and the first server for the first database as second server for the second database (you might need to read this sentence multiple times, in short: they are each other's fall back but also provide their own primary data-

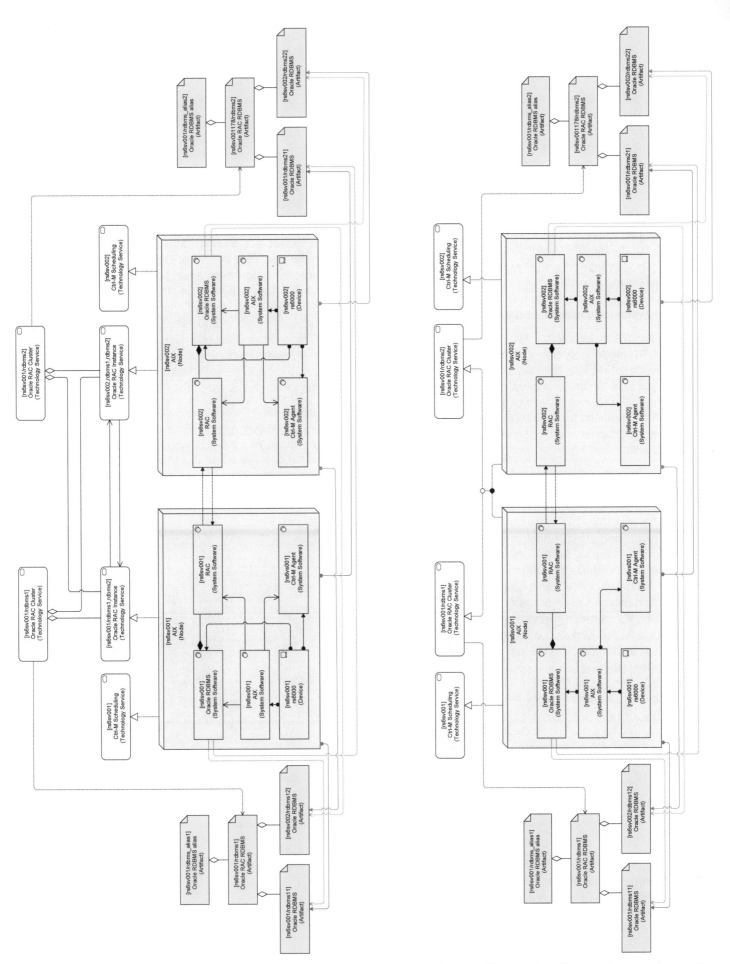

View 118. *Infrastructure Pattern: Database Cluster. Set up pioneered by colleague/hired gun Roy Zautsen. Right (bottom when page is turned):*
ArchiMate 3 solution (see text)

base). So, it is a pretty efficient setup. The fall back server is used and not just idling expensively in the background. Of course, this requires that — in the case of a failure of either of the Nodes — the applications can do with roughly half the database performance. As extras I have modeled the upper Artifacts. They are aliases in the database's naming scheme. They may be used by some applications and we therefore need them in our model. The nodes also contain a batch-job agent. Both devices need such an agent, e.g. to start jobs on them during the night (e.g. a backup job for rdbms2 on rs6sv002 and a backup job for rdbms1 on rs6sv001).

Now, applications that access this cluster always go to 'rs6sv001'. For the outside world, that is the name of this cluster. In this specific example, the Oracle RDBMS has its own databasename-to-system mechanism that handles this (as far as I know, I'm not an expert) This is modeled as an extra Aggregation layer of Technology Services.

Variations are of course possible. We could for instance have chosen to model only one abstract Node but that would have meant we lose the information on which Device the actual physical databases are, unless we would have Assigned them to the Device instead of the Node. Alternatively we could have modeled an extra layer of Node-embedding and just have the top Technology Services being Realized by that outer Node.

So far, everything in our example is ArchiMate 2 compliant. Now have a look at the second variant. This is ArchiMate 3 compatible. It uses Assignments for System Software deployed on System Software, instead of Assigning them all from the Device and using Serving relations instead. This makes the inside simpler. And it uses Junctions to make a simpler construction to model the simple 'clustered database service' being Realized by both Nodes. It prevents us from having to make an extra layer of Technology Services, which — in case they are used as part of an Aggregate 'Exploitation' Technology Service (see 15.6 "Infrastructure 'Building Blocks'" on page 69) — would increase the number of levels from two to three. This way, we can keep all infra patterns to two layers. I've also shown the ArchiMate 2 pattern here, but from now on in the book I will generally not pay a lot of attention to ArchiMate 2 compatible solutions (after all: there is Edition II for that).

15.19 Infrastructure Pattern: High-Availability Server

The third example of clustering is a high-availability operating system or server. Here, two devices run an operating system and on top of that they run software that makes them act as a single system. So, we can approach the cluster as a single system on which we can for instance install software. In the example in View 119, we see a Node that contains two RS6000 Devices

running IBM's AIX. On top of AIX, Power-HA software (originally: HACMP, which stands for "High Availability Cluster Multi-Processing") has been installed which delivers a HA Service. The flows between the HA system software elements are used to model the clustering dynamics. The result is in fact a virtual single operating system, which has been modeled explicitly.

In this example, Tibco has been installed on this virtual operating system. Tibco itself is unaware that there are *two* Devices and *two* operating systems it runs on: it sees only a single operating system and a single file system thanks to Power-HA.

I have also modeled three installed scheduler agents here. One on the operating system of each device and one on the cluster. If, for instance, a batch job for Tibco needs to be started (e.g. a scheduled restart), the scheduler must use the "[rs6sv001 Cluster] Scheduler Agent (Technology Service)", but if for instance some housekeeping job on one of the underlying devices is necessary, it should use "[rs6sv001] Scheduler Agent {Technology Service)". Not visible in the view: the Tibco and 'cluster' Scheduler Agent System Softwares have been Assigned to the Node.

This is one of many ways this can be modeled and it is actually not the one we use. There are often constraints to the way you want to model things, based on the way your model is used. More about this in Section 22.3 where the actual pattern I ended up using is discussed.

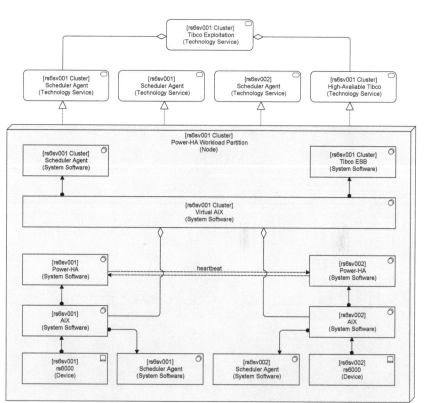

View 119. *Infrastructure Pattern: High Available Server. This set up pioneered by colleague/hired gun Roy Zautsen. (services approach from Edition I was dropped)*

15.20 Using Collections and Abstraction in a model

When you make large models to describe your current state architecture, it tends to become useful to have certain groupings in your model. I am not talking about grouping in a view, but grouping elements 'together' in a model, e.g. via Composites, Aggregations or Specializations. For instance, if you have multiple versions of MS Excel in your landscape, you might want to group all instances of Excel 2003 and Excel 2007 in your model so it is easy to find them when, for instance, you have to do an analysis that has to do with upgrading one or the other (e.g. which business processes are affected when I upgrade all MS Excel instances to MS Excel 2010?). You might think of doing it as shown in View 121.

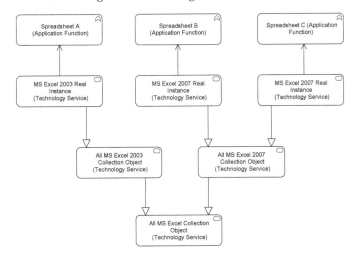

View 121. *Adding collections to your model by Specializations*

Here abstract elements have been created to stand for the different types of Excel we have in our landscape. After all, the 'real' MS Excel 2007 on a PC somewhere, is an instance of a generic type 'MS Excel 2007', which in turn is a subtype of 'MS Excel'. (Incidentally, most organizations would love to be able to account for all the spreadsheets that are used in their business, but few do). A different approach would be to use an Aggregation as in View 120, which looks almost the same.

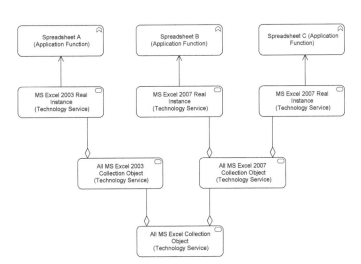

View 120. *Adding collections to your model using Aggregations*

The first has the advantage of using a true abstraction relation for the abstractions: in other words: these generalizations do not exist in reality, they are *types*. Hence, using a specialization is 'proper'. The second suggests not so much a Type/Class, but sees all those Excels out there as a large *collection* of real instances. That is a more down to earth 'abstraction' and it is 'proper' too. The second has the advantage though, that derived relations from the abstract elements to the real elements are possible: 'Spreadsheet C' uses 'Excel'.

You can probably get pretty heated discussions amongst architects over one or the other. But if your tool does not restrict your analyses to only derived relations, they both work out equally in practice. In practice I have settled on using the second because of the following unlikely scenario: If my tool ever in a new release restricts me to doing analyses through proper ArchiMate derived relations, that pattern will still work.

More on using abstractions in Chapter "Reflections" on page 199.

15.21 External Data Services

Suppose you have an application that uses an external data provider. For instance, you have a pricing process that uses a system that gets its data from a price feed from a data vendor. There are generally two ways to model this. The first is to model the external provider as an Application Service as

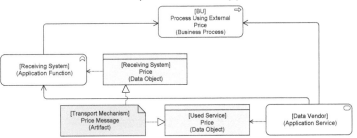

View 122. *Data Vendor modeled as Application Service*

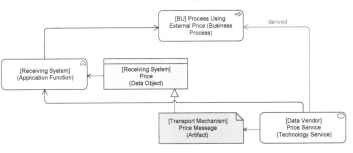

View 123. *Data Vendor modeled as Technology Service*

shown in View 122. The second is to model the Data Vendor as a Technology Service as shown in View 123.

Following the same argumentation as in section 15.14 "We only model what we can see/'change'" on page 76, my preference is the second one for data services. The first has the advantage that you can directly model the dependency of the business process on the data provider, but the second one only contains items we can 'change': elements that we can actually see and verify at our end. 'Change' in this case means of course that we can either use the service or not. These Technology Services are kept outside an 'exploitation' Aggregate (see View 110 on page 73 for an example).

If all is well, the relation between the data vendor's service and the process still exists as a derived relation.

Note that if the service used in the process has direct human interaction, like a SaaS-solution, there is of course an externally provided application in play, which should be modeled as an Application Service.

15.22 Multiple Realizers

In ArchiMate, a function or a process can Realize a service. Nothing in ArchiMate stops you from having multiple functions all Realizing the same service and you often see it in models, see example in View 124. But what does it signify? In my experience, it is meant by those that use the pattern that both functions together Realize the service. But as of ArchiMate 3, the ArchiMate designers have weighed in and say that the "usual interpretation" is that each source by itself completely Realizes the target, hence it is an 'either function can Realize the service' situation. It is not a hard rule of ArchiMate, just the preference of its authors.

This construct, however, is somewhat problematic. Let's start with the intended meaning, of two different processes that *together* realize a service. Now, if these two functions provide the service together, we have two options:

- Both functions together realize a single unified service;

- Both realize a sub-service of the overall service.

The first can be modeled using Business Interaction (and if active components are added: Business Collaboration). See View 125. Note that we do not strictly follow ArchiMate here as ArchiMate says an Interaction is the behavior of a Collaboration and not so much an Aggregation of functions or processes like a Collaboration is an Aggregation of Roles or Application Components. But this is in the spirit of Archi-Mate. The second (sub-services) looks like View 128.

If you expand the Nesting of View 128, it looks like View 126 (ignore the red associations for now).

Now, the question is: what is the relation between Function A (or B) and the 'Service provided by Functions A and B'? In the image, these relations are depicted by the red lines. Well, since the Realization between the Function and the corresponding Sub-Service has a direction opposite to the relation between the Sub-Service and the overall Service, there is no official derived ArchiMate relation. And if you look at dependency in a certain way, it is also logical: Sub-Service A does not depend on Function B. So, if we have two independent sub-services, we should not model a Realization between each function and the overall service because *they do not exist*.

In the case of a collection of independent sub-services that are offered to the outside in a

'package', you can probably better use the Business Product element as in View 127.

Finally, since ArchiMate 3, we can make use of Junctions. If we want to show that *both* functions are required for the service, we get View 129, using the (AND-)Junction. Here, the Sales and Legal Business Functions together Realize the Offer Contract Business Service. If we want to show that either function can Realize the service, we get View 130, using the OR-Junction. Here, either the Sales EMEA or the Sales US Business Functions may Realize the Offer Contract Business Service. This implies that there never will be single contracts for both parts of the world. Not preferred

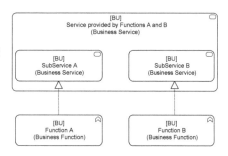

View 128. *Two Business Functions each Realize a Sub-Service of an Overall Business Service*

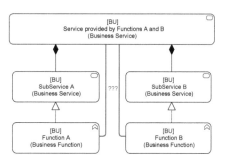

View 126. *Two Business Functions each Realize a Sub-Service of an Overall Business Service, expanded*

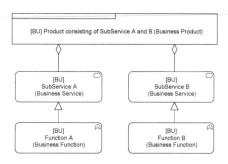

View 127. *Two independent (Sub-)Services make up a single Product*

View 124. *Two Business Functions Concurrently Realize One Business Service*

View 129. *Two Functions together Realizing a combined Service*

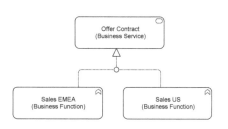

View 130. *Either of two Functions Realizing a Service*

View 125. *Two Functions Interact to Realize a Service*

by large customers, probably, so you have painted yourself in a corner here.

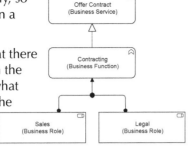

To drive the point home that there are many ways to approach the same modeling question, what if we use the Junctions on the Assignments from the Business Roles? The example is shown in View 132. Summarizing:

View 132. *Sales and Legal Roles Collaborate on the Contracting Function*

- If an overall Business Service is truly realized by two or more functions (or processes) in collaboration/interaction, you can use an AND-Junction (ArchiMate 3) or model the true collaboration/interaction;

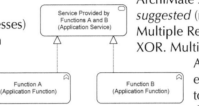

- If it is not function A *and* function B Realize a Service together, but function A *or* function B Realize the *same* Service *independently*, we could use the OR-Junction (ArchiMate 3) or the pattern in View 124 on page 82 (though the latter is technically ambiguous);

View 131. *Application Service Realized by Two Application Functions*

- And if functions A and B Realize Sub-Services for an overall Service or Product, we can best use View 128 or View 127.

All in all, unless you are explicitly using Junctions, I suggest to stick to a 1:n relation between:

- In the business layer: Business Process (or Business Function) and the Realized Business Service;

- In the application layer: Application Function (or Process) and Application Service;

- In the infrastructure layer: Technology Function (or Process) and Technology Service.

More on this in section 34 "Why Model? (And for Whom?)" on page 200.

Realizing a service by two functions is also possible in the application layer of ArchiMate, as can be seen in View 131. Here too, you need to wonder what is meant. If two independent functions can provide the same service, this is a possible pattern. You might think of two applications that both provide the same and you can use either of the two to do what you need, as in "there are two applications to calculate travel distances for your travel expenses".

But as a pattern showing two functions Realizing a service *together* (which is how you will see most modelers using it), you run into the same sort of questions as above. Of course, ArchiMate also offers the Application Collaboration and Application Interaction as an element to model the way two Application Functions may offer a single service. I personally think this should be avoided in your models, as I'll explain in Section 16.1 "Application Collaboration is an Anthropomorphism". As such, this would for me be an example of an 'anti-pattern'.

15.23 Other Parallel Relations

There are more examples of multiple identical relations ending up in an element and where we may employ a Junction in ArchiMate 3. Examples are:

- A Function or Process being Served by multiple Services;

- A passive element being Accessed by multiple Functions or Processes;

- Multiple active elements Assigned to the same behavioral element;

ArchiMate 3 is a bit of a mess with respect to the *suggested* (not formal) meanings of these constructs. Multiple Realizations to the same element imply XOR. Multiple Servings to the same element imply AND. Multiple Assignments to the same element imply XOR again. Multiple Access to the same element is not mentioned, though what is mentioned is that multiple Access relations *starting* at an element usually imply AND. My personal guidelines are:

- Multiple identical relations *ending at* or *starting from* the same element imply OR (not XOR, so "one or more"). This also covers informal collaboration (see Section 8.2 "(Formal) Collaboration and Interaction" on page 33) and shared data such as with messaging, see for instance Section 28.2 "DevOps Ready Data Center (DRDC)" on page 151);

- For AND and XOR, the Junctions are used.

15.24 Summary of Basic Patterns

A summary of the most important points of the patterns above (and a bit more):

- As mentioned in Section 15.2 "A Basic TI Pattern: A Database" on page 63, I generally do not model interfaces. As I keep a 1:1 relation between interfaces and services, and a 1:n relation between internal and external behavior (hence, no (ambiguous) 'concurrent Realizations' for instance), interfaces do not add anything to the model, they are that 'other side of the coin' and nothing else;

- I use a Node to encapsulate infrastructure. Technology Services are Realized directly by the Node, Artifacts are Assigned-To the Node. With a few exceptions (throughout the book) there are no relations between elements outside the Node and elements inside the Node;

- I Aggregate Technology Services as 'building blocks' into a Technology Service explicitly meant to model the support for a certain application. Relations between the child-Technology Services (e.g. Serving relations) are optional;

- I only model what I can change/see. I do not model assumptions about matters I cannot check (e.g. internals of counter-parties, unless required).

16. Some Anti-patterns

16.1 Application Collaboration is an Anthropomorphism

The designers of ArchiMate added the collaboration concepts to the language: a Business Collaboration, Application Collaboration, and (since ArchiMate 3) Technology Collaboration. In Section 18.2 "Business Function or Business Process?" on page 92, we will see that Business Collaboration has an equivalent in the real (business) world. But this is hardly true for Application (and Technology) Collaboration (though with an exception, see below).

In ArchiMate there are two basic `cooperation' patterns. One is Serving. A behavioral element (process, function) can use another behavioral element (service). We repeat View 40 on page 33 here in View 133.

The other is a Collaboration. We repeat View 41 on page 33 in View 134.

In the business layer this is both an understandable way to look at it. But when do you choose one, and when the other? If you look at the concept of 'collaboration' from a

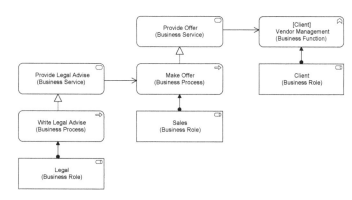

View 133. *Collaboration: Sales Uses Legal on Order Creation*

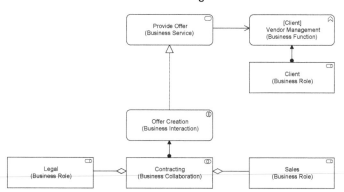

View 134. *Collaboration: Sales and Legal Collaborate on Order Creation*

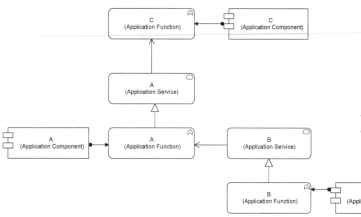

View 135. *Application C uses Application A which uses Application B*

human perspective — which is OK at the business level — it is about decision making. I would go for Collaboration when both processes must actively negotiate to make decisions *together*. An example is the 'exception collaboration' as we will see shortly in Section 18.2 "Business Function or Business Process?" on page 92. I would use Serving when

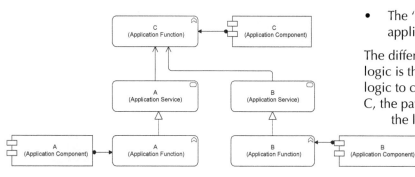

View 136. *Application C uses Application A and Application B*

the process or function used has no real say in the matter, the decision power all lies with the 'user' and not with the 'used'.

If you try to imagine how a real Application Collaboration would work, you have to differentiate between the two uses of Serving (see Section 7.2 on page 21). One is an application used by a business process or business function, the other is an application used by another application. In the latter case, the question is: which application provides the service that the 'user' application connects to? Basically, there are two options:

- The 'user' application C uses another application A which itself uses yet another application B as can be seen in View 135;

- The 'user' application C uses both application A and application B as can be seen in View 136.

The difference between these two is where the application logic is that *combines* the functionality of A and B. If A has logic to combine itself with B and then deliver the result to C, the pattern of View 135 on page 84 is the case. If C has the logic to combine the results of A and B, then the pattern of View 136 on page 84 is the case.

Now suppose we would draw this using an Application Collaboration as can be seen in

View 137. It neither fits the first nor the second option. It introduces elements that are abstract and that do not exist in reality. It certainly does not fit the second option: the actual interaction does not take place outside of C, it takes place *inside* C. And in the case of the first option, it suggests an equality between A and B that is not there.

So, in the case of applications using a service provided by two other applications, we shrink the amount of elements from 8 to 7,

View 137. *Application C uses a Collaboration of Applications A and B*

but at the price of introducing 3 elements that do not exist in reality and that muddy the picture of what is really going on in a substantial way.

And that is not all: try to add the Application Interface to the mix and you get View 138. Given that an application can only use *one* interface for a service, we have now also introduced an interface that *cannot* exist in reality. In terms of creating a good model of what is going on, matters have gone from problematic to bad. To make matters even worse, if you use an Interaction to describe behavior (and properly document the Application Interaction element), you will still need to fully document the separate behaviors that make up the Interaction if they are used elsewhere in solitary form or in another Application Interaction. The same documentation will be in different places and it will be difficult to keep it in sync (a typical thing for IT-people to forget: documentation).

Is it possible to think of a pattern where Application Collaboration makes sense when the 'user' is another application? Yes, but it is pretty convoluted. Here is an example:

View 138. *Application C uses a Collaboration of Applications A and B, with Application Interface*

Suppose there are multiple applications that provide the same service, say a search service. A request for such a service is given concurrently to all that can provide the service. All possible search providers calculate a quality of the answer they can provide: how much 'trust' they have in the answer they can give. All write this 'trust' value in a common data object. After a fixed interval, all reference the common data object to see whether they have the highest trust value and only the one with the highest trust value delivers the service. Basically, what is described here is a sort of AI with autonomous software agents: on the basis of internal rules (which they all share but have implemented separately, which in this case is possible in a practical sense because the rule is very simple) the applications amongst themselves decide who is going to provide the service. Given that all applications participate in making that decision, you can argue that there is a single application function that is in effect distributed across multiple application components: hence

a collaboration of all applications is assigned to that single function. The interface for that solution will be a nice piece of engineering too. In practice, software engineers will most likely design a 'master application' and the architectural relation reverts to the Serving relation of View 136.

So, using Application Collaboration for a pattern where applications are using multiple other applications is not a very good idea, I think. Basically, what the Application Collaboration element in most cases breaks is the guideline "the best model of the world is the world itself". This is an old saying from AI where they learned over a couple of decennia that creating abstractions actually decreased usability. The same is true for Enterprise Architecture modeling, especially when you are busy modeling your Current State or the end state of a Project. I do not think using such abstractions is always wrong, they are perfectly reasonable. Enterprise Architects, being creatures that love the simplification that comes with abstraction, especially love it. My problem with too much abstraction in your Enterprise Architecture models is that it is pretty unmanageable, just like in AI. Stay close to what is really there and less confusion and more usability is your reward.

Anyway, what about using Application Collaboration for an Application Service that is used by the business and that is thus described more in business (human) terms? Well, an Application Service for the Business is of course defined in business terms and as such, a collection of services thrown together is possible from a human point of view. But think again of the interface which messed things up before. Each of these applications has its own GUI. Using an Application Interaction again forces you to create a non-existent (abstract) Application Interface that under the hood consists of the two separate GUIs collected in one.

All in all, you're generally better off not using multiple realizers for one service at the application or technology layers. It looks simple, but it also introduces many 'nontrue' (false or misleading) aspects in your model, so in many cases there will be a too high price to pay.

But there is an exception.

Recall the multiple-tier application deployment patterns like for instance View 112 on page 74. There the presentation layer of the multi-tier application and the business logic layer are each an Application Component Realized by an Artifact. In that View, the complete system was modeled as an Application Component with each of the Artifacts Realizing a sub-component. And while technically it is the presentation layer that *Uses* the business logic layer, it is quite nice to model this as a true Application Collaboration, as my colleague Jos Knoops proposed. This is shown in View 139.

I must admit I rather like this use of Application Collaboration. We also decided not to use it, though it is more aesthetically pleasing. The reason was that it meant we had to change our analysis viewpoints such that everywhere the script is looking for an Application Function, we would also have to model the alternative route. But we might still do it, because it is also nice to have a way to differentiate be-

View 139. *Using Application Collaboration to model a multi-tiered software system*

tween single- and two-tier applications where the business logic resides with the presentation in one component, and three-and-more tier applications where the business logic is spread out over multiple components working together.

Question 3. If you want to add an Application Interface to '[System X] Service Name (App SLA) (Application Service)', of which Application Component is it a Composite child?

Answer 3. '[System X] Presentation Layer (Application Component)' and derived from the '[System X] {Application Component)'.

16.2 Using the Association Relation

The Association relation has a several official uses in ArchiMate. As the Association relation is allowed between all concepts, it is also a kind of catch-all. It is always allowed and it is always possible.

As far as I'm concerned, most of the time, the Association relation is for wimps. It is a sign that you haven't thought out what the real relation is. It is often a sign of sloppy modeling. So, here are my rules regarding the use of the Association relation:

- Don't use the Association relation where another more specific relation can be used;

- If you cannot use a more specific relation, consider whether elements are missing that would make modeling without the Association relation an option. Only fall back to the Association relation if a complete model would be too complex or detailed for the use you are going to make. In that case, develop a fixed pattern for the situation using the Association relation and reuse that exact pattern in comparable situations. In such cases, you should at least once have modeled (analyzed) the complete situation in full without the Association relation as the underlying foundation for the choices in your pattern. An example will be given later in the book when we will be talking about modeling ownership of applications and such;

- For the rest: only use the Association relation in its formal roles in the meta-model.

Summarizing: use the Association relation only where it appears in the meta-model and in situations where doing a real model of what happens becomes too unwieldy. A pattern where we use Associations that way can be found in Section 19.9 "Making it Practical: shortcuts" on page 108. In Section 28.2 "DevOps Ready Data Center (DRDC)" on page 151 I will be using Associations to hide the actual complicated way (automated continuous delivery pipeline) in which elements are related.

16.3 Using properties too much

There is also an anti-pattern that has not so much to do with ArchiMate itself, but with tooling. Most tools let you add all kinds of information to an element or relation that is modeled. This is a good thing, for instance if the tool (almost all do) let you add the documentation for that element to that element.

Some tools also have the option to add explicit properties to an element type. This can even be in the form of free fields where you can add information. For instance, you could add the cost of a Technology Service to the element and use that information to provide analysis of running costs of your Architecture. I know an organization that uses this approach very effectively.

Properties of elements and relations can be very useful. They also have a danger: they are largely invisible. ArchiMate is a graphical grammar and those properties do not always show up when you want and they are not always available for the easy analyses you can make on the basis of a model. So, for instance, you might add the application's owner as a property to an Application Component, but that makes it impossible to connect that property to that same Actor that lives as a real Actor element elsewhere in your model.

So, the bottom line is: only use properties for things you cannot model and even then be careful as they live outside of ArchiMate's grammatical structure.

The same limitations hold for labels. Labels do have a positive role to play in readability of course (see Section 14.6 "About labels" on page 61), but do not rely on them for analysis and structure.

17. An Example from the Real World

Ending this chapter I want to present you with a real-world example. This is about receiving files from an external data provider and using them. These files have to be received, moved to the right location in your landscape and then loaded in some application.

For this, the company employs a Managed File Transfer system, a Scheduler System and a human. The MFT System is programmed to receive certain files and depending on what it receives from whom, move those files to a directory on a server in the landscape. There, the Scheduler watches for the file to arrive and if it does, it starts a script that copies the file over to yet another location, using simple copy commands and shared file systems. After having done that, the Scheduler is done. The human (supposedly at some time of day) looks for the received file and loads it into the application by hand.

Now this situation is unnecessarily complex. After all, you could let the MFT system drop the file on the server where the receiving system can read it. Assume that there are reasons not to do it that way.

In View 142 on page 88, this setup has been modeled. The MFT system works like this. In the Demilitarized Zone (DMZ) of our network, a 'Relay Server' (srv001) receives communication from the outside, e.g. an SFTP file transfer initiation. It checks if the sender is authorized and if so, patches the incoming communication through to a 'Gateway Server' (srv002) on the inside of our network. Here the actual reception of the file happens and the file (Artifact filexxx.yyy) is stored locally. Here the MFT system runs a work flow that decides where the file has to go. In this case, it goes to srv003, a dedicated MFT transport end node: it receives all files together with signal files for the Scheduler. From here the Scheduler takes over.

But before we go further I want to draw your attention to the other two Artifacts on srv002.

- One is the distribution of the MFT Gateway System. This Artifact Realizes the '[Transporter] Workflow Maintenance (Application Component)'. This application is used by IT Management to control the MFT System, create work flows for it etc.;

- The other is '[srv002] Transporter Workflow Configuration' (Artifact). This Artifact Realizes two different elements. One is the '[Transporter] Workflow (Data Ob-

ject)', which is the *passive* element that is maintained by the 'Workflow Maintenance' application. The second is the '[Transporter] Workflow (Application Component)'. This element represents the workflow as an *actor* in our landscape which is responsible for automatically performing the 'Receive Incoming Files (Business Process'. What you see here is both the architecture of *using* the workflow as well as *creating or maintaining* the workflow. In Section 19.3 "Secondary Architecture: Development" on page 104, this will be explained in detail.

The same primary (used by the business) and secondary (created/maintained by the developers) split is modeled again for the Scheduler.

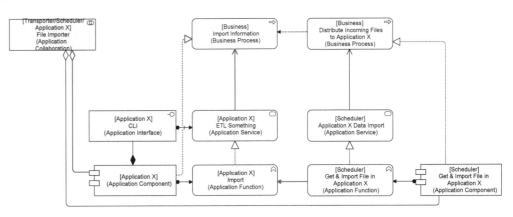

View 140. *Scheduling example: Scheduler triggers ETL*

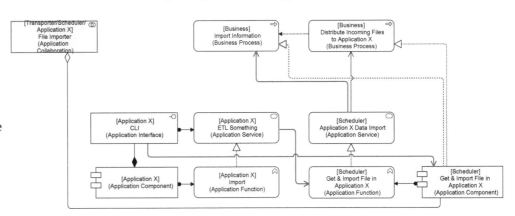

View 141. *Scheduling example: Scheduler uses ETL*

I also want to draw your attention to the way the file ends up on srv003 from srv002. On srv003 an MFT software agent is running that can receive files. This System Software Realizes the 'Dedicated Transporter End Node Service' that is used by the software on srv002. Following our deployment patterns, we do not model this in fine detail but we model this as a dependency between both Technology Services.

The fine details of the Scheduler starting local scripts (jobs) on servers which then use mounted file systems to copy files are not modeled. There is no need. A shortcut is modeled, the File Share of srv004 is used by the Scheduler. Agent on srv003.

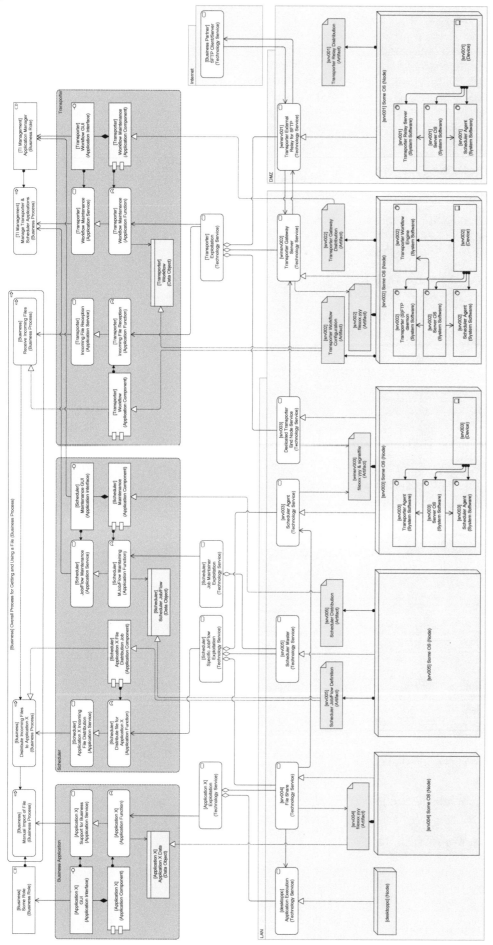

Have a look at the '[Scheduler] Specific Job/Flow Exploitation (Technology Service)'. This is the 'exploitation' service we saw before (see View 104 "TI Building Blocks" on page 69). It is made up of the File Share where the file has to go, the Scheduler Master, which is in control of the whole operation and the Scheduler Agent, which is needed to do the actual copying. The Scheduler Agent therefore needs the File Share and that is modeled by the Serving relation between them.

Finally, at the top of the view, you see the entire business process. Two subprocesses/steps are automatically executed by applications (the Transporter and the Scheduler systems) and one is performed by a human.

But that doesn't need to be the case. In many organizations such business processes are fully automated. This has been modeled in View 143 on page 89. This view is identical to the previous one, except in the upper-left corner. If the final step is not done by hand (by a human Business Role) but by a system, there are two ways to look at this (and probably more), shown in red and blue in View 143 on page 89.

- Following the blue relations and shown separately in View 140, we model the loading as being done by Application X, behavior that is *Triggered* by the Scheduler;

- Following the red relations and shown separately in View 141, we model the loading as being done by the Scheduler which *Uses* Application X.

Both are correct. But the one with the *Trigger* does not depend solely on structural relations, while the one with *Serving relation* does. I find the latter somewhat cleaner.

There is another advantage for using the one with purely structural relations. I generally do not model Interfaces, something that is more or less superfluous when you model the behavior well. (If someone disagrees with me, he or she can write his or her own book ;-). So, without those

View 142. *Modeling the use of a Managed File Transfer and a Scheduler for your business, a human user loads the retrieved data*

Mastering ArchiMate Edition III.TC1

(and without the collaboration that I generally also avoid because in Archi-Mate, I cannot model a Collaboration of automated and non-automated actors) you get the result shown in View 144 on page 90. And for the entire setup, only one relation is left.

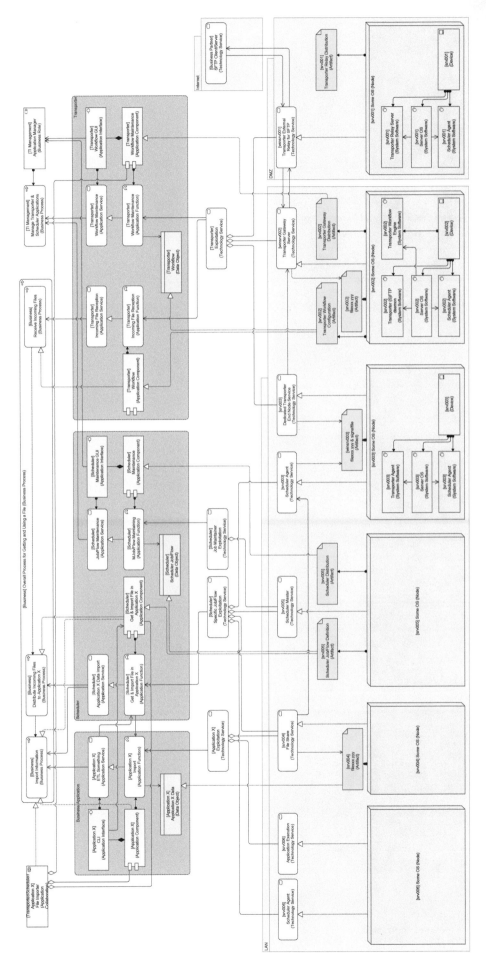

View 143. *Modeling the use of a Managed File Transfer and a Scheduler for your business, fully automated loading*

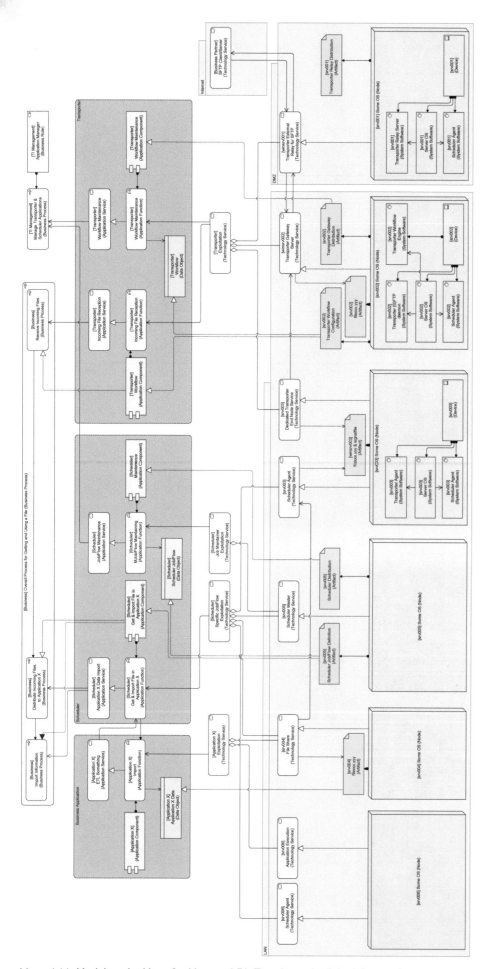

View 144. *Modeling the Use of a Managed File Transfer and a Scheduler use for your business, fully automated loading (cleaned up)*

18. Business Function and Business Process

18.1 On ArchiMate's divide between behavior and structure

ArchiMate is divided into structure and behavior. Active structure elements (like Business Roles and Application Components) perform behavior (like Business Processes/ Functions and Application Functions) and these behaviors act on passive structure (like Business Objects and Data Objects). This division is a fundamental property of the language, but it is slightly different than other ways to look at architecture (e.g. traditional view of software architecture or business architecture) and that does sometimes lead to discussion.

What I have noticed is that ArchiMate's Business Function element is especially problematic in this sense. It has been customary in some circles to see a Business Function as a somewhat visible 'part of the *organization*' that *performs* a certain function in that organization. And that description shows already where the problem lies. In non-ArchiMate business architecture speech, a business function often *performs* something and both there and in ArchiMate terms, something that *performs* behavior is an *active* structure, while ArchiMate's Business Function is not an active structure element at all, but a *behavioral* element that *is* performed.

Application Function also suffers from this problem. In the field of software engineering, a function is both a piece of code (which is structural) as well as the behavior of that piece of code. Historically, there have not been two terms in software engineering to separate that structure and its behavior (nor in the related subject of mathematics, where formula and behavior of a function are one and the same). Also, coming from software engineering, in UML the division between structure and behavior is different from that in ArchiMate. In UML, we have a set of elements, some of which may play both a structural and a behavioral role, depending on the type of diagram they are in. Take for instance an Object Diagram in UML, which is structural, and a Sequence Diagram, which is behavioral, and both may use the same objects in either a structural or a behavioral role. In other words: UML allows objects that can be both structural and behavioral, depending on the views they appear in (structure type of view or behavior type of view). This follows the paradigm of Object-Orientation in software engineering, where objects are structural but encapsulate behavior (and some data even). In ArchiMate, there is but one type of view (even if you are free to restrict yourself to certain element and relation types in different viewpoints) which combines structure and behavior, but the elements *themselves* are separated in behavioral and structural (active and passive). Coming from one world, the other doesn't fully match. (UML is big, complex and mostly directed at the world of object oriented software engineering, it is not really a good placeholder in this section for software engineering in general and much more can be said about it, but I thought the juxtaposition was nice).

So, both in business descriptions and in software engineering, many people see structure as something that 'encapsulates behavior'. In ArchiMate, it is possible to suggest a structure that encapsulates behavior as can be seen in View 145.

On the left you see the un-Nested model, with an Assignment relation between the Application Component and the behavior of that component: the Application Function.

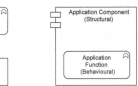

View 145. *Nesting a behavioral object inside an active object to suggest encapsulation*

On the right, a visualization suggesting encapsulation using ArchiMate's Nesting relation, here used for Assigned-To (nesting is one of those parts where ArchiMate is pretty unclear as it can mean (a mix of) three different relation types. I personally almost exclusively use Nesting for Composition between elements and, with a bit of reluctance, Aggregation). Note: though this nesting suggests encapsulation, it does not *mean* encapsulation. "Encapsulation of behavior equals structure" does not exist in ArchiMate.

Back to the business layer. ArchiMate 3's definition for a Business Process is:

> A business process represents a sequence of business behaviors that achieves a specific outcome such as a defined set of products or business services.

ArchiMate's definition of a Business Function is:

> A business function is a collection of business behavior based on a chosen set of criteria (typically required business resources and/or competences), closely aligned to an organization, but not necessarily explicitly governed by the organization.

In summary, both are behavioral and both group the *same* activities, but from a different perspective. ArchiMate also suggests in its explanation that both process and function are the behavior of a *single* role and that if you want to model behavior of multiple roles, you should use a Business Interaction, which is the behavior of a Business Collaboration. The suggestion used to be a requirement, but certainly with the possibility to use a Junction to combine multiple Business Roles to perform behavior, it has become obsolete.

So, a Business Process groups behavior based on what it *produces*. It is a grouping based on an 'outside' parameter: the *result* of the activities. A Business Process is therefore an 'outside-in' grouping of behavior. A Business Function groups activities based on an 'inside'-parameter: what resources and capabilities it needs. A Business Function is therefore an 'inside-out' grouping of (potentially the same) behavior.

Business Process and Business Function both are *behavior* in ArchiMate. For Business Process, that is not surprising for most of us. But for Business Function, that differs from other approaches where a function is considered 'structural'. In ArchiMate, Business Function is *purely* behavioral, it is itself behavior that may be a grouping of (sub)behavior. So, where is the structure that performs it? Well, according to the definition, a (single) Business Role (in practice often a role fulfilled by a department). So, where a business function in other approaches may be a structure that encapsulates behavior and thus be structure and behavior in one, in ArchiMate, a Business Function is *pure behavior* and it is performed by a *different*, structural element: a Business Role.

And what about grouping/encapsulating of Application Component and Application Function? Same here, and even nicer. Because at the application level, ArchiMate kind of sees the same sort of 'encapsulation' on both sides. Application Function may be an encapsulation (by means of a composition) of other Application (sub)Functions and Application Component may be an encapsulation (by means of a composition) of other Application (sub)Components. Between the Application (sub)Functions and Application (sub)Components is a one-on-one Performed-By relation. As can be seen in nested form in View 146.

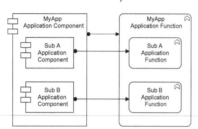

Seeing the composition of Application Functions on the right of that diagram easily makes one use the word 'structure'. And indeed, in a sense, there is a 'structure' in the Application Function, as it is a compo-

View 146. *Encapsulation of Application Sub-Components and Application Sub-Functions*

sition of Application (sub)Functions. But though there is a 'structure', that does not mean the element itself is 'structural' *in ArchiMate's sense*. Paraphrasing Uncle Ludwig: watch out for 'bewitchment by language'. The fact that you are using (almost) the same word ('structure') does not automatically make it the same meaning.

18.2 Business Function or Business Process?

So, a rather tricky part of ArchiMate is the difference between Business Process and Business Function. Both stand for behavior at the Business Level. Both generally encapsulate in the end the same activities. Choosing between a Business Function and a Business Process is sometimes difficult. It is like the eternal question about the chicken and the egg. Note: there is a large part of the architectural community that thinks it is not difficult at all. For them, a process is a chain of functions. But the story is more complex.

Question 4. Now that I'm mentioning it: Which *was* first, the chicken or the egg?

Answer 4. The egg. The first chicken egg was a mutation laid by a pre-chicken from a mutated seed or egg cell. A chicken is the means by which an egg makes another egg.

ArchiMate in its prenatal form used to have a concept called Business Activity. This would stand for a lowest level, indivisible, piece of business behavior. It was not to have any con-

stituent parts. Business Function and Business Process would then be an Aggregation of- business behavior elements, either Business Function, Business Process or Business Activity. In an 'unfolded' picture that lacks the abstract 'Business Behavior' concept, it looks like View 147.

TOG dropped activity in the 1.0 spec. I do not know why exactly, but I can imagine a couple of reasons:

View 147. *Pre-ArchiMate 1.0 relations between Business Process, Business Function and Business Activity*

- It is difficult to decide when something becomes indivisible;
- It is difficult to come up with a clear distinct definition of Business Activity that is neither inside-out nor outside-in.

My initial approach to combining the different roles of Business Function and Business Process in our ArchiMate models was close to this original, but with a small twist. In our company it was still customary to think of Business Processes as being a sort of 'chain' of Business Functions (as is often the way architects look at the division, but watch out: this is the *structural* ('performing') function not ArchiMate's *behavioral* one) and in ArchiMate this can become a Business Process that has aggregated Business Function children. I proceeded to make that view symmetric in that one could

also say that a Business Function aggregates the Business Processes it contributes to. This can be seen in View 148.

View 148. *A Business Process Aggregates Business Functions and a Business Function Aggregates Business Processes*

(I had removed activity as it is not part of ArchiMate 1.0) In this way, I took the classic approach and made it nicely symmetric. Both are then just overlapping (not necessarily orthogonal) views of the *same* business behavior. Say, a wave/particle view of something that is essentially the same thing, one 'measured' from the aspect of what it produces (process, outside-in) and one of what it requires (function, inside-out). I can personally live with that Quantum-Mechanics-like ambiguity, but it is not to everybody's liking. Therefore, I dropped that way for another as we actually can be more precise in our thinking using ArchiMate's core relations from the meta-model as guidance.

Suppose we do indeed see process as a kind of 'chaining' of 'functions', what are we actually saying, ArchiMate-wise? Chaining is not an ArchiMate relation, after all. Luckily, ArchiMate has a good relation for this: Serving. So, what we can say is that a Business Process *uses* the Business Functions in some way (instead of both being aggregates of each other). But, in ArchiMate, how does a process use a function? Well, a Business Process can use a Business Service, which in its turn is provided by a Business Function.

But if you want to model the behavior that *Realizes* something (like a Business Service), the preferred option is a Business Process and not a Business Function. After all a Business Process is 'intended to produce a service'. So we must ask ourselves: if a Business Function Realizes a Business Service what *process* actually realizes that service? Well, that must then be an *internal* process of the Business Function. The result is something like View 149. Here we see a Business Process that uses ('chains') two different Business Functions to realize a Business Service. The roles are assigned to the functions, that according to ArchiMate should be performed by a single role. The internal processes of the functions have here been modeled as composites of the function, not aggregates. That is logical, because the *internal* process of a business function ceases to exist if you delete the business function.

This pattern can of course be repeated infinitely, i.e. the internal process uses multiple internal sub-functions and their internal sub-processes. I think you should be careful with that, as it fragments your model. It depends on the future questions you want to answer with the help of the model wether those details are really useful.

View 149. *A Business Function's internal process Realizes a Business Service*

You may prefer nesting to strengthen the visual message here. Under the hood, the composition relation is still there, but showing it embedded is kind of nice in this case, as can be seen in View 150.

Now, the question must be asked: which role(s) actually perform(s) "Business Process P" in View 150? This depends on the organization of the company. Maybe there is an explicit steering role for that process (which has some difficulties if you go into it). In the absence of such a steering role, we might think that both Role A and Role B are assigned to Process P. But the (ArchiMate) derived relations between said roles and process from the model above are not Assigned-To but *Serving* (performs+composite+realizes+-Serving = Serving), so it would be confusing to have both Assigned-To and Serving from roles B and A to process P. Therefore, we need another separate role to assign to process P.

A solution is to use a Business Collaboration consisting of the roles in question here to assign to the process. This is not that far from what in reality often happens. In many companies we will see some sort of very loose and thin 'collaboration'. Payments just pays what Claim Handling has

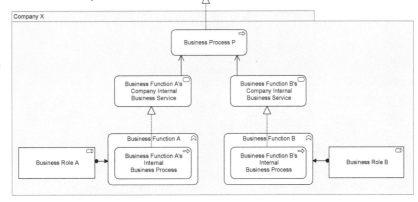

View 150. *A Business Function's internal process Realizes the Business Function's service, nested view*

approved and they only communicate when it is about the process itself or when something is amiss (which in turn is often all that they collaborate about). There is no separate role making sure that everything happens. Yes, there are (as oversight) process owner roles for the internal processes of function A and B so their internal process is such that collaboration *can* actually happen. But these, as we will see in Section 19 "Secondary and Tertiary Architecture" on page 104, are quite different roles from those that are assigned to performing the function. Anyway, an example of loose/thin collaboration would be something like View 151 on page 94 (note: the collaboration is assigned to a process and not to an interaction).

Depending on how the operating model of your organization actually is, a different picture may emerge of course.

If instead of using an 'end-to-end' process that *uses* functions, we model the End-to-end process as a Business Interaction and notice that it can Realize a Business Service, you can wonder about the internal setup of that interaction. ArchiMate just says the interaction is performed by the collaboration and leaves it at that. But if you look deeper, what happens when different roles collaborate?

The first thing is that if different roles collaborate, it is their separate behaviors in the collaboration that *together* create the interaction. These separate behaviors will somehow be recognizable as such also, or you will not be able to define the interaction in your business manuals. If two Business Functions together somehow create the Business Interaction, it is either an 'interaction of processes' or 'an interaction of functions'. Since an interaction is directed at *realizing* something (a service for instance), it is best to use processes. We'll show an example below when we look at the relation between ArchiMate Enterprise Architecture modeling and Business Process Modeling.

The *Business Process P* in View 151 on page 94 is modeled as some independent entity: a separate process that uses the services provided by the internal Business Processes of the separate Business Functions. But a problem exists: that separate process using the services of others does not really exist. In reality, that process is made up of the processes of the different functions. So, we can simplify. The first step in simplification can be seen in View 152 on page 94. Here the Business Services have

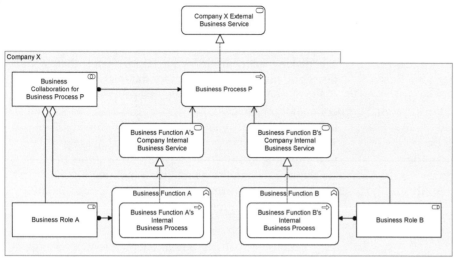

View 151. *A Business Process using Business Functions is performed by a (loose) Business Collaboration*

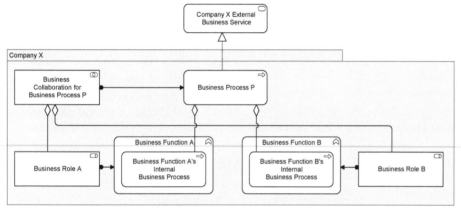

View 152. *End-to-end process made up from parts of functions instead of using independent functions*

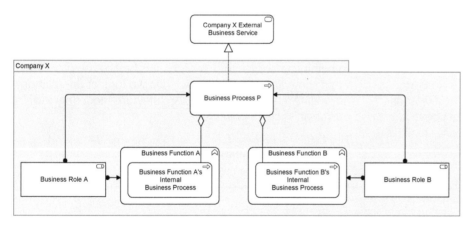

View 153. *End-to-end process made up from parts of functions instead of using independent functions, with informal collaboration*

been removed and the internal Business Processes of the Business Functions have been Aggregated into the End-to-end Business Process P.

Actually, we can simplify once more. Using the 'informal collaboration' technique (see section 8.2 "(Formal) Collaboration and Interaction" on page 33), we can make a very simple diagram indeed. Using 'informal collaborations' has the added advantage that you do not have to name that collaboration, which is especially advantageous if you

have many of these that nobody but your Enterprise Architecture modeling language requires. View 153 just communicates a lot easier than View 151.

In section 30 "A Possible Linking of BPMN and ArchiMate" on page 164, we will encounter an even more drastic simplification when the whole process structure of the enterprise has been siphoned off to BPMN models that are linked to ArchiMate models.

If we take the approach in View 151 and map it to the application layer, we would get the situation where we might say that an Application Function has its own internal Application Process, which (with Technology Process) is available as a concept as of ArchiMate 3. As such, it might be preferable to use Application and Technology Processes to Realize Services. I keep to using the functions in the lower layers. Inertia is one reason. But also that at the lower levels, it is less important in general to speak of process instead of function. Certainly in the digital arena, both are often almost indistinguishable. But if you make a fresh start, deciding on the use of Application and Technology Processes instead of Functions is certainly an option.

18.3 Good Old Fashioned Business Function

In Section 18.1 on page 91, I discussed the structural/behavioral divide in ArchiMate and how it differs from the 'old school' Business Function (something I call the GOFBF or Good-Old Fashioned Business Function in honor of Hubert Dreyfus, the philosopher who wrote about 'Good Old-Fashioned AI', or GOFAI' in *What Computer's (Still) Can't Do*, but I digress), the 'structural' function that encapsulates 'behavior'. Here, I'll show a way to model this in ArchiMate.

The full world of a Business Function delivering services to the organization can be modeled like View 154. The gray

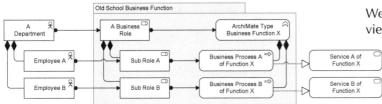

View 154. *An ArchiMate Business Function, with two internal processes, roles and services realized*

box contains the 'old school' business function. The structure (role with sub roles) and the behavior (function and internal processes). That doesn't look like 'encapsulation' yet, but using ArchiMate's Nesting visualization, we can make a view that suggests the encapsulation as in View 155.

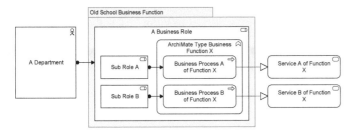

View 155. *An ArchiMate Business Function, with two internal processes (nested), roles and services realized*

It is a bit nasty, this one, because the relation between 'A Business Role' and 'ArchiMate Type Business Function X' is Assigned-To, something not always expected of an ArchiMate Nesting.

We can simplify this picture further as can be seen in View 156 (note, all these views come from the same model, they are just presented in different ways to convey a different message). The Realization relations from 'ArchiMate Type Business Function X' to 'Service A of Function X' and

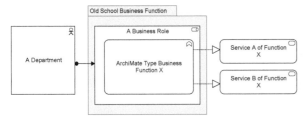

View 156. *An ArchiMate Business Function realizing two services with internal processes omitted from View 155*

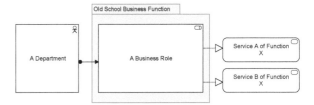

View 157. *A Good-Old-Fashioned-Business-Function becomes a Business Role in ArchiMate, further simplified from View 156*

'Service B of Function X' are derived from Composition (from function to process) and Realization (from process to service).

We can remove ArchiMate's Business Function from the view and summarize one level further to get one single element in the gray grouping of View 157. And there you have it: a GOFBF viewed as a structure encapsulating behavior. Conclusion: If you want to model a GOFBF, you should use Business Role in ArchiMate. Incidentally, ArchiMate says that a Business Function or a Business Process must be seen as the *internal* behavior of a Business Role. So, there you have it, the solution was there already from the start...

18.4 The 'End-to-end' Business Process

In Business Process Modeling many model without business functions at all. They model so-called 'end-to-end' processes that consist of steps and subprocesses that are performed by different roles. This is different from ArchiMate and that has to do with ArchiMate's split of active and behavioral elements.

To explain this, I am starting with a view that depicts the approach of a process modeler (View 159 on page 96). The process modeler looks at the end-to-end process as a series of subprocesses or process steps that are performed by different roles or actors in the organization. Note: View 159 suggests something not exactly ArchiMate. For instance, though the subprocesses are nested in the roles (thus modeling swim lanes), the subprocesses are *also* embedded in the end-to-end process. In my model, the subprocesses are aggregate children of the end-to-end process, but in the view, the end-to-end process is positioned *graphically* behind the role 'swim lanes'. (I can also nest the roles inside the end-to-end process in my tool, even if they stick out.)

The first thing you may wonder about is this: where are the Business Functions? And indeed, most of the time I have talked with business process modelers they tend to ignore the functional division of the organization, other than the roles. In fact, this is one of the ways the GOFBF-thinking manifests itself. The process modelers do not make the separation of role and function too clearly. Process modelers tend to see a business function as an 'actor' of sorts in the GOFBF way. The Process Modeler's 'business function' X *performs* Y, whereas in ArchiMate the business function is just another categorization of behavior *of* actors (X is *performed by* a role).

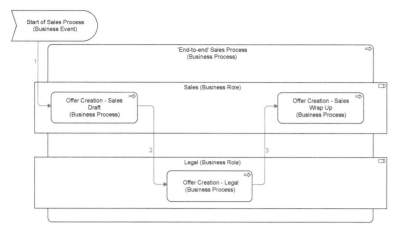

View 159. *How the process modeler looks at the 'end-to-end' process in a 'swim lanes' kind of view*

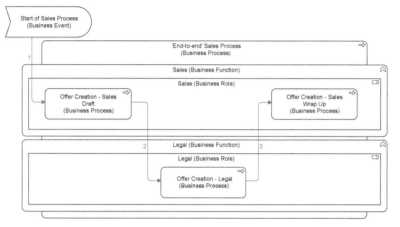

View 158. *Business Functions added to the process modeler's View 156, the GOFBF way*

We can add the Business Functions for which the subprocesses are internal processes. This can be seen in View 158 and View 160.

If you think in the GOFBF-way, where 'functions' are structural with roles inside them, you get View 158 (note, this all is not proper ArchiMate) In ArchiMate, the nesting of roles and functions toggles: a function may be nested *within* a role (thus depicting the Assigned-To relation to the roles' behavior). This can be seen in View 160.

This is borderline clean modeling in ArchiMate. The Nestings of processes inside functions depict Compositions, the

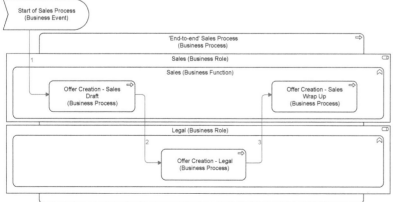

View 160. *The process modeler's View 159, with functions added the (kind of) ArchiMate way*

Nestings of functions inside roles depict Assignment and the Aggregation relation between the end-to-end process and the subprocesses is not really shown, we would need two diagrams to show the different Nestings.

We can model the end-to-end process in ArchiMate also according to the patterns used in Section 18.2 "Business Function or Business Process?" on page 92. View 163 on page 97 is in fact equivalent (with the exception of the added client) to View 160, though some relations are now shown explicitly instead of in the form of Nesting.

We have another option. We can use a Business Interaction to model the 'end-to-end' process. After all, the 'end-to-end' process is performed by a collaboration of the roles that perform the processes that 'make up' the interaction. This can be seen in View 161 on page 97.

If we follow strictly what ArchiMate says about interactions being just the behavior of a collaboration (ArchiMate, remember, says nothing about the interaction being an Aggregate collection of processes like it says the collaboration is an Aggregate of roles), we get View 162 on page 97. The problem here is that you lose the direct relation between the 'end-to-end' process and its constituent parts. Since ArchiMate does not forbid the approach of View 163 or View 161, these can be used. The advantage of using the Business Interaction as in View 161 is that you can see for every 'end-to-end' process which roles are required where and this remains the case when you start to get more complex models with sub-roles, etc.

18.5 Business Process Modeling versus Business Layer Architecture

There is one aspect of modeling where I have encountered a fundamental different outlook between some Business Process Modelers and ArchiMate. That difference is their attitude towards automation.

When these process modelers look at the position of automation in the business processes, some tend to focus solely of what they can describe of the *human* part of the process. The automation part has to be described elsewhere (in the documentation of the systems). This means that — in the eyes of these business process modelers — if a process is automated, it disappears from the radar. It has become automation, not process. ArchiMate, however, looks at it differently. Even if a business process is automated, there still is a business process.

Personally, I think ArchiMate is superior. The way to look at automation as something that is 'Serving' human processes is only part of the story. More and more, automation runs processes entirely by itself. For most companies, fully automating certain processes and making the business architecture 'STP'

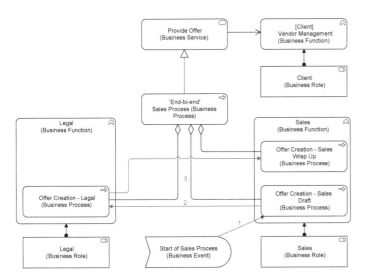

View 163. *The end-to-end process as a chain of processes, without using collaboration and interaction*

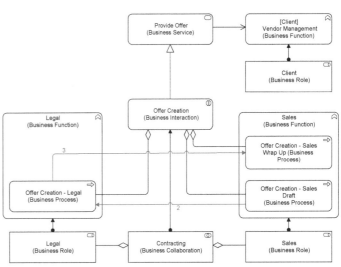

View 161. *End-to-end process modeled as Business Interaction (with added Aggregate relations to the subprocesses)*

(Straight-Through Processing) and 'Exception Based' is the norm. But process modelers are seldom well aware of Enterprise Architecture's integral view of the landscape and look at it 'the old way'. The best way to confront the issue is to ask what would happen in their models if a process was fully automated. Where, in that case, do we find the process?

Note that the process modeler's view is easier on the business user who generally does not think in abstractions like a 'Report Definitions (Business Object)' but thinks of the 'reportdefinition.xls' file. Abstractions scare them off.

18.6 Dividing your enterprise's behavior into Business Functions

Having discussed how to combine Business Functions and Business Processes, let's look at an actual discussion I once had with other architects. For this, I first need to make a short and simplified description of what was under discussion.

In Asset Management, portfolio managers (or fund managers, etc.) manage assets. They have a portfolio of holdings, stocks, bonds, ownership of shopping malls, etc. They manage these holdings generally along three aspects:

- Performance: what does this investment actually deliver in profits?

- Risk: what is the risk associated with this investment? How uncertain are the profits or the value of this investment?

- Compliance: are we following the restrictions set upon us? An example may be that the client has told you not to invest in weapons. Or the organization has generic risk-minimizing rules such as: you are not allowed to invest in certain countries, or trade with certain counter-parties, or invest in certain types of instruments (like junk bonds).

Asset Managers try to maximize financial performance while minimizing financial risk. In the meantime they all work under the assumption that there is generally an inverse relation

between the two, so if there are more risks, they will want to see more performance. E.g.: riskier bonds have to pay out more interest, safer bonds deliver less. They try to mix assets with different risk profiles as these combine generally into a lower risk of the portfolio. They also try to minimize their own cost and they have to comply to the compliancy rules.

Now, the process (simplified) is as follows. Each day, the portfolio manager inspects his portfolio and the news in the world. When inspecting his portfolio, he tries to assess future performance, he assesses risk (often based on all sorts of statistical calculations) and then he may decide to buy or sell something. When he has decided (say, buy $100 million worth of Zimbabwean diamond mining stock), there will be a phase of so called 'ex ante' (Latin for 'before') compliance checking. There are many kinds of checks, based on rules set by a different department, the `investment control` department. Generally, this department monitors performance, risk and compliance and sets the rules for compliance. One of those rules may be that there is a limited list of countries the portfolio manager is allowed to invest in, and Zimbabwe is

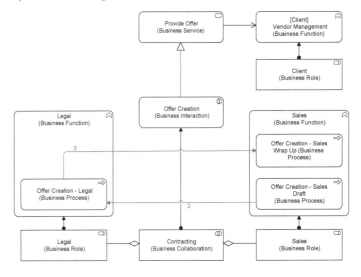

View 162. *The end-to-end process modeled as a Business Interaction, strictly following the description of Business Interaction in the ArchiMate 2.0 specification*

not on that list. The check bears this out and such the order is not passed on to the trading desk.

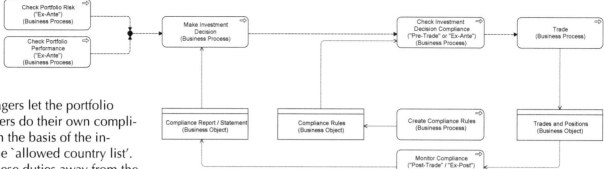

View 165. *Simplified Portfolio Management without Business Functions*

Some asset managers let the portfolio managers or traders do their own compliance checking on the basis of the instructions, like the `allowed country list'. Some separate these duties away from the portfolio manager to make it less likely a portfolio manager enters into a deal that has to be rolled back. Of course, the risk difference between the two are limited as any compliance break will turn up when the 'ex post' (Latin for 'after') checking at the end of the day is performed by investment control.

Now, here is the discussion: When architects discuss the business architecture of this asset manager and they want to divide the activities into business functions, the question arises: is 'ex ante' (what happens before the deal) compliance checking part of the 'portfolio management' business function or part of the 'compliance control' business function, which also has 'ex post' (after the deal) checking?

Two things get easily mixed up here: functions and processes on the one hand and roles and actors on the other. But let's start with an initial view of the processes and objects involved as seen in View 165. `Investing' processes are:

- Check the portfolio against performance and risk parameters;

- Make an investment decision;

- Check the decision against compliance rules;

- Make the deal (trade).

The compliance processes (we have limited ourselves to compliance here, you have also processes that measure risk and performance) are:

- Create the compliance rules and objects;

- Monitor the trades and positions against compliance rules;

- Check the decision against compliance rules.

The latter can be seen as part of both 'investing' and 'controlling', it seems, and in fact organizations disagree on this point. Some see it as 'investing', just as checking performance and risk are part of the normal activities of a portfolio manager (View 164). Others see it as part of all of the 'compliance' activities that are performed by a different group than the portfolio managers, say the investment control de-

partment (View 166 on page 99). This difference is in fact based on difference in actors more than in other differences. In ArchiMate that is actually a pretty decent reason for separating activities into different Business Functions as functions are groupings based on shared resources, skills, etc., which are performed by a single role.

So far, so good. Let's add those roles and actors to the main Business Functions in both solutions. The Portfolio Manager role performs the Portfolio Management Business Function

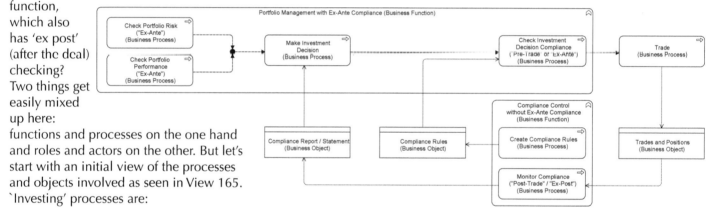

View 164. *Simplified Portfolio Management with Ex-Ante Compliance as part of Portfolio Management function*

and the Compliance Officer role performs the Compliance Control Business Function. When the 'Ex-Ante Compliance' is seen as part of 'controlling', performed by a compliance officer, it looks like View 167. When 'Ex Ante Compliance' is seen as part of 'investing', it looks like View 169. Both are pretty clean views.

But 'being performed by a compliance officer' is just *one* possible reason to separate activities into a Business Function. There are many more, other resources, for instance. And suppose we would have the following situation: the portfolio manager does the 'Ex Ante Compliance' check, but 'Ex Ante' compliance checking is still seen as part of the 'compliance' *function*, e.g. because it is supported by the same IT services as the other processes that are part of the compliance function. Well, that is possible as well. It looks like View 168 on page 100. The 'compliance' function now has two processes that are performed by the compliance officer and one that is performed by the portfolio manager.

View 170 on page 101 contains the reverse split: the compliance officer role performs a step in the portfolio management function. ArchiMate has no formal problem with writing it this way (though it may be frowned upon), we look at Business Functions and Business Roles independently and we can have a Business Function where the internal processes are performed by multiple roles. The question that arises of course is: what Business Role needs to be assigned to the overall 'compliance' Business Function in View 168? We have a function, but who performs it? It must be a single role, according to ArchiMate. The solution is to use a Collaboration, as in View 173 on page 102.

Summarizing: if you want all 'compliance' activities in one Business Function, but not all processes of that function are performed by the same role, you end up with a Collaboration that is needed in your model to perform the function. To make the set of examples complete, have a look at View 175 on page 103. Here the Portfolio Management function is performed by a Collaboration.

Though ArchiMate suggests that a function should be performed by a single role, this role can well be a Collaboration (which itself is a type of role), though the function then becomes an interaction. Function and *actual* Role being disjunct could therefore very well be the case if you have other characteristics that drive your grouping into Business Functions. I personally would advise against it, though, because if your Business Function landscape differs widely from your Business Role landscape, it will be very difficult for everybody to keep track. In other words: being performed by a single recognizable role is an important potential dividing characteristic for dividing your landscape into Business Functions, just as ArchiMate suggests.

Now, if you step back from all the possibilities of modeling for a while, and you look at it from an Asset Management perspective, some of these models will be considered as plain silly by investment professionals. But that is in fact more about how they are used to view their affairs, than that the models are actually 'false'.

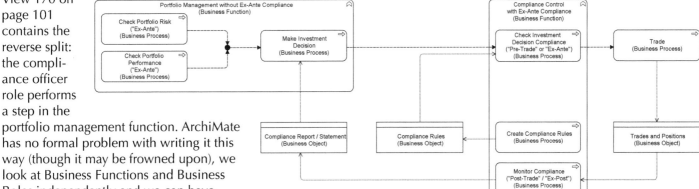

View 166. *Simplified Portfolio Management with Ex-Ante Compliance as part of Compliance Control function*

Personally, I would indeed use the 'single Business Role' as an important characteristic for separation into Business Functions. So, at an Asset Manager where the portfolio manager does 'Ex Ante' compliance checking, I would go for separating into Business Functions according to View 169 on page 100 (and not like View 167). But if the compliance officer does the 'Ex Ante' compliance checking, I would probably *still* go for View 175 on page 103 and not View 168 on page 100, the reason being that the whole chain of portfolio management to trading has quite a different beat to it (continuous, straight through processing) than the batch-like daily measurement of *the rest of* compliance, let alone

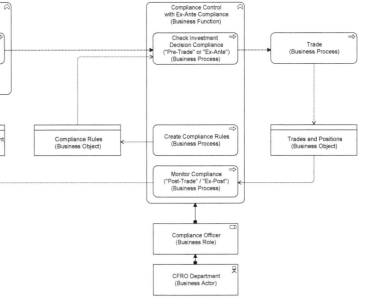

View 167. *Simplified Portfolio Management with Ex-Ante Compliance as part of the Compliance Control Function*

the once in a while change (creation) of compliance rules. In other words: Business Role is an important characteristic for separation into Business Functions, but it is not by definition the *only* characteristic. Time patterns may be an important characteristic as well. And there are more. In fact, 'Ex Ante' compliance checking is so weakly connected to the skills of either portfolio manager or compliance officer, if you choose View 169 or View 175 on page 103, your main division into Business Functions stays the same, even if the company decides to change the assignment of 'ex ante' compliance checking from a portfolio manager to a compliance officer (or the other way around).

So, here you see it again: there is no simple answer on how you should model, just as having a grammar does not mean you know which sentences evoke the best effect in your reader.

18.7 Concurrent Functional Landscapes

So, among the most difficult Enterprise Architecture discussions are discussions on separating your business into Business Functions. The previous example already gave an example on how something can easily (and properly) be seen as a part of two different functions. But even after you have created your ideal functional decomposition, keeping it for all uses may not be the best thing to do.

Take the following example: in Asset Management, we can have — amongst all our functions — the following two functional decompositions: 'fund accounting' on the one hand and 'payments & cash' on the other hand. Both generally have to do with business objects that are being held in the outside world: banks have the bank accounts where the cash is, custodians have the custodian accounts that hold the non-cash assets, e.g. stocks and bonds. If we buy stock from another party via the stock exchange, we enter into a deal, which is then confirmed by both sides and then follows 'settlement'. Settlement means: we instruct our bank to send cash from our bank account to the other party's bank account and they instruct their custodian to send stocks from their custodian account to ours. It often takes some time for this to be completed, say 3 business days. At the end of each day, our bank sends us a bank statement with all our transactions of that day and the end cash position on that account. The custodian does the same on our holdings. When we strike the deal, we put in our accounting system that we will receive the stocks in three days, and we also put there

that we will have to pay out cash which they will receive in 3 days. But in both cases, we also check afterwards if what has actually happened is the same as what we said would happen. Such checking is called 'reconciliation'.

Functionally, we might have a 'Cash & Payments' Business

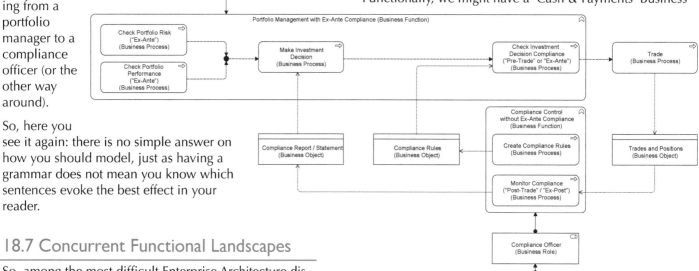

View 169. *Simplified Portfolio Management with Ex-Ante Compliance as part of the Portfolio Management function*

Function and a 'Fund Accounting' Business Function. This is because managing custody and managing cash are quite different in terms of processes, outside contacts, skills, etc. So, our 'Cash & Payments' Business Function contains a daily 'Reconcile Cash Accounting with Bank Statements' Business Process, while the 'Fund Accounting' Business Func-

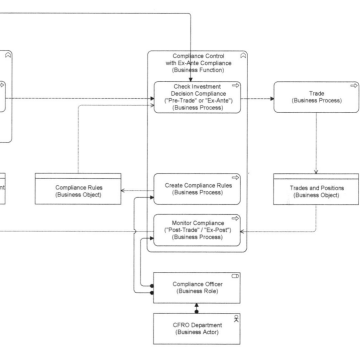

View 168. *Simplified Portfolio Management with Ex-Ante Compliance part of the Compliance Control function but performed by the Portfolio Manager role*

tion contains a 'Reconcile Holdings against Custodian Records' Business Process.

So far, so good, but reconciliation is a pretty basic set of activities: you have the records of someone else, you have your own records, you compare records and you handle the exceptions (called 'breaks' in reconciliation lingo). In terms of IT support, the activities are almost the same, even if they differ substantially at the business level. Hence there are systems that in a generic fashion support 'reconciliation': comparing two sets of data and support the work flow of those checks and the handling of any finding.

So, when you let Enterprise Architects — instead of the Business — discuss the functional decomposition of your business, they — knowing how much each reconciliation technically and operationally looks like another — tend to want to group all reconciliation in a 'Reconciliation' Business Function. They look not just at the business layer, they are focused on the effects on the IT landscape and when you take those underlying operations into account, a single grouping of all reconciliation seems logical, especially if in the back of your head, you are already thinking forward to the process of selecting the right platform for 'Reconciliation'. Feeling strongly, both sides, business and architecture, fight fanatically for what they see as the 'correct' separation in disjunct Business Functions.

The simplified view without a separate Reconciliation Business Function looks like View 171.

The Cash & Payments Business Function is supported by the Payments System, the Accounting Business Function is supported by the Accounting system. Both have reconciliation processes, which are supported by the Reconciliation system. Note: I am not saying Asset management is to be modeled like this, say, that the Cash & Payments Business Process does not need the Accounting system, I am just making a theoretical example as simple as possible. The real world is more complex.

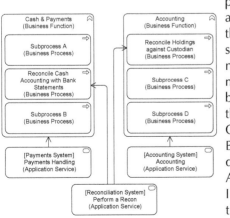

View 171. *Cash & Payments function and Accounting Function both have a reconciliation process*

When we model a separate Reconciliation Business Function, it might look like View 174 on page 102.

I have, however, not been entirely complete. Because even if technically and operationally the actual data reconcil-

View 170. *Simplified Portfolio Management with Ex-Ante Compliance part of the Portfolio Management function but performed by the Compliance Officer role*

iation only requires the Reconciliation system, handling 'breaks' (exceptions) will still require the Accounting System for holdings reconciliation and the Payments system for the cash reconciliation. If these are added, it looks like View 172 on page 102.

The added red Serving relations show that the reconciliation (as seen from a *business* and not *IT* perspective) still requires access to the accounting or payments system. In fact, in a derived way, these relations were already there in View 171, so one could argue from this example that you need not create a separate Reconciliation Business Function in your model, but that is not the point of this story.

The point is that if you look at it from a technical point of view, there is something like the bare technical and operational capability to handle reconciliations generically. In the views, it is what the 'Perform a Recon' Application Service supports. And if you start looking for ways how your IT is going to support your business, it is not a smart idea to handle both reconciliations separately. You might end up with an IT solution for the first one that is incompatible with the second one, forcing you to two systems or a migration. It is a smart idea to look at supporting the technical and operation aspects of doing a reconciliation in one go. The fact that business-wise, the reconciliation processes need access to their respective source systems to handle the exceptions does not mean that reconciliation itself is supported by either an Accounting or a Payments Application Service.

The two ways of looking at it are based on the two different approaches to separation into Business Functions that we described above. One approach sees a Business Function

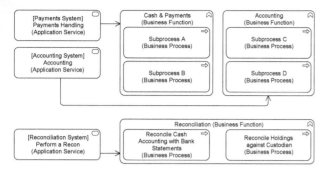

View 174. *A separate Reconciliation Business Function*

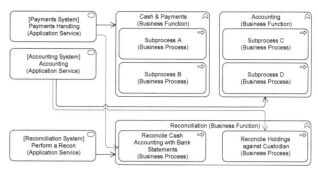

View 172. *A separate Reconciliation Business Function still uses the accounting and payments systems for exception handling*

akin to a capability to *do* something. The Business Processes make use of that capability or are made up of 'strings' of those capabilities. From that viewpoint, the 'Reconcile Holdings against Custodians' makes use of both the Reconciliation capability and the Accounting capability. Both capabilities offer services to that Business Process. In this approach, the Business Processes are not the internal structure of a Business Function, the Processes are 'on top' of the Business Functions. Both ways of looking (as described here) are valid, in my opinion.

If you want to choose between making Reconciliation (or whatever your choice) a separate Business Function or not, ArchiMate helps in the sense that it says that a Business Function should preferably be performed by a single Business Role. So, in case you have a clearly defined single Business Role that performs all 'reconciliations' (e.g. in an operational or technical sense that hands the results to other functions like Accounting or Payments to handle the exceptions), there is a decent reason to have a separate Business Function. But in a case like this, it is probably more important to combine monitoring and exception handling of 'holdings reconciliation' into one process that is performed by a single role: someone with knowledge of accounting and custodians and their processes. And the same is true for cash reconciliation. So, though we have reconciliation capabilities in our business, they will be performed in many places by many different roles in different contexts. Creating a single function of it at the business level that is performed by a single *real* role is not a good idea.

Now suppose we do indeed conclude that reconciliation is not a separate Business Function in our business because it is more like a capability that is part of different separate processes. How do we make sure we can take account of all those separate processes when we are looking at supporting the business with IT? Because in that

case, it *is* useful to have a 'reconciliation function' that is to be supported by reconciliation Application Services.

The answer is that you nothing stops you from having a different separations into separate Business Functions for that specific goal. Let's go back to ArchiMate's description of what a Business Function is:

> A business function is defined as a behavior element that groups behavior based on a chosen set of criteria (typically required business resources and/or competences).

And the specification continues with this explanation:

> Just like a business process, a business function also describes internal behavior performed by a business role. However, while a business process group's behavior is based on a sequence or "flow" of activities that is needed to realize a product or service, a business function typically groups behavior based on required business resources, skills, competences, knowledge, etc. that 'make up' the behavior.

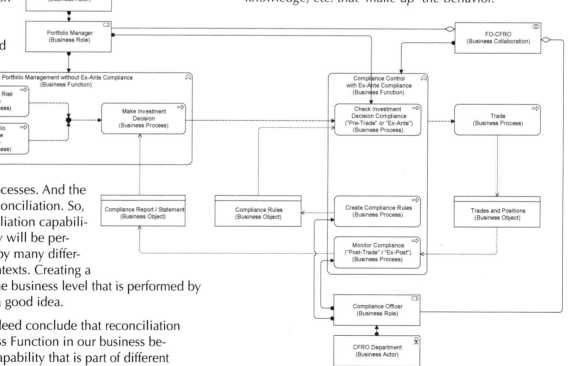

View 173. *Simplified Portfolio Management with the Compliance Control function performed by a Collaboration of Portfolio Manager and Compliance Officer*

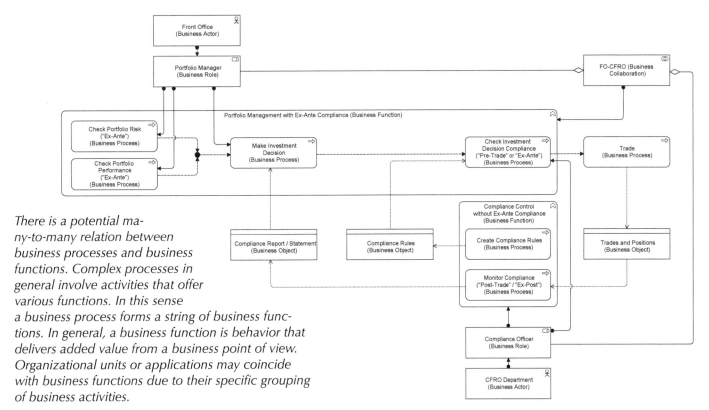

There is a potential many-to-many relation between business processes and business functions. Complex processes in general involve activities that offer various functions. In this sense a business process forms a string of business functions. In general, a business function is behavior that delivers added value from a business point of view. Organizational units or applications may coincide with business functions due to their specific grouping of business activities.

As described in Section 18.2 "Business Function or Business Process?" on page 92, if a Business Function is to deliver added value, it has to provide a Business Service. But as a Business Service is to be produced by a Business Process, a Business Function must logically have *internal* Business Processes that actually Realize those Business Services. Other, higher level, Business Processes may be based on that 'string of Business Functions', but that means the *internal* Business Processes of a Business Function are Serving the (to the Business Function) *external* Business Processes.

But when we use a different set of criteria, we get a different grouping of behavior. If we want to group our business behavior on the basis of the criterium of IT-use, we get a different landscape. In that case, we might prefer the model where Reconciliation is a separate Business Function. In our example, if we follow the criterium 'competences', we get one landscape and if we follow 'IT-resources' we get another.

In summary:

- You divide business behavior into Business Functions based on criteria;

- Different criteria produce a different landscape;

- Always forcing everybody into one specific landscape produces irreducible conflicts. Hence, you might end up using multiple 'landscapes';

- Any landscape is based on a grouping of the internal Business Processes of the Business Functions. These must be the same for all landscapes to make sure that landscapes do not contradict each other.

View 175. *Simplified Portfolio Management with the Portfolio Management function performed by a Collaboration of Portfolio Manager and Compliance Officer*

I call the separate IT-resource based enterprise landscape the BITMAP: Business-IT Mapping*.

18.8 Application/Technology Process or Function

As of ArchiMate 3, ArchiMate also has a Process element in the application and technology layer. As I started out years ago, I tend to use only Application Function and I have infrastructure patterns without Technology Function or Process. Grammatically, there is no difference in ArchiMate between either a function or a process, using either is thus — apart from the differences described before — a matter of taste. But especially for physical processes that create products, it is more appropriate to use Technology Process.

In general, when you are concentrating on the outcome, you use Process, when you are concentrating on the 'input' (such as skills or resources), you use Function. One word of warning: using both interchangeably means more difficult automated analysis. So, when automated handling of what is in the model is important, I would advise against using multiple patterns that only differ in the choice between function or process unless you have a good reason to do so.

---

*   Given the developments in automation it is not unlikely that the split between 'business' and 'IT' will start to become more and more meaningless over time.

19. Secondary and Tertiary Architecture

19.1 Introduction

A while back, when we were building our Current State model somebody posed the question: How are we going to add the 'application owners' to our model? The question arose, because we had decided to use our Current State ArchiMate model as source for our CMDB on which the help-desk software was based. In that database, the help-desk people needed to be able to find the owner of the application if something is wrong with it. In fact, our ArchiMate model partly became our CMDB.

Now the easiest and most simple way to connect a Business Role to an Application Component is with an Association. But working with ArchiMate a lot influences your thinking.

So, when somebody came up with the word 'owner', my thought was: "Wait a minute, that sounds like a *role*...". So, if owner is a Business Role, what Business Process is ac-

tually assigned to that Business Role? What, in other words, is 'the owner's process'? What does an 'owner' *do* actually? And that made me think about other roles surrounding the use of IT: application manager, developer, exploitation manager, architect maybe even. The thinking resulted

in an approach that I have christened 'Primary, Secondary and Tertiary Architecture'.

19.2 Primary Architecture

Primary Architecture is what it is all about and what is generally on everybody's mind and what we have been using for examples most of the time. An example summary is in View 176.

This is what generally is the sole focus of Enterprise Architects: how the business processes are supported by IT. More or less, you see here a small summary of the essentials of the Archi-Mate meta-model.

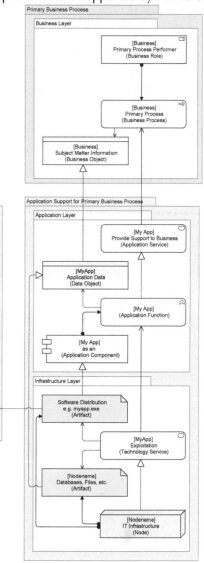

View 177. *The Primary Architecture with the Secondary Development Architecture*

19.3 Secondary Architecture: Development

But as we all know, there is a lot that is needed for this 'Application Support for the Business' to work. Assuming we build our own application (comparable things happen when the application is not built but bought), we need to model the *development* of the application. Application develop-

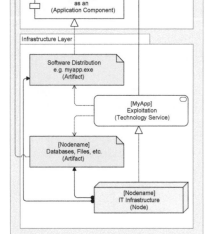

View 176. *The Primary Architecture: Business uses an Application that uses Infrastructure*

ment is a Business Process in itself, which as a result produces the application to be deployed and run. Suppose, this is a simple application and it is supposed to run in a Windows environment. What the development process *physically* has to produce is an executable ('.exe') file. That file is already in our Primary Architecture view. To *produce* that executable, the developers have their own Business Process, they employ their own Application Support, the latter generally some sort of Integrated Development Environment (IDE), an application that produces applications. This is shown in View 177 on page 104.

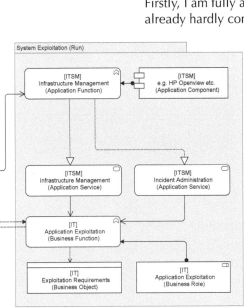

View 178. *The Primary Architecture with the Secondary Exploitation Architecture*

dated by the development environment which supports the development process.

In other words, what for the business user is an application, is data for the developer. The user Uses the Application Component, the developer Accesses a Data Object. Looking at the development process, we see the development environment that is used to create the application. That application is used by the 'Application Change' Business Function which is Assigned-To the 'Application Development / Change' Business Role. Note: I have used a Business Function here, more or less because this behavior is not application-specific. Alternatively, I could have used a process.

Lastly, there are two Business Objects:

- The requirements for the application. This is an important input for the development process;

- The development requirements. There are some things the development function cannot handle. For instance, there may be policies regarding the development languages to use, because supporting every development language ever created is just too expensive and risky. Each of these languages comes with restrictions. If a business requirement would be in conflict with the restrictions of the development function, there is a conflict that needs to be resolved. We get back to these later.

19.4 Intermezzo

Firstly, I am fully aware that in most organizations it is already hardly common practice to model everything that is part of the *primary* architecture. So, modeling the development process is something that is generally thought of as 'nice to have'. I agree, and that is why I call this 'secondary'. However, the development role must see this as its own *primary* process and would do well to actually get it under control. Having said that, I am not expecting you to model every nook and cranny of your organization. I am using ArchiMate modeling here to make an analysis of the situation, in the end, I will present a short and usable summary that only slightly extends primary architecture.

Secondly: the labeling of the business layer elements has between the []-brackets the proposed part of the organization responsible, generally 'business' or 'IT'.

19.5 Secondary Architecture: System Exploitation

When the developers have delivered the application, it needs infrastructure to function. The application may be deployed on the hardware (the Node), but the 'run' people keep the infrastructure running smoothly, etc. The 'run' people also have a help desk, to which users can go with

I want to point your attention to the fact that the executable Artifact now realizes *two* elements in the Application Layer:

- For the primary (business) process, the Artifact Realizes an Application Component: an active element that supports the primary process with automation;

- For the (secondary) development process, however, that same Artifact Realizes a Data Object, that is created/up-problems. An example is modeled in View 178 on page 105. The 'run' people also have Business Processes that are supported by their own Application Services Realized by IT Service Management (ITSM) software. Two are modeled in the example:

- Infrastructure Management, which means keeping an eye on the infrastructure to check if it is still running properly;

- Incident Management to keep track of incidents, requests etc.

In the example, the Technology Service that the Node Realizes for the Infrastructure Management software to use has been left out. What you see is the derived relation between Node and Infrastructure Management software. Additionally, the incident and request information and answers that flow from the primary process to the exploitation process (and back) have been modeled as Flow relations.

In reality, all of this is far more detailed and complex, but the idea of this example is to show how the various aspects of using IT in your organization are related.

19.6 Secondary Architecture: Application Maintenance

The last aspect of Secondary Architecture is application maintenance. Application maintenance consists of things like managing settings of an application, such as user profiles, authorizations, or other maintenance jobs like management reports and such. Generally, in an organization, the larger applications have dedicated application managers who are responsible for these activities.

View 179 contains an example in which two patterns have been modeled:

- the application MyApp itself offers application management (e.g. screens to modify user's rights and so forth);

- some other editor (not shown) is used by the application manager to edit configuration files which are Accessed by the application.

Furthermore, the business users will communicate with the application managers. This has been modeled by a Flow relation between both Business Processes. And finally, the application management for MyApp has been modeled as being part of an overall Application Management Business Function.

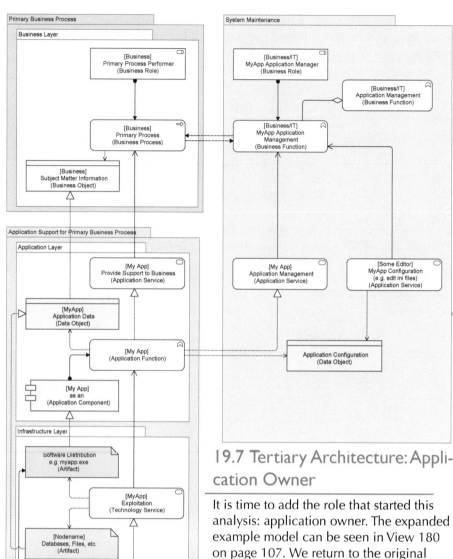

View 179. *The Primary Architecture with the Secondary Application Management Architecture*

19.7 Tertiary Architecture: Application Owner

It is time to add the role that started this analysis: application owner. The expanded example model can be seen in View 180 on page 107. We return to the original question: "What does an application owner do?", or — since the 'application owner' is clearly a Business Role — "What is the application owner's process?". Here you need to separate the 'application owner' role from all the other roles that actual person may be assigned to, e.g. information manager, department head or whatever. If you think about it that way, then the 'application owner' is above all about one thing: determining the 'requirements'. The 'application owner' may tell the developers what to build (remember: a comparable situation arises when systems are bought instead of built) and probably foots the bill. The 'application owner' is a spider in the web: he or she communicates with the users, the developers, the application managers, the infrastructure managers, all of whom have a role to play with regards to the requirements. The users want a change? That is a change of the requirements that has to be decided upon by the 'application owner' role, all the while communicating with other stakeholders like developers and infrastructure managers. Infrastructure managers have their own requirements and so have the developers whose requirements have to be aggregated into the system requirements as well.

You can see there are more spiders in this web: the application managers communicate with all stakeholders and so do the infrastructure managers. After all: whom are they going to call when there is a problem with the application which needs a change of that application?

19.8 Tertiary Architecture: other roles

We're almost done with this description. In View 181 on page 108, the final expansion of the example is shown. It adds a few other tertiary roles in summary form. These are: Process Owner, Data Owner and Enterprise Architecture. Remember, these are *roles* (the actual actors may overlap with other roles). They are shown here primarily because they also have requirements that have to be taken into account by the application owner.

The 'process owner' is responsible for the process description and decides how a business process should run. Often, the 'process owner' is the same as the 'process executive'

(which is not shown in this example), the one who is responsible for the execution of the process. Think of a department head who is responsible for the execution of the business process while a business control department may in the end be responsible for the way the process must be executed (the process description). The user generally is a subsidiary of the process executive and often either the process executive or some 'information manager' of his unit fulfills the role of application owner. Anyway, the process description is part of the requirements for an application, as the application is there to support that process after all.

The Data Owner may set policies for data, like retention, security, etc. This role also adds requirements.

Enterprise Architecture may set policies and goals for the way applications are set up and how they interrelate: another addition to the requirements an 'application owner' has to manage.

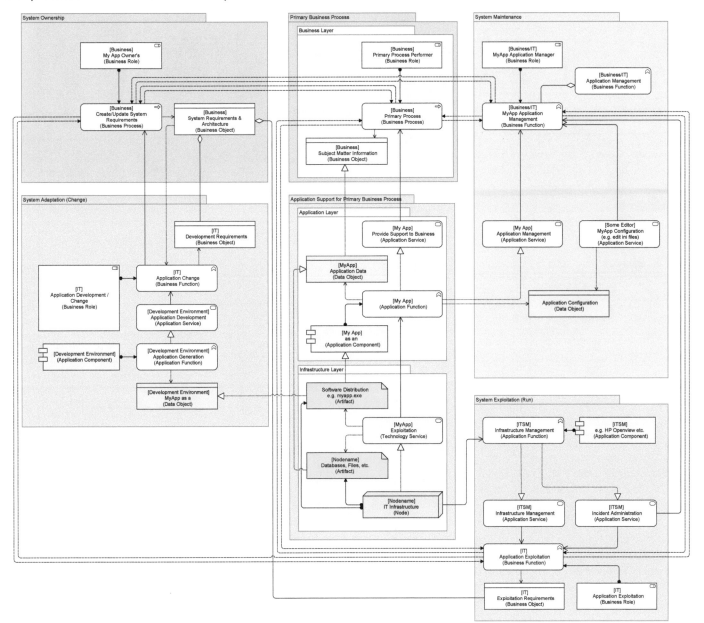

View 180. *The Primary and Secondary Architectures and the (Tertiary) Application Owner Architecture*

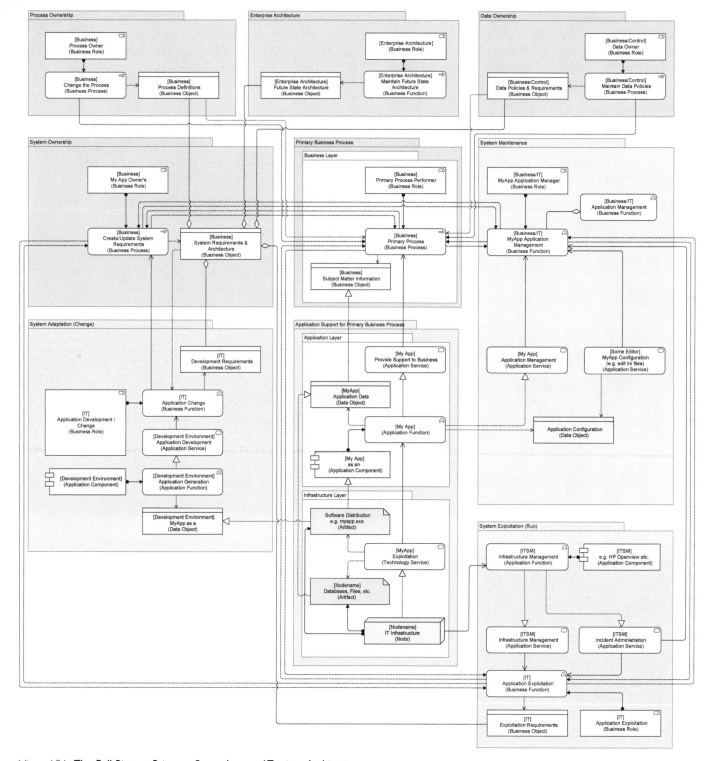

View 181. *The Full Picture: Primary, Secondary and Tertiary Architecture*

Finally: the purple groupings in the diagram are clearly 'business', the orange ones are clearly 'IT' and the gray ones can be either.

19.9 Making it Practical: shortcuts

Now if you're in an average organization, you are probably far from realizing the complete model coverage of primary, let alone secondary or tertiary architecture. Maybe, when our discipline matures in a few decennia, it will be normal to do so. But for now, if you have to model all the secondary

and tertiary aspects, it is probably a bridge too far. However, it might be good to model the most important roles regarding IT without fully modeling their processes and relate them to the primary architecture. The following set of 9 roles (as seen in View 182 on page 109) may be sufficient in most cases:

- Run Manager. This is the role that is responsible for the smooth maintenance and running of the infrastructure. This role may be accountable for any SLA that has been agreed on Technology Services, hence we model this as an Association Relation from the Run Manager Role to the Technology Service. The role is generally fulfilled by the IT department.

- **Application Manager.** This is the classic application manager, the role that changes application settings (e.g. adding/deleting accounts or authorizations, changing application settings). It is the application functionality that is changed by this role, so we Associate it to the Application Function. This role is in practice fulfilled by many different actors in organizations. Some application managers are part of a business function, some are part of the change/development function, some are part of an IT delivery organization. In View 182, the role is Assigned to the IT Delivery organization.

- **Change Manager.** This role is responsible for the delivery of the application. If the application is built, these are the people responsible for development. If it is bought, these are the people doing the implementation and configuration. This role is generally fulfilled by IT-oriented (but business-aware) people.

- **Application Owner.** In the full Secondary-Tertiary approach, this role is responsible for the requirements of the system. What these requirements above all describe, is how the system is going to support the business. This is, so to say, the primary requirement, whereas the requirements from others (run, change, application management, architecture, etc.) are in the end always secondary. That primary part of the requirements is realized by the service the application delivers (to the business), so we Associate the Application Owner role to the Application Service. This role is often fulfilled by a Business Executive or in larger organizations this is delegated to an 'Information Manager'. A nice consequence is that we mirror the difference between 'owner' and 'user' of ITIL, a widely used framework for aligning services with business needs.

- **User.** This is simple, this is the person using the system. We do not need an Association relation, because the User role is part of the primary architecture and the role is already Assigned-To the process that uses the Application Service.

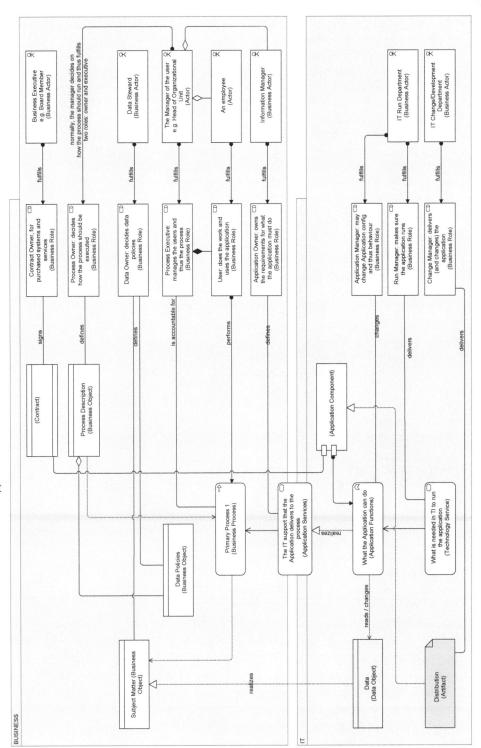

View 182. *Simplified way to model roles from the Primary/Secondary/Tertiary Architecture Analysis*

- **Process Executive.** This is the role that is accountable for the execution of the process. It is generally fulfilled by the management of the user's department. The Process Executive is often not recognized in these descriptions and is often confused with the Application Owner. But in my setup, there is a difference. For instance, in a scenario with a major disturbance to the process because of IT failure, you inform the one responsible for the *process* (the User in this setup) and the one accountable for the *process* (the Process Executive, generally the management). The Information Manager as such does generally not have accountability for the process's execution — he has no operational role. Note: if these roles are fulfilled by the same person, you end up talking to the same person, but that does not mean that person is at that time fulfilling all his or her roles. In the example, I have made the Process Executive the manager of the Information Manager by Aggregating the latter under the former. What I have done here is using the Head of a Department and the Department interchangeably. How you model the manager role of a department is an interesting subject, by the way, which I'm not going further into here, I am just using this shortcut.

- Data Owner. Often, policies, regulations and laws govern data use. A separate owner of the data of a system may be used to design that role.

- Process Owner. This is the role accountable for the way a process is run. In the example, I have Assigned it to the Manager of the User, who also fulfills the Process Executive role. Indeed in practice, these roles are often fulfilled by the same executive. However, in larger organizations, it may be delegated to, for instance, the Information Manager. Note that I have not been perfect with RACI (Responsible-Accountable-Consent-Informed) here, I am just creating a shortcut to model a few stakeholders into your Enterprise Architecture without modeling in full the Enterprise Architecture of those stakeholders.

- Contract Owner. Often, a system is (in part) purchased. There will be a contract that is important when looking at requirements etc. I have modeled this role separately and Assigned it to a top executive, who is generally supported by a Vendor Management function & department.

The most important ones to start with in my experience are the ones from the IT exploitation perspective: Application Owner (Associated with the Application Service), Application Manager (Associated with the Application Function) and Change Manager (Associated with the Distribution). But a usability problem appears when you have applications that Realize multiple independent Application Services or have multiple recognizable Application Functions that need to be modeled.

Note: The summary relationship between Change Manager and the IT system has changed with respect to Edition I of Mastering ArchiMate. The association used to be between Change Manager and Application Component. Why this is and more on complex applications is described in Section 27 "Complex Environments" on page 138.

19.10 Exploiting ArchiMate 3's improved flexibility

As we saw in section 7.16 "Who is in Charge?" on page 30, ArchiMate 3 has the possibility to have the Serving dependency not only 'bottom-up' but also 'top-down'. It then becomes possible to model, for instance, application management as a Business Service that Serves an Application Function. I've added this as the red Serving relation to an excerpt of the previous diagram in View 183.

You can do this, but if you only do it this way, you cannot see how this application management Business Function itself uses the application. As we saw in that introductory section, you cannot show the role of the maintenance-specific application behavior (or interface if you want to model these).

Note that if we would add interfaces, we might have the Application Interface used by the Business Role and the Business Process used by the Application Function. We would use both aspects for the different types of dependency.

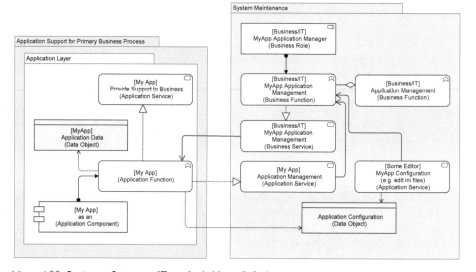

View 183. *Business Supports IT — ArchiMate 3 Style*

20. Modeling Risk & Security with Motivation Elements

As far as Enterprise Architecture goes, one of the most underdeveloped areas is Security Architecture. It has been mentioned in most Enterprise Architecture frameworks and there are some new frameworks under development. Most of those that I have seen have a fundamental problem, which I'll illustrate with an analogy (always dangerous, analogies).

When Apple launched its own calendaring application (iCal) in 2002 they introduced a new architecture for the concept of a calendar. The calendaring application could hold multiple calendars. You could for instance load the calendar of all the sports matches you want to keep track of. Or you could load a view on another person's calendar (served by iCal Server) in your iCal window. Apple did not (it now does) offer the option to make appointments in your calendar *private*. Apple reasoned: it is not the *appointment* that is private, it is the *calendar* that is private or public. If you want to withhold details of certain appointments in your calendar, you need to make a second calendar for yourself with the private appointments.

Now, there is a basic flaw in this reasoning. As I am just a single person, I have only a single life. Which means that for people to be able to see whether I'm available as a person, they have to see all my appointments. Hence, just granting them access to my public calendar and not to my private one does not work. Apple fixed this, probably under the market force of Microsoft Exchange, but it took them years to come around to the correct point of view (such hopeless inertia probably comes with the territory of being right too often ;-).

The analogy with Enterprise Architecture is that there is just a *single Enterprise reality* and thus, that having a separate Security Architecture is nonsense. To be useful, Security Architecture must be fully integrated with your Enterprise Architecture, it must — ideally — be an *aspect* of it.

20.1 Security Architecture

The core aspects of information — that are addressed in Security Architecture — are:

- Confidentiality: Information is *only* accessible for those that should have access to it;

- Integrity: Information is correct. In practice this means that it cannot be modified undetectably;

- Accessibility or Availability: Information is available for those that need access to it.

These are the original CIA-aspects. Many frameworks add other aspects, like legally driven aspects such as:

- Authenticity: The source of information can be established with certainty;

- Non-repudiation: In practice this means that a party cannot deny certain information, e.g. having received something.

There are many more details with respect to modeling security, depending on the framework used. In fact, there are many discussions on these (maybe even more than on Enterprise Architecture frameworks, who will say). All these aspects have an effect on *risks* that are related to handling information. E.g. a leak in your confidentiality might result in a financial risk, or a damage of your reputation or it might even land you in jail. Which brings us to the fact that these aspects used in Information Security are what in Risk Management are sometimes called *Control Objectives*.

20.2 Risk

If you move over to Risk Management, you find generally a division in three:

- Risk: The damage that can be done. The main aspects of risk are *impact* and *likelihood*;

- Control Objective: What state of affairs you want to achieve with regard to the Risks. In the most simple form, Control Objectives often take the form of the inverse of the Risk. But in more mature approaches, the Control Objectives are separate, as a single Control Objective may be a state of affairs that fights multiple Risks and for a single Risk, multiple Control Objectives may be important;

- Control Measure or sometimes Countermeasure or just Control: What you actually *do* to get to this state of affairs that is the Control Objective.

This division can be found in many frameworks, like ISO27001, ISA 3402. The main issue for us here and now is that if we are able to model the most important aspects of Risk Management in our Enterprise Architecture, we also have the framework to model the most important aspects of Security Architecture. I am not saying that everything related to Security or Risk can be brought back to a few simple elements and relations. Risk and Security merit a far more comprehensive approach than that. But modeling Risk, Control Objective and Control Measures in your Enterprise Architecture may offer a good link between your Enterprise Architecture and the Security and Risk Management in your organization.

So, we come to the question of whether ArchiMate can support adding Security and Risk Management aspects to our Enterprise Architecture. And — since ArchiMate 2.0 — it can. I am presenting to you here an approach (first collaboratively pioneered at my company by colleagues Jos Knoops and Roy Krout), using ArchiMate's Motivation Extension (see section 10.3 "Motivation" on page 44).

20.3 Modeling Risks and Controls

I am not a big fan of modeling the 'why' of Architecture using the Motivation aspect of ArchiMate. The why is too human a concept and human concepts cannot be modeled very usefully with discrete elements and relations. Generally, you can make something simplistic that adds little value, or you can make something more realistic that is unwieldy. The limitations of the usefulness of this approach are related to the limitations the AI community ran into in the 1970's-1990's (see the aforementioned *What Computers (Still) Can't Do* book by Hubert Dreyfus). Besides, I'm more a fan of using scenario/uncertainty planning for enterprise architecture and I find the way architects try to control the development of the enterprise with architecture principles and such a lost and mistaken battle (see my other book: *Chess and the Art of Enterprise Architecture*).

But the Motivation aspect can be made useful in another way. Apart from the generally useful element of Requirement, the Motivation aspect can be used effectively to model Risk & Security. When modeling Risk, you can use the following mapping:

- A Risk can be modeled using ArchiMate's Driver element;

- A Control Objective can be modeled using ArchiMate's Goal element;

- A Control Measure (sometimes just 'Control', sometimes referred to as 'Countermeasure') element can be modeled using ArchiMate's Requirement element.

We Associate a Process for which there is a Control Objective with that Control Objective. For instance, a payments process may have as Control Objective that it is not possible for a single person to authorize a payment. Such a Control Objective is then modeled as a Goal element that is Associated with the process it is a Control Objective for.

In the overview of View 184 on page 113, the patterns for modeling Risk (including Security Risks), Control Objectives (including Security Aspects of Information) and Control Measures are shown.

In the green grouping, we find a (primary) Business Process 1 that consists of three subprocesses Sub 1.a, Sub 1.b and Sub 1.c, where information flows from Sub 1.a to Sub 1.b and Sub 1.b to Sub 1.c.

Furthermore, 4 Risks have been modeled: Risk X, Y and Z and a Risk called 'Security'. Note that these can in the real world be replaced by a complex tree of Risks, using for instance Aggregation and Composition relations. The Risks X, Y and Z are Associated with Control Objectives 1, 2 and 3 in an n:m way. For instance, Risk Y is Associated with Control Objectives 1 and 2, while Control Objective 2 is Associated with Risk X, Y and Z. The Risk 'Security' is Associated with three Control Objectives: Confidentiality, Integrity and Availability.

The Control Objectives are not only related to the Risks (red Associations) but also to the elements for which they are Control Objectives (blue Associations). In the case of Control Objectives 1, 2 and 3 and Control Objective Availability, the Control Objectives are Associated with Business Process 1. In case of the Control Objectives Confidentiality and Integrity, they are Associated (blue Associations) with the 'Subject Matter' Business Object for which they are Control Objectives. Note that the color of the Associations here is

only to make the explanation easier, I am not advocating per se that blue Associations are used for linking Risks to Control Objectives and blue Associations for linking Control Objectives to the elements they are Control Objectives of. But to be honest, I find the idea attractive, as you can easily focus on the specific type of relation in a view.

Control Measures (or just 'Controls') contribute to the Control Objective. This has been modeled by using the Influence relation from Control Measure to Control Objective. For instance, the '99% uptime' requirement (Control Measure) for the Technology Service contributes positively to the 'Availability' Control Objective.

All Control Measures are either Realized by a Business Process, by an Application Service or by a Technology Service. For the last two, it holds that the Control Measures are requirements to the service.

Three patterns show how Control Measures can be Realized by Business Processes:

- First, there can be a separate process that Realizes the Control Measure. This can for instance be a separate audit process. This is the case for Control Objective 1 in View 184. The audit process requires a flow of information from the audited process and this is true for any external process that realizes a Control Measure for a core process.

- Secondly, the actual Business Process that the Control Objective is about might have to be *changed* because of the Control Objective. For instance, there might be an extra step required in the Business Process to perform a check or an authorization. In View 184: This extra step Sub 1.b is really part of core process 1. To denote that this part/subprocess is there *because* of the Control Measure, it has also been made an Aggregate child of the (possibly unrelated) collection of process steps (subprocesses) that together Realize the Control Measure. This aggregation therefore is a collection of all the changed parts of processes that have been changed because they are part of what Realizes the Control Measure.

- Thirdly, a separate process may influence the core Business Process. This can be implemented in different ways:

  * First, a process may produce information that is used in another process. For instance, as a Control Measure to prevent trading with prohibited parties or in forbidden countries, the control function may produce a list of allowed parties or countries that is then used in the trading process.

  * Secondly, a process may provide requirements for how a core business process is run. For instance, requiring a four-eyes principle on certain activities. Such requirements become part of the process's documentation and adhering to the requirements can become again part of an audit type realization.

The first pattern is the pattern that also offers the proof that Control Measures have been taken and that therefore Control Objectives will be met.

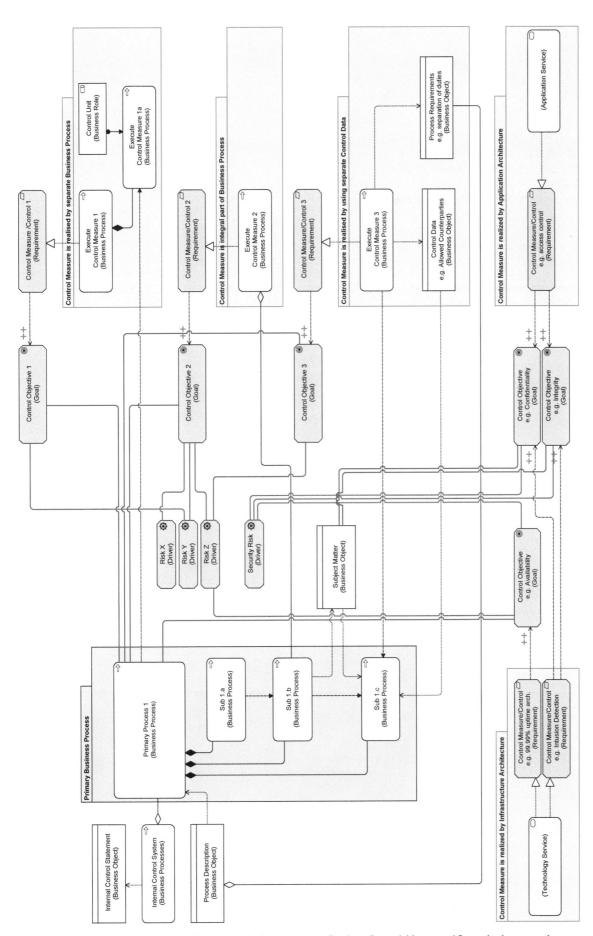

View 184. *Five ways (patterns) the Enterprise Architecture can Realize Control Measures/Controls that contribute to Control Objectives that are associated with Risks*

21. Using the Implementation and Migration Extension

Now that we've used the Motivation Aspect, we might as well look at using the Implementation and Migration Layer. We described the Implementation and Migration layer of ArchiMate in Section 10.2 "Implementation & Migration" on page 43)

I am personally not a big fan of the view on enterprise architecture that is underlying these approaches. I do believe in the importance of (extensive) modeling in Enterprise Architecture of 'the enterprise itself', I don't think it is realistic to expect that strategy and motivation can be usefully modeled. I do not expect more than superficial annotations. More on this in Section 33 "The Role of ArchiMate in Enterprise Architecture" on page 199, part of the "Discussing Archi-Mate" Chapter).

Now, for the Motivation Extension, as you saw in the previous section, I found a useful application within risk modeling. For the Implementation and Migration Extension, I have not encountered such an application yet within the domain of 'the enterprise itself'. Modeling implementation and migration is useful, but here, ArchiMate again can only be of limited value and tools must be much smarter to make it practical.

I personally think that —though it may seem nice to be able to connect architectural landscapes to this sort of change modeling — it becomes (except for the most simple of cases) rather unwieldy pretty quickly. Nice for simple examples but it does not scale well and as such does not offer any advantages over simpler ways. Real support for implementation and migration processes require software that supports project management or agile approaches. That is much, much more than just creating a model and viewing it. That is why I only offer the basic explanation in the introduction chapter. Meaning is use, and I cannot see any deep use. Even though — as a separate modeling structure for change — it works fine.

In other words:, in an ivory tower it works well, but connecting to the actual change processes in the enterprise will be a problem (let alone in a DevOps/Agile approach). So, as an architect you end up with your own description of implementation and migration of the enterprise itself. That may in some cases be useful, but it will always be 'yet another model of something that is modeled differently elsewhere' and thus it will add to the chaos of the enterprise if used at a large scale or in a fundamental way while driving change.

The positioning of implementation and migration modeling is also problematic. If you relate it to modeling 'the enterprise

itself' it is a description at an entirely different level altogether: it is about the *change* of 'the model of the enterprise itself'. What ArchiMate does here is conflate the model with the change of the model. Managing change is in my view more a domain of the tooling than it is of the language. Yes, Work Packages, Deliverables, Gaps and Plateaus are useful concepts, but a tool that can keep different models (versions) of 'the enterprise itself' (or 'the solution itself') and let you move between them, analyze their differences is much more useful than you as an architect modeling these explicitly. *Every* actual change in the landscape effectively defines a new (micro-)Plateau. Besides, Deliverable overlaps with Requirement, Gap overlaps with Assessment, and Work Package overlaps with Process. The whole lingo of Implementation and Migration is also closely related to a rather old-fashioned approach to change (not agile) and that also limits its usefulness.

View 188 contains all Implementation and Migration elements and the Core elements that may be related to them in a very simple example: a server must be updated from version 1 of the operating system to version 2. I would like to draw your attention to the following aspects:

- You must decide which Realization relations you want to draw from either Work Package or Deliverable (shown in orange). I would suggest using only a 1:n relation between Work Packages and Deliverables (both of which can be Aggregated/Composed to create more comprehensive ones), and not modeling any Realization from the Work Package to Core elements, but only from Deliverables, which are more specific if you keep to 1:n;

- In the example, the device is not changed, only the operating system installed on it. This happens often when your landscape changes, not everything changes. So, I would not model Realizations from Work Package or Deliverable to elements that do not change. The

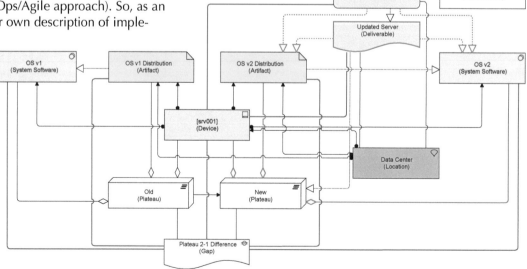

View 77. *Basic Structure of the Implementation and Migration Extension*

ArchiMate standard does not allow any other relation, but in the spirit of ArchiMate, I would suggest using Associations (shown in blue) for affected but not changed elements. I would also not model this from Work Packages but from Deliverables only.

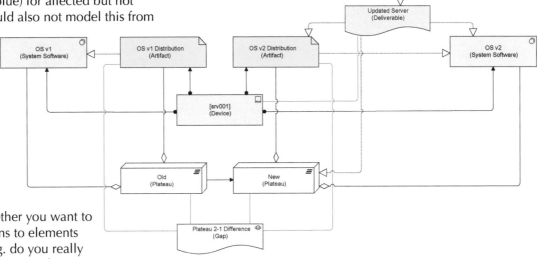

- You need to choose which elements to Aggregate in a Plateau (shown in green). In the example you need to choose if you want to Aggregate affected but unchanged elements (e.g. the Device) and you need to choose whether you want to model direct Aggregations to elements that can be 'derived' (e.g. do you really need to Aggregate the System Software if you have Aggregated the 'distribution' Artifact?).

- If you want to model Locations, do you Aggregate both Work Packages and Deliverables in them? It is possible that something is created at Location A and used at Location B, so you might have to. Personally, I would not use Locations at all.

- Gaps are Associated with the Plateaus they represent the difference between. It is ok to Associate them as well with the Core elements that the Gap analysis is about (shown in violet). Do you include Associations to elements that remain the same but that are relevant?

View 78. Proposed pattern for using the Implementation and Migration Extension

- You need to choose wether you use a single element or a multiple for each element that changes. In the example, two are modeled, but with many Plateaus that becomes messy. Use single objects, though, and the result may be difficult to read. Tooling may help here, e.g. by offering viewing options and element versions depending on plateaus, but this is not part of the ArchiMate standard itself.

The proposed pattern is shown in View 78.

22. Organizational Structure

22.1 Basic Organizational Structure

The actors in the business layer generally form an organization with a discernible structure. This structure can for instance be found in HR systems where the formal hierarchy is often put down in some sort of tree structure. But the HR system is generally only about humans, it is not about Departments or other more abstract structures. The department is there virtually, but only the job profiles normally have actual data in them. This is illustrated in View 185 on page 115 where – on the left hand side – you see a typical HR structure of the organization. If you want to add more abstract actors like departments or the organization itself, you need the right hand side.

The structure in View 185 is too simple of course. Because in HR we do not only have actual persons, these persons fulfill specific job profiles. In fact, the structure of departments and such from an HR perspective is a structure of job profiles, where the manager profile sits above

View 185. Very Basic Organizational Structure

the various employee profiles. Such a Job Profile is in fact a Business Role, but without the specific Business Processes to perform Assigned from it. The HR department has no use for 'job descriptions of a *department*', that's more something for Enterprise Architecture (Business Role Assigned from that department and Business Function Assigned from that Role). But if we model the Job Descriptions as Business Roles, we can create the structure seen in View 186 on page 116, where I've also added (orange) Associations between the departmental abstractions and their managing roles (this pattern will be derived in Section 30.6 "The Process Landscape in ArchiMate" on page 179 when we look into linking process models in BPMN with Enterprise Architecture models in ArchiMate). Now, of course, we would probably almost never model an organization to the employee level. But this exercise is to get to the bottom of the structure. Later we might look at which patterns to use for what. Looking ahead: if you want to model rights management, for instance, the HR structure does not al-

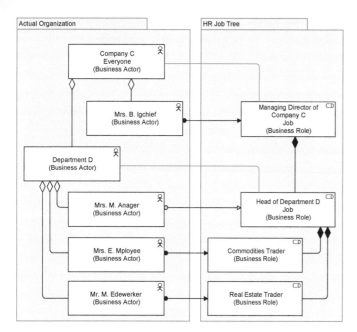

View 186. *Actual Organization and HR Job Structure*

low you to Associate rights with a Department. You might for instance want to give all the employees of the department, including the manager, the right to access a certain part of the building. But the right hand side of View 186 does not have an easy element to Associate these rights with. You do not want, for instance, for the employees to inherit all the rights of the manager (right hand side) as you would like all employees (including the manager) to inherit the rights of the department (left hand side). This illustrates a limitation of the HR structure.

Now, a Business Role is 'responsibility for certain behavior'. How should we model this behavior? It must be either a Business Process or a Business Function. Here, it is clear that for the 'Job' roles, the Business Function is most appropriate for the behavior. But the actors themselves are executing internal processes. We are going to ignore the Business Function aspect now and look at the relations between actors, roles and processes and their IT support. We will get more into process details in Sections 29 "A Very Short BPMN Primer" on page 159 and 30 "A Possible Linking of BPMN and ArchiMate" on page 164.

Our simple example can be expanded with a few systems P, Q and R that are used by the business. To start with: there is no formal

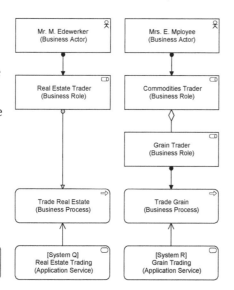

View 187. *Process Landscape for Organization Example*

process description that uses System P. Think of the application people use to report their worked hours, for instance. It is something everybody of Department D has to do, but there is no formal process description. System Q is being used by the Real Estate Trader Job in Process 'Trade Real Estate', where the Real Estate Trader performs some tasks. Finally, System R is used in Process 'Trade Grain', in which Job 'Commodities Trader' performs some task, but the process description is more detailed than that. For example, the job is 'Commodity Trader' but the role as mentioned in the process descriptions is more specific, like 'Grain Trader'. The elements are shown in View 187.

Process 'Trade Real Estate' is behavior performed by the (Business Role) 'Real Estate Trader' job and thus *may be* performed by Actor Mr. M. Edewerker. Process 'Trade Grain' is performed by the 'Grain Trader' job which is one of the Business Roles that is contained in the job 'Commodities Trader' and thus Process 'Trade Grain' *may be* performed by Actor Mrs. E. Mployee.

Question 5. Can you *derive* a Serving relation between Application Service 'Real Estate Trading' and Actor Mr. M. Edewerker? If you created one, what would it stand for in ArchiMate?

Answer 5. No derivation. Application Service 'Real Estate Trading' is Serving Actor Mr. M. Edewerker. It is a direct relation. If you want a derived one: the Trade Real Estate Business Process Realizes a Business Service which is Serving Actor Mr. M. Edewerker. As he also performs the process, he would be serving himself.

22.2 Using an ArchiMate landscape to design an object model

Now that we have a basic pattern for a detailed view on our organization, coupled to real jobs and real actors, we can use that to design a setup for rights management. I include this to show as an example how you can use an Archi-Mate-based analysis to design a informational structure. I will be using View 188 on page 117.

First, note that I have completed the process landscape by adding an (Informal) Business Process 'Keep Time' and (Informal) Business Roles 'Time Keeper' elements. These are useful for our analysis. Now, we are going to answer the question: which Actors may use which Application Services and how should rights be granted?

Let's start with Mr. M. Edewerker. He is assigned to Job 'Real Estate Trader'. Job 'Real Estate Trader' performs Business Process 'Trade Real Estate' which uses Application Service 'Real Estate Trading' from System Q. Mr. M. Edewerker therefore needs access to the Q System because he is fulfilling Job 'Real Estate Trader'. *It must therefore be possible to Associate a right to use an application (or part thereof) to a Job from our HR Job Tree.* This is shown by an Association from the 'Real Estate Trader' Job to the 'Real Estate Trading' Application Service.

Next is Mrs. E. Mployee. She fulfills Job 'Commodities Trader'. She is also Assigned-To the process-specific Business

Role of Grain Trader. By checking both routes (direct from Mrs. E. Mployee to 'Grain Trader' and the pink relations via her job description), we can see that she may perform that role. Everyone who fulfills the role of 'Grain Trader' must have access to System R and its 'Grain Trading' Application Service. *It must therefore be possible to Associate a right to use an application (or part thereof) to a Business Role that is a performer of a Business Process.* This is shown by an Association from the 'Grain Trader' Business Role to the 'Grain Trading' Application service.

There is however a problem in View 188. Mrs. E. Mployee is Assigned-To (in red) the 'Trade Real Estate' Business Process, but she is a 'Commodities Trader' and not a 'Real Estate Trader'. So either this is an error or maybe we have an exception on our hands. Maybe our Real Estate Trader has left and we need a temporary solution. That does not mean we let Mrs. E. Mployee fulfill two jobs formally. But she will still need access to the 'Real Estate Trading' Application Service of System Q. She will get a personal exception. *It must therefore be possible to Associate a right to use an application (or part thereof) to an Actor (a specific person).* This is shown by an Association between Mrs. E. Mployee and the 'Real Estate Trading' Application Service.

Next, everybody who is part of Department D has to keep time using System Q's 'Time Keeping' Application Service. A Business Process and a Role are not really defined for that, so we cannot attach it to the role. But if we put the role and process in temporarily, we can see that the routes in blue provide a way to link Department D with the 'Time Keeping' Application Service. *It must therefore be possible to Associate a right to use an application (or part thereof) to a Business Actor that represents a Department.* This is shown by the Association from 'Department D' to the 'Time Keeping' Application Service.

Then, one Friday afternoon, we find Mrs. M. Anager using the 'Real Estate Trading' Application Service. This is OK, because every manager is allowed to order their subordinates around in our example organization. As a result we say that every Actor that fulfills a Job that is up the tree from a Job that is allowed to use a System may use that same system. Of course, the rules in a real organization may be different (and probably are), but in our example, the orange Assignment from Mrs. M. Anager to the 'Trade Real Estate' Business Process means she also is allowed to use that system because of the purple relations.

The elements that have green borders in View 188 are elements you will normally find in business layer of your enterprise architecture models. In reality, the granularity of your process descriptions are far finer than is shown here in this pattern example. We will return to this later, when we will go into process details in BPMN and how they may be linked to ArchiMate. There we will see that we can link Business Roles and Application Services from ArchiMate to

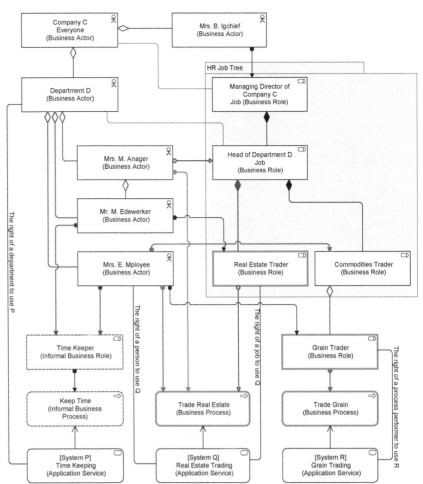

View 188. *Designing Rights Management using ArchiMate*

detailed Activities in BPMN and thus link actual relations between roles and application services. If you have a detailed BPMN model and a detailed ArchiMate model linked to each other, you will have a serious foundation for providing some basic business information to your rights management environment.

What is left now is the final step. Now that we have identified the relations between the various elements, we can turn it into an information model for rights management. After all, the rights management system does not manipulate real actors (let alone abstract notions like roles) but representations of them as information. This is like a client of a company: that client is an *Actor* in your EA model, but it is also a *Business Object* in your EA model, realized by 'client records' Data Objects in your applications and the database Artifacts realizing these Data Objects.

The information model is shown in View 189 on page 118. On the left are the sources of information we can import automatically. The purple outlined elements are the source information we need to maintain in our rights management system and which are the basic building blocks of the rights. All these can be automatically derived from the sources on the left. On the right, we see the four different types of rights we have found. Each right is a Business Object that is an Aggregate of an Application Service and something else:

- The right for any employee of a department requires that we know which department an employee is in. This can be generated automatically using the orange relations;

- The right for an employee that performs a process (using blue relations) can be derived automatically if the role that performs the process is an HR Job Description. If the role is a process-specific role, we need to manually link the employee with the process-specific role, this is illustrated by using a thick relation (all thick relations require manual interventions);

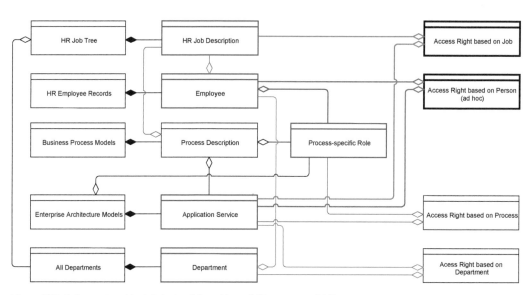

View 189. *Information Model derived from View 188 on page 117*

- The right for an employee based on his job description requires a manual link of that job description and the Application Service (green relations);

- The right for an employee directly (ad hoc) requires a manual link of that employee and the Application Service (green relations).

We can likewise identify the processes that are needed for Rights Management, some of which can be automated.

Now this is a simplification of the real thing of course, where we will also have requirements like separation of functions, (limitation of) access to Business Objects and Artifacts, and much more than just access to Application Services. Furthermore, the rights management processes and affected systems are pretty complex. Because your rights management system may keep the right of Employee X to access an Artifact like Directory Y on your file server (based on whatever right from View 189), in the end it needs to be configured like that on the file server itself and the right in one system must translate to actual settings in another.

23. Virtual Machines (Parallelization)

There used to be a time when computer hardware was simple. Computing even started with only hardware: hard-wired analog components, together performing a mathematical function, like calculating shell trajectories for naval guns — war, indeed, being the great innovator that it is.

When computers were built for breaking enemy encryption — war again — they had to be digital, because their

subject matter was digital. Soon thereafter, digital computers became 'general purpose' computers. Their architecture was generic. *What* they did was left to software. What you did was that you loaded the program in the computer memory somehow and then started it by telling the hardware to start executing the instructions you just did load. Any application ran directly on the hardware. Soon, this loading became a program itself: the system software, or the 'operating' system, the system that operates the hardware. This was a permanently running program that was capable of loading and starting other programs and if they finished, the control was handed back to the still running operating system. This program was the *supervisor*, nowadays called the operating system (literally: the application that supervises the hardware so that humans don't have to[*]).

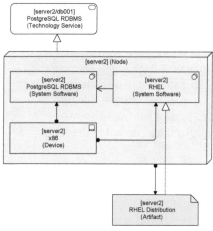

View 190. *Two real servers which we will turn into virtual servers*

---

[*] Automating the work of infrastructure engineers is apparently much older than today's brouhaha surrounding 'infrastructure as code' — see Section 28.2 "DevOps Ready Data Center (DRDC)" on page 151 — would suggest...

But still, the situation was simple: there was a *single* device, on which ran a *single* operating system. On large mainframes, the operating system soon became (pre-emptive) multi-tasking: this enabled running various programs in parallel. Now, this parallelization is an illusion: what happens in modern pre-emptive multi-tasking is that there runs a clock and every 10 milliseconds or so, the operating system gives a little bit of operating time to another program, thus creating the *illusion* of parallelism to the end user. Today, by the way, some of it is real, with multiple computing cores and all.

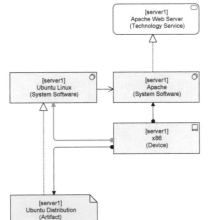
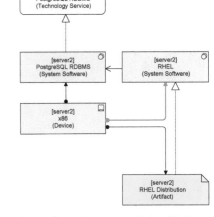

View 191. *Two real servers which we will turn into virtual servers, but without the encapsulating Nodes*

Over the last decade, in operations of computer infrastructure for organizations, parallelization of operating systems (initially often called 'server consolidation') has become popular, as it enables the efficient use of expensive to acquire and run hardware by multiple independent operating system instances. (Of course, there are risks, e.g. regarding software licensing or performance, but virtualization vendors won't tell you the extent of this.) Surprisingly, this type of parallelization/virtualization (the possibility to run various *operating systems* side by side on the same hardware) is also pretty old. It is also more complex than running multiple applications in an operating system which is designed for such parallelism. Because the operating system is supposed to be low level, some of the tightly coupled interaction of the hardware and operating system must not be interrupted or overwritten.

The operating system is the *supervisor* of what happens on the computer. Being able to run multiple hardware supervisors in parallel, each with its own 'supervisor state' was invented by IBM as long ago as the 1960's. To manage these

supervisors, a special piece of logic is needed (in hardware or in software) for which *hypervisor* was the logical name.

These days central processing units of computers often have hardwired support for hypervisors. In other words: hardware devices have become capable of supporting operating system parallelism. The hardware can keep multiple independent 'states'.

So, the question is: how do we model that in ArchiMate? We will start with two simple servers that we are going to consolidate on single hypervisor-ready hardware using one of two approaches:

- *Bare-metal*. This means that the hypervisor sits directly on top of the hardware and the operating systems sit on top of that. Examples are VMWare ESX or Microsoft Hyper-V;

- *Hosted*. This means that there is an operating system on top of the hardware and in it runs an application that also contains a hypervisor. This is the case for instance when you use Parallels Desktop or VMWare Workstation.

The distinction is not always clear, but that is not important for our goal. Now, when we start to model virtualization, we are going to look into detail first, before thinking about what the practical approach might be (e.g. when modeling a Current State Architecture). We start with a standard pattern (see section 7.9 "Using a Node to encapsulate infrastructure" on page 25) in View 190 on page 118 for two independent servers that we will transform into virtual servers using the *hosted* virtualization approach. First, we remove the Node that we use to isolate the server's contents from its surroundings. This gives us View 191. Note the two Assignments from each

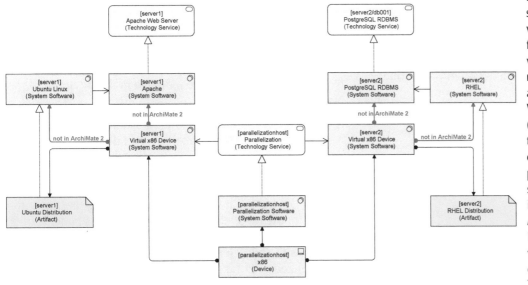

View 192. *Our two real server Devices transformed into virtual server System Softwares, hosted on a new Device*

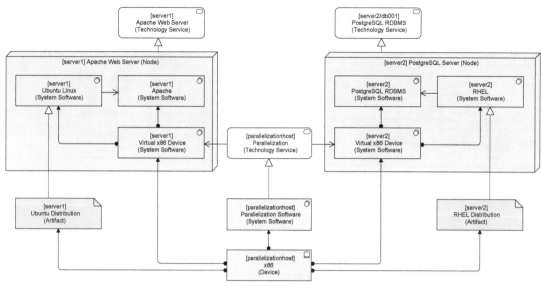

View 193. *Our two virtualized servers encapsulated in Nodes following the standard pattern*

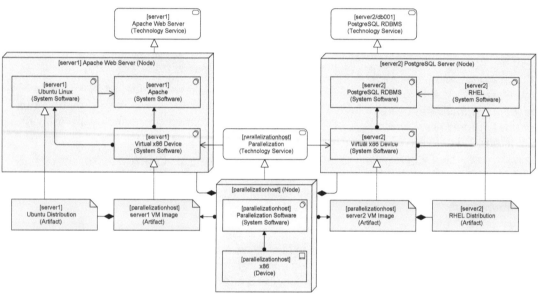

View 194. *Our two virtualized servers with a Node-encapsulating pattern for the parallelization host and partial Artifact modeling*

The virtual device System Software elements are of course Assigned from the real device (the Parallelization Host). To show that the OS with hypervisor capability is required to actually run the virtual servers, I have added a Serving relation between a Realized 'Parallelization' Technology Service and the virtual devices.

We now add the encapsulating Nodes again, so that our virtualized servers are modeled in a pattern comparable to the real servers. This can be seen in View 193. And if we add Node-encapsulation to the parallelization host as well we get View 194. In this view, I have added the virtual machine images to the mix. This illustrates that it is also not a bad choice to use Composition as the relation between the System Softwares of a virtual machine, as it mimics the structure of the Artifacts that Realize the System Software elements. We can argue that the Linux System Software is a part of the Virtual Device System Software, as the Virtual Device System Software is Realized by an Image that also Realizes Linux. I have left out the sub-Artifact for Apache in this example. I have also added Composition relations between parallelization host and the (virtual) guest computers.

Note that there is no Device modeled in those 'virtual' Nodes.

A version of View 194 with partially different Nestings is shown in View 195 on page 121. As I do not model internal Technology Services, I have left these out in that view. View 194 keeps the overall model simpler in terms of the number of different patterns employed (except for that missing Device), so it would be my preference (for now): the pattern for the parallelization host itself, for instance, is in fact a standard server pattern. Also, for architectural discussions outside the IT infrastructure provider, whether a server is virtualized or not is — apart from the cost issue — in *most* cases not very relevant (as long as the applications run and

Device. One goes to the software distribution Artifact which Realizes the System Software element. The other directly goes to the System Software element. We will discuss the orange one in a bit more detail in a Chapter "Discussing ArchiMate" on page 207, when we discuss ArchiMate's (often historical) peculiarities.

Now, when we want to turn our real servers into virtual servers, we turn *hardware* into *software*, to be precise: software that mimics hardware. Software at the infrastructure level means using the System Software element. So, we are going to introduce new hardware (the virtualization host) and on it is deployed an operating system and hypervisor on which our virtual devices will run. This is shown in View 192 on page 119.

Let me first draw your attention to the red Assignments. These were not allowed in ArchiMate 2. If we wanted to remain within ArchiMate 2's formal prescriptions, we needed to use another relation. I opted for Composition in that case.

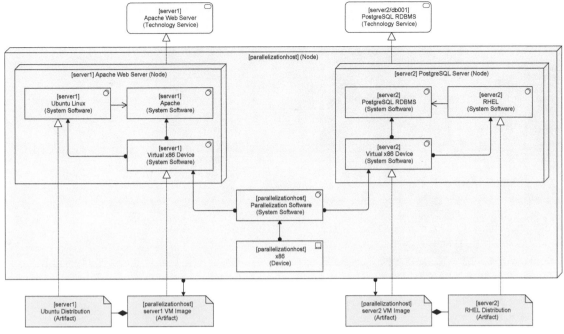

View 195. *A Nested version of View 194.*

are supported, everybody is happy regardless of a server being real or virtualized).

In View 196 you see a new example with a real server on the left and virtual servers on the right. This view shows a number of possible solutions to relate the parallelization host to the (virtual) guest devices. The blue Composition relations and the route via the VM Image Artifact are equivalent to what has been used in View 194. The other alternatives shown are:

- The orange Assignment shows the relation between the active parallelization host element and the virtual device.

- The green Serving shows that the virtual device requires the parallelization host to function.

- The red Realization is derived from the route via the VM Image Artifact.

There are of course many, many more ways to model hosted virtual servers. There is a myriad of choices in what you show, leave out, etc. Here again, it becomes clear that you need to find your own pattern based on what you like and need. A small reminder: this book is in the end about understanding the language and which options it gives you.

Now, with all these details for just a few simple servers, you do get a rather complex picture. It could be worse (e.g. recall the development of the basic server pattern in section 15.2 "A Basic TI Pattern: A Database" on page 63), but still, there is a lot of detail.

As always, you need to answer the question: do you *need* all this detail? Via an approach to model the *bare metal* virtualization (instead of *hosted*), we can come to a pretty simple solution. The first step can be seen in View 197 on page 122. Instead of modeling the virtual devices as System Software, we model them as *Devices*: Composite children of the Device of the host. (A bit confusing this virtualization nomenclature: you have *native/bare-metal* versus *hosted*, but the parallelization machine is always called a 'host'). This might feel as a misuse of the Device element for something it is not intended for (software), but what we say here is that virtualizing is in fact partitioning the parallelization host in 'sub-hosts'. These sub-hosts are not space-separated but *time*-separated, as in: they never exist concurrently but 'existence' switches very rapidly between them. In fact, as we are talking 'hardware supported virtualization' (*bare metal*) here, we can thus see the virtualized Device as part of the hardware.

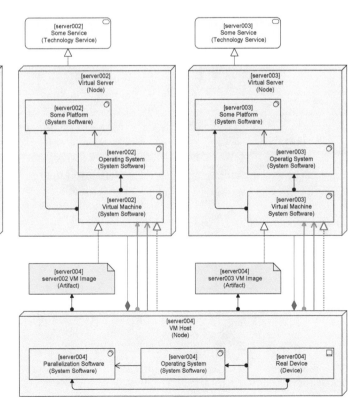

View 196. *Another real server versus virtual server, side by side*

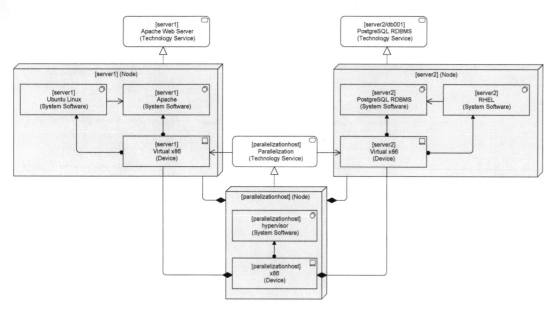

View 197. *Virtual servers in a 'bare metal' variation, where the virtual servers are modeled as sub-Devices of the host device (a suggestion from colleague Jos Knoops)*

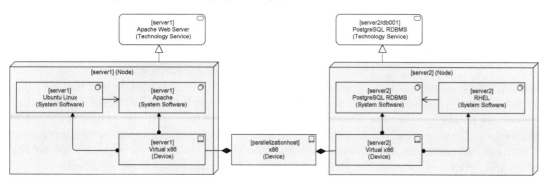

View 198. *Virtualized servers in a simplified pattern where, from the parallelization host only, the Device is modeled.*

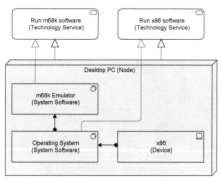

View 199. *Emulated hardware*

Which leads me finally to a minimal pattern for hardware virtualization: View 198. The whole issue has been simplified by making the Devices Composite children of the parallelization host's Device, without encapsulating the parallelization host in a Node.

I would use the pattern of View 199 for *emulation*: a software program that emulates hardware of a different type (actually another IBM invention from the 1960's).

Since hardware virtualization has become widespread and common (it might even be found on the desktop of a normal user, whose Mac runs Parallels Desktop so he or she can also run MS-Windows-only programs in a virtual machine, or in other words: me using my ArchiMate modeling tool) this is seldom seen anymore, except in attempts to keep software for obsolete hardware platforms (e.g. older game consoles) running.

View 198 is just View 197 with some elements left out. It can easily live in the same model. View 197 might be useful for the architect designing or describing the details of the parallelization approach. Again: what you model depends on what you (potentially!) need from a model. Do you need to show or analyze with the software that creates and/or manages the virtualization? Add it.

Question 6. Can you spot the ArchiMate 'error' in most of the views in the section?

Answer 6. There are many elements with multiple Composite parents as the Node Nestings represent Composites. An element informally not allowed to be a child of multiple Compositions.

24. Modeling Information Aspects

So far, we have mostly ignored the informational aspects of our landscape. From an Enterprise Architecture perspective, this is mostly not a problem. The active structure and its behavior are generally the key to your landscape. Besides, modeling the Artifacts in your landscape often feels like modeling brick and mortar while all you wanted to show was a house. But there are cases when informational elements (Business Object, Data Object, Artifact) are essential.

24.1 Messages and File Copies

In the real world of organizations connected to the outside world, there is a lot of data going in and out. An Asset Manager, for instance, gets price and other master data from data vendors, cash positions from banks, holdings positions from custodians, the list is endless. And most of that data these days is still transported by shuffling files around, often via a very antique mechanism called FTP (albeit in a secure version). Take for instance price data. To get that from a data vendor, you may have to create a file in a certain format that contains information about your holdings. Then you upload that to an FTP site of the data vendor. The data vendor creates a reply, which again is a file with all the missing data (price and other aspects) filled in. This file you either have to collect yourself or they drop it on your own FTP server. This is a rather essential process for the business, and it is almost all low level data manipulation where the systems involved (like file transport, scheduling) are not interested in or aware of the content of the file.

Data transport has already been modeled before. In section 17 "An Example from the Real World", in View 144 on page 90, we see an essential piece of data transport modeled. Brought back to the file copying essentials, this becomes View 200.

On the right of this view, no Artifact is modeled. But if we want to add one that represents the data that is transferred from [srv001] to [srv002], we get View 201.

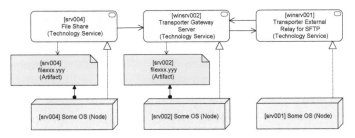

View 200. *Data transport: copying a file*

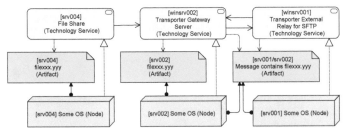

View 201. *Data transport: File copying and messaging side by side*

I am taking a bit of liberty with ArchiMate when I model a message as something that is Assigned to multiple Nodes. Of course, if one digs deeper, even the messages become little stored Artifacts and 'moving' something is implemented as copying and deleting the original. In fact, that is fundamentally true of digital technology. The Internet is a good example: All those data streams are in fact built on top of IP (the 'Internet Protocol') which is just copying data over and destroying the original when successful receipt has been acknowledged. Do that copying and deleting quickly enough and you have an abstraction that looks like moving data around.

Now, the question obviously is: when do you choose one and when the other? Why not, for instance, use a single Artifact for the copying pattern? An example is shown in View 202. But suppose this Artifact is used by some application

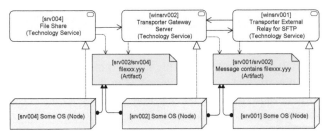

View 202. *Data transport with single Artifact for copied file*

and represents a real Data Object? If we add a Data Object it looks like View 203. Now, this suggests that System X de-

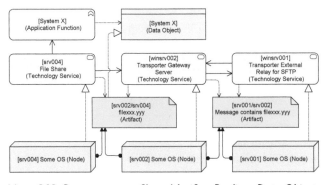

View 203. *Data transport: Shared Artifact Realizes Data Object*

pends on srv002. Now, in a 'loose' way, this is true: If srv002 dies, no more new files can be copied to srv004. But if you start to reason that way, soon everything depends on everything. So, to prevent drawing weak conclusions too easily, the multiple-Artifact pattern is better in this situation. This is shown in View 204 on page 124. Other problems appear when there are multiple systems employed to transport the Artifact around in a couple of steps, if the Artifact changes name, etc.

Now, suppose our message contains price data which is created by one system and imported by another. An example is shown in View 208. Note, this example leaves out a lot of my standard patterns for modeling, like Infrastructure Building blocks, etc. What this view shows is that there is a

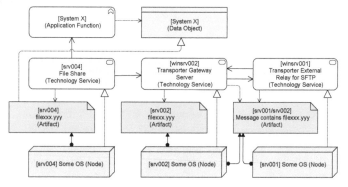

View 204. *Data transport: Multiple Artifacts and Realized Data Object*

'Provide Prices' Business Process that uses both systems to get the price from one system into another. Both systems use the MQ Messaging Service for this, one as sender, the other as receiver. The message is modeled as a shared Artifact. But in the application layer, both systems have their own Data Object, these need not necessarily be the same, both may have different extra properties, for instance. But both Data Objects do represent that same abstract Business Object: a Price. Note also that System B also keeps price data in a database (the infrastructure of which is not modeled). In fact it may read the price message but it writes its price data Object to permanent storage. I have modeled that as two Access relations (because my tool is unable to create a true read-write).

It is fair that System A is in some way dependent on serv001 via the message Artifact, because without srv001, the message, and thus the Data Object cannot exist, whereas in the file copy example, it cannot be created anew, but it can exist.

If our 'Price' Business Object is highly sensitive information, we can from this model deduce that we need to pay close attention to the security of srv001 and srv002 (and srv003).

24.2 Informational Structure

Now, from the explanation it is clear that our 'Price' Business Object is represented independently by both '[System A] Price Data (Data Object)' and '[System B] Price Data (Data Object)'. But what if we have a Business Object that is some sort of abstraction that is not kept in a single application, but that is distributed across multiple? Such things happen. The 'Customer' Business Object may be Realized by Data in the CRM system in combination with data in the Accounting system.

Or what if we have two systems, each holding half of the representations of a certain Business Object? Such things happen too. We may have a single 'Price' Business Object, but the vegetable prices are kept in a different

system than the meat prices.

Here we hit on a weak spot of ArchiMate: it does not have much to help us model this clearly. Those two Realization relations from two different Data Objects to that single Business Object (as in View 205) can have many different meanings that are not immediately clear from the model.

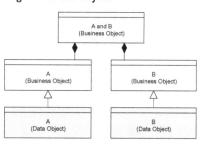

View 205. *Two Data Objects Realize a single Business Object*

You might be tempted to use Composition and Aggregation at the business layer to solve this. View 206 has the AND-structure modeled as Composition. Technically, you lose the relation between the Data Objects and the overall Business Object, as a derived relation is not possible. But as we have seen more often, keeping to strict 'derived relations' when you think of meaning is generally too limited. The same is true for the relations in View 207 where an attempt to model the OR-structure is shown.

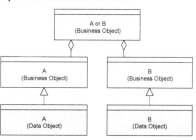

View 206. *Using Composition to model an informational AND-structure*

View 207. *Using Aggregation to model an informational OR-structure*

The problem with both is that the meaning is still not clear. First, the Aggregation in View 207 generally means that its constituents have independent existence, which is not the case in our situation. And the Composition might be interpreted as the fact that the constituents cannot exist without the parent, that does not say they *must* exist in all cases. And we haven't even tried to model the difference between OR and XOR.

All in all, ArchiMate does not allow you to model informational structures precisely and unambiguously.

Note that the same ambiguities exist when modeling Services as Realized by multiple Functions (or Processes) in the same way as in View 205.

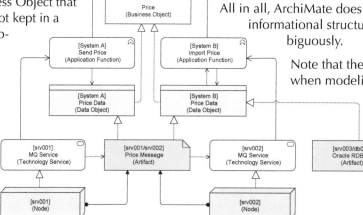

View 208. *Message Realizes two data Objects which Realize a single Business Object*

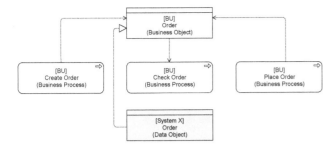

View 209. *Status Change of Business Object: Ignored*

24.3 Status Change of Informational Objects

Suppose you have a process where an order needs to be checked by a supervisor before it can go ahead: an example of the four-eyes principle. The order's content itself does not change at all, it is only checked visually, e.g. in the system or via a printout.

If you have a situation like this you have a few options. The first is to ignore this in the informational part of your architecture. You model access of the check behavior to the Business Object and leave it at that. This is shown in View 209.

But being able to prove that the four-eyes principle was actually followed may be important in our enterprise design. For instance, we can show that only checked orders are placed. This is shown in View 210. Note that we could probably move this modeling better to BPMN, but we'll get to that later in Chapter "BPMN and ArchiMate" on page 159. For now, we remain in ArchiMate.

But since both Business Objects are Realized by the same Data Object, and assuming that we do not notify this check in the Order Business Object itself, we still cannot prove that we only place checked orders. We need some way to prove that. One way is to use the audit trail of the supporting system, which is a separate Data Object, for that. Together with the order, the audit trail can Realize a checked order. This is shown in View 211.

Having separate Business Objects for order and checked order does clutter our informational landscape though. We could do with just a single 'order' abstract entity and depending on the availability of the audit trail, the order is either checked or not. Because we can show that checking the order leads to a proof in the audit trail, and because the processes are modeled such that the order in which they are executed mean that no unchecked order can get placed, we might simplify our business architecture. This is shown in View 212.

Finally, View 213 and View 214 show the version where the proof is on a signed printout, modeled with a Representation element. Of course, there might be both an audit trail in the system and a paper trail, in which case these are combined. All in all, I would in most cases not model status changes by creating additional Business Objects, though if you want to be very precise, you can.

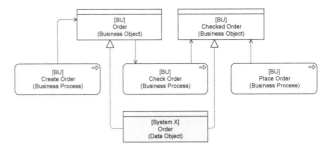

View 210. *Status Change of Business Object: in business layer*

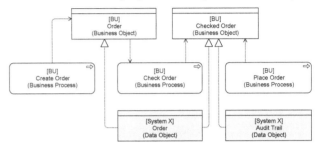

View 211. *Status Change of Business Object: in business and application layer*

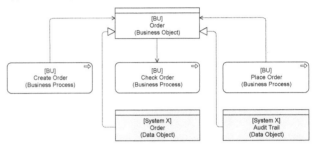

View 212. *Status Change of Business Object: in application layer*

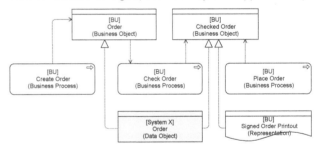

View 213. *Status Change of Business Object: in business layer and as Representation*

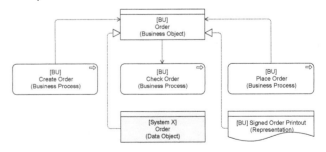

View 214. *Status Change of Business Object: Representation only*

24.4 Access passive element from internal or external behavior?

The ArchiMate meta-model allows you to Access informational objects from both the internal and the external behavioral element. The two are shown in View 216: the blue

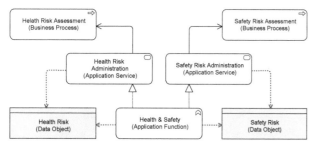

View 216. *Two ways to Access Information*

Access relations from the external behavior (service) and the red ones from the internal behavior (function). The same pattern applies in the business layer and the infrastructure layer. Incidentally, the red Access relation is also the derived relation from the route via the Realization relation and the blue Access relation.

Now, in this book, I have most of the time modeled Access from internal behavior, but the other one is quite valid as well. The question of course is: when to use one and when the other. Here, I think there are a few aspects to take into account. First, using both means that your analyses in the model get yet another route to manage. And as you know it is important to keep your routes to a minimum if you want to use seriously large models. If you are willing to pay that price, then it depends on what the information stands for. If you follow the line that you do not create service abstractions (i.e. services Realized by multiple functions/processes), in other words you keep the relations between internal and external behavior as 1:n, then relating external behavior to information is more specific.

Personally I prefer:

- Access information normally from internal behavior. It is after all that behavior that generally accesses that information for more than just the service;

- Only Access information from the service if that information is the content of that service (and nothing else).

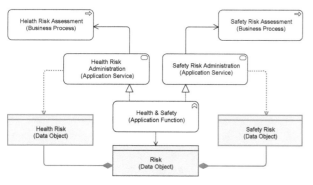

View 215. *Basic Access Pattern with optional service-specific objects*

This is shown in View 215, with the optional service-related information and its relation in orange.

Of course, we could be as specific without services at all in ArchiMate 3 by using Flows with payloads. This is shown (without Serving relations as they are superfluous in this case) in View 217.

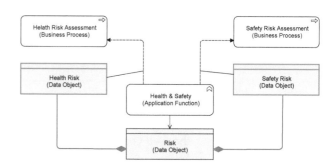

View 217. *Using Flow instead of Services to be specific*

24.5 Low Level Data Entry

Recapitulating our approach with respect to software:

- If it has business logic / functionality used by the business, it is an Application Component. As a result, that spreadsheet your business uses is an Application Component and Excel itself is System Software that Realizes a Technology Service (see Section 15.3 on page 65);

- If it does not have business logic / functionality used by the business, it is either something very generic, e.g. a database system or it is a platform of sorts (see Section 15.5 on page 68) or both.

But consider the following scenario: you have an application (App A) that requires you to load certain data via an Excel 'spreadsheet' document. That is, you need plain vanilla data entry in Excel to create that .xls file. That file is then later loaded into the application. You do not use Excel as a Technology Service *platform* to run business logic in an Excel spreadsheet, you create the *data* using Excel as the *application*.

In ArchiMate 2, that System Software could not Realize an Application Service itself, nor could it be used directly by the Business Process. I suggest you do not read on immediately, but instead consider for a while how to solve that puzzle.

Now, that you've thought of a solution, I'd like you to go back to Section 17 "An Example from the Real World" on page 87. What happened there was that a platform was *both* used as Technology Service for some sort of logic written for that platform (e.g. a Scheduler or Transporter workflow) *as well* as its own maintenance tooling. So:

- The system's distribution Artifact Realized the System Software that Realized the Technology Service (the *platform*);

- The system's distribution (Artifact) Realized the Application Component that was the *maintenance/development*

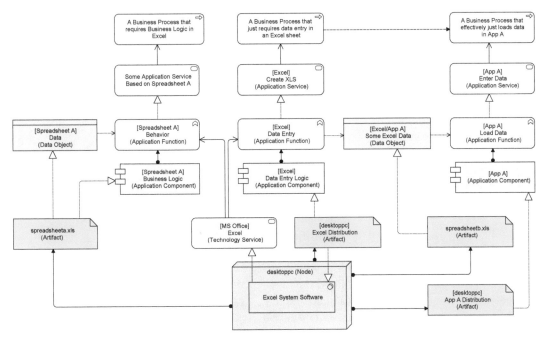

View 218. *Using Excel for Data Entry for a Business Process*

an Excel spreadsheet is data entry when it is just entering data in cells for other applications to read. Or it is just a different way of writing a different kind of document, e.g. a report. But as soon as you start using macros and formulas, you are in fact using the Excel development environment to write an *application*, which is an Excel spreadsheet that runs using the Excel Technology Service as in 15.3 "Modeling Spreadsheet Applications" on page 65. This is not different from the maintenance environments shown in Section 17 on page 87.

ArchiMate 3, however, enables a much simpler solution. It is possible to model abstract Application Services that represent an abstraction of an underlying Technology Service. This is shown in View 220 with elements from View 218. The Application Component and its Application Function for Data Entry Logic from the previous approach could be dropped. Instead we model that the Create XLS Application Service is Realized by the basic Excel Technology Service. We move the Access relation to the Service, as per the previous section.

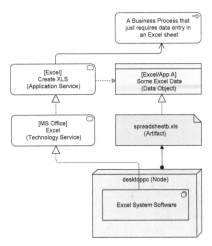

View 220. *UsingArchiMate 3 abstraction to represent a Technology Service as an Application Service*

part (directly used by a 'secondary' business aspect) of that platform.

Actually, this is a pretty common pattern if you reason from the distribution Artifact. Now, go back to the Excel distribution (in fact MS Office, but that is not an important distinction). That distribution Realizes the Technology Service for the spreadsheets that 'run' in the platform. But that distribution *also* Realizes the Excel 'maintenance/development' Application Component just like in the example of Section 17. Summarizing: Excel is not just a Technology Service, but it is *also* a *development environment* (when you write business logic in Excel) and a *data entry environment* (when you have to enter just data).

So, in those cases where data entry in an Excel spreadsheet (say a spreadsheet with user names and authorizations that some SaaS service requires to be uploaded to be able to set the users and authorizations) is an essential step in your business process, something you should not leave out because it is very important, you can use for instance a basic '[Excel] Spreadsheet Maintenance (Application Function)' in your landscape. Worked out in detail the reasoning can be found in View 218. (Incidentally, I would personally leave the Application Component, the distribution Artifact and maybe even the Application Function for Excel's 'maintenance' mode out of my model. Just use the '[Excel] Create XLS (Application Service)' and leave the rest out. In fact the solution to model Excel to create a file becomes pretty simple. It is shown in View 219. The argument for the Realization relation from Node to Application Service is left as an exercise for the reader (I always wanted to write that since having to study Gasiorowicz...).

What this also shows is that Excel is its own development environment. Creating

View 219. *The 'Create Spreadsheet' Excel Application Function*

25. Integration

25.1 Service-Oriented Architecture / The API Economy

These days, there is a lot of talk about the 'API Economy': a world filled with systems providing services to other systems using (RESTful) services. It would be easy to miss the fact that this isn't new at all. It used to be called 'Service Oriented Architecture' (SOA). That these are the same becomes rather clear when you try to model them in ArchiMate. In ArchiMate, the active element is ultimately modeled separately from the behavior it performs. Yes, you can leave out the details, but if you don't, you get the picture in View 225

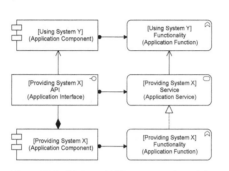

View 225. **SOA and API are two sides of the same coin**

The 'API Economy' term focuses on the interface. The 'SOA' term focuses on the service. But a small ArchiMate model shows that — in ArchiMate at least — these are two sides of the same coin.

25.2 Who is Serving Whom Anyway?

Now that we've been looking at lots of patterns, it is time to have a more in-depth discussion on the meaning of the Serving (formerly Used-By) relation. Of all the relations it is the one — with the exception of Association of course — which is the least well defined in terms of what it exactly means. To start the subject, we will look at the following situation: one application sends data to another. Let's say: the Sales application sends an Order to the Accounting application. Somehow, a message bus is involved to get the Artifact across. This is shown in View 221

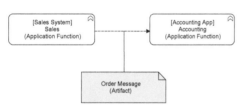

View 221. **Basic Flow with Associated element**

We are using the very useful improvement of ArchiMate 3 — the possibility to Associate elements with relations — here. In ArchiMate 2 (and we can still do that), we could also have used Access relations, but we could not have used Access relations to an Artifact, only to a Data or Business Object. We can expand View 221 to View 222. I've added the business layer as an abstraction of what goes on in the application and technology layers. Note that I've chosen to have Application Functions Realize Business Processes. I could of course have used Application Processes but I don't, because I often have Application Functions already and using an extra variant only makes it harder to analyze my model in

an automated fashion.

The Business Object and the attached Access relations (in orange) are an ArchiMate-2 compatible alternative between the Business Processes for the Flow with Associated Business Object. The red Association relation shows an alternative to depict the content of the Flow between the applications. The blue Realization relation is derived via an invisible Data Object.

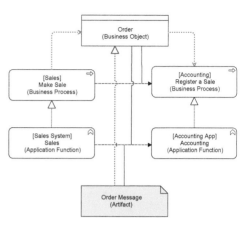

View 222. **Basic Flow with Associated Element, expanded to business layer**

Anyway, now that we know what is going on, what if we want to denote the structural relation between both Application Functions? This is depicted in View 223.

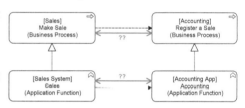

View 223. **Which way should the Serving relations go? (Note: depiction is not ArchiMate-compliant.)**

What direction should we draw the orange Serving relations? This is not clear, because it depends on your interpretation of the term 'serving'. Logically, it is simple: the Sales application can do sales even if Accounting isn't running. But Accounting needs the input from Sales to do its work properly. So, the Sales application serves the Accounting application: the same direction as the flow of information.

But suppose for instance that the Sales application has to use an API/service offered by the Accounting application to send the Order data to the Accounting application? In that case, it is technically like View 224.

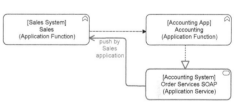

View 224. **Sales pushes the order to the Accounting API**

And that means that, technically, the Sales application uses the Accounting application. Maybe the Sales application actually is programmed in a way that it throws up errors if it cannot post the sale to Accounting. There may be a real dependency.

But suppose that our Accounting application doesn't have an API/service, but it has to get the orders from the Sales

application on
a regular basis?
Suppose the Sales
application has
an API/service for
the Accounting
application to
use? Then we get
.View 226.

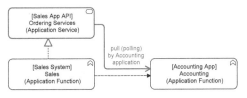

View 226. *Accounting pulls the orders from a Sales API*

So you see: there are arguments for either direction. ArchiMate doesn't tell you that you have to use 'logical reasoning' or 'technical reasoning'.

Especially now that ArchiMate allows Associating elements with Flows, it becomes possible to model the dynamic behavior more specifically. So, my personal approach is to use the Serving structural relation to model structural dependency, that is: 'technical' dependency. So, I model the 'callee' Serving the 'caller'. However, that becomes a bit awkward (though there are exceptions) in the business layer, so there I ignore the actual 'technical' side and model Serving along the more abstract dependency that generally runs in the same direction as Flow. Summarizing: the Serving relation can in the application and technology layer generally be used for the same meaning in both directions, depending on your reasoning.

25.3 Associating with Trigger and Flow

A lot of integration between different parts of your Business-IT landscape has to do with the flow of information and the triggering of activities. Before ArchiMate 3, Flow was a pretty limited relation in the sense that you could model that 'something' flowed from A to B, but not what. ArchiMate 3 lets us Associate any element with any relation, which opens up a lot of possibilities, almost none of which have very clear semantics. But there are a few that are useful and have a relatively clear interpretation from the start.

The first is the Association of passive core elements with the flow to signify that the passive core elements are the content of the flow (the payload). We have already seen this for instance in View 221.

Another that is pretty intuitive semantically would be between behavior and Trigger and Flow, signifying that it is this behavior that realizes the Trigger or the Flow. We'll see an example below.

For the rest, I am very careful not to use Association between elements and relations too much.

25.4 Routing and Orchestrating Middleware (ESB and APIs)

How do you model an Enterprise Service Bus (ESB)? An ESB is a system that many organizations deploy these days to connect different systems to each other. What an ESB generally offers is a way to 'loosen' the dependencies between the applications that use each other's data. Instead of a large bowl of spaghetti of custom-built point-to-point connec-

tions, the ESB offers a more generic solution: a central agent in between that makes sure every application gets its data from other applications. There are a few uses where middleware shines. All are a form of decoupling.

One decoupling has to do with translating from one data-model to another. Systems have data, but they all have their own specific data model and data formats. The systems that need access to that data all need it in their own data model and formats. The middleware relieves each system from having to translate to/from all those different dialects, by using a 'common data model' (CDM) and taking care of translating all the connected system's data to and from that CDM, thus making sure that each connected system can keep talking its own lingo. So, when the sales system needs to ask the warehousing system how much of a certain product is available, it asks the middleware instead, which routes the question to the warehousing system and routes the answer back to the sales system.

The second form of decoupling has to do with spreading data around. E.g., when an order is entered in the sales system, that order needs to be shared with accounting and warehousing. To prevent the Sales system needing knowledge of every system that uses its data, this task is passed to the ESB. The Sales system just publishes the data on the bus, the bus takes care that any system that has subscribed to that kind of data gets it. In ESB-terms, 'kind of data' is called a 'topic'. Of course, such a publish-subscribe setup also uses the data-lingo decoupling. Partly, this is process automation.

The third form is not a pure decoupling, but it is adding (business) logic to the middleware environment. This is often frowned upon in the ESB-world, and it is indeed a dangerous route there. Before you know it your ESB becomes just another application platform with spaghetti-like logic linking everything to everything. And this platform then often suffers from all kinds of issues, such as performance degradation. But organizations often do have a need for more complex abstractions than just routing, such as providing coarse-grained services on top of existing fine-grained services. As an example: take the middleware that wants to offer a service for planning an itinerary of a trip and that is connected to various hotel and flight reservation backend systems. Several requester systems need this itinerary service, so we want to offer this integration to the outside world. We seemingly can do this in two ways. We build the logic as part of an 'orchestration' inside the service bus. The implementation of this 'orchestration' has logic that enables it to ask other systems that are connected to the bus for the required data, combines it, and delivers a set of answers. Or we build a separate system to create itineraries and connect it to the service bus. In that case, we route the outside 'itinerary request' to the 'itinerary system' and this system again uses the bus to ask for possible flights and hotel accommodations. However, with that last pattern we run into another problem: if the 'itinerary system' is outside the bus, it has no knowledge of which connected systems can deliver hotel and flight reservation information and thus, we still need some logic inside the service bus that knows which systems to ask for what kind of information, whether we need to return any answer or all answers in a set, etc. That is why there is almost always some orchestration implemented in a service bus and why we need to see the ESB (also) as an application platform.

The question is: how to model all of this? Logically, when the ESB is only routing, it is just infrastructure tying applications together (application A serves application B). But if it is orchestration, it is more appropriately modeled as application layer structure. Let's start with distribution, but modeled as application services and keeping the information modeled in the business layer only for now. This is shown in

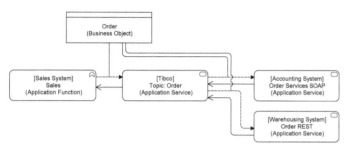

View 227. *ESB: The Sales system uses the ESB to route orders to both the Accounting and Warehousing systems.*

View 227.

Actually, the fact that we use an Application Function for the sender and Application Services for the receivers will get us into trouble with our standardized patterns as soon as Flows in the other direction are added. So, a full display of this approach would be like View 228.

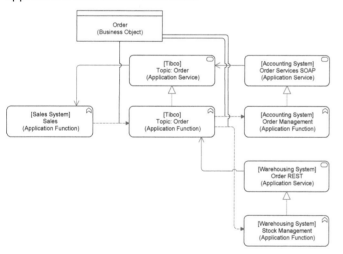

View 228. *ESB: Expanded version of View 227*

A good way to see this kind of ArchiMate combination of dynamic and structural relations is this: The red structural relations are what make the blue Flow relations possible. Note that this structure enables us to follow the routing of the Order across the landscape by combining the Flows with the passive elements they are Associated with.

How would distribution look if we would model the ESB service providing it as Technology? Well, it could initially look like View 229.

This is a very simple structure, but it tells us enough. Too bad, by the way, we cannot let the Flow be Realized by the Tech-

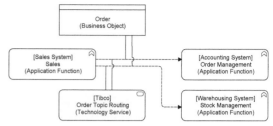

View 229. *The ESB as infrastructure 'Realizing' the Flows*

nology Service, it would have been a correct way of relating them. Just as Aggregation from the Flow to the Business Object would have been appropriate. But ArchiMate only allows Association, so we have to make do with it. Anyway, let's start by modeling the publish-subscribe information routing with our ESB, based on the choice to model the ESB as part of the technology layer (quite appropriate for messaging infrastructure). This is shown in View 230 on page 131.

I'd like to draw your attention to a few aspects of this diagram. First of all, the whole ESB has been introduced to realize the blue Flows. Note that I have drawn the Flows directly from one connected system to another. While in a structural sense, the systems are decoupled, I have chosen to use the Flows to model the actual (loose) coupling. If I would have drawn a Flow from publishing system to ESB and again from ESB to the subscribing systems, I would have needed some extra structure on the inside of the ESB. E.g. I could have let the Sales application Flow to the Sales Adapter from the ESB, then internally to the other adapters and from them to the subscribing applications. I would have had to Associate all these Flows with the Business Object. That is extra complexity, but on the other hand I now have to Associate the Sales Adapter to every Flow from Sales (I could do something with Junctions of course), and by using a separate Flow from application to ESB, I could simplify that.

Secondly, the red outlined elements are the ones we generally have to build ourselves if we install an ESB platform. Of course, some platforms might come out of the box with a few adapters. Or there might be some sort of market place for them. The point is that, by itself, the ESB platform doesn't perform the function our organization needs. For that, we have to set up something, and that something is the red-outlined stuff.

Thirdly, the orange Serving relations run from application layer to technology layer. This would have been impossible before ArchiMate 3 and the freedom is a welcome addition to the standard as it becomes easier to mix technology and application layers. In previous versions of ArchiMate we would have to restrict ourselves to the application layer to be able to model the use of the application services by the ESB.

And finally, have a look at the violet Serving relation. It is internal to the ESB (so we might not be interested) and it shows that the Sales Adapter requires the services of the Order Topic Routing. What I haven't added is the same dependency on the subscribers' side. If I would, it would add some complexity to get it right. Can you see why?

We can strip most of View 230 to show only what is required for the publish/subscribe of the order from the sales system to the other systems. This is shown in View 231.

And if as an alternative, we could use the red modeling in View 232 instead of the blue in View 231. You can see that it quickly becomes very complex. I can't stress enough: it all depends what potential use of the model you need, of course. If you want to model this detail and have readable views: just make views with smaller selections. At some point in large detailed models, the views become maintenance tools for the model more than communication diagrams. Using the model then becomes more a matter of automated analysis and reporting.

An ESB can be used for more than just publish-subscribe. It can be used to connect all kinds of systems together. For the rest of this section I'm going to use the open source Mule ESB as an example because of the way Mulesoft, the firm selling support for the Mule, position their ESB. Mulesoft markets Mule as the solution for companies that have older 'legacy' systems that have trouble getting up to speed in the new world of apps and such. This, by the way, is exactly the same story as was told during the previous phase of 'the rise of SOA'. Mule has stamped this with their own brand of marketing lingo, calling it the 'API-led' approach. Now, as we have already seen through ArchiMate-tinted glasses, API and Service are two sides of the same coin. Two words for the same concept.

The story behind API-led architecture is not that silly, though (and the implementation is nice), and it goes as follows: we have 'System APIs'. A 'System API' connects to ('legacy') backend systems. There can be many System APIs for a single backend system. Often those System APIs will have some shared intelligence, e.g. how to connect to the underlying system, authentication and so forth. A System API thus exposes some aspect of an underlying system, such as 'Order Queue' or 'Inventory'. Actually, if the underlying system is a bit less 'legacy' and already offers a good CDM-based RESTful service, you can just tell Mule to use it (Mule creates a proxy for it). Again: the term 'legacy' is often marketing jargon to sell the ESB as a solution for the complexity of connecting all

View 230. *Publish-Subscribe by an ESB*

kinds of systems that are already in place. I personally think the term (reusable) 'Producer-Defined API' is a much better term, as it focuses on the exposure of the backend system, 'legacy' or not. At my firm, for instance, we had to build System APIs for brand new Cloud-based services that had to be connected to the landscape, the reverse of legacy.

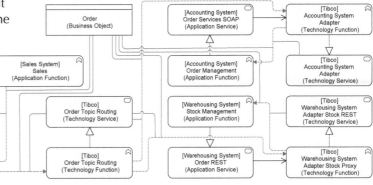

View 232. *Showing the Flows of Publish-Subscribe to and from the ESB instead of the logical direct Flows from system to system.*

When things become a bit more complicated, when for instance you need a more complex API that combines different backend systems you may need what Mule calls a 'Process API'. An example would be a robust 'guaranteed free inventory' service which takes the inventory from the warehouse service and subtracts the inventory that hasn't

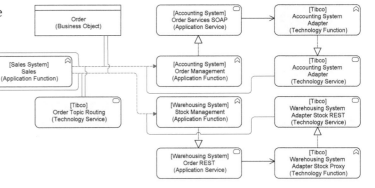

View 231. *Simplified version of View 230*

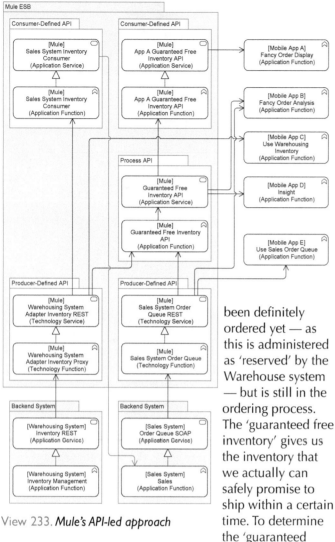

View 233. *Mule's API-led approach*

change around four times a year or so. Hence, it is unwise to let System APIs depend on Process APIs.

Now we come to Mule's third API-type: the 'Experience API'. This is what Mule calls services that may be created in the Mule environment by some product or project team. These are built when it is impossible to let a consuming system consume a Process or Producer-Defined API directly, and it is economically not viable to change the consuming system. These Experience APIs may change frequently and they are not reused (by other projects or product teams). In fact, one could see these as part of the product that the team is building or maintaining, it just happens that this part is infrastructurally run within the ESB platform. In fact, looking back to our earlier discussion about platforms, we have a system here that consists of parts that run on different platforms.

These APIs are meant to enable consuming applications to use existing System or Process APIs without having to change the consumer. They are not meant to be reused, they are consumer-specific. Hence, I prefer to call these Consumer-Defined APIs. So, the Guaranteed Free Inventory intelligence is part of a (reusable) Process API, while the App A Guaranteed Free Inventory API is just a way for App A only to consume that Process API which it cannot consume directly. If App A changes, the App maintainers may have to change their specific 'Consumer-Defined API'.

So, the team building Mobile App A decides it needs Guaranteed Free Inventory intelligence in Mobile App A. They build that Consumer-Defined API and they let it be used by Mobile App A for a Fancy Order Display. Then later, they want Fancy Order Analysis in Mobile App B and this combines the Sales System Order Queue System API with the Guaranteed Free Inventory Process API.

been definitely ordered yet — as this is administered as 'reserved' by the Warehouse system — but is still in the ordering process. The 'guaranteed free inventory' gives us the inventory that we actually can safely promise to ship within a certain time. To determine the 'guaranteed free inventory', an application could do it itself, but if the concept is useful for others (reusable), it could be implemented in the Mule system as a Process API.

At this point, have a look at View 233 on page 132.

At the bottom we see the backend systems and on top of them the Producer-Defined APIs. The Producer-Defined APIs are modeled as Technology (as they just help to translate, they have no real business logic). But the 'Guaranteed Free Inventory' service comes from a Process API. In the View, Mobile App E and Mobile App C use the System APIs directly. Mobile App D needs smarter insight and uses the Guaranteed Free Inventory service.

According to Mule, the System APIs should be owned by IT and only change once a year or so. A change is a major event as it is used by many consumers. The Process APIs should be owned by the business (as they contain business logic) and these normally

Now, not just some mobile apps or other frontends, but our (backend) Sales system itself needs to access the (backend) Warehousing system, but it is unable to do so out of the box. Say, our Sales system is some platform we bought and configured, and we may be able to define a non RESTful service in it that it can connect to. Changing this Sales system is beyond our means. So what we do is define a special API in Mule for the purpose of giving our Sales backend system access to our Inventory RESTful service. This is shown as the red Serving relation in View 233 and the — specifically for the Sales backend system defined and built — 'Consumer-Defined API'.

When we dig somewhat deeper into this environment, we may look at the realization of these services in the Mule environment. This is shown in View 234. Most of this is pretty straightforward given the patterns so far. Some piece of infrastructure (the

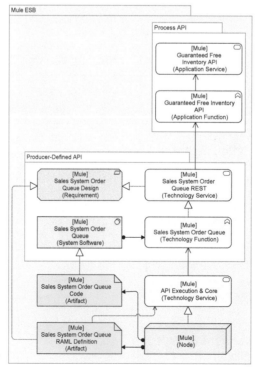

View 234. *Internals of the ESB*

Node) Realizes a service that enables execution of the Producer-Defined API, modeled as System Software. (Aside: I keep adding the ArchiMate types to improve legibility, but in the case of System Software is quite a misleading name for the concept. System Software sounds too much like an operating system and we may use it for many more purposes.)

Finally, in Mule, the services are defined by RAML contracts. In the case of Mule the actual service definition in RAML is even used by the runtime environment to check the correctness of the call by the service consumer and broken calls never end up in the function (to wreak havoc, possibly).

In View 234 I've added the RAML definitions as Artifacts because — next to the code — they are Artifacts we actually have to create. I've chosen to add the RAML contract in a second way: the service behavior has to conform to the specification, so it is also a Requirement. Looking back at our story about Secondary and Tertiary architecture in Section 19 "Secondary and Tertiary Architecture" on page 104, we probably also have a (development) process that creates this Requirement. The Requirement is thus also a Business Object. I've not gone so far as to add this (but I'll get back to this issue in the chapter that discusses ArchiMate, because there are problems here).

26. Additional elements for model use

We are going to take a little detour via model analysis, as this gives us an opportunity to introduce a few structures that are also useful for modeling some more complex structures.

A model — and Uncle Ludwig would agree — is only meaningful if it can be used. ArchiMate is not a language for yet another way of creating pretty pictures. It is mostly a grammar that can be used to create *models*, and the nice thing about models is that you can analyze them.

To ease these analyses, or to provide better ways of integrating your model with other models in your organization, it is often useful to add extra elements. Some of these we have already encountered, such as the roles from secondary and tertiary architectures in a way that enables practical use (see Section 19.9 "Making it Practical: shortcuts" on page 108 and their use in Section 31 "Construction & Use Views" on page 189).

26.1 Using extra elements to facilitate analysis

An example would be to model which development language is used for applications. Development language and Run platform are not necessarily linked, e.g. a program written in C may be intended for Windows or on Linux. But sometimes it is: application developed inside the SAS-stack will also be developed using SAS-tools and SAS-language. As there is no 1-to-1 mapping from the runtime environment (via the Technology Services that are used by the Application Function) and the development aspects, it may be useful to model these.

There are – as always – multiple ways to do this, but in this specific situation there are generally two:

- Add properties to elements. E.g. have a 'Development Platform' property in each Application Component and System Software component and fill these with appropriate information;

- Create additional model elements, e.g. a 'C# (Application Components)' element in which you Aggregate all Application Components that are developed/maintained in C#.

And — as always — both have advantages and disadvantages. A disadvantage of the former is that it is often hard to make this visible in your views and analyses require some sort of scripting that accesses those properties. So it depends on the tool if this is doable. Besides, what if you have a hybrid such as 'Application E' in these views? How many property fields are you going to use? It gets pretty complex quickly. Modeling is far more powerful.

The disadvantage of the latter is that you will sometimes run into restrictions set by ArchiMate, e.g. before ArchiMate 3, you could not Aggregate both System Software and Application Component in a single element that says 'C#'. So, in ArchiMate 2, in View 235 a second Aggregation was required so we could Aggregate both Application Components and System Software.

You could get around this by using Associations, as partly shown in View 236, but that trick could only be used once in your model, or the same pattern (e.g. Application Component Associated with Application Component if you do it for

View 235. *Model analysis elements: Aggregation example*

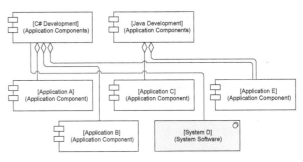

View 236. *Model analysis elements: using Association to overcome type differences*

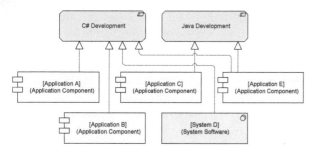

View 240. *Model analysis elements: using Constraints (or Requirements)*

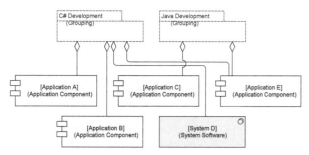

View 241. *Model analysis elements: Grouping example*

the entire collection) might get two different meanings and become ambiguous.

You can also creatively use elements from, for instance, the Motivation Extension. E.g. you could let each Application Component (for which you need to know the development platform) Realize the (in your model) single Constraint 'Must be maintained in C#' as is shown in View 240. I prefer this one, as it also has a meaning I can understand: without C# maintenance skills to actually do the maintenance, you are helpless.

Luckily, as of ArchiMate 3, one of my requests to the ArchiMate Forum became a reality: a real Grouping element that could actually be a real element in a model and not just a graphical construct. Grouping enables us to Group anything, so it enables View 241.

This one also enables the right Nesting if you want this at any point, so it is my preferred option when using ArchiMate 3.

Of course, if you do not run into the limitation above, you can use the same element type as the ones you want to aggregate for analysis (abstraction) and use Specialization or Aggregation between parent and children. I personally prefer the one in View 240, as it simplifies the analysys to combine this aspect with other requirements in a single analysis.

26.2 Keeping in sync with other administrations

In Sections 23 "Virtual Machines (Parallelization)" on page 118, 15.18 "Infrastructure Pattern: High-Availability Database Cluster" on page 78, and 15.19 "Infrastructure Pattern: High-Availability Server" on page 80, we already saw some slightly complex infrastructure diagrams.

Most of the infrastructure I model is generally simple: a repeat of the same basic pattern: a Node encapsulates the Device and System Softwar elements inside it and all the Technology Services are Realized directly by the Node. We can have several Nodes, such as in 15.15 "Deployment Pattern: Providing a local SaaS" on page 76, but the basic pattern remains fairly simple. Even the final pattern for hardware virtualization (View 198 on page 122) was simple.

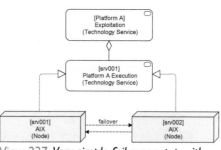

View 237. *Very simple fail-over setup with a single Realized Technology Service*

But there are exceptions. Server Clusters in several variations present a challenge. Not so much designing a pattern, as we saw in View 119 on page 80. But what is difficult is to have patterns that give a good representation of what is going on, while not having too many pattern variations, as they make

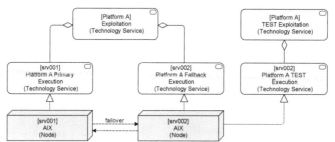

View 238. *Very simple fail-over setup showing separate Technology Services for primary and fail-over and showing the use of the fail-over device for testing*

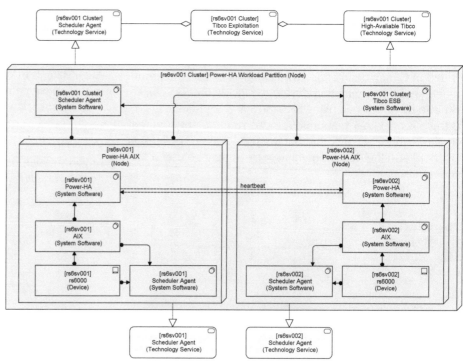

View 239. *The High-Available Server of View 119 on page 80 modeled to fit the IT department's administration*

automated analysis more difficult. Besides, in case of large scale Current State Architecture models, we also want to be able to synchronize our models with other models that exist in our organization, e.g. CMDB models of the IT department.

Take that high-availability server from View 119 on page 80. That outside 'cluster' Node might be something that cannot be found in the IT department's administration. Instead, we might find just two Nodes, one for each device. The fact that they are set up to form a cluster is part of the unstructured information, say some sort of design or maintenance document. Whichever way it is documented (and hopefully it is), when we want to remain in sync with their administration, we need to adapt. We need a pattern for this high-availability server setup that can be matched to their administration of separate Nodes, while we want our landscape preferably to show that those Nodes form an integrated and interconnected whole that as a whole Realizes the Technology Services we need.

The simplest form of 'clustering' is a simple 'fail-over' setup. Here, one Node Realizes a Technology Service and when it dies, we can fail over to the other one, maybe even requiring a manual intervention. Basically, that setup looks like the pattern of View 237 on page 134, where I have left out the internal structure of the Nodes, but still show the approach of Section 15.6 "Infrastructure 'Building Blocks'" on page 69. The approach, though simple, contains an abstraction that can limit the use of our model: starting from the Technology Service, we cannot see which one of the Nodes is the primary and which one is the fail-over. This may be important information, as we might try to save money by using the fail-over Node as a test environment as long as the fail-over is not needed. As soon as fail-over is needed, the test device is switched to a production configuration and restarted. A very error-prone, low-tech, labor-intensive example of fail-over, but it does exist.

View 238 on page 134 shows the basic pattern in which we have an independent Technology Service for primary and fail-over, of course both again Aggregated in a single 'exploitation' Technology Service that acts as a simplifier towards the application layer.

This all still fits nicely with both our basic infrastructure pattern and with the IT department's administration. But our high-availability server pattern of View 119 on page 80 does not. It consists of a 'cluster' Node that is unknown to the IT department and that also has a setup (with two devices and three operating systems) that is alien to the infrastructure people. So we need a solution that fits both our idea of the fact that this high-availability cluster acts as a single Node and the IT department's idea that we are talking about just two Nodes (and the rest is just configuration). A solution is shown in View 239 on page 134. Both 'internal' Nodes now perfectly fit the administration of the IT department. We also let these Nodes Realize their specific maintenance-services. But for us, the important Node is the outer one. For us, that Node is a single element that Realizes the Technology Services our application landscape needs.

To

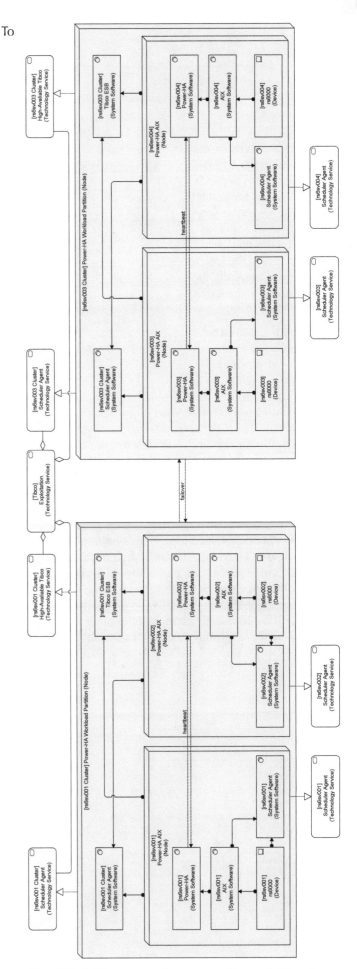

View 242. *A fail-over setup between two high-availability clusters*

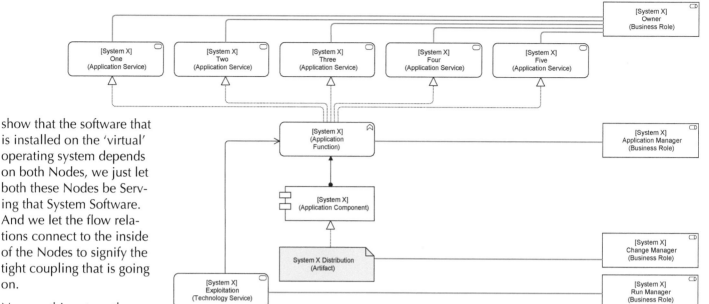

View 244. *Application Realizes many Services - cluttered owner relations*

show that the software that is installed on the 'virtual' operating system depends on both Nodes, we just let both these Nodes be Serving that System Software. And we let the flow relations connect to the inside of the Nodes to signify the tight coupling that is going on.

Now, nothing stops the really paranoid from creating a fail-over situation between two high-availability clusters. Some things should *never* fail, after all. Such a setup is modeled in full in View 242 on page 135. If anything, diagrams like that prove that ArchiMate is not just a language for abstract high-level boardroom diagrams. Of course, we can create a simplified diagram. This is shown in View 243. I have removed the details from the sub-Nodes and the Technology Services for the secondary 'Exploitation' architecture (see Section 19.5 "Secondary Architecture: System Exploitation" on page 105) and for good measure added the data center locations. At this point it may be good to stress a point I have not stressed much in this book: both View 242 and View 243 are part of the *same* model, they are just different views of the same underlying reality. That means that if you change the label on an element in one view, it will automatically change in the other. It means that relations are there, even if they are not shown.

26.3 Reducing clutter through Aggregation

Suppose you have modeled an application as in View 244 on page 136. We see here some basic pattern approaches, namely the logical setup of an Artifact (the distribution of the application), which Realizes the Application Component, which is Assigned-To the Application's Function, which — in this case — Realizes five different Application Services. Following the approach laid out in 19.9 "Making it Practical: shortcuts" on page 108, we have Associations between a number of Roles like the application's Owner, the Application Manager, etc. I have colored the Associations orange in View 244 and the other views in this section.

As we can see, the fact that we want to link the Owner to the Application Service means we get five links; one for each Application Service. This clutters the view, and we would like to get rid of that, even more so if we have an application where this substructure approach is necessary on many levels, as can be seen in View 245 on page 137. There is another problem: those Owners, Application Managers, Change Managers and such do not think of themselves as owners of 'five services' or 'five functions'. They look at the system as a single whole. The Owner sees him- or herself as owner of 'System X' and not of 'the five Application Services of System X'. Reporting from the model in a way that produces this substructure is therefore not acceptable.

This can be solved by putting the substructure in an Aggregation or Composition and relating management to those. The result is in View 246 on page 137.

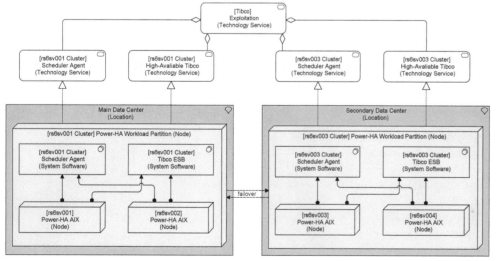

View 243. *Simplified version of View 242 on page 135.*

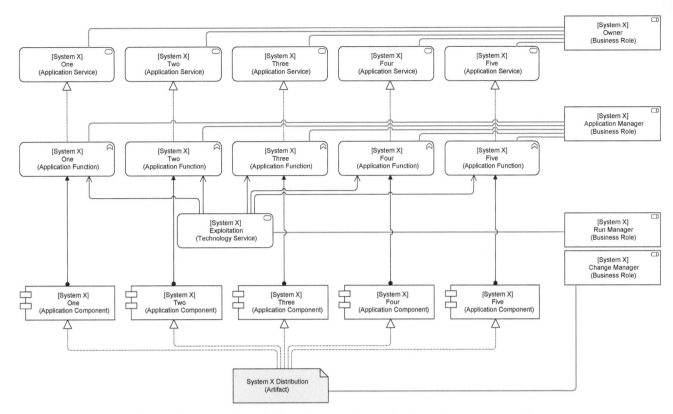

View 245. *Application with Sub-Structure: cluttered relation between the application and management roles.*

That solution immediately poses its own questions, namely: "do you want the red relations in View 246?", or even: "do you want red relations instead of some of the other ones?".

The answer for me is no, because your model will end in chaos if you do. The problem is that not all applications have this complexity. Some are really simple. They are just

a basic one-on-one from Artifact to Application Service. Others might be complex in any of the other areas of Application Architecture. Some may just have multiple Application Services as in View 244. Others may have just a single Application Component, but multiple Application Functions and Application Services. Some may have all aspects of the

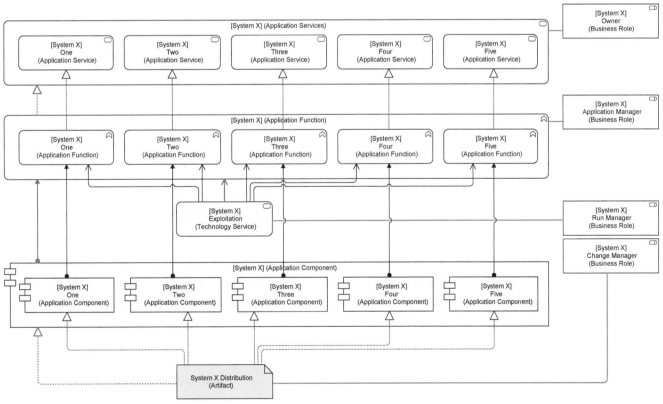

View 246. *Using Aggregation to simplify the management relationships to systems*

application landscape in multiple ways as in View 246 on page 137. To illustrate what happens when some applications have and some do not have the Aggregation structure, I have created View 247. On the left you see the simple application. Now suppose you want to use your model to answer the question: which distributions relate to which owners? The left column is simple: there is only one route. In the middle column you see what happens if you add the Aggregation at the Application Component 'level'. Suddenly, we have three different routes from distribution to owner: the original blue one and two red ones (one follows the Aggregation that is depicted by Nesting). Add another Aggregation and the number of routes becomes five if you only count routes that are valid as ArchiMate derived relations (and more if you don't). The example is not perfect (creating a real example would mean that you get a very large picture with many patterns and relations), but I think you will get the picture from this. If you have all these routes, trying to answer questions from analyzing your model becomes rather difficult, because you need many, many variations of 'route traversal' in your analysis to make sure you do not miss anything relevant. And if there are multiple routes, pruning becomes a problem because you will find many conclusions multiple times.

This is why I think you should stick to as few patterns as possible. Hence, in View 246 we do *not* add the red relations and we model everything between Artifact and Application Service with the same pattern: the left column in View 247. We do not try to get a combination of both.

We accept that *if* there is a need to model substructure, we model it all the way. We do not model only sometimes. So, deciding to model substructure or not also means answering the question: do we need it?

Sometimes we do need those additional structures though. With only the model as in View 245 on page 137, we can-

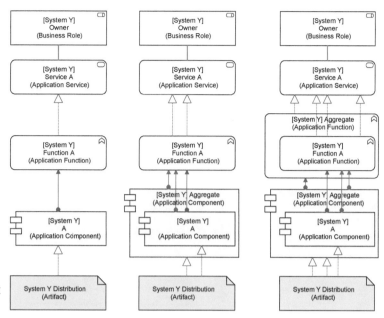

View 247. *Side-by-side illustration of the existence of multiple possible routes from distribution to owner, depending on pattern*

not provide the owner of the system with a simple 'you own System X'. To be able to say that to the owners and managers of the system, we do need the Aggregations of View 246. That is why we keep to the dictum: we may add additional structures to the core modeling patterns, but we make sure that they cannot confuse each other in analysis. Thus, the Aggregations to link owners and managers only exist for that goal.

This problem exists because ArchiMate offers more freedom in how you model something than a very formal approach would (especially one without derived relations). ArchiMate is less formal, there are (like with natural language) more 'correct' ways to say something.

27. Complex Environments

The examples so far have been mostly minimal, to address certain aspects of basic patterns. But in reality, especially applications maybe be far more complex than those simple basic patterns. That same large system your organization deploys may offer many, many Application Services to the business.

Incidentally, this is one of the reasons why 'application rationalization' initiatives are useful, but do not deliver the expected ultimate simplification of the application landscape of an organization. Replacing those twenty different applications with one big system in part only shuffles complexity around instead of removing it. This is especially true when you are using platforms that are in themselves just rich development environments: install one and it doesn't do anything useful for your business yet. You need to create all kinds of configurations that are just again forms of applications, just running in your new platform instead of directly on top of the operating system. One instance of business

complexity has been transformed into another instance of that same complexity. The new platform is richer and supporting this typical need will probably be simpler. But the cost is often that the platform itself is an architecture that also limits you in certain ways, as its core application architecture does not necessarily fit your organization very well, and complexity-increasing workarounds are often needed. You win some, you lose some.

Going back to our core subject, modeling in ArchiMate, this section addresses some of the aspects and consequences of complex application landscapes and platforms.

27.1 Server Farm

Now that I have my structure for complex clusters of Nodes, we can easily adapt this to 'farms'. A farm is a collection of Nodes that are all (generally) identical and that may all provide an identical service. Often, such a farm is combined

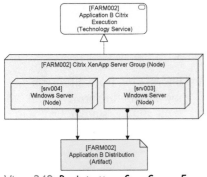

View 249. *Basic pattern for a Server Farm*

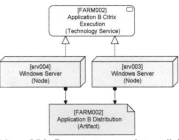

View 250. *Farm pattern with parallel Realization*

with some sort of 'load balancer', which makes sure that labor is divided over all the Nodes. A typical use these days is Citrix or other terminal services to provide applications to thin clients. Other typical uses are heavy-duty web servers or streaming services.

The basic pattern for a farm is rather simple, just a Node that contains a number of other Nodes and the outer Node providing a service (or more services). It is shown in View 249. This pattern replicates some of the chosen aspects of the high-availability server, namely Node-Within-Node, where the Nodes have some sort of independent existence. Another standard pattern (for me) is that the Technology Service is Realized by the outer Node, not by the actual System Software that is somewhere on the inside.

What is different from the high-availability cluster is that the outer Node has no real 'existence', we cannot, for instance,

deploy System Software on it. View 249 shows another aspect as well: since all the Nodes of the Farm must be completely identical, any installed software must be identical on all the Nodes. This is shown by Assigning the Artifacts of the software distribution to all Nodes of the Farm.

By the way, as an alternative, we could have also used the solution of View 250, taking parallel Realization of the Technology Service to signify 'either'. I don't use this, because in our practice the farms do have a recognizable entry in the IT department's documentation and also because this parallel Realization is ambiguous and because both parallel relations have opposite meanings: the Realizations mean 'either', while the Assignments in my practice mean 'both'.

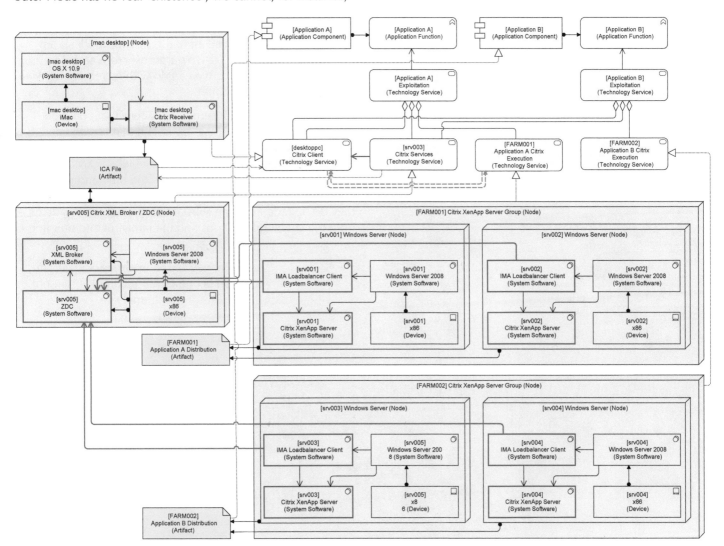

View 248. *A Citrix setup with two XenApp farms and one Node for both XML Broker and Zone Data Collector.*

27.2 Citrix

Finally, now that (via our detour) much is in place, I can show a pattern for Citrix XenApp. For those who do not know what Citrix (or another Terminal Services solution) does, it allows organizations to run certain desktop applications in a controlled server environment instead of on the desktop: while the application runs on the server, e.g. in a data center, the user's in- and output (keyboard, mouse, screen) are connected to the application. Any movement of the mouse, any click on the keyboard on the user's desktop is sent to the server and handed to the application, any graphical output of the program is sent to the user's desktop and presented to him. For this, a special proprietary protocol is used that requires very little bandwidth so it can be used to offer applications to users in situations where there is little bandwidth. Terminal Services are bad at handling graphics-intensive programs like video, because it is hard to compress that kind of graphics for fast transport over a network.

Citrix is a suite of different kinds of solutions, from virtual desktops to streamed applications and may be used locally on a company network directly or provided via a web server intermediary. In that last form it is often used for working with your organization's applications from home via the Internet.

View 248 on page 139 contains a detailed display of the architecture. Note that many items and relations are there for explanation purposes, not all of these are by definition useful as addition to your model.

When a user starts an application under Citrix, the following happens (I have left some bits out):

1. The Citrix Receiver on the mac desktop sends a request to the XML Broker to start Application A. In View 248 this is shown as the violet Serving between the Citrix Services and the Citrix Client Technology Services;

2. The Citrix XML Broker requests information on the load of the servers in the FARM001 from ZDC (the Zone Data Collector), shown as internal Serving in srv005 in View 248;

3. ZDC constantly collects information from all servers in the farms on how busy they are (load). Shown as the red Servings from the farms to the ZDC System Software in View 248;

4. Based in part on the information from ZDC, the XML Broker creates an ICA file. This contains the address of the server that is going to serve the Citrix Receiver on the mac desktop. The mac desktop gets this file. This is shown as the Assignments to both srv005 and the mac desktop. It is also part of the Serving from Citrix Services to Citrix Client Technology Services;

5. Based on the ICA file received, the Citrix Receiver sets up a connection with one of the servers in FARM001. The application is launched on either src001 or srv002 and XenApp Server connects its interface to the mac desktop's Citrix Receiver, where the user can interact with it. This two way interaction is modeled in View 248 as the orange Flow relations between the Citrix Client and Application A Citrix Execution Technology Services.

The purple bordered Software System elements are Realized by the (not shown) Citrix distribution Artifact. Now, as stated, you do not need all of this in your model, I am only showing it for illustrative purposes. From an Enterprise Architecture perspective, we can do with fewer details. After all, why model that ICA file?

View 251 shows the infrastructure pattern that could be used in a Construction Views approach that is explained in Chapter "Model Use & Maintenance" on page 189. In this view, I only keep the red flow to model which XML Broker is managing which farm and remove the blue and green flows. These are also Citrix flows, but they can be omitted as they do not add anything substantial to what we can deduce from the structural relations and the infrastructure building block setup.

For a web-based intermediary, the situation becomes more complex, but not extremely so.

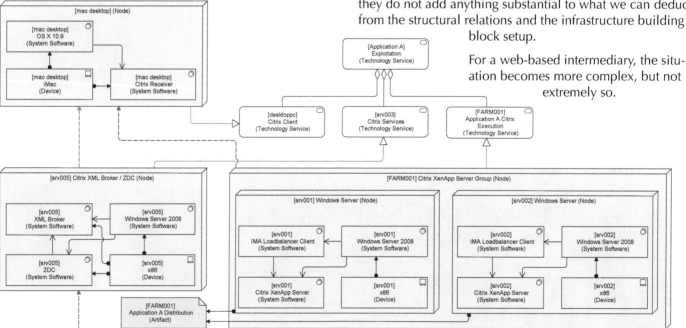

View 251. *Current State infrastructure pattern for Citrix based applications*

27.3 Complex Software Stacks

A platform is a software program that can load and execute software that is specifically written for it. We encountered the platform-approach from this book, for example in sections 15.3 "Modeling Spreadsheet Applications" on page 65, 15.4 "Modeling an Internet Browser" on page 67, 15.5 "More 'application platforms'" on page 68, 17 "An Example from the Real World" on page 87, and 25.4 "Routing and Orchestrating Middleware (ESB and APIs)" on page 129.

The pattern used in this book follows ArchiMate's definition of System Software: "System software [...] is used to model the software environment in which artifacts run. This can be, for example, an operating system, a JEE application server, a database system, or a workflow engine. Also, system software can be used to represent, for example, communication middleware". We take the idea of software being deployed in a platform one step further: if an application can be `configured', the configuration can be seen as an Artifact that Realizes an Application Component which runs in the platform. This use of System Software enables us to make clear that there is little difference between configuring on the one hand and building on the other. The difference between the two has become blurred anyway by graphical programming environments.

The possibilities that a system offers in configuration can be seen as a programming environment in its own right. For some systems with scripting languages and such, it is clear that the system is not only an application, it is also a platform in which to run those scripts. For systems that on the other extreme contain just 'configurable settings', we might feel uncomfortable calling those configurations 'programs' and the possibilities a 'programming environment'. So, we don't do that, we stay pragmatic and practical. But specifically defined workflows, checks, etc., are clearly business logic that is 'programmed' and 'executed' within the system and that makes the system a platform. Complex Application Platforms, as we have seen are often a collection of both. A very common pattern is that the complex system has a couple of applications to monitor, maintain/develop, etc., and that specific modules are implemented in that system which are programmed according to the requirements of the users.

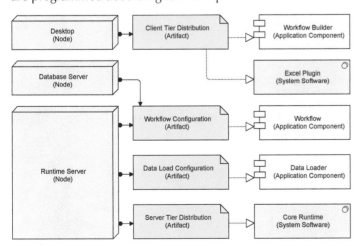

View 252. *Example of software 'tiers' with an irreducible part*

Some systems which are called applications are often little more than glorified toolboxes, e.g. master data management, warehousing, reconciliation systems are often 'empty'. You need to build your own business logic (work flows, data manipulations) in them. The fact that implementing these toolboxes in complex business environments often costs millions is a clue that a lot of 'programming' goes on, even if it isn't labeled as such.

Now, suppose you buy a scalable analytics platform. This platform consists of a couple of separate architectural domains:

- A Client, consisting of a couple of native Windows programs that talk directly to the back-end, like:
  * A workflow builder;
  * A report definition builder;
  * A monitoring application that enables you to keep track of what your workflows are doing;

- A runtime environment capable of running those workflows that use the report definitions to create actual reports;

- A database that is used by the back-end.

And it also requires (though it is not strictly part of its architecture) a file share to which the reports are written. To produce a report we need a definition of that report and a workflow that uses the data and the definition to produce that report. Report creation does not require human intervention, the workflow (once started) does it automatically.

An example is modeled in View 253 on page 142. In this slightly silly architecture we see:

- The report definition lives on the file share as does the produced report;

- The workflow definition lives partly on the back-end and partly on the database server. Think of a description that partly consists of stored procedures written to a database (I know systems that work like that). The model shows that the workflow is created by a combination of data on the CS Server and the Database Server. Modeling this explicitly helps you when the time comes to access the possible migration of one database system to another: knowing that there are 'programming Artifacts' in that database makes you extra careful: do they still work the same? Passive data is far less vulnerable. This pattern might look like the type of pattern that we saw earlier when we modeled a message as a single Artifact to be Assigned to all the Nodes that have access to it (See section 24.1 "Messages and File Copies" on page 123) but this is more like the 'informal collaboration' (See section 8.2 "(Formal) Collaboration and Interaction" on page 33) as the Artifact is not something identical on each Node but consists of something that is separated across both Nodes;

- The red bordered Application Components and the red bordered System Software together form the platform that you bought. Here you find the reason why (compared to Edition I) the Change Manager is Associated with the distribution Artifact and not an Application Component. The problem is that there is no good way in ArchiMate to aggregate System Software and Application Components in a single element. You may group them in a Grouping, but that has no structural relation, you cannot use that for analysis easily. But if you look at the example in View 252 on page 141, you see that the 'Client Tier', consisting of a real application and a plugin for Excel consists of *both* System Software and an Application Component. So, how can I model this 'tier', so that I am in line with what the business knows from its vendor? The only structural option I have in ArchiMate at this time is falling back on the distribution Artifacts. This is acceptable maybe from the perspective of Associating the Change Manager with everything in and of this platform (both the core distribution and the stuff we have added ourselves), but to create structures that enable our model to be linked with the outside world is problematic;

- The orange bordered Application Components are the applications you have built in the platform. These contain your business-specific logic

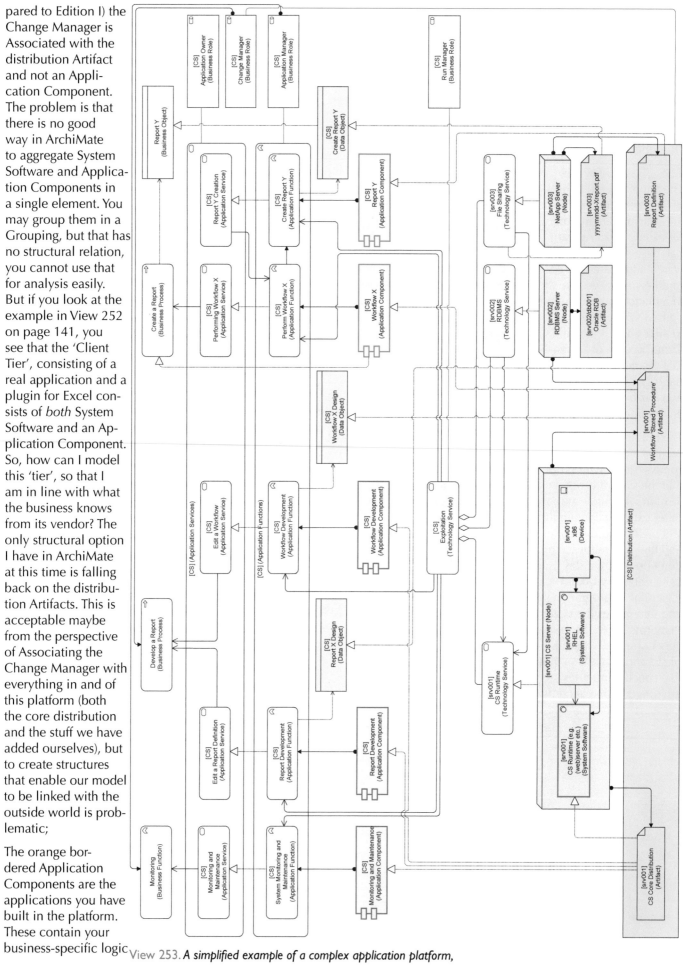

View 253. *A simplified example of a complex application platform,*

and the reason for which your organization bought the platform in the first place;

- Business process Monitoring is done by the Application Manager, who is also associated with the application functions of the system;

- Developing a report means writing both a workflow and a report definition. In this simple example, the workflow is entirely internal. But in many setups you will find some sort of scheduling system kicking things off from the outside, e.g. at a certain time of day or when a certain piece of data has arrived;

- The business process of creating the report is fully automated. The workflow we have written performs that process. This is shown by letting the Workflow X Application Component Realize (derived) the Create Report Business Process.

A good example of pretty generic complex application/platforms are SAS and Tibco. The MS Office Suite is also a collection of true applications (like MS Outlook) and application/platforms (such as MS Excel, MS Access).

27.4 A completely alternative platform approach

A quite different approach was suggested by Thomas Barnekow during a discussion on the LinkedIn ArchiMate Group. Before we describe it, we will first revisit the basic complex application pattern, where a system is both an application and a platform. A diagram is shown in View 254. The orange bordered elements make up the complex application/platform including what you have built/configured in it. There are three components:

- The System Software element. This represents what is needed in the core to run any applications in the suite and any specific modules you have created;

- An Application Component representing the full applications that are part of the suite. Here they are modeled as one application that has two functions you can use out of the box: monitoring and developing/configuring/maintaining. This is part of secondary architecture (see section 19.3 "Secondary Architecture: Development" on page 104);

- An Application Component that represents a module/configuration you have created yourself.

In the example the first two are Realized by the distribution Artifact. The third is Realized by an Artifact you have created using the developing/configuring/maintaining Application Component. The Artifact Realizes both an Application Component (primary architecture) and

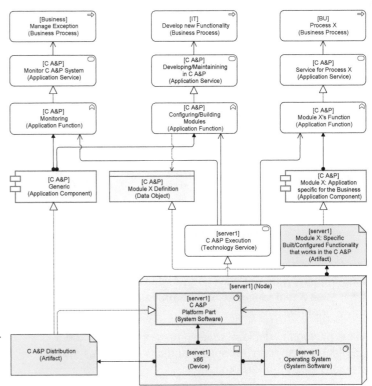

View 254. *Basic Complex Application/Platform system*

the Data Object (secondary architecture). This is a simplified example of course: for instance the infrastructure support is very simple, whereas in reality it will be more complex.

Now, Thomas Barnekow suggested a different pattern. His solution has the platform part modeled not as System Software (as what the ArchiMate standard more or less suggests with its definition of 'platform') but as an Application Component as well. Running your own built/configured modules then makes use of the internal 'run' capability of

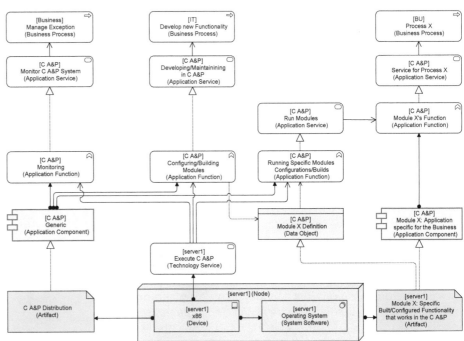

View 255. *Complex Application/Platform system with platform aspect modeled in application layer. From a suggestion by Thomas Barnekow*

your application. Or in other words: running your module requires not the use of something from the *infrastructure* layer but something from the *application* layer. This creative use of applications using applications (see section 7.2 "The double use of the Serving relation" on page 21) makes it possible to Aggregate the entire suite into one Application Component, solving the problem depicted in View 252 on page 141. It can be seen in View 255 on page 143.

I am adding this example because it is a beautiful example of the fact that ArchiMate enables you to model something in many different, sometimes even fundamentally different, *correct* ways. In any language (I know no real exceptions, though strictly logical ones — ArchiMate is not, as it requires interpretation — will have multiple ways that are *exactly* equivalent), you can say the same thing in many different ways. And ArchiMate is not even a real language, it is technically only a grammar.

I have personally decided to keep my approach to model the platform aspect of complex application suites as System Software. I think Thomas' solution is perfectly correct and has some advantages, but also some disadvantages. Automated analysis becomes slightly more complex, I think, as you will be using the 'application uses application' pattern for two different meanings. Adding to that: our existing pattern choice (View 254 on page 143) serves us well. So, I keep to my existing setup. Besides, in ArchiMate 3, we can more freely mix the layers in the sense that an application can by used by a platform (see Section 7.16 "Who is in Charge?" on page 30), so several limitations have been lifted and even more patterns have become possible.

There is one thing I cannot stress enough: Whatever you choose, make certain that you do it always the exact same way in all your models.

27.5 Complex Application Components

Not every organization can buy its software from vendors. Even if they do, we have seen the 'applications' are often (partly) platforms that require quite a bit of configuration and/or building before the application does exactly what your business needs.

But for those organizations that cannot purchase a platform that meets their requirements, there is no other route than building the software in-house. Generally this is only the case for very large organizations, whose needs (e.g. regulatory or technically) are so specific that a commercial tool vendor will be confronted with a market size of (close to) 1.

So, we will find still complex 'monolithic' applications built in-house. Maybe less so that a few decennia ago, and more of them are interconnected, but it still happens. Besides, those application/platforms you buy are in themselves often (partly) 'monolithic' applications. There is no free lunch: a true web of small interconnected programs (as envisioned by the people who gave us Unix) has never really materialized.

So, these are applications that contain a lot of internal complexity. A lot of sub-applications and parts that weave everything together (the 'orchestration' inside the monolithic application). How do we model that? Let's start with a simple example in View 256.

Our BigSystem monolithic application provides two Application Services for the business: '1' and "2. Of course, in reality there may be tens or hundreds of specific services, but for the exposé, this will do.

View 256. **Big Monolithic Complex Application**

Typically, when we want to model that the Application Component is made up of many sub-components, we model those sub-components as Composite children and Nest them, as in View 257.

However, there is more to the structure than just the division into sub-components. These sub-components have relations which — in the case of a large monolithic system — become as interesting for an enterprise architect as the landscape of applications is for less monolithic solutions. After all, the inside of the monolithic application is a landscape in itself that might have to be managed as parts may interact with the rest of the world. So, View 258 shows us some (derived) relations between the sub-components.

View 257. *Typical substructure modeling of monolithic complex application*

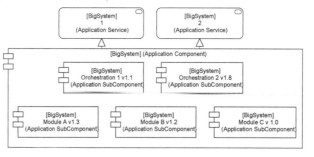

View 258. **The original substructure of BigSystem**

Not shown is that 'Orchestration 1' Realizes Application Service '1', etc.

If you wonder why this may be interesting from an Enterprise Architecture point of view, let's assume our big monolithic application needs serious rebuilding. In fact, the work that needs to be done would be comparable to changing application *landscapes* in cases without monolithic systems. Such efforts are substantial enough to put them under Enterprise Architecture governance. Take for instance the following two phases that we foresee (View 259 and View 260 on page 145): the two-step phasing out of 'Module B'. First we will update 'Orchestration 2' and 'Module A' such that 'Orchestration 2' becomes independent from 'Module B'. The new 'Module AB' is going to use 'Module B' itself, provide 'AB' to 'Orchestration 2', so we have two sub-component updates. Then, we will change 'Orchestration 1' so it uses 'Module AB' and we will have 'Module AB" create 'AB' without the help of independent 'Module B', which subsequently can be removed.

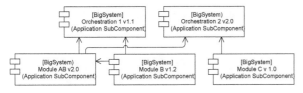

View 259. *BigSystem Update Phase 1*

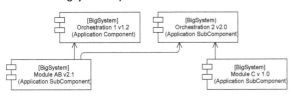

View 260. *BigSystem Update Phase 2*

So, the stage is set for a series of changes to our Complex Application Component 'BigSystem'.

We will now return to the situation of 'Update Phase 1' as seen in View 259 on page 145 to illustrate a very small problem in ArchiMate. Diagrams so far did show the dependencies used derived Serving relations between the various sub-components. The first thing we want to do is to add the internal Application Interfaces so we know what we are actually saying with those derived relations. This is shown in View 261.

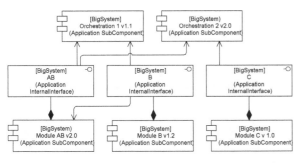

View 261. *BigSystem Update Phase 1 with internal interfaces added*

What happens if we Nest this again in the BigSystem overall Application Component? This is shown in View 263.

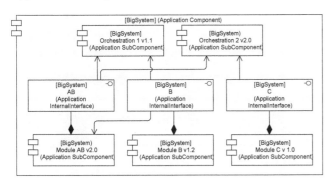

View 263. *BigSystem Update Phase 1 with internal interfaces in Nested fashion*

But what is the relation between the overall BigSystem Application Component and its constituents? Well, we know that the sub-components are Composite children of the overall component. They do not have an independent existence after all. The relation between the overall Application

Component and the Nested (internal) Application Interfaces is likewise a Composite. There are two ways in which this is true, but they end up in the same way as shown in View 262.

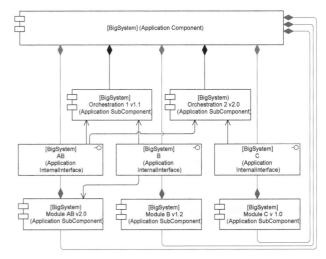

View 262. *BigSystem Update Phase 1, expanded version with all relations.*

- There is a direct Composite relation (red) between the overall Application Component and the Nested (internal) Application Interfaces. What this means is that these interfaces are interfaces of the overall Application Component, directly. This, of course is problematic.

- Even if you say that the interfaces are not of the overall Application Component but of the sub-components, there still is a derived Composite relation (red) between the overall Application Component and the internal Application Interfaces (blue route).

And the (very) small grammatical problem is this: the Application Interfaces now have *two* Composite parents, but ArchiMate forbids any element from being part of more than one Composite, and it does not limit that constraint to direct (versus derived) Compositions.

Even if we only use a direct relation, we have a small problem: Nesting is allowed to represent a relation (Composition, Aggregation and Assignment for the core meta-model), so if you nest the internal Application Interface in the overall Application Component, there must be a relation. A direct Composition relation would mean that you let the internal interfaces be owned by the overall component, leading to the same multiple-ownership problem. So the only relation allowed between the overall Application Component and the internal interfaces in View 262 is an Aggregation.

In fact the only solution entirely without grammatical problems is that you not only Nest, but you Nest all the way down (this is shown in View 264 on page 146) *and ignore derived relations*.

If you do *not* ignore the derived relations, the situation presents a true contradiction in ArchiMate: rules for derivation say the Composition from the overall Application Component to the internal interface is allowed. But the rules for composition itself say it is forbidden.

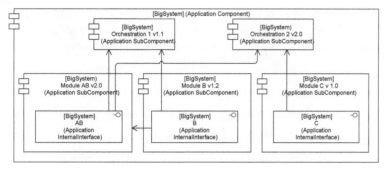

View 264. *BigSystem Update Phase 1, in double-Nested fashion*

So, you need to prevent the derived Composition relations. This can be done by using Aggregation instead of Composition between the overall Application Component and its constituents. This is shown in View 265. The orange Aggregations are derived from the blue Aggregations and Compositions. But, frankly, that is not what you mean when you have that big system and you want to show the substructure. After all, it *is* a single monolithic system and you only want to show substructure that is not independent from it.

There is another way to prevent the technical problem in ArchiMate 2. We could say the overall BigSystem application is a platform modeled as System Software. This is shown in View 266. Though technically correct ArchiMate, this is pretty artificial. After all, this allows us to let the overall application exist without its constituent parts. Besides, we have

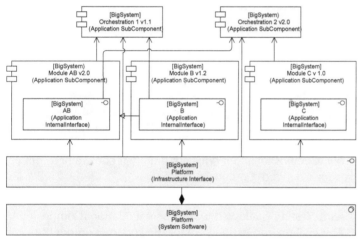

View 266. *BigSystem Update Phase 1, overall application modeled as System Software (platform)*

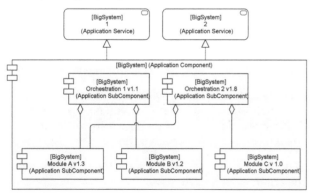

View 267. *The substructure of the Current State of BigSystem (View 257/View 258 on page 144) modeled with Aggregation instead of Serving*

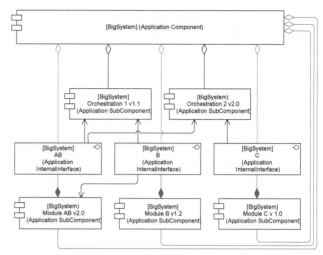

View 265. *BigSystem Update Phase 1, overall application modeled as Aggregation instead of Composite*

to make up an Infrastructure Interface that in reality does not exist.

There are more ways to model this substructure. View 267 has the relations between subcomponents modeled as Aggregations. This view says that the subcomponents refer to each other. View 268 models their relation with (derived) Flows, here the dynamic character of the relation between subcomponents is stressed. And, finally, View 269 leaves out the orchestration elements altogether. This functionality is modeled as being part of the overall Application Compo-

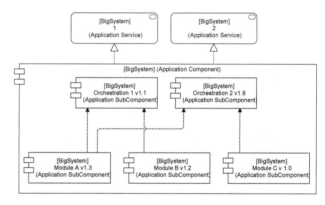

View 268. *The substructure of the Current State of BigSystem (View 257/View 258 on page 144) modeled with Flow instead of Serving*

nent. As you can see that there are many ways of modeling application *landscapes* or application *structures* (or hybrids of these) in ArchiMate.

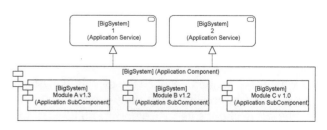

View 269. *The BigSystem system modeled without explicit orchestration subcomponents*

Personally, I would just use the pattern in View 263 on page 145, and ignore that small grammatical problem and just do something that might formally be illegal in ArchiMate. We might even see ArchiMate solve this issue in one way or another in a next release. Or we might use a Nested version of View 259 on page 145, but personally I would prefer having the interfaces in this case as they are important for development and maintenance.

So, why did I make such a big production of this non-issue about the Composition relation? It is to show you another example that there are many ways in ArchiMate to model the same state of affairs. And secondly, that you should not be fanatical about following the standard in its literal detail. You use patterns that suit you best (and hope an upcoming release of your tool does not forbid the pattern in the future).

27.6 Business logic at the infrastructure level

So far, the modeling approach has been to make the split between application layer and technology layer largely on the basis of the question of whether there was business-specific logic or not. If not: the software would be modeled as System Software in the infrastructure layer, otherwise, as it was business-specific, the software was modeled as an Application Component in the application layer.

This choice has the advantage that business-specific logic is always in the application layer and can thus be coupled (used by) the business layer in an appropriate manner.

There is a disadvantage to that approach as well: application logic cannot manipulate Artifacts and sometimes the business logic is just about manipulating Artifacts. This becomes especially clear when your business uses Business Process Modeling, which — other than Enterprise Architecture — generally does not make a split in layers. More on BPM in Chapter "BPMN and ArchiMate" on page 159, but coupling Business Process Models — where Activities (from an EA perspective in the business layer) may directly manipulate Artifacts (e.g. files) — to Enterprise Architecture models in ArchiMate — which does not allow that — is obviously problematic.

We can model business logic in the infrastructure layer, but we run into problems if we do. An example is shown in View 270. This example is adapted from the Managed File Transfer (MFT) - Scheduler example of section 17 "An Example from the Real World" on page 87. In it, we see the MFT solution that is responsible for (somehow, not modeled) receiving the file 'filexxx.yyy' and then acting on that. What is has to do with the file is defined in a business-specific 'Workflow X'. This workflow copies the file to a file share (not very realistic as we have an MFT so we get rid of all those file shares, but it will do for now).

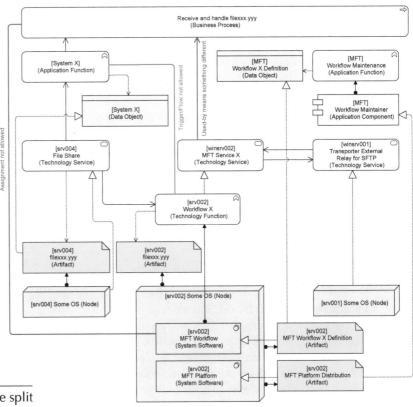

View 270. *Business Logic in the Infrastructure Layer*

The MFT system comes with a development/maintenance tool that we can use to define (develop) workflows. For the development/maintenance application, the workflow is data. But the Artifact that Realizes the Data Object also Realizes the System Software that stands for the application logic which is now modeled in the infrastructure layer. Before, we modeled such logic in the application layer, e.g. the Primary/Secondary architecture pattern seen in section 19.3 "Secondary Architecture: Development" on page 104. As the 'MFT Workflow X Definition' Artifact Realizes System Software, its behavior is a Technology Function or Process. Basically, this is all just like the modeling we did in the application layer, only now with infrastructure components which are able to handle/manipulate Artifacts directly. Earlier, we were unable to model how the 'workflow' handled Artifacts as we cannot relate application layer elements with infrastructure elements that way (an Application Service cannot manipulate an Artifact).

But this comes with issues:

- If the whole Business Process is automated, we cannot Assign the System Software as 'performer' to it in ArchiMate. I've modeled a purple Association to show where we would like to have an Assignment instead;

- We *can* technically let the Technology Service Serving the Business Process. But, though allowed, this relation means quite something different than a direct usage. It is a derived relation that assumes that some application sits in between. And that application does not exist.

- Since ArchiMate 3, we can use Realizations to model application and business layer behavior as 'abstraction' of technology layer behavior. We now have this abstraction in the passive and the behavior column, but not in the active column. This still does not give us the option to let a business process Access a Technology layer passive element (Artifact, Material) directly, though. It just enables us to model everything in multiple layers and relate these.

So, though we can do it and solve our 'Artifact manipulation by a Business Process' by it, current ArchiMate doesn't make it as easy as for instance BPMN.

27.7 Bitcoin (Blockchain)

As a next example on modeling reasonably complex IT in its context, we're going to create a blockchain explanation in ArchiMate.

If I have to explain blockchain, I'd say it is a "trusted distributed ledger of transactions".

These transactions are put in blocks that are made trustworthy. For bitcoin, this means that they are 'cryptographically' signed to make them tamper-proof. Those blocks also contain the signature of the previous block, thus creating a chain of signed blocks of transactions. The deeper the transaction resides in this chain of blocks, the more difficult it becomes to tamper with it for two reasons:

1. The total ledger (all the blocks) are shared by many participants who each have independent means to check the validity of the cryptographic signature. You can overrule if you have more than 50% of the 'vote';

2. It is computationally difficult to find a cryptographic signature for any block of transactions.

Creating a signature for a block of transactions is called 'mining'. In bitcoin, someone who finds a signature for a new block of bitcoin transactions is compensated for the effort with a fee (in bitcoin) for the block as well as the fees (see below) for all the transactions that are in the block. Hence, it looks a bit like mining, you spend the effort and you get bullion. Other blockchains may use other means to create 'trust'.

But more even than mining gold during the gold rushes of the past, bitcoin mining is a lottery. Because there is no causal relation at all between time spent on mining and the reward received for the effort. The process of mining is to take some random number (the 'nonce'), use it as one of the parts in the process to create a cryptographic signature for the whole, and then check whether that signature conforms to the requirement that it starts with a certain number of zeros. If this isn't the case, you try again with another number. And another. And another. Millions of them. It is impossible

to predict which number will lead to a signature with the required number of zeros.

Bitcoin is set up so that all the miners in the world together stumble across an acceptable signature (with the appropriate number of leading zeros) roughly once every 10 minutes. As trying to hit a solution takes a lot of computational work (many 'nonce' numbers are tried until a valid hashcode is found) the resulting hashcode is called "Proof of Work" ('PoW' in the diagram). As soon as such a hashcode is found, a new block can be added to the chain, and the resulting new block is broadcast over the network to all peers. This means that all the miners in the world have to start over again: all their 'failed' random 'nonce' numbers for their idea of a current block could easily be valid for the new one. The relation between the 'nonce' and the signature is mathematically unpredictable.

We start with modeling the data in View 271. Here, a nascent blockchain of just 4 'mined' blocks is shown. All participants in the blockchain share the data labeled "[SHARED]". We will not go into the deep details on how this sharing takes place and how conflicts are resolved. But generally, transactions are created by participants and spread in the network of participants. These participants include the transactions in the block they are trying to 'stumble upon', depending on a fee that comes with the transaction. Miners are encouraged to mine blocks as they get a fee for each mined block and for all the transactions that become part of the block. As the 'block fee' will get smaller as the bitcoin blockchain grows (this is built in), in the future it will be mostly the fees that come with transactions that drive the miners. It will also become increasingly difficult to mine blocks, hence there will come a slow stop to the increase of the amount of available bitcoins. It is off topic for a book on modeling, but economically it is interesting to see what happens over the long term.

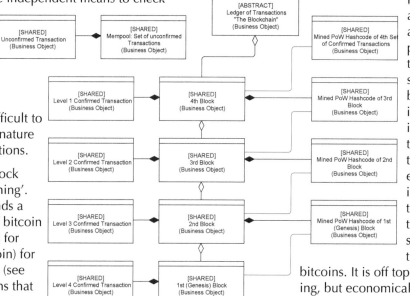

View 271. *A data model structure for blockchain*

Anyway, as soon as a miner finds a valid hashcode for the block he or she is working on, he or she publishes the new block to the network. All participants check the validity (stumbling upon the hashcode is computationally intensive, checking is not) and if it checks out, they add it to their own copy of the chain and remove all transactions in the new block from the pool of unconfirmed (or *unsigned by the collective actions in the bitcoin network*) transactions. Many of these transactions will be in the block the other participant miners are currently working on, so the other miners ditch their prospective blocks and start over again with the transactions that remain in the Mempool.

The diagram shows a single element labeled "[ABSTRACT]", which represents the 'blockchain' itself. In fact, the blockchain is just the chain of blocks below it, and it is addressed by addressing the last mined block in the chain.

Transactions that are part of a mined block become tamper-resistant. It is theoretically possible to tamper with transactions that are already part of a mined block (interesting stuff, by the way), but it is very, very difficult. However, when transactions are part of an earlier block this becomes more difficult as you have to tamper with many more blocks and 'convince' the rest of the bitcoin network that your solution is the correct one. It regularly happens that blocks are mined almost simultaneously by the network. In that case, people temporarily work with a 'fork' and as soon as one of the sides of the fork gets a block added, the other fork is lost and removed from the chain. A fork of two deep is already rare but a fork of three deep is almost unimaginable. This is why many sellers only deliver their end of a bitcoin transaction as soon as the input end of a payment transaction (more below) is three levels deep in the blockchain. Given that bitcoin operates to create an average of one block every 10 minutes world wide, transactions are generally not immediate as the transaction that created the money for a new transaction is only trusted after it has been buried a few levels deep in the world wide shared bitcoin blockchain.

Next, we look at transactions in the bitcoin network. A transaction is very simple. It lists a number of past transactions, each having an output of bitcoin registered to the one spending the bitcoin now, and a number of new transactions of where to spend the total of those past (confirmed) outputs. The sum of all available outputs minus all available inputs is the fee for the transaction and is collected by the miner when a new block is created. So, if in the past X has paid you B10 and Y has paid you another B10, and you want to pay B15 to B, You create a Transaction that takes the previous two transactions as inputs (together worth B20) and two new ones as outputs: one paying B15 to B and one paying B4.75 *to yourself*. The remainder is the B0.25 fee that is offered to the prospective miner who includes this transaction in a successfully mined block. Different from a system where a balance is kept somewhere (e.g. a bank account), you only make *transactions* and you pay the remainder to yourself as a transaction you can then later again use as an input. Creating a transaction is shown in View 272.

As soon as the transaction hits the bitcoin network, everyone in the network knows that the two transactions used as input for this new transactions have been spent and thus cannot be used again. Thus, these 'inputs' are not accepted as inputs for another transaction, so you cannot spend your money twice.

Finally, we can show how the mining of blocks works. In View 273 we see that the miner runs a few processes. First there is the process that receives new transactions from the peer nodes in the bitcoin network. This transaction goes into the local copy of the mempool where all yet unconfirmed transactions are kept. The transactions (that conform to the fee requirements that the miner has set) go into the block the miner is currently trying to 'stumble across a solution for'. If a solution is found, the result is broadcast by the miner to all the peers.

If you are a miner, your income depends on your chances of being the one to find a next block first. That chance is small. Most of the time your efforts will be reset by someone else broadcasting a new block on the bitcoin network. Or you join a collective, a mining pool, where ranges of potential 'nonce'-values are spread out over the members of the pool to try, and the profits are shared likewise. Most mining happens in pools these days.

Mining also takes a lot of computing power (and thus energy). So you find a lot of miners where either energy is cheap (more than 50% of miners are next to old Chinese coal-fueled power stations as I'm writing this) or cooling is cheap (e.g. on Iceland).

A word about the modeling (after all this book is about modeling, not about bitcoin). I've not created a coordinated full model of the diagrams here. I've just been using ArchiMate as a way to help explain how something works. Firstly, the Constraint is Associated with the Access relation that depicts transactions accepted for inclusion in the block the miner is working on. Secondly, I'd like to draw your attention to the colored Aggregations in View 273. As a modeling choice, the red Aggregation shows that the new transaction becomes part of the mempool. This is always the case, so the choice is safe. But while the blue Aggregation shows that a new transaction is part of the set of transactions accepted for inclusion in a new block, this is not by definition so. We have therefore Associated the Constraint with that Aggregation also. You can easily imagine that this use of Associations to relations can make your model rather complicated quickly.

View 272. *Creating a bitcoin transaction*

View 273. *Mining a block of transactions in a blockchain*

28. The Data Center

We have already seen a lot of infrastructure, up to modeling virtualization of computing hardware. That virtualization is part of a larger whole: the data center. Except for very small organizations, the Data Center is not going to disappear if we move as much as possible to the cloud: the cloud just becomes part of your infrastructure and you still need to manage a lot before you can actually use all those different cloud solutions properly. It is ironic, in a way: more outsourcing of stuff to 'other people's data centers' is just going to make it more and more important that you pay attention to your own. Two subjects will be shown in this section: ways of modeling networking and the issues we may have to confront when we are modeling software-defined data centers.

28.1 Networking

But we will first make an attempt at using ArchiMate's 'networking' elements as intended.

Basically, we have a Communication Network (for information, bits, Artifacts) and a Distribution Network for (physical) Material. On top of that there is the more abstract Path element.

The Communication Network element can be used to link Nodes that make use of that Communication Network (that are connected to it so they can exchange bits). This is done by *Associating* the Nodes with the Network.

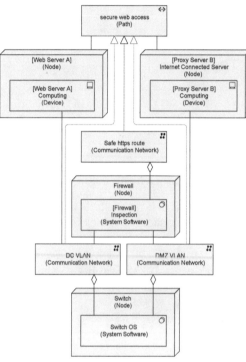

View 274. *Attempt at modeling networking with ArchiMate's networking concepts*

There are also Nodes that make the Network *possible*: switches, routers, firewalls. ArchiMate 3 says about these:

A communication network [...] can aggregate devices and system software, for example, to model the routers, switches, and firewalls that are part of the network infrastructure.

Interestingly enough, while ArchiMate 3 finally has a larger example than just a 100Mbps LAN connection between a Desktop PC and a Mainframe, it doesn't show this Aggregation at all in its example. Networking is quite 'below' the architects' attention, it seems.

In View 274, I've given an example of modeling a typical (though simplified) networking/security situation using ArchiMate's networking elements. We have a web server that needs to serve the outside world. Such a server is not exposed directly. Instead, in a special secure 'zone', the demilitarized zone (DMZ), a special hardened server is run that safely accepts the connections and passes these on to the inside where the actual web server lives that has to handle the request and that itself may connect to other sensitive parts of our landscape, such as applications, databases and so forth.

The separation is created by having two separate 'Virtual Local Area Networks' (VLANs). A VLAN can separate network traffic and is realized by a switch. Normally switches create LANs by copying network packets that arrive on one port by an attached network cable to all other ports, but smarter ones can create virtual LANs, which keep network data packets logically apart across the landscape of all switches by tagging them. This enables dynamic changes in network design without having to physically rewire systems to different switches.

In ArchiMate, I may represent the VLANs by a Communication Network element. View 274 shows that only Proxy Server B and the Firewall are connected to the DMZ VLAN (Communication Network). Proxy Server B is configured such that it sends all its data to the Firewall ("default gateway"), but we cannot really show that. The Firewall is also connected to the DC VLAN to which the actual web server is also connected. Traffic from Proxy Server B to Web Server A only occurs if the Firewall routes it from the DMZ VLAN to the DC VLAN.

These VLANs are created by the switches. So, I have to model a switch that is Aggregated by the Network. A nasty limitation of ArchiMate is that I am not allowed to Aggregate *Nodes* in a Network to show the Nodes create the Network, it *must* be Device or System Software. It is testament of how the original designers looked at networking, an area they had even less feeling for than infrastructure in general, it seems. For them, a firewall apparently was a 'device': the lowest rung on their hierarchy of architecture, something as low as a 'dumb switch', where you put your networking cables in, like an electrical socket.

Now, I could Associate the Web Server A and Proxy Server B *Nodes* with their respective VLANs, but I don't, for a reason that will soon become apparent.

I've modeled that the Firewall's routing capabilities create a safe https route (Communication Network) for the traffic between Proxy Server B and Web Server A. While the VLANs are 'layer 2' networking, the routing is 'layer 3'. There is no good way to model the relation between both layers. I can make one Communication Network a child of another, but that is not what is really happening here. The layer 3 (routing) network sits 'on top of' the layer 2 switching network. Anyway, between both servers (Nodes) we are supposed to model a Path. In this case, I have modeled a Secure web access (Path) between both Nodes by Associating the Nodes with the Path element. This Path must be Realized by (a) Communication Network(s), but I cannot let it be Realized by the VLANs, because it's not the VLANs that realize the Path, the separation is (also) realized by the firewall. Hence the addition of the Safe https route (Communication Network) element. The red Realizations are optional if you want to show that the Path is created by a combination of the VLAN separation in layer 2 and the routing/filtering in layer 3.

I use Association between Path and Nodes as I should. I'm of course allowed to create Associations between Communication Networks and Nodes as well (just not the Aggregations that show who creates the Network), but if I did that, it would become confusing: both Paths and Networks would be Associated with the Node. So I have chosen to Associate the Networks that represent layer 2 networking with System Software or Device and the Path with Node. I might have complicated things by adding System Software to the server Nodes and Associate these with the Safe https routing (Communication Network) that is created

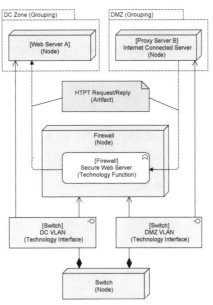

View 275. *Networking modeled without ArchiMate's networking elements*

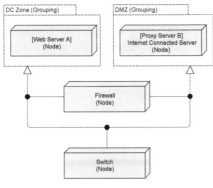

View 276. *How the Security Zones are Realized by Switch and Firewall*

by the Firewall, but frankly, all that extra detail doesn't add much to the understanding.

In reality, today, a firewall, a router, even a switch is a complex appliance, with hardware, an operating system, data, applications to manage them with user interfaces, APIs to manage them in an automated fashion, and so forth. The switches of today constitute 'fabrics' and all kinds of smart and complicated operations on bits happen. They play important roles in performance and security, especially now that we get more and more connected (micro)systems.

While networking was a bit like a simple utility for those who created ArchiMate, it is an important part of the enterprise these days. Boards of Directors have to confront serious issues about cloud computing, security zoning, software-defined data centers and so forth. The choices are often strategic. Designs of networking and security have become difficult and complex and we need to express our networking landscape as clearly as the infrastructure and applications on top of it. Seen that way, the choice of ArchiMate to have the Network and Path elements to model all that is clearly insufficient.

Summarizing: ArchiMate, as well as its current inspiration TOGAF, are not overly interested in the part of the enterprise that is the data center. ArchiMate's official support for networking is extremely limited (and abstract) and has issues. It has never received proper attention and I have never seen it used in any serious manner. The concepts are not clear enough about what is happening and they assume a very rough and abstract use where networking is not worthy of further attention than to model in a rough sense who is associated with it, not how it all fits together. The ideas are based on the complexity of a small home LAN or a company network of a quarter century ago. Outdated is the right adjective here.

Luckily, you don't have to use the 'networking elements'. After all, routers, switches, firewalls are Nodes as well. They provide services and interfaces to their environment. The reasoning here is a bit like the one from Section 19 "Secondary and Tertiary Architecture" on page 104. There it was: everything in the enterprise is its architecture, so that includes security, development, risk and even enterprise architecture itself. Here it is: networking is infrastructure too, so we should be able to model it with the standard infrastructure elements and without those special 'networking' elements.

The result is in View 275. The Communication Network elements have been replaced with Infrastructure Interfaces (with the accompanying services, but these are not modeled in this example). The networked Nodes in the landscape use (are served by) the layer 2 infrastructure of the switches. The Path has been modeled by the Flow, and we can be more clear about what functions are used and what payloads we have.

I use Groupings for the security Zones. In View 275 they seem to be just visual aids. But have a look at View 276. Here we have modeled that Switch and Firewall together Realize our security zones. Both diagrams come from a single model of course, we are after all modeling, not just drawing pretty pictures...

28.2 DevOps Ready Data Center (DRDC)

These days, we're about as far away from the largely ignored and undervalued infrastructure of the 1990's, the thinking that apparently influenced the basis of ArchiMate (that, or the likewise inappropriate ideas that infrastructure is not 'strategic' or that details can always be ignored). Anyway, these days, infrastructure is becoming more and more like software, and quite complex software at that. The idea that infrastructure is a (hardware) Device with some 'System Software' running on it (originally, ArchiMate 1 had even tagged 'System Software' as the *behavioral* aspect of a Device, a role now taken by Infrastructure Function/Process), connected by some rather undefined networking was already outdated when it got into ArchiMate, it is totally inappropriate today. That is one of the reasons few people have started to use ArchiMate for infrastructure modeling. But — as we saw in the previous section — ArchiMate 3 has some improvements that enable us to express at least networking better.

The changes in the rest of the infrastructure world have been at least as dramatic. Driven by the virtualization of infrastructure (see Section 23 "Virtual Machines (Parallelization)" on page 118), most of what is infrastructure these days is not hardware but software.

And even more recently, the challenges of coherently managing all that (virtualized) infrastructure have become huge, as most of it has so far been managed by infrastructure engineers using GUI or command-line tooling. Such 'operations by people' is slow, costly and error-prone. Especially the 'cloud providers' have been driving ways to automate this management in order to get reliability up and cost down. Cloud companies like Amazon, Google, Spotify, Facebook, and also the likes of Microsoft and Apple, have huge numbers of identical 'machines' that make up their landscape. It is not an option to manage all those machines by hand.

As I'm writing this, the 'rest' (starting with banks, insurers, retail, government agencies, etc.) are also getting in on the act. But their situation is much more challenging. These players don't have huge homogenous landscapes, they have mid-sized heterogenous landscapes, often in large parts made up from systems they have bought, not built. My term for the architecture of those systems is 'canned architecture'. You, as a buyer, hardly have any influence over them. The vendors can only support a small part of the possible landscapes their systems have to land in and chances are that your particular exact set of infrastructure standards is not part of them. This challenge drives all sorts of vertical integration. Some vendors are now shipping their systems as 'virtual machine images', including everything needed to run their system, the operating system, database, application server, and so forth. Others offer their system as a cloud-based 'SaaS' solution. Vertical integration is in my analysis a much more important driver for this than the Internet, in fact the Internet only *adds* problems, like latency. The Internet is an enabler, but not the reason for the solution. But I digress, and I've written elsewhere about that.

The complex heterogenous landscapes of 'normal' organizations are now being automated, the management of the infrastructure being performed by software instead of by human infrastructure engineers. We are going to take a look at one of the aspects: *desired state configuration*.

Desired state configuration is where software is in control of the configuration of infrastructure. One of the products that is widely being used for this is Puppet. Puppet is a system where a central server — the 'Puppet Master' — controls the configuration of many other servers. Those servers all have a 'Puppet Agent' on

board that regularly checks itself against the 'desired state', which it gets (at request) from the Puppet Master. It reports its state to the master and it continually (normally every 30 minutes) enforces the state it is given by the Puppet Master.

Well-designed Puppet setups do not just have a large bunch of separate definitions, one for each server to control. They use (cascading) roles and profiles. For instance, a Tomcat Applet Server reuses the configuration of a generic RedHat Linux server. A WildFly Java application server reuses the configuration of that exact same generic RedHat Linux Server. It looks like (though it is not technically exactly the same as) object-oriented programming.

To make matters more challenging, adding a server to a landscape generally not only means managing the 'desired state' of that particular server. It also means managing the desired state of the environment in which it must function: firewalls (e.g. opening it up so that your new server can communicate with specific others), routers, switches and so forth. It also means allowing the systems that support running your data center (centralized logging, dashboards, event management, discovery, etc.) to be able to actually work with your server. E.g., if you setup centralized logging using the ELK-stack (Elastic, Logstash, Kibana) and you add a Windows IIS-server to the mix, the Windows server must know where to ship its logs (this is part of the desired state of the IIS-server itself), but the ELK-stack itself needs to be told how to handle IIS-specific logs.

Finally, our engineers need to interact with the systems. E.g. start or stop a web server or application pool. These interactions may require configurations and installations on the server.

What follows is based on actual experience, but notably slimmed down to just a few aspects. It's about the modeling, not about the DRDC (which could fill an entire book by itself; and I expect my former colleague Luc Raeskin — who initially drove this development at the company I work for — to write one...).

We start with the code. After all, we are talking about 'infrastructure as code'. View 277 shows part of it. The code is separated into the parts that make up the DRDC core (here labeled IT4IT), the servers that needs to be there for any new server to function properly. E.g. the above-mentioned

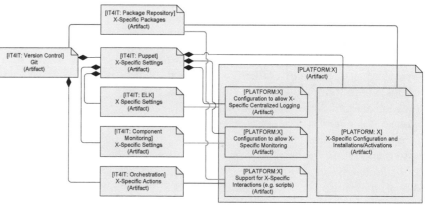

View 277. *The code for some aspects of a new server*

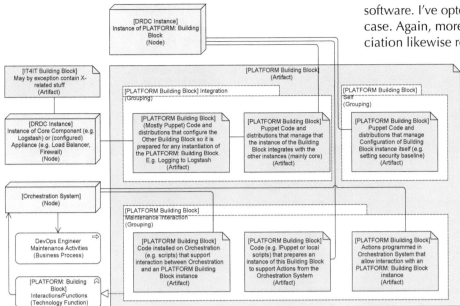

View 278. *Overview of a Building Block in a DRDC*

ELK-stack for centralized logging, a component monitoring solution (e.g. Icinga2) that is used to check if systems are still running properly and — last but not least — the support for component self-configuration, i.e. Puppet. All code is under version control (e.g. Git). To roll out and manage a server for a certain platform X (e.g. a WildFly Java application server) we need to code how such a platform is monitored, which logs it must ship to centralized logging, how component monitoring is determining its status, and so forth. I'm leaving a lot out here, e.g. discovery, event monitoring, deployment of software on servers, and so forth.

First, have a look at the pink Associations between code that affects the desired state of the server for Platform X itself and that affects the desired state of the related (IT4IT) servers. An example is that the code for a Windows IIS (IIS being the 'Platform X' in this case) server must know what logs to ship to the central Logstash server, but the central Logstash server must also be configured to be able to handle those logs. Hence, the new 'Platform X' server and the Logstash server have parts of their 'desired state' that are related and that has been modeled in View 277 by using an Association. In reality, we can go a lot deeper and actually model how the continuous delivery process for these two related parts of code works, but we're not doing that here.

Next, have a look at the red Composition from the Package Repository to the X-Specific code Artifact. Part of the desired state of a server might be that certain software packages are installed. E.g., part of the desired state of a Tomcat server is that Tomcat is actually installed on that server. So, the self-configuration of a Tomcat server means that the Puppet Agent on the Tomcat server must make sure the right version of TomCat is retrieved from the Package Repository and installed locally. Modeling-wise this presents us with a dilemma: what is the relation between the Package Repository and the locally installed package? The software *as installed* is not a composite part of the repository, and it is also a bit strange to Aggregate the repository in the locally installed

software. I've opted (once more) for an Association in this case. Again, more detail could resolve it. The orange Association likewise represents installing for instance (packages of) scripts that are required on a server to support interactions with our orchestration solution. E.g., we might have to build a specific Python script to have some specific interaction with a web site running on our server, an interaction that can be triggered from our orchestration, the relation between which is modeled by the purple Association here.

Now have a look at the blue Association between the Git repository and the Package Repository. As we noticed above, the Package Repository contains packages that are part of the self-configuration of a server. In the reality of a DRDC there is a continuous delivery pipeline that builds those packages to be in sync with the rest of the desired state configuration definition (another aspect that needs to be closely coordinated). After all, a new version of Tomcat might change something as mundane as the name of logs that need to be shipped to the Logstash server. A detailed model of the delivery pipeline would resolve the Association here.

Next, have a look at the [IT4IT: Puppet] Artifact. This one contains the settings for the core IT4IT servers such as the Logstash server and the Component Monitoring server, but also for our Platform:X server that has to be integrated with them. And of course it contains the Platform X-specific 'desired state' as well.

You will have noticed that I'm using quite a few Associations here, despite having written earlier that I do not like them much. I still do not like them, but here, they do what they are meant to do: hide the actual relations between the different parts of code, just showing that they *are* related. The explanation is not in the structure of the model (here, at least) but in the text you are reading now. This is a nice example of the choice you often have to make: what do I put in a (structured) model and what do I put in (unstructured) text? Where do I stop? I cannot repeat it often enough: there is no definitive answer to those questions, it all boils down to what you want to use the model *for*. Meaning, use, and all that, you might recall from the introduction.

In View 278, a rough overview of the different kinds of code that make up infrastructure as code in the DRDC is shown. We have organized the code in a 'building block' of the DRDC. Here we see that a building block contains code to integrate a server with the overall landscape, code to support interacting with the server and code specifically for making the specifics of a server be in a desired state. A good example of the latter would be for instance that a Linux server has to conform to the organization's security baselines.

The different parts of the code have to do with different systems. In the example this has been brought back to the server itself, the orchestration system and (for instance) the Logstash server.

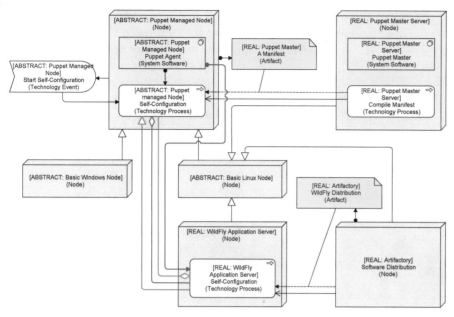

View 279. *Inheritance used to model different types of Nodes*

The example of the security baselines for a Linux server brings us back to the fact that (as mentioned above) a decent setup for all of this uses inheritance as much as it can. It's a bad practice to model the security baselines for each Linux-derived system (Tomcat, WildFly, Logstash, etc. etc.) more that once. An important rule is "Don't Repeat Yourself" (DRY). So, the code for a Tomcat server to self-configure into a 'desired state' contains the code to self-configure any Linux system. In Puppet this means that the code is organized in a hierarchical way. The hierarchical way the code is set up mimics a landscape of 'abstract' Nodes. We may say that every server that reuses the standard code for a Linux server is a Specialization of an (abstract) Linux server.

Now, if that code is used, what kind of infrastructure landscape do we get? How does our landscape look? Here, we might employ ArchiMate's Specialization relation to show how our landscape fits together. An example is shown in View 279.

Three actual Nodes from our landscape are shown: the just instantiated WildFly Application Server, the Puppet Master and the Artifactory server where the WildFly Application server gets its WildFly distribution from. But also shown are a few 'abstract' Nodes that represent this re-use of configurations we described above. In the diagram, we see that our WildFly Application Server inherits from a Basic Linux Node. This Node is nowhere real in our actual landscape. What it does is represent the 'basic Linux' part of any 'desired state configuration' of a server that is based on Linux. DRY, right? We also see that Artifactory server is a Linux server and even our Puppet Master itself is one, so they also inherit this desired configuration.

We also show that *every* server in our landscape is managed by Puppet. We do that by introducing another abstraction, the 'Puppet-managed Server' Node. From that Node, we show how any server in our landscape relates to its Puppet Master, it calls the Puppet Master (which *Serves* the Pup-

pet-managed Server') and it receives (Flow) a manifest that defines the 'desired state'

This setup also comes with a challenge. The WildFly Application Server needs — as part of its desired state — to download (and install) WildFly from the Artifactory server. We can't let the Infrastructure Function of the 'Puppet-managed Server' do that, because this is specific for the WildFly Application Server. Here we have solved that by creating an Infrastructure Process in the WildFly Application Server to manage that part of the 'desired state configuration'.

This, by the way, is strictly speaking technically misleading. There is no recognizable subprocess on the WildFly Application Server that is not just the Self-Configuration Infrastructure Process of the (abstract) 'Puppet-managed Server'. In the view, three options for connecting the Puppet Agent to the WildFly Application Server's self-configuration process are shown. We might see the WildFly Self-Configuration as a recognizable subprocess (red Aggregation), but that is — as we have already seen — a lie. We might say that the generics of the Self-Configuration are an Aggregate part of the specific WildFly Application Server's Self-Configuration (orange Aggregation) (might be acceptable) and we might say that the WildFly Application Server's Self-Configuration is a Specialization of the more abstract version of the Puppet-managed Server (green Realization). The last one is probably the most correct one, but it begs the question: what active element is performing that Infrastructure Function on the WildFly Application Server? The answer given here is: the Puppet Agent on the (abstract) Puppet-managed Server (blue Assignment). It becomes a bit difficult to see, but we can also conclude (though not derive) that the manifest flows from the Puppet Master to the WildFly Application Server.

There is a major issue with View 279 though. How does the Puppet Agent (let alone Linux or Windows) *itself* get installed on the WildFly Application Server? It cannot be installed by itself in Baron Münchhausen-style 'bootstrapping'. In reality, thus, something else happens. There is a 'bare Linux server' that is created from an image by the hardware virtualization environment (e.g. VMWare). This 'bare server' contains the Puppet Agent already and it is booted up, then a few prerequisite configurations happen before Puppet gets into the act (e.g. telling the Puppet Agent which Puppet Master to connect to). Then, the Puppet Agent is triggered, it goes to the Puppet Master which tells it to become a WildFly Application Server. *Time* enters the picture: for a short while there is a basic Linux server in your landscape, which then transmogrifies itself into a WildFly Application Server.

View 280 on page 155 shows this in an initial solution. Instead of the 'Puppet-managed Server' abstraction, we have two independent 'bases'. This view also shows an attempt at a modeling solution for other 'profiles' that can be part of the well-designed Puppet setup. For instance, each server in our landscape must be able to ship its logs to our central Logstash server. This has been modeled by introducing an (abstract) 'Server that Logs to Logstash' Node, which has a relation with the (real) Logstash server. Now, every Node, abstract or real) that must be able to log to the central Logstash server can be made to do so by Specializing from the abstract 'Server that Logs to Logstash' Node. In the diagram, this has been added for our WildFly Application Server, but also for our Puppet Master and our Artifactory Server. This, however, will become troublesome if we want to show *what* exactly the WildFly Application Server is transporting to the Logstash server. For that we will need a separate Flow to the Logstash server in the same way that we have a separate Flow from the Artifactory server to the WildFly Application Server. Hmm. It turns out that if we use these Specializations to simplify the number of Flow relations shown (we only show a Flow from the abstract 'Server that Logs to Logstash' Node to the Logstash server, not from each individual server type) we lose the possibility to show unambiguously *what* is flowing. I've put this example in to show you an example of the price one always pays for abstraction. Abstraction is useful, but one must pay the price in a conscious manner. In the risk domain, the definition of safe is: "Working safely is consciously taking acceptable risk". With abstraction the rule is: "Abstraction is consciously leaving out irrelevant details". This is why there is never a single good 'level of abstraction' in Enterprise Architecture, it depends on the situation*.

Removing that unhappy abstraction, leaving the further unused Windows side of things out, and introducing the temporary real bare Linux server results in View 281. I am using the opportunity to address a few other aspects lightly:

- The whole automated delivery would be a mini 'implementation' in ArchiMate parlance. That is, if people were still doing the work, you would have some Work Package(s) that deliver(s) the bare Linux server (first plateau) and then the fully running WildFly Application Server (second plateau). Agreed, these are almost nano-plateaus, they would normally not be the target of using the Implementation and Migration part of ArchiMate. However, the whole part of actually delivering servers is part of the core operations of the organization, these days, so you

View 280. *More on abstract Nodes*

would like to show how that automated part of the organization's operation is working. There is still a bit of bias in ArchiMate that looks at IT as an object of attention, not as an acting subject. This might have been true long ago, but it isn't anymore and it is one of the places where ArchiMate's age/heritage still shows.

- I have nonetheless shoehorned a bit of Implementation and Migration in, by stating that the bare Linux server is a plateau (it does — even though only fleetingly — exist in your landscape). However, if you look at the Automated Delivery Work Package, it does have to Realize the actual finished WildFly Application Server (in orange). And we know that the transformation from bare Linux server to fully running WildFly server is *actually*

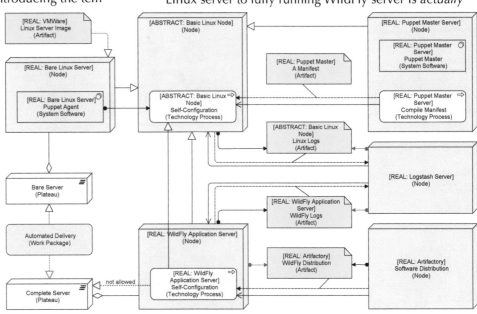

View 281. *Abstract Nodes and the Real Nodes that exist during and after the delivery*

---

* I've written more about this in Chess and the Art of Enterprise Architecture (and yes, I am plugging the other book, but also to point you to a (pragmatic) way of doing Enterprise Architecture that fits well with a good (and pragmatic) modeling practice and which I neither can nor should repeat here).

done by the Puppet Agent. So, what we would like to have shown is the red Realization, but that one is not allowed, again, because ArchiMate still is married quite strongly to the world where humans and their projects deliver changes to your landscape and not that systems do it themselves.

- The Artifacts that are Flowing have been Assigned to the source Node. There they exist in the first place. Optionally, you can *also* Assign them from the receiving Nodes (where they exist too, after all), which is shown by the blue Assignments.

- All Flows/Servings are modeled as a combi (Flow and Artifact to show what Flows and in which direction, Serving relation to show who takes the initiative), see Section 25.2 "Who is Serving Whom Anyway?" on page 128 for the discussion on the ambiguity of the Serving relation. In a Puppet world, by the way, the difference is actually meaningful. If the Puppet Master dies, the whole landscape keeps running happily, after all everything *Self*-Configures. So, while I have added the Serving relations above, it might in this case better not to model them, and use Serving only if the caller fails when the callee is not available, i.e. a 'live dependency'.

In this section I've not been strict in using patterns. Sometimes the relations start.end at the Node level, sometimes at the 'internal' behavior level. I've used this freely.

This section started with Donald Knuth's 'dangerous bend' sign because we are now deep in many valid-and-less-valid options for modeling patterns and it becomes very hard to argue for one or the other. At this point, it must be very clear to you that there is no single 'correct' way to use ArchiMate. And adding abstractions like Specializations to the mix makes for even more possibilities. Personally, I have been wrestling a lot with these patterns, because more often than not, I ended up with models that to easily led to wrong conclusions.

This page intentionally not left blank

BPMN and
ArchiMate

BPMN and ArchiMate

Why is there a chapter on BPMN and ArchiMate in this book on ArchiMate? Well, there is a very good reason: powerful and flexible though ArchiMate is, it can't do everything. It is a language for Enterprise Architecture modeling and not for, say, software design (for which we may use UML) or process design (for which we may use BPMN). Business Process modelers need more than ArchiMate can provide, e.g. in detailed sequence flow modeling, decision point modeling, etc., and they often require tooling that not only lets them model, but maybe also simulate or even directly execute a modeled process. Given that you cannot really support the needs of process modelers with ArchiMate, they will generally use their own language. But their processes are part of the Enterprise Architecture and thus also of your EA models of Current State or Project in ArchiMate. And as there is only one reality, the two models should not tell incompatible stories about your enterprise. There is, therefore, a need to use both, but to keep them in sync. In fact this is true for many, many more models that exist about your enterprise, be it the content of the Help Desk system where incidents are linked to systems and people, the Operational Risk models that link risks, controls and processes, etc. They might not be immediately recognized as 'models', but they are. That Excel spreadsheet with a list of applications and their security or business continuity classifications is also a model (a poor one, though).

ArchiMate, being the language that covers all layers of the enterprise and having a decent and flexible meta-model is a natural hub for all these models. For Business Processes, that superficially means that you may have Business Process elements in your ArchiMate model but that they represent processes modeled in more detail by the process modelers. There are many proprietary process modeling environments for sale and only one Open Standard: BPMN. Therefore, we will take BPMN as our process modeling language and show how an Enterprise Architecture modeled in ArchiMate can be in sync with a process landscape modeled in BPMN.

There is one other important aspect to consider. Business process models are generally used by, discussed with and therefore must be understandable by 'the business'. Enterprise Architecture models, especially those detailed models for Current State and Project Architectures far less so. Yes, the high-level abstracted models in ArchiMate can be used for discussions with the business (in a way not very different from presentation slides with a few graphical elements), and yes, ArchiMate is not rocket science, but complex ArchiMate models will still not be very usable in communication with your average business person. Process models on the other hand, must be understood by the people who actually perform them and that means there are important aspects to guard, especially with respect to too much abstraction. A nice example is that while in ArchiMate, a Business Process cannot directly Access an Artifact (it needs to be abstracted up to Business Object or a Representation may be used instead), the business will demand to see a description where a 'process' directly handles an 'Excel spreadsheet document' which is then for instance loaded into a system. Business process model views used for the documentation and design of human-based processes must be grasped more intuitively than Enterprise Architecture views.

29. A Very Short BPMN Primer

BPMN stands for *Business Process Model and Notation* (or *Business Process Modeling Notation* depending on which BPMN documents you read) and it is an open standard for Business Process Modeling which is managed by the Object Management Group (OMG). This book is about ArchiMate, so in this chapter I am going to assume you are familiar with BPMN. However, for those that want to read on regardless (I would) here is a very short primer. Note: if you want to learn BPMN Modeling, I would strongly suggest using Bruce Silver's book *BPMN Method & Style 2nd Edition*.

We start with a simple high level process. A Portfolio Manager of an Asset Management firm daily checks his portfolio of investments against his or her targets with respect to performance, risk, etc.. And if he or she decides that the portfolio needs adjustments (buy or sell assets) he or she will have to come up with an investment idea (which may be selling as well: a de-investment). After the creation of an

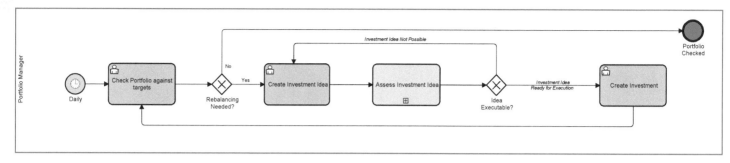

View 282. *BPMN Example – The Basic Portfolio Management Process*

idea, this idea has to be checked. This generally consists of many possible checks, like running simulations, checking against compliance rules, checking against the mandate from the client, etc.. If the idea is executable, an investment will be created and then it is back to the check whether the portfolio is now balanced with respect to the targets. If the portfolio is still 'out of balance', this 're-balancing' process continues with the next investment idea. This goes on until the portfolio is back into a state that lets the portfolio manager sleep well at night. A basic overview in BPMN can be seen in View 282.

The large overall outer rectangle is called a Lane. A Lane in BPMN is nothing more than a visual organization of the process model. Lanes are generally used to group activities that are performed by a single role, but BPMN does not prescribe this. You may use a Lane as you want, it is more or less meaningless in BPMN. You might use it to divide activities into those that are done in different locations, have different risk profiles, etc..

In the Lane, we see a couple of elements and relations:

This is the Start Event of this process. The process starts here and a sequence of events follows. What follows depends on the arrow that leaves the Start Event. In this example, the Start Event is a timer event, it occurs at a certain point in time, in this example: daily.

⟶ This is a Sequence Flow. A Sequence Flow is used to model the order in which activities occur. In our example, after the process starts, the next thing that happens is the first activity, which is connected to the arrow head of that first Sequence Flow.

This is a Task. A Task is one of the possible types of Activity. In our example we see two of these and this is the simpler one. A Task is a 'not further detailed' set of behaviors. As you can see, there is a little person-icon in the top-left corner of this Task. That icon says this is a User Task.

Here we run into a peculiarity of BPMN. BPMN has three types of simple Tasks: a User Task, a System Task (little gears as icon) and a Manual Task (no icon). In our example, the Task is a User Task and it is performed by a person. The definition of the three types of Tasks in BPMN leaves an interesting white spot. According to BPMN a Manual Task is performed with the help of *any* kind of automation and examples given are like digging a hole or something other purely physical. The User Task is defined as a Task that is orchestrated by a process engine but performed by a person.

The System Task is performed by a computer. As you can see, there is formally no room for a Task that is performed by a user but that still uses automation, e.g. writing a letter using a word processor.

There are more curious parts of BPMN (one of which we will encounter below). One of the reasons there are peculiar parts of the BPMN specification is probably that its development has been driven largely by the desire to model automated processes that are orchestrated by workflow engines. The fact that a few large companies that sell workflow engines have financed the development of BPMN is probably to blame.

This is a Gateway. Gateways require some attention. From the view it is clear what effect this Gateway has: the sequence is split and the process proceeds with *either* of the outgoing sequence flows. It follows either of these, because this type of Gateway is an XOR Gateway. The large X signifies that. As the XOR Gateway is also the default Gateway, you may leave out the X icon inside. But I like to be explicit in my modeling, so I always explicitly show it. It is important to realize that a Gateway is not an activity that is performed. The Gateway only *represents* something, namely the possible outcomes of the Activity that went before it.

There are many types of Gateways. Some have multiple inputs and multiple outputs and are very complex. They are seldom used. The ones generally used are the XOR Gateway above and the Parallel Gateway. The Parallel Gateway has a large + as icon. The Parallel Gateway signifies that all outgoing Sequence Flows will be followed.

What is useful to remember when handling Sequence Flows, Gateways, etc. is the concept of the *token game*. Think of a token as a marble that travels along the Sequence Flows. Every Start Event produces a single marble thus creating a single *instance* of this process. Our marble rolls into the first Task and when that Task is done it comes out at the other end. Then the marble rolls into the XOR Gateway. Here the marble goes either way. Had it been a Parallel Gateway with two exits, *one* marble would have gone in and *two* marbles would have come out. The idea behind the marbles is that when the process is finished, all marbles must have been consumed. The most common and obvious consumer of a marble is an End Event. But a Parallel Gateway can also consume all marbles of all incoming Sequence Flows and then spit out only one.

 This is the End Event in our example. It consumes the marble and the process ends. A process may have multiple end states and all should be represented as an End Event. We will get back to this below.

It might be good at this point also to explain that a process description contains a generic description of a single instance of a process. That is, it is possible that the same process happens simultaneously multiple times in your organization. Bruce Silver gives a good explanation in his book, including situations that you have one process that has to work together with multiple instances of another process. Think of a sale to a customer that happens many times and billing to that customer that happens only once a month. Or more to the point: the single process of filling a specific position in your company related to the multiple instances of a process to handle a single applicant for that function. Again: if you haven't been studying BPMN a lot, I can recommend Bruce's book.

There is only one element left in our example in View 282 on page 160.

This is a SubProcess. A SubProcess is a kind of activity that has details that are available and are modeled as a separate process. You can expand this Activity in place, but here it is shown in a collapsed state. We see the details of this SubProcess activity in View 283 on page 161.

This SubProcess models what happens when we 'assess an investment idea'. The first thing we do is check if this idea is actually allowed by the mandate that we have from our client. If this checks out OK, we check if for this type of investment a portfolio is available. Assets are generally organized in portfolios and we need to decide in which portfolio this asset must reside. If a proper portfolio is available we prepare the idea for execution and move to the end state 'Investment Idea Ready For Execution'. All these Tasks are performed by the Portfolio Manager, hence they have been modeled in a Lane that is labeled with 'Portfolio Manager'.

But there are two situations where we are forced to leave this 'happy flow'. The first one is if the client's mandate actually does not allow the portfolio manager to make this investment. If he or she thinks the idea is good enough, he or she might try to get the client's mandate updated. But that is not something

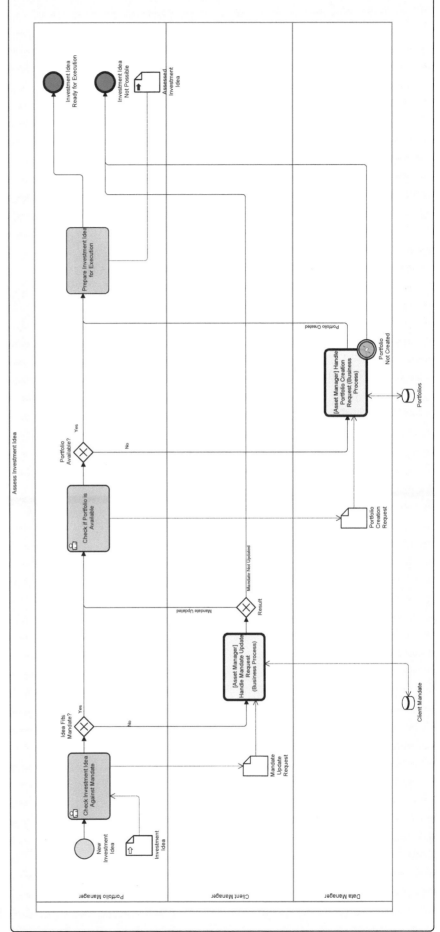

View 283. *BPMN Example – Expanded SubProcess from View 282 on page 160*

that the portfolio manager does by himself in our example organization. So, he shoots off a request to the Client Manager for an update to the client's mandate. The outcome of that activity might be that the client's mandate is either updated or not. If not, we move to the end state 'Investment Idea Not Possible' and the SubProcess finishes. If the client mandate is updated and the idea becomes allowed, we move back to our 'happy flow'. The same kind of thing happens when we do not have a portfolio ready to accept the investment: a new portfolio has to be created. In our example organization this is the domain of a Data Manager. The outcome of this is a new portfolio and we return to the 'happy flow'. Unless, that is, some error occurs and the portfolio cannot be created. In that case we move to the 'Investment Idea Not Possible' end state. The green activities are of a new type:

This is a Call Activity. What it represents is that we are going to *call* another process. This looks like the SubProcess of before, but while the SubProcess is an integral part of our process, the Call Activity is a temporary handover to another process, generally some sort of 'reusable process' that can be re-used from within many other processes. Technically, in BPMN, Call Activity and SubProcess look very much alike. You are allowed, for instance, to expand the called process in place in the Call Activity, just like a SubProcess.

Having come so far I must make an important remark on using color. BPMN, like ArchiMate, is color-neutral. Color has no official meaning in BPMN. The other aspects of form, like thin/thick borders, rounded corners or not, etc., are part of the BPMN specification.

Note: I do not follow Bruce Silver fully here. Bruce advises to put the Call Activity in the Lane of the role that 'makes the call'. I agree that this is more correct, but it has a slight prac-

tical disadvantage when communicating with the business. By putting the Call Activity in a Lane of the role that performs the called process, the view itself immediately shows who is involved and that improves understanding of what happens by people who do not model for a business.

Our Call Activity 'Handle Mandate Update Request' is followed by an XOR Gateway with two outgoing Sequence Flows: 'Mandate Updated' and 'Mandate Not Updated'. In fact, this only makes sense (as we shall see) as the process called has two End States, one for each outgoing flow.

More to the right in View 283 there is another Call Activity. This one has a single Sequence Flow coming out, but something else too:

This is an Error Boundary Event. BPMN has a rich set of event type elements which make up for pretty sophisticated modeling. I'm not going to describe them at all, just this one because it is used in the example. What happens here is that the process called by the Call Activity throws an error. Here it means that some error in the called process interrupted the process in mid-flow, thereby also killing it. It is often a matter of taste if you consider something a normal situation or an error. Personally, from long ago working with Abstract Data Types, I find the difference not that important: you need to be complete (all non-error end state and all errors need to be accounted for to be robust).

Both Call Activities in the example have two possible outcomes, one is modeled with two proper end states (not seen yet) and a Gateway, the other is modeled with a single outgoing Sequence Flow and one coming from an error that was produced.

The only remaining elements of View 283 on page 161 not yet described are the informational elements. While tasks, activities, subprocesses etc. are not that uncommon from the

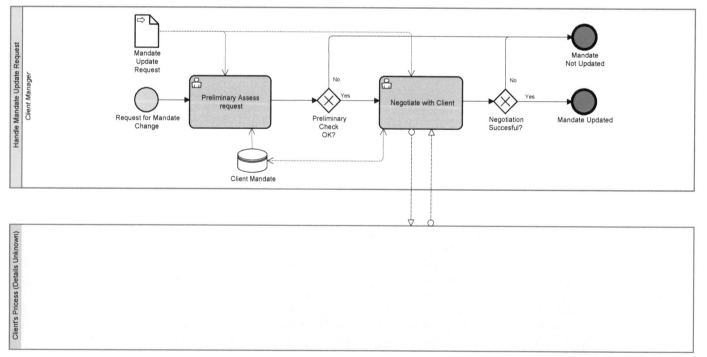

View 284. *BPMN Example – Collaboration between the Asset Manager's (our) process and the Client's (their) process*

ArchiMate perspective (they are all business behavior, most likely to be modeled as a Business Process), the informational perspective from BPMN is quite different. BPMN knows about data and has generally two types:

This is a Data Store. A Data Store stands for data that exists independently from a process. This is *permanent* data. BPMN thinks about data in quite a technical perspective, coming from its 'process engine' background. So, in terms of ArchiMate, these are best seen as permanent Artifacts in ArchiMate. From an ArchiMate perspective BPMN (and other process modeling notation styles) often seem to link the business layer (process) and the infrastructure layer (artifact) indiscriminately. However, they make sense without automation too: that "locked filing cabinet stuck in a disused lavatory with a sign on the door saying Beware of the Leopard'" is a Data Store in BPMN terms too. Still, it is a rather physical approach and is easiest associated with infrastructure.

This is a Data Object. This is *temporary* data that only exists as long as this process instance still runs. Again, this makes perfect sense from a technical perspective with 'process engines'. This is data that is kept 'in memory' of the process engine for that particular process. In that sense, it is easiest associated with ArchiMate's Data Object at the application layer. Some modelers say that data like this should not be modeled as internal data is implicitly available to all Activities in the Process, but sometimes it can be useful, for instance if you need to document certain aspects of that data. And of course, in executable processes running in workflow engines you will need to model it explicitly.

The Call Activities in our example call other processes. The first Call Activity in View 283 on page 161 calls a process named 'Handle Mandate Update Request'. As this process communicates with another independent process (that of the client) we draw visible proxies for both processes. One for our process and one for their process. We do not know the details of their process, so we leave them out. But we do know we communicate with them, asking their permission to update the mandate and getting a decision in return. This is shown in View 284. There is a new element here, that is shown in its two possible appearances.

This is a Pool. To be precise: this is a Black Pool as it does not have any process details in it. A Pool is a somewhat troublesome element in BPMN (as far as I'm concerned) as I'll explain below.

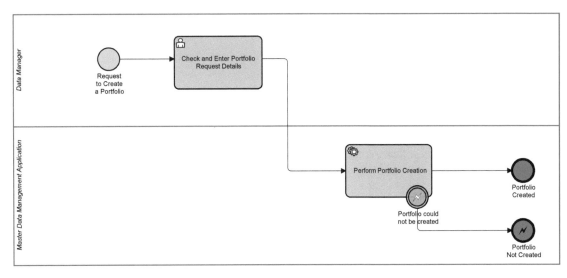

View 285. *BPMN Example – Handle Portfolio Creation Re-usable Process*

Technically, 'Pool' is not even the right name for this element. The correct name from BPMN's meta-model is Participant and a Pool is the 'visual representation of a Participant'.

If a Pool has process details in it, like Lanes and Activities it is a normal Pool. A Participant/Pool just may or may not contain a Process. If it does not contain a Process it is a Black Pool, but still a Participant.

This is a Message Flow. An important thing to know about Participant/Pools is that between Participant/Pools only messages may flow. A sequence of activities is only allowed *within* a Process (using Sequence Flows) and communication (using Message Flows) is only allowed *between* Processes. Message Flows can be connected to either Activities or to the Pool/Participant itself (the latter generally in the case of Black Pools).

Now the trouble with Pool/Participant in BPMN is this: the text of the BPMN 2.0 Specification clearly suggests that a Participant is a kind of role or actor in the collaboration. A 'Client' or a 'Seller' or 'Company X'. But the meta-model of the BPMN 2.0 Specification suggests something quite different. A Participant is a kind of ephemeral proxy. It sits between Party or PartyRole (e.g. 'Company X' or 'Seller') and the Process. A Participant may — according to BPMN's meta-model — only 'have' one Process or none (in case of a Black Pool). Now that does not sound right for a Party; after all a Client may participate in multiple Processes, e.g. 'Buy Something' and 'Complain'. Also interestingly enough, the Process can be 'of' multiple Participant/Pool elements. That does not make sense at all, unless all these different Pools/Participants are proxies for the Process itself or for the Party behind it. I have written elsewhere in more detail about this and I do not blame you if you find it confusing. But it becomes important later on when we are talking about integrating BPMN and ArchiMate.

Something else that becomes important later on is that the BPMN language does not have a visual representation for Process. Yes, you read that right: *The most important Business Process Modeling language (BPMN) does NOT have a visual representation of its 'Process' element*. This, again, becomes an interesting fact when trying to link BPMN and ArchiMate.

Back to our example, we see that the called process as shown in View 284 ends with two possible End States: 'Mandate Updated' and 'Mandate Not Updated'. When you go back to View 283 on page 161, you see that those two End States match with the Sequence Flows that leave the Gateway immediately following the Call Activity. There is nothing in BPMN that says that this must be so and that forces this kind of a correctness upon you. It is a matter of 'Method & Style', as Bruce Silver has written. In this case, I normally slightly digress from Bruce's advice as he differentiates between '2' and '3 or more' End States. In the first case, he suggests using the name of one of the End States as the label for the Gateway that follows and 'Yes' and 'No' for the Sequence Flows leaving that Gateway. I know from private communication he does not disagree with using his rule for '3 or more' for '2 or more'. The advantage is that you may get tool support for that, while changing an End State label into a 'yes/no answerable question' is something quite beyond digital computers and thus cannot be supported by automation. The hard link between End State labels and Sequence Flow label can be supported, though and good modeling tooling will help you here to keep your models internally consistent and maintainable (not something easy to do with word processing files and images).

Returning to our BPMN example, we have one called process from View 283 on page 161 left. That process is shown in View 285 on page 163. There is one new element here.

 This is a System Task. A System Task is a Task that is fully performed by a computer, a fully automated task. Now, as you can see, since the task is performed by a computer, I have labeled the Lane in which it is modeled with the name of the application that performs it. In fact, you can probably already guess what this means in ArchiMate terms where an automated Business Process can be performed by an Application Component by assigning one to the other.

The process in View 285 is pretty simple: the Data Manager enters the details and then the application goes on to create everything that is necessary. That should always succeed, so if it does not it is considered an error. This error leads to an Error End State of the process 'Portfolio Not Created'. Here again, if you go back to View 283 on page 161, you see that the label of this Error End State corresponds with the label of the Error Boundary Event in View 283. Not something BPMN prescribes, but it is good practice anyway.

30. A Possible Linking of BPMN and ArchiMate*

 Now that we have introduced the basics of BPMN (or for some readers, rehashed what they already knew) we can discuss how ArchiMate and BPMN can be linked.

Thinking about this linkage starts simple: use ArchiMate for the Enterprise Architecture and BPMN for the details of the business layer, more precisely the business processes, that are shown in ArchiMate. There are various overlapping questions that arise:

- How should we link the processes themselves? For one, though BPMN does have a Process element in its meta-model, it does not have it visually;

- What to do with the Pool/Participant in BPMN? It is tempting to use it for ArchiMate Actor (for the high level BPMN 'Parties'), for ArchiMate Business Function or GOFBF, for some high level Business Role;

- As far as Process is concerned, one visual option is to create an outer Lane level for any process that holds the link to the ArchiMate Business Process but that means that for simple single-Lane processes you still will have two levels of Lanes;

- You can choose to take Pool/Participant as a proxy for a Process instead of a proxy for a Partner. A Process then more or less always requires a Pool visually, unless you can find some way to link a Process view without a Pool to the ArchiMate Process;

- The BPMN Data Objects seem a bit more difficult to pin down. BPMN separates them according to their 'permanence' while ArchiMate separates them according to the layer (infrastructure, application, business) they belong to. The easy answer is that you can link whatever you want here, it is a matter of style/taste what pattern you prefer (only, as always, choose a pattern and stick to it);

- Then there is the question of where to maintain specific linkages: at the ArchiMate side, the BPMN side or both?

Less problematic is the use of an Application by a Process. You may link any Activity or Process to an ArchiMate Application Service in some way. Also, linking an ArchiMate Application Component to a BPMN Service Task or entire Process will be a good way to link fully automated behavior between BPMN and ArchiMate.

Working together with Dick Quartel from BiZZdesign, who did test implementations in the BPMN module of BiZZdesign Architect and discussed options with me, choosing solutions and abandoning them again because of problems and disadvantages, this is what resulted:

---

* Note: the ArchiMate patterns in this Section have not all been redone for ArchiMate 3 (only visually updated) and the reasoning is based on limitations in ArchiMate 2. The reason is that my tool has stopped supporting the mechanism. I will mark the outdated choices based on ArchiMate 2 limitations with the color of this paragraph. One should consider this section as 'informational' and 'experimental'.

30.1 An ArchiMate–BPMN Linkage Pattern

First: I wanted to have a linkage that was independent of tooling. Though it is necessary to add things (especially to the BPMN side because that is the side where the actual links have to be maintained as the details are there) it is necessary to design something that could be implemented for ArchiMate and BPMN models to be part of different modeling environments.

The basic technical/syntactical structure of linkage is like this:

- Added to the BPMN model are objects in 'Other Domain' libraries. These objects become available in the BPMN modeling tool in a way described below. Example 'Other Domains' are 'EA Application Services', 'EA Application Components', 'EA Business Roles', 'EA Locations' and 'EA Business Processes'. In these domains, we can load the elements from another environment, in our case we load the elements that we have exported from the EA tool. We can also create new 'Other Domain' elements ourselves in those libraries, as these are just simple elements with a name and a type, e.g. name: *Data Manager* of type *EA Business Role*. Three 'Other Domains' are available in the setup we use (the icons are provided by the tool I use):

  ▨ The Enterprise Architecture domain;

  ♡ The Locations domain;

  ⚠ The Risk Domain.

  While the BPMN tool supports these three separate domains, we fill them all from the same ArchiMate model. A separate risk environment could be the true source of the elements in the Risk Domain, but we provide them via the central ArchiMate model;

- We add links from the BPMN elements to these 'Other Domain' elements. These links are stored as properties of the BPMN elements. This is an extension of BPMN. Examples are:

  * If we link an *EA Application Service* to a *BPMN Task*, it means that the Application Service (from ArchiMate) is used in that Task;

  * If we link an *EA Application Interface* to a *BPMN Task*, it means that the Application Interface (from ArchiMate) is used by the performer of that BPMN Task. As the performer is not an official part of visual BPMN, we must later infer the real connection to a real performer;

  * If we link an *EA Business Process* to a *BPMN Pool*, it means that the Process embedded in the BPMN Pool is the equivalent of the ArchiMate Process linked to it. Note that we have chosen to use the BPMN Pool as proxy for the *process*, not for the *party*. We also do not use (ugly) constructs like always having an outer Lane Set that can carry the name of the Process. Not using the 'extra Lane Set' construct means that when we have a BPMN Process visualization without a Pool, we do not have a direct way

to link the two, because as said before, the amazing situation is that BPMN does not have a visual representation for its foundational element: Process. But tooling can offer a way around this (as we will see);

  * If we link an *EA Business Role* to a *BPMN Lane*, it means that this role performs the BPMN Activities in that Lane;

  * If we link an *EA Application Component* to a *BPMN Lane*, it means that this application performs the (automated or 'System') Tasks in that Lane. In ArchiMate 2, this leads to an Assignment from Application Component to business behavior, signifying an automated Business Process. In ArchiMate 3, this relation becomes a Realization. All Tasks in such a Lane should be Service Tasks of course. It also means that we will have to be strict in using BPMN Lanes for Roles/Application Components;

  * *BPMN Data Objects* and *BPMN Data Stores* may be linked at will to *ArchiMate Artifacts*, *ArchiMate Data Objects* or *ArchiMate Business Objects*. The relation between ArchiMate's passive structural (informational) elements and BPMN cannot be made very hard. Business Process Models are generally not described in a very abstract way and do not link well to more abstract notions like ArchiMate's Business Object. Also linking with internal application architectural structure like the ArchiMate Data Object does not work very well. If the modelers are also very much aware of the EA structure as modeled in ArchiMate, some more links are possible;

  * *BPMN Activities* and *BPMN Data Stores* may be linked to *ArchiMate Location* elements to signify where the activities are performed or where data is stored;

  * *BPMN Activities* may be linked to *ArchiMate Requirement* elements, for instance when these elements are used to model Risk Controls. But we can also use data from other environments (e.g. a specific Risk Management environment) to fill this 'Other Domain' in the BPMN model;

- In some situations, the link is a type of 'equivalence' link. For instance, when linking a *BPMN Process* to an *ArchiMate Business Process*, we want it to mean that they represent the same in both models. The same may be when we use *BPMN Lanes* for performers and link them to either an *ArchiMate Business Role* or an *ArchiMate Application Component*). If we want 'equivalence' we must make sure that the labels of the elements in both models are the same. Given that we have added the ArchiMate elements as 'Other Domain' to the BPMN environment, we must have the means to link the label of the BPMN element to the linked ArchiMate element. E.g. if you link multiple ArchiMate elements to a single BPMN Process, e.g. a Risk Control, a Location, a few Application Services and a Business Process, the last one is an equivalence link and we want the BPMN Process in the BPMN model to have the same name as the ArchiMate Business Process in the ArchiMate model. This we call the 'label link';

- At the BPMN side we ignore ArchiMate's Business Functions or any other functional concept like GOFBF (see 18.3 "Good Old Fashioned Business Function" on page 95) or abstract roles. The 'business functional landscape(s)' are ignored at the BPMN side. I tried looking at ways to make a linkage with a business functional approach, but none of these worked out properly and it is therefore left to the EA side to have this structure.

Now that we have introduced the basic setup, we can expand our example BPMN with a linkage to ArchiMate and show how such a linkage can be represented in the Archi-

- Have the Human Task in the upper Lane linked to the Application Service that is used by the human's behavior. The little icon is an ArchiMate Application Component icon inside an ArchiMate Service icon in my Application-Behavior color;

- Have the Service Task in the lower Lane linked to the Application Service that defines what the application actually does.

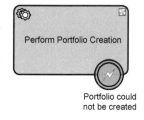

View 288. *Icon in top-right corner shows there are links to the EA Domain*

In my environment, when I add a link to a BPMN element, it shows up as a little icon in the element as can be seen in View 288 where we see one of the Tasks from View 285 on page 163.

If I click that little icon a graphical object becomes visible displaying the names of the linked ArchiMate elements. In View 286 this is shown. As you can see, I have linked ArchiMate elements to both Tasks and to both Lanes. The Task elements have been linked to ArchiMate Application Services,

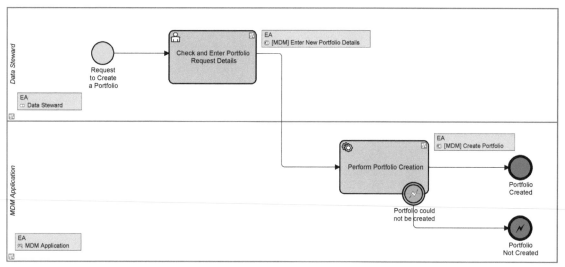

View 286. *View 285 on page 163 with added EA Domain links (visible)*

Mate model. We start with the BPMN Process in View 285 on page 163. What we want to do here first is:

- Have the ArchiMate Business Process linked to the BPMN Process and make it a 'label link';

- Have the upper Lane linked to the right ArchiMate Business Role and make it a 'label link';

- Have the lower Lane linked to the correct ArchiMate Application Component and make it a 'label link'. The little icon showing there is a 'robot' to signify automated performance by the application, it could of course simply be the icon of the Application Component;

signifying that these are the Application Services that are used by those tasks. It is a good idea to let the Business Process modelers define these services if possible, unless you already have a set that is usable by them. In any case, they must have a strong say in their definition when you are designing a new solution.

If you look at the Lanes in View 286, you see that not only are there ArchiMate elements linked to the Lanes, but the Lanes have changed names too with regard to the situation in View 285 on page 163. That is because I have also set these linked ArchiMate elements to be the 'label links'. The Lanes now have labels that are copies of these ArchiMate el-

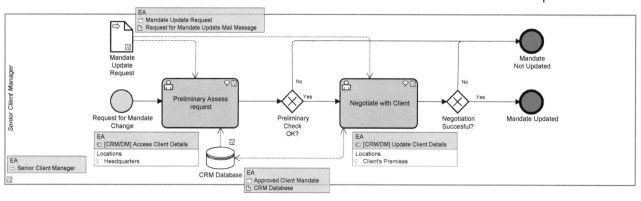

View 287. *The Process from View 284 on page 162 expanded with some Other Domain links.*

Mastering ArchiMate Edition III.TC1

ements. To show that a label is linked, my tool shows that label in *italics*. If you go back to View 282 on page 160, you will see some other labels in italics, namely the Sequence Flows following the Gateway that follows the SubProcess. That is because I have linked these labels to the End States of that SubProcess before the Gateway. As that is not about the relation between ArchiMate and BPMN, but about elements within the BPMN model I will ignore that here.

Our setup has more 'Other Domains' in BPMN. As mentioned above, we have a 'Risk' domain and a 'Location' domain. These are also filled from the ArchiMate model, but we have chosen to model them as separate domains in BPMN. That makes it easy for instance to use an Operational Risk Management system as source for Risks, etc. As an example, I have added a Location to the Human Task in View 286 and I have added Risk Controls to both Tasks. The result can be seen in View 289.

Question 7. Can you see what is wrong with View 289 (best seen in the lower expanded version) from a BPM perspective?

Answer 7. The RC1 Risk Control suggests that the human can decide not to enter the portfolio but there is no Gateway or End State for that.

161 has been extended with a Lane representing the Fund Manager who has to OK the request to update a Client Mandate to illustrate something on the ArchiMate side which we will address below. In this example, we have defined a few Application Services that are used in certain Tasks, e.g.:

- *[PM/OM] Enter Order*, the 'Enter Order' Application Service from the 'Portfolio Management/Order Management' Application, used in the 'Create Investment' Task;

- *[PM/OM] Access Portfolio Details* and *[DSS] Calculate Portfolio Characteristics*, DSS being the Decision Support System used in the 'Check Portfolio against targets' Task.

The first question is: Which processes should be visible as Business Process on the ArchiMate side when we do a roll-up of process details on that side? I choose to show two types of processes on the ArchiMate side: The *End-to-End* process and the *Re-usable* process, so, for instance, subprocesses are not shown separately in the ArchiMate model. The End-to-End process is a process that starts with an important business event and that runs to its full completion producing something of value to the business. This includes every part that has to contribute, even if we are talking about wildly dif-

Now the question becomes what the effect of all these links should be on the EA side in the ArchiMate model where the process details are aggregated but all the business-IT links should be visible. We do not want to replicate all these SubProcess and Activity details of BPMN in the ArchiMate model. After all, the whole idea was to have only a rough identification of Business Processes and such in the EA ArchiMate model while keeping a synchronized detailed description of the processes in a BPMN model.

Before we see what the result might be, we complete the rest of the BPMN model with some 'Other Domain' links in View 290 on page 168. Note: the expanded Assess Investment subprocess of View 283 on page

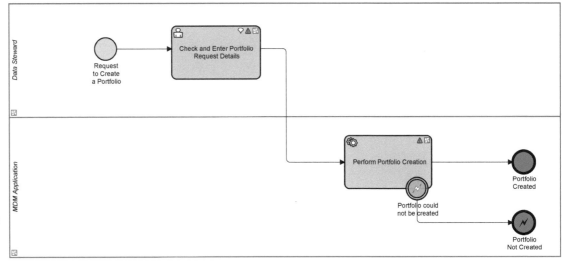

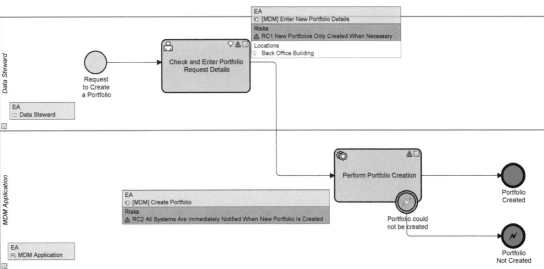

View 289. *View 286 on page 166 with added Location and Risk Domains. Above with only the icons that there are such links and below with the contents of the links of the Tasks visible.*

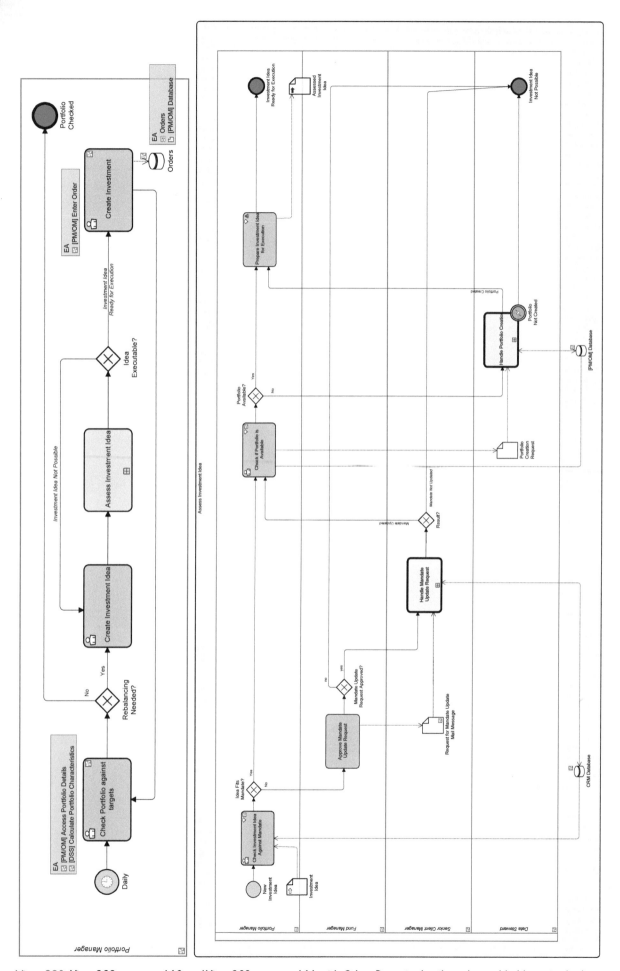

View 290. *View 282 on page 160 and View 283 on page 161 with Other Domain details and an added Lane in the latter*

Mastering ArchiMate Edition III.TC1

ferent Business Functions and the widely different Business Roles assigned to them. In our example, we have a single End-to-End process: Daily Rebalance Portfolio. Though this process is generally seen as part of the Fund/Portfolio Management Business Function, we have already seen that in it other functions, like Master Data Management and Client Management may play a role.

The Re-Usable processes are those that I model as started from another process via a Call Activity. We have two of these in our example model.

In View 293 on page 170, you see such a *possible* Roll-Up of the links that have been created in the BPMN Model. All the red-rimmed elements have been used in the BPMN Model, linked to a BPMN element. All the orange (structural) and purple (dynamic) relations can be constructed from the links in and contents of the BPMN Model. Of course in a real Current State model, you would not model everything in a single view, it would become too unwieldy to read (this one could probably be organized better too and I've left a few things out even). And you can choose what you want to model depending on how you want to use the model.

Here are some things to note:

- It is possible for a Business Process to have assignments from more than one performer (Business Role and/ or Application Component) as a result of this roll-up. ArchiMate suggests that you should assign only one Business Role or Application Component to a Business Process and use Collaborations and Interactions if multiple performers work together to perform a process. I have ignored that (see also section 8.2 "(Formal) Collaboration and Interaction" on page 33 and 16.1 "Application Collaboration is an Anthropomorphism" on page 84 and 18.2 "Business Function or Business Process?" on page 92 about the use of Collaborations and Interactions) and instead have modeled de facto 'informal' collaborations and interactions (see View 26 on page 28). In our example, Business Process, 'Handle Portfolio Creation' has two performers, one of which is an application that performs an automated part of the process. And our main end-to-end process 'Daily Rebalance Portfolio' has two human roles assigned to it: the 'Fund Manager' and the 'Portfolio Manager';

- The Roll-Up of View 293 on page 170 ignores the Call Activities when deciding which Business Roles are assigned to a Business Process on the ArchiMate side. That means that Business Roles 'Data Steward' and 'Senior Client Manager' are not assigned to our main 'Daily Rebalance Portfolio' end-to-end Business Process, even though they do play a role in some situations. Instead: the Call Activities in a BPMN Process result in that, in ArchiMate, the main-process and the re-usable-process-that-is-called are linked via Trigger and Flow relations. I prefer — and this is illustrated in View 294 on page 171 — showing the dependency

on the called processes by modeling (structural) Aggregation relations;

- The ArchiMate Artifacts that have been used in the BPMN model to link to BPMN Data Stores are not the real Artifacts as I should have in an ArchiMate model, certainly not a Current State or Project model. That is because an Artifact like "[server1/db01] Oracle DB" is meaningless for the business modeler. So, I have extended my normal modeling patterns with 'abstract' aggregates that hold the Artifact names that can be understood by the business (modeler). You will need very good cooperation between architecture modelers and business modelers anyway to make linked models like these work;

- If a project starts out with designing the rough processes and imagining what Application Services (or automated tasks) are needed, you get a very nice start for the IT side of the project in terms of what is to be realized by the applications. Also, if you already during the rough design phase identify which processes or activities need to be performed automatically (hence, by applications), you already start both detailed BPMN business process modeling as well as detailed EA modeling on the right track.

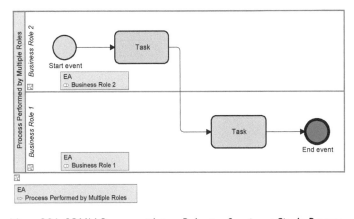

View 291. *BPMN Process with two Roles performing a Single Process*

Now, let's address a few basic patterns, some of which have already been hinted at in the previous example. The first is a simple one.

30.2 BPMN/ArchiMate: Multiple Roles performing a Single Process

On the BPMN side, this is a very simple pattern shown in View 291.

As my tool can show it, you see the EA 'Other Domain' elements displayed. The process itself is linked to the ArchiMate Business Process and the Lanes are linked to the ArchiMate Business Roles. Rolled-up in ArchiMate this becomes View 292.

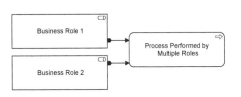

View 292. *ArchiMate Roll-up of BPMN Process performed by two Roles*

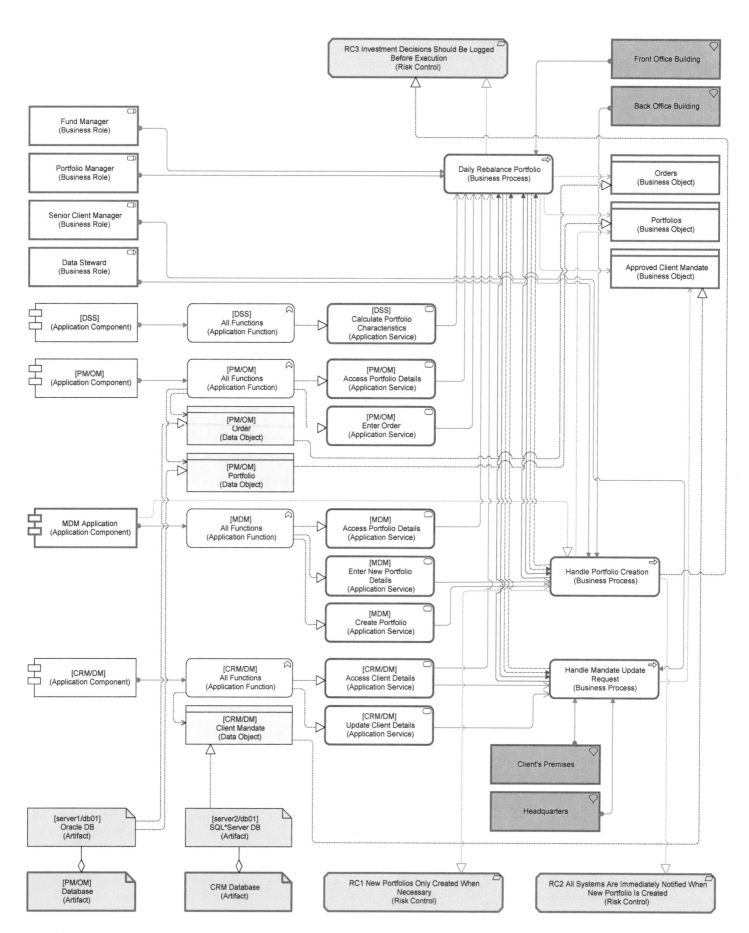

View 293. *ArchiMate View Containing a Roll-Up of Links in the Example BPMN Model*

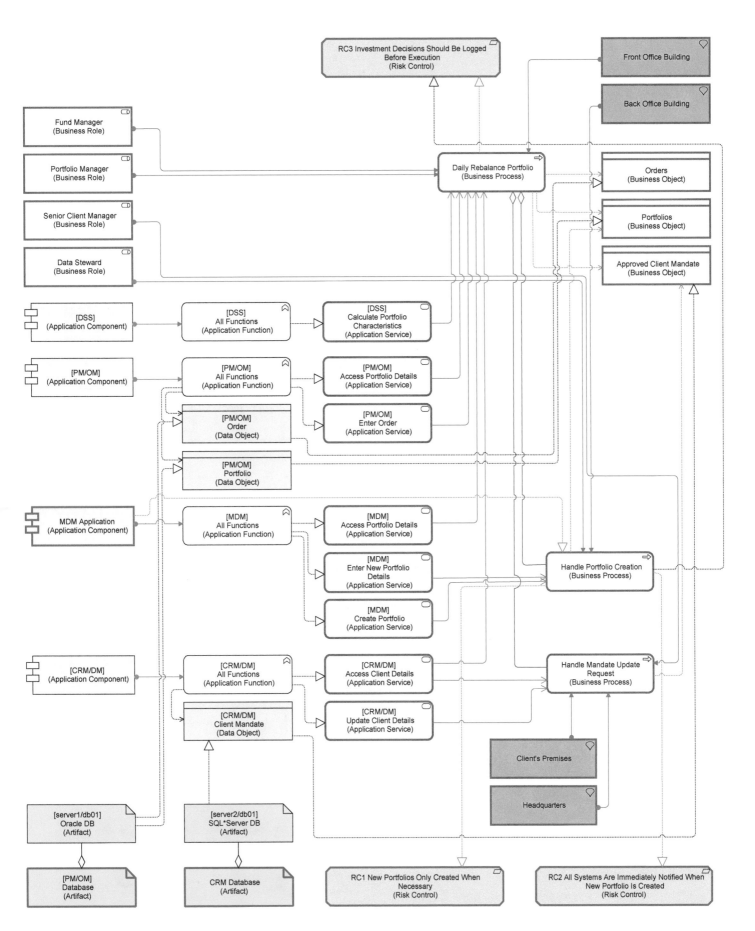

View 294. *ArchiMate View Containing an alternative Roll-Up of links in the Example BPMN Model*

This is not quite how ArchiMate purist modelers would like to see it, as I should have either used an Aggregation of those two Business Roles in a parent Business Role or in a Collaboration. In the latter case, the process would have to change into an Interaction.

The first option (just Aggregate the roles in ArchiMate) results in View 295.

View 295. *ArchiMate Roll-up of BPMN Process performed by two Roles – Aggregate Business Role performs the Business Process*

There are a few disadvantages:

- Formal ArchiMate now does not allow you to draw a derived relation between each of the roles and the process. This is not really a problem in the real world. It just illustrates that ArchiMate's idea about derivation doesn't always really work out in practice;

- The aggregated Business Role needs to be modeled explicitly in ArchiMate (it is implicit in BPMN) and it needs a name. You cannot create that name in an automated way, that would require artificial intelligence, unless you do something like "A collaboration of Role 1, Role V, Role X, etc.". So, you end up having to maintain these aggregates in the ArchiMate model by hand and the logic on updates of both models becomes very complicated. Furthermore, for every combination of roles that perform a process another explicit aggregated Business Role is needed. Apart from the ArchiMate model, nobody in your organization looks at it this way; nobody has a lot of 'named' sets of roles in their head when they think of roles performing processes in collaboration.

You can even do it in a pure ArchiMate way, which means using a Collaboration of Business Roles for every collaborative behavior. That results in View 296.

View 296. *ArchiMate Roll-up of BPMN Process performed by two Roles – Business Collaboration performs a Business Interaction*

Though ultimately most correct in terms of ArchiMate 2, this has the same disadvantages as the previous solution and an additional one: all your Business Processes will be Business Interaction elements, another bottleneck in your communication with the business.

Most importantly, these aggregates, both Business Collaboration or Business Role, do not add any information to your model, they only make matters more complex than needed and you cannot draw extra inferences.

As an aside: in very complex BPMN cases, where for instance meetings are modeled, it may be a pragmatic necessity to keep the meeting as a single Task in a single Lane. In that case one could decide *not* to link a role (or a Collaboration in ArchiMate terms) to the Lane, but instead link all roles to the Task and label the Lane independently.

30.3 BPMN/ArchiMate: A Process calling another Process

The next one is also pretty simple: Some process is calling another independent process through a Call Activity. In a very simple form this looks in BPMN like View 297.

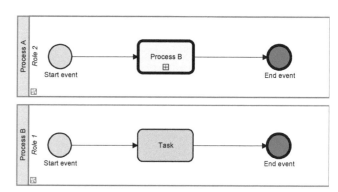

View 297. *BPMN Process calls another Process*

I've shown both processes in separate pools for clarity and to be able to show the process name (as the Pool name). In ArchiMate, the Roll-up becomes View 298.

Modeling the triggers and flows between these processes assumes the BPMN processes exchange information (which is optional) and trigger each other (which is a necessary result of the call and return). In BPMN, modeling the information exchange explicitly would require Data

View 298. *ArchiMate Roll-Up of BPMN Process calling another Process*

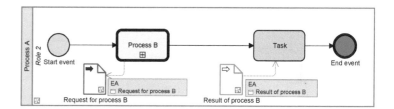

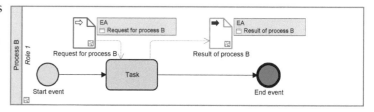

View 299. *BPMN Process calls another Process – with Data Inputs and Data Outputs*

Outputs and Data Inputs (neither using a Data Store nor Message Flows would be proper, I think). Now, with Data Inputs and Data Outputs it could look like View 299 on page 172.

What I did in this view was use two Business Objects at the ArchiMate side: 'Request for process B' and 'Result of process B' and linked these (label link) to the Data Inputs and Data Outputs. Hence, via the ArchiMate model, the Data Output of Process A and the Data Input of Process B have been linked together. BPMN itself does not offer this, though of course tooling might. But in BPMN these objects are fully independent.

The ArchiMate Roll-up now can show Business Objects for the data that was passed from Process A to Process B and back. This is shown in View 300.

To ease the comparison, I have color coded the elements in both views. The red BPMN Association relation corresponds with the red ArchiMate Access relation. The purple bordered BPMN Data Input and Data Output correspond with the purple bordered ArchiMate Business Object.

In the ArchiMate Roll-up, the information flow is in fact modeled twice now. Both the Access actions to the Business Objects and the Flow relations repre-

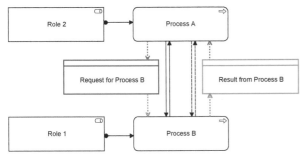

View 300. *ArchiMate Roll-Up of BPMN Process calling another Process – with Data*

sent the same.

Given that, when information flow is not explicitly modeled in BPMN with BPMN Associations to Data Objects/Inputs/Outputs, there might be no ArchiMate Flow at all, it is I think best to forget about ArchiMate's Flow relation. Just model the Triggers and model Access via Business Objects if the Data Objects/Inputs/Flows are explicitly modeled in BPMN and linked to ArchiMate Business Objects. That looks like View 301 (with data) and View 302 (without data).

30.4 BPMN/ArchiMate: BPMN has no Architecture 'Layers'

So far, the previous pattern was pretty easy and linking BPMN and ArchiMate worked well. The more details BPMN has, the more can be represented in a Roll-Up in ArchiMate. But there is a snag.

When ArchiMate models information, it is available in three versions:

- Artifacts for the low physical level at the technical infrastructure, generally used for files, data bases, etc.;
- Data Objects for objects inside applications, generally (if permanent) Realized by those infrastructure Artifacts;
- Business Objects which are Realized by those Data Objects and are more abstract concepts, like for instance 'Bank Account' or 'Invoice'.

BPMN does not have abstraction at all. It is intended to model executable processes and the way BPMN separates data into different concepts is not by abstraction but on the split temporary/permanent: Data Objects/Inputs/Outputs exist as long as the process is running, Data Stores exist independently from processes. In ArchiMate, the closest equivalent is a Data Object in memory versus a Data Object Realized by a file or a data base Artifact.

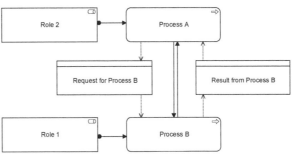

View 301. *ArchiMate Roll Up of BPMN Process calling another Process – with data*

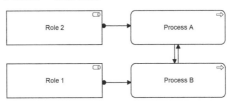

View 302. *ArchiMate Roll-Up of BPMN Process calling another Process – without data*

When business modelers model non-executable processes, these are often described in what from an ArchiMate perspective is a mix of layers. Tasks (clearly business behavior performed by a human role) 'access' files (clearly Artifacts from the infrastructure layer). This cannot be modeled in ArchiMate; Business behavior cannot access Infrastructure Passive Elements. An ArchiMate Business Process cannot Access an ArchiMate Artifact. But that is exactly how the business sees its actions and one of the reasons why the layered Enterprise Architecture approach generally feels

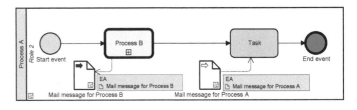

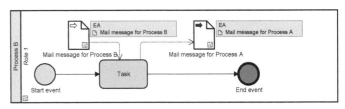

View 303. *BPMN Process calls another Process - Data Objects are infrastructural (e.g. mail messages)*

alien to them. They do not think in abstractions, they think in concrete activities and objects.

Suppose we change our processes of View 299 on page 172 so the data represents ArchiMate Artifacts instead of Business Objects? This is shown in View 303. Here, the process designer had to model a process where the business tells him "we have to handle this or that incoming mail message' and he models Data Objects that are those mail messages (or 'Excel file' or 'Word file with allowed counter-parties').

Now, when we Roll-up this into ArchiMate, the basic structure can be seen in View 304.

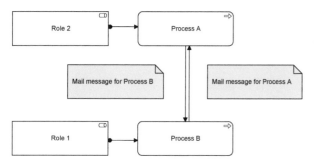

View 304. *ArchiMate Roll-up of BPMN Processes in View 303*

The problem is that we are not allowed to draw Access relations from an ArchiMate Business Process to an ArchiMate 2 Artifact. So, how are we going to represent what is in the BPMN model? We cannot 'invent' a Business Object separate from the Artifact. There might not be a clear intermediate ArchiMate Data Object (e.g. the Business Object 'Customer Complaint' is directly Realized by the 'Mail Message' Artifact). And even if we ignore the ArchiMate Data Object issue, a single Artifact may in the end Realize many Business Objects. How do you choose which one? You can't. We have some options:

- We can silently promote the Artifact on the BPMN side to a Business Object on the ArchiMate side. In the example above we would get a 'Mail message for Process B' Business Object, etc.. This will work, but as soon as there is also a real Business Object at the ArchiMate side, say 'Customer Complaint', it becomes tricky. You can't overwrite the name of the BPMN Data Object 'Mail message' with 'Customer Complaint' just like that, the business after all thinks in (and requires the visibility in their process descriptions of) mail messages and not in abstract business objects;

- We can use Associations between the Artifacts and the Business Processes. This is pretty ugly as it adds a new incompatible pattern to our ArchiMate landscape.

A possible solution is this: if the BPMN model contains only links to Artifacts from a Data Object/Input/Output/Store, they are represented as Artifacts in ArchiMate with Associations to the Business Process. But if the ArchiMate modeler finds out which Busi-

ness Object is meant by the Artifact, he or she models that Business Object and creates an Access relation from the Business Process to the Business Object and a Realization Relation from the Artifact to the Business Object. He produces View 305.

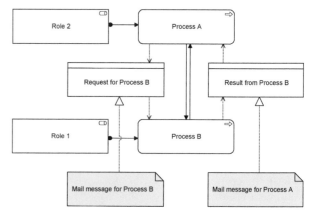

View 305. *ArchiMate modeler expands Artifact link from BPMN to Business Object*

And when synchronized back to the BPMN model, this turns into View 306.

On synchronization back to BPMN, the Business Object is represented as an 'Other Domain' object and it is linked to the same BPMN Data Object/Input/Output/Store elements as the Artifact is.

The whole setup above is not a perfect real world example. For instance, an ArchiMate setup may have the Mail Agent (e.g. MS Outlook or Apple Mail.app) at the application layer and the mail message then becomes a Data Object Realized by a (probably never modeled) Artifact. A better example might have been to model an application maintenance Process that gets an Excel spreadsheet with names to add to the application's user table. But I'm too lazy to change all the images and text at this point. Maybe later.

The whole link-up requires quite a bit of technical sophistication and there are no tools yet that support this in full.

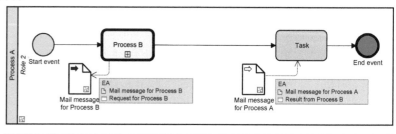

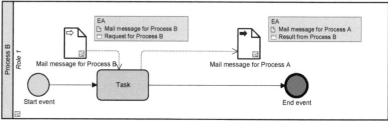

View 306. *Artifact links in BPMN model expanded to Artifact + Business Object links.*

Mastering ArchiMate Edition III.TC1

30.5 The Process Landscape in BPMN

Most companies I have seen wrestle with linking their processes up to some other structure. Not long before writing this, a senior consultant of a major world-wide operating consulting firm presented to an acquaintance a process framework he had just designed for a company. What is noteworthy about this is that he had to do this at all. What is strange is that after all these years of modeling businesses there isn't a standard way to do it. The consultant had invented a new setup. To this day, many hours are spent in many companies on yet another way of modeling a process landscape.

At a high level, there are many variations of a single theme: processes as a chain of functions. Such a pattern was expanded in 18.2 "Business Function or Business Process?" on page 92. Incidentally, the framework presented by that consultant was fundamentally flawed even: the end-to-end processes that consisted of behavior of various departments, (various business functions) was presented as an *internal* process of one of these departments. No surprise then, that as soon as people tried to use it in earnest, it died a quick death.

Starting from BPMN Processes, I am going to build yet another process landscape setup. I am starting with a sketchy end-to-end process for investing in stocks. It is a Process Chain of three processes of three parts of the company: Portfolio Management creates an Order, Trading receives the Order and makes the deal, Administration receives the

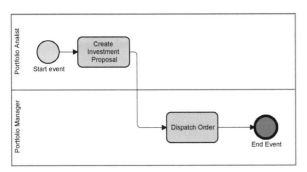

View 307. *The Sketchy Create Order Process*

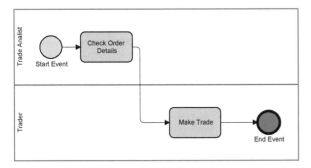

View 308. *The Sketchy Create Trade Process*

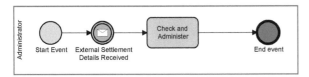

View 309. *The Sketchy Settle Process*

details of the deal and administers it. I am at this point purposely vague about what 'Portfolio Management' stands for — a Business Function?, a Business Role?, a Business Actor? — as we get to that later.

The three processes (caricatures of the real thing, I can assure you) are shown in View 307, View 308, and View 309.

- Process 'Create Order' begins when the analyst starts to create an order for some reason we do not know. This analyst does two things: first create the investment proposal (e.g. invest in X for amount Y). This may mean running all kinds of calculations and reading a lot of company documents, newspapers and web sites. When he has decided what to invest in, the second task is creating an order for the trading desk. This task is done by the portfolio manager, presumably using some order entry system.

- Process 'Create Trade' starts when the order has been received. A trade analyst checks whether the order can go though, e.g. adding missing information, checking correctness, etc. Then the order is handed to the trader who goes to the outside world to make the trade.

- When a deal is struck, the trading process ends. Now the trade must be settled. Settlement means "you get your money and I get my goods" (or the other way around of course). It means that we have to instruct our bank to wire the money to our counter-party and they have to instruct their custodian to wire the stock to our account. The administrator waits for the settlement details as received from the outside world, checks them against what was expected and administers.

Note, all messy exceptions that can occur are left out of these caricatures of processes.

Question 8. Can you see what is wrong with View 309 from a BPM perspective?

Answer 8. The description assumes that the External Settlement Details arrive *after* the instructions. But what if there is a problem and it happens the other way around? There is no process waiting for those instructions..

None of these processes have any use without any of the others. The processes are related. They form what is generally called a 'Process Chain'. Note: a 'Process Chain' is not necessarily a single thread of processes, there may be branching, merging, etc.. In fact, there is no modeling difference between a 'Process Chain' and a 'Process', but we need a different name, because organizations generally see a difference between a process that exists inside a certain responsibility and one that crosses multiple responsibilities.

Everybody agrees about the existence of these chains, but the question is, how does these chains fit in the company? The chain crosses departments, responsibilities, etc. and thus becomes a subject of intense discussion. The consultant I mentioned earlier sidestepped the issue by making a setup where you did not see those responsibility conflicts. As there is no standard model to use, I'm going to use one of my own. This one works from the practice of most organizations. Top-down, it is created from the responsibilities within the organization, which starts from the top. I am not using ArchiMate here (but we'll return to ArchiMate later). In my approach, the highest level is a *Mandate*, something that a board member of a company or business unit has. Such a mandate is a combination of people, roles, resources, etc., everything the high level manager is accountable for and makes the final decisions about.

Now, this Mandate is often a collection of recognizable different 'units of business' of the company. Say, the Chief Financial and Risk Officer may be responsible for (surprise) finance and risk. And the Chief Operations Officer may be responsible for Administration and IT Support. Such responsibilities may in practice be swapped about. A Mandate of a C-level officer may be any set of these (with some constraints, like separating risk or auditing from the primal process). So we might see a Chief Finance and Operations officer, etc.. These 'swappable' units of business could — in my view — be the *capabilities* of an organization. *Note: at this stage I am not talking about ArchiMate's Capability element yet.* ArchiMate's Capability element is positioned as a rather pure abstraction of the enterprise in a way that makes it

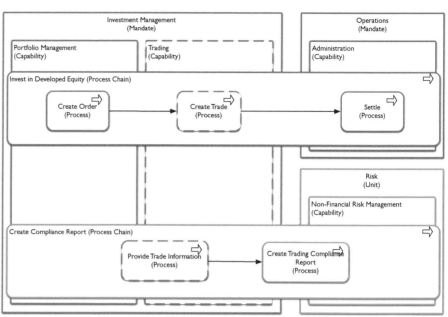

View 311. *Example from a potential process framework (not really ArchiMate)*

hard to integrate with 'the enterprise itself' (ArchiMate's Core). I'll pay some attention to the way this could be modeled with ArchiMate's actual Capability element below. In the remainder of this text, I will use the capitalized Capability term for ArchiMate's Capability element and 'capability' for the 'sub-mandates' in the process landscape approach.

Generally, a capability has a manager too, one level below the C-level. Of course, a capability can be subdivided in sub-capabilities etc.. What then is the definition of capability? There are many around, but here is one: resources giving the ability to undertake a particular kind of action. Remember: *ArchiMate* sees Capability as the purely *behavioral* element that has both passive and active Resources Assigned to it and which (see section 10.1 "Strategy" on page 42) is an abstraction of 'the enterprise itself'.

All these capabilities can contribute to processes and (end-to-end) process chains. In fact, technically I would find the term 'Cross-Capability Process' a far better name than 'Process Chain' as the term 'chain' gives a misleading one-dimensional suggestion.

In View 311 there is an example. We see the capabilities 'Risk', 'Operations', and 'Investment Management' and the Cross-Capability Process (or Process Chain) 'Invest in Developed Equity', which is made up of the three processes we described above: 'Create Order', 'Create Trade' and 'Settle'.

Below it, we see another Cross-Capability Process 'Create Compliance Report', which we will use down below to illustrate a variation on our theme.

Now, interestingly enough, BPMN has three ways to model this 'Process Chain':

- The processes can be in a separate Pool each and communicate via messages. This is shown in View 310. Note the message start and end events;

- The processes can be SubProcesses of an overall process. This is shown in View 312 on page 177 (with

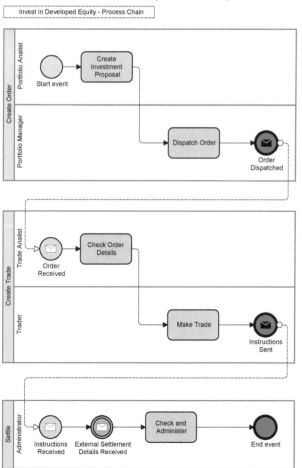

View 310. *Process Chain depicted as a Collaboration in BPMN*

Data Inputs and Outputs to take the place of the messages) and in a collapsed state in View 313 on page 177.

- The processes can be called from an overall process via Call Activities. Those called processes look exactly like the ones depicted as SubProcesses.

The question of course is: which one do you take? To begin with, in our example, the Process Chain is not really a process that is performed where such a thing makes sense. Our Process Chain is a managerial abstraction that is performed by a loose collaboration of the roles that perform the individual processes the Process Chain is made up of, as depicted in View 151 "A Business Process using Business Functions is performed by a (loose) Business Collaboration" on page 94. That would suggest using a 'chain of Pools' (technically a Collaboration in BPMN) as in View 310. BPMN does not have a graphical representation for the total, i.e. you cannot embed the pools in some outer object, so you are restricted to having some sort of view represent the 'process chain'. The sequence of the 'Order', 'Trade', and 'Settle' processes cannot be modeled using Sequence Flows, but that seems at first hand not to be a big problem. In fact, sending a message from a Message End Event to a Message Start Event as in View 310 effectively creates a sequence, even if our 'sequence token' is consumed by the end event and produced new by the connected start event. Even if the 'chain' is more complicated than a straight chain, but has branches we can do without the gateways. After all, each end state of a process can send a message to a different 'next' process. Sadly, though, we seem to be stuck when we have processes that do not clearly send messages to other processes. What if the Create Order process just writes the Order in a Data Store and the Create Trade process has a continuous loop of looking at the available Orders in that Data Store? This is in fact a pretty common pattern. However, following the principle that we should stay as close as possible to reality, we can in fact show what happens. After all, each process in the 'chain' can read from or write to a store (of Orders, of Trades) and it will still work and it can be modeled. In fact, it is what really happens, the sequence of processes in the chain is 'loose' and implied, not 'hard'.

The second and third ways are identical in most respects except one. Modeling the 'process chain' as a process in itself makes it possible to use Sequence Flows and Gateways to

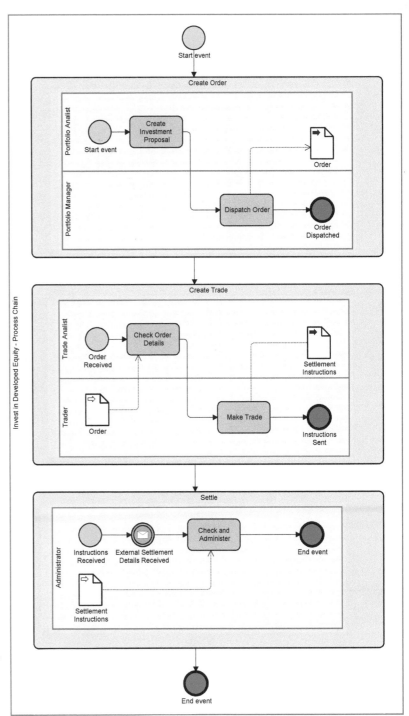

View 312. *Process Chain depicted as a Process with SubProcesses in BPMN*

produce more realistic complex chains directly. An example using SubProcesses can be seen in View 312. Though it can of course be left out, I have modeled the data too, so you can couple the BPMN data elements to 'other domain' ArchiMate informational elements. SubProcesses can be collapsed and a nice simple overview of a process chain can be created as can be seen in View 313. Creating a 'simplified view' or 'collapsed view' of the process chain of Pools as in View 310 might be possible as well, depending on your tooling. It might look like View 315 on page 178 (my tool cannot really do it well, so you cannot see the difference here between the collapsed state and a black pool).

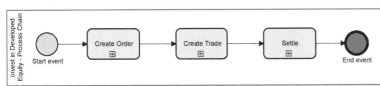

View 313. *Process Chain depicted as a Process with SubProcesses in BPMN — Collapsed*

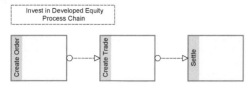

View 315. *Process Chain as a Collaboration in BPMN – Collapsed*

Using SubProcesses for the processes in the process chain has a serious disadvantage, though. Say that you have a process chain for 'Investing in Developed Equity' (as shown in these examples) but also a process chain for 'Investing in State-backed Credits'. The processes for creating an order or a trade are quite different and require different capabilities, but the settlement is handled by the exact same generic 'Settle' process. When you use SubProcesses, you need to define that same 'Settle' process twice and keeping them in sync will be a problem. Luckily, BPMN has a way of re-using processes using Call Activities and the example is shown using Call Activities in View 314. You can of course use a mixture of SubProcesses — for processes that are unique to the chain — and Call Activities calling Re-Usable Processes — for processes that are not exclusive to the chain.

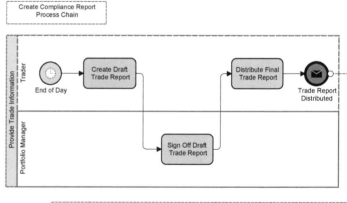

View 314. *Process Chain depicted as a Process that calls other Processes in BPMN*

Which brings us back to the question of what to use. Using different Pools has the disadvantage that you cannot really model process chains that —as a chain — are under workflow engine support: Sequence Flows cannot be used. It has the advantage of having natural visible elements (the Pools) for the processes. Whether you like to use Pools for processes that are wholly internal to your organization is a matter of taste, but in principle there is nothing against it. In fact, as Bruce Silver shows in his 'hiring' example: sometimes multiple Pools are the only way possible to model certain processes, especially when there are 1:n relations between aspects of them (one 'fulfilling vacancy' process and many 'screen applicant' processes for instance, see Bruce Silver's excellent book). Looking at it now, my personal preference is using Pools for the processes in the process chain. One aspect that plays a role here is that these processes are still very high level and require detailing in actual subprocesses and call activities anyway.

Now that we have decided what to use, we can look at a slight variation. Our example processes above were processes that clearly belonged to a single 'capability'. But this is not always the case. Take the bottom process chain in View 311 on page 176. This is a process chain 'Create Compliance Report' consisting of two processes 'Provide Trade Information', which comes from the Trading capability and 'Create Trade Compliance Report' which comes from the 'Non-Financial Risk Management' capability. These processes are depicted as crossing capability boundaries, however. That is, because in both processes a Task needs to be done by another capability. In 'Provide Trade Information', there is a small task for the Portfolio Manager, he has to sign off on the data generated by Trading. And the same thing happens when the report is created, the final report needs

to be signed off by Trading. For these small and simple steps it is overkill to create entire processes (or SubProcesses if you chose to model chains that way). So, we accept that it is possible that, not only a process chain can cover multiple capabilities, the roles that are part of the capabilities may perform a task somewhere else. In fact, this is one of the reasons why we might use the 'capability' concept, to differentiate between a role performing activities that are part of a capability and performing activities that are part of another capability. The processes in this second example chain are shown in View 316. I have color coded the edges of the Pools and Lanes so it relates to View 311 on page 176.

The upper Pool contains a process from the Trading capability that contains an action of a role that 'belongs to' the Portfolio management capability. The lower Pool contains a process from the Non-financial Risk Management capability that contains an action of a role that 'belongs to' the Trading Capability. How it is shown in View 311 on page 176 cannot always be realized: suppose it is the Portfolio Manager who has to perform a Task in the 'Create Trading Compliance Report' process? The element would overlap Trading which has no part in the process at all. So, though (not quite ArchiMate) View 311 on page 176 looks nice, its method of displaying a role belonging to one capability performing a Task in a process from another capability does not scale. In reality, I think such processes should be shown just as the ones from the upper process chain: inside the capability where it belongs to. The detail that a role from yet another capability does something is then ignored.

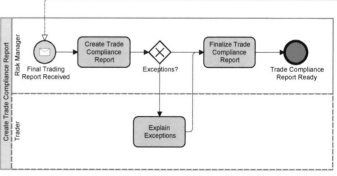

View 316. *Create Compliance Report Process Chain*

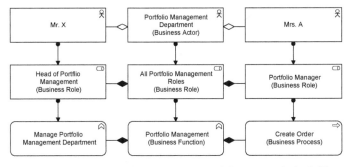

View 317. *The Portfolio Management capability in simple ArchiMate 2.0*

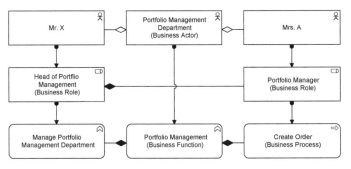

View 318. *The Portfolio Management capability in simple ArchiMate 2.0 using HR's Job Tree from View 186.*

Before finishing this slightly off-topic exposé and return to modeling in ArchiMate, I'd like to say something about ownership of processes and process chains. For me, a process should be owned by the one who is responsible for its results. Which means that in View 311, the 'Settle' process is owned by the Administration capability under the Operations Mandate. But the 'Settle' process is also part of the 'Invest in Developed Equity' process chain (or cross-capability process, or end-to-end process). And the Capability that drives this process, the process that owns the results, is Portfolio Management. We do not do Portfolio Management because of Trading and we do not do Administration because of Trading. We do all of this because we want to do Portfolio Management. But we do the 'Provide Trade Information' because of 'Create Trading Compliance Report', so here Non-Financial Risk Management owns the chain. Often, owners of processes are afraid that they lose effective ownership of their process if a 'process chain owner' is appointed. But that should not be so. If there is disagreement between Trading and Administration about what happens in the 'Invest in Developed Equity' process chain, the Portfolio Manager should make sure that 'Create Trade' and 'Settle' are aligned. That means talking with the Trading and Administration Capabilities (who still own their own processes) to solve the issues.

30.6 The Process Landscape in ArchiMate

How would the landscape of View 311 on page 176 look in ArchiMate? We need to choose what to use for 'Mandate', we start in the details and we try to abstract away until we get something resembling View 319. Here we have adapted View 311 so that 'nested' elements are not nested by 'performer' but by 'owner'. The former, after all, is not really possible in real situations (we would

need a rather large number of dimensions to do this 'nesting' coherently and we only have two...).

Suppose we think of a capability (sub-mandate) as some sort of department with its behavior. For instance for a Portfolio Management capability we could start with View 317.

I have created a Business (sub)Function for 'managing the department' because that is not really a single process with a single recognizable result.

Now, if we want our 'Jobs' to be compliant with what is in HR's systems (we want this because otherwise we have to (a) make things up and (b) maintain them ourselves) as in View 186 on page 116, there is no Composite element containing 'all Portfolio Management roles'. Leaving it out (and using the HR Job Tree as pattern) produces something like View 318. As we wrote before, there is something to say for this HR Hierarchical Job Tree as the manager is generally able to overrule (and thus perform) the role of the managed employee. That is what hierarchy is about.

Now, modeling this hierarchy presents us with something ugly: to keep the Portfolio Management department as the performer of the Portfolio Management function we can draw a direct Assignment between them. But that Assignment is in fact a derived relation of some role that sits (hidden) in between. We might have removed that 'All Portfolio Management Roles' element from the view, but its existence is still assumed in the background (as otherwise the derived relation would not be possible).

To solve it we can instead Assign the 'Head of Portfolio Management' role to the Business Function of the behavior of the department. In that case, the specific 'manage department' (sub)Function can be removed as well as can be seen in View 320 on page 180.

This result was used in 22.1 "Basic Organizational Structure" on page 115. Hiding relational details and using Nesting may produce View 321 on page 180.

If we model the details of our Process Landscape of View 311 on page 176 in ArchiMate, using the pattern of View 320, we get something like View 322 on page 180. Let me reiterate: examples like these are not meant as example

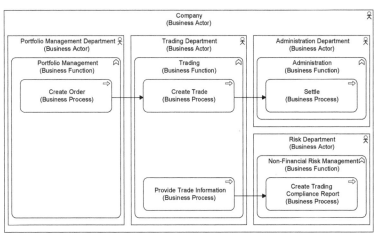

View 319. *Process Landscape attempt in ArchiMate (from View 311 on page 176)*

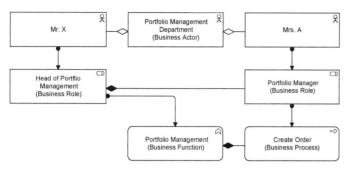

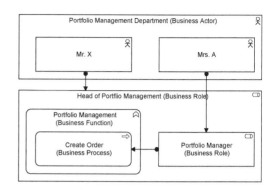

View 320. *The Portfolio Management capability in simple ArchiMate 2.0 using HR's Job Tree and using only direct relations.*

View 321. *Nested version of View 320*

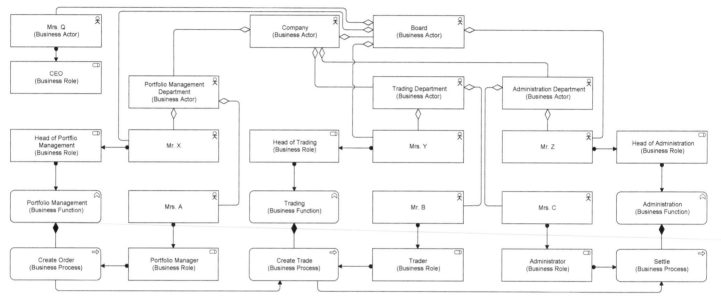

View 322. *The Process Landscape of View 187 on page 116 in ArchiMate with far too much detail*

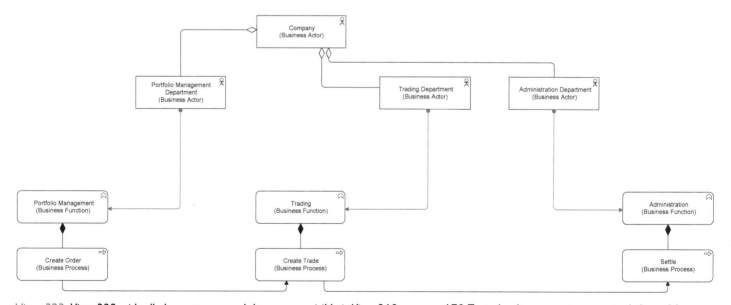

View 323. *View 322 with all elements removed that are not visible in View 319 on page 179. To make the connections required, the red Assignments have been added.*

patterns for Enterprise Architecture models, I am just using ArchiMate as tool to help with analysis.

Now, if I remove all the elements from View 322 that are not in View 319 on page 179, and I add missing relations, I get View 323. This can be shown nested and if you do

that, View 319 on page 179 (which was derived from the non-ArchiMate View 311 on page 176) results and that was what we set out to do.

What does this show us? Well, for one, that thinking in terms of Board Mandates leads to defining a 'mandate' as the responsibility for a unit-of-business (department) which somewhat represents a (non-ArchiMate) 'capability'.

In summary, with respect to process landscapes:

- Processes need to be grouped by 'owner' (and not 'performer') to create a coherent landscape that can be correctly shown in a simplified 'nested' form;

- A process chain (end-to-end process) requires its own separate owner;

- Ownership is based on who requires the result of a process or process chain.

30.7 Processes handling Artifacts

In ArchiMate, processes do not handle Artifacts, they handle Business Objects. But if you look at actual business process documentation, it often happens that there are actual steps in the process (Activity, Task, SubProcess) that manipulate for instance files.

Take the following example. We have a situation where we have to report to a regulator. These reports are created and sent. But there is also an 'ad hoc' question handling process, which is shown with a lot of detail in View 324. The regulator asks us a specific ad hoc question, maybe a clarification question after we have sent our generic report. For this, the people responsible for answering those questions need to collect a number of files, then use these files as input for a new report and send that as the answer to the regulator. In this process, there

requirement is that in the process documentation we have to describe a process activity — which in ArchiMate terms is part of the business layer — that accesses a file — which in ArchiMate terms is part of the infrastructure layer.

Now, earlier we decided not to model the details of the process on the ArchiMate side. For this section, we are going to step away from that a little to make our options clearer. So, we are going to start with the process, but modeled in detail in ArchiMate, which is shown in View 325. Here we have modeled the activities on the BPMN side as Business Process on the ArchiMate side. On the BPMN side, the ArchiMate Business Roles have been linked to the Lanes, as was proposed before.

Now, the question is: how do we model the passive side (data) in the ArchiMate model?

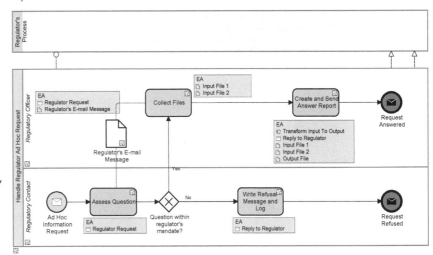

View 324. *A process that handles artifacts with much detail shown*

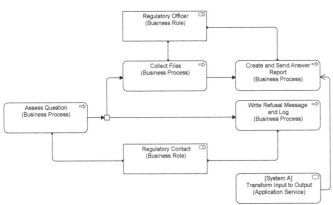

View 325. *Detailed ArchiMate 2 version of process of View 324, without data*

is a step where we 'collect files' and a next step where these files are loaded into a system which makes sense of them, e.g. extract exactly the right information from them.

Now, suppose from the process modeler's perspective, the step of collecting the files is crucial and needs to be explicitly described, e.g. because its effect is that the performer of that step needs access to specific information. The effect of that

A first attempt could be to follow ArchiMate strictly and use Business Objects for the passive elements. The simplest way is to make a Business Object that represents the file to be handled. This is shown in View 326. From an ArchiMate perspective, this is definitely weird. We have passive elements

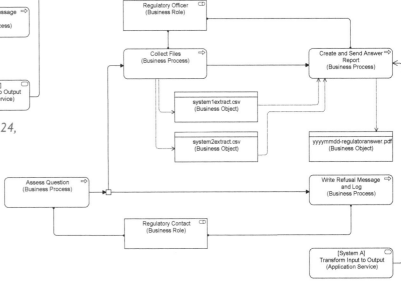

View 326. *The Process of View 324 in ArchiMate 2 with files represented as Business Objects*

that are obviously Artifacts, but they (unnecessarily) end up (unwanted) in the model as Business Objects.

A second attempt would be to represent the artifacts in the BPMN model as Artifacts in the ArchiMate model. This is shown in full in View 327 on page 182, where I have left out the Application Function as it is not relevant to this analysis. Now, we have Business Objects that represent the Artifacts, and these have gotten a more logical name, e.g. instead of 'system1extract.csv' the Business Object has been named 'System 1 Extract'. Though much better from an Enterprise Architecture perspective, we now have two (and adding the application layer even three) elements all representing what in the eyes of normal people (such as the business) is just a single easy to understand thing: a file. It is not surprising that you run into trouble sometimes when the tools and mechanisms of Enterprise Architecture have to be read or used by the business. It is a 'light' version of confronting a couch potato with the schematics of his or her TV.

There is a special problem in View 327 on page 182 as well, and it is illustrated in red. What happens in this view is that we have a full layer route from Artifacts to Business Objects because one of the processes also uses an application to manipulate them, hence, there is also an intermediate Data Object. But leave out that application, and what we need to do to model both Artifacts and Business Objects are Realizations such as the one shown in red. Now, these Realizations are valid ArchiMate 2 relations. But there is a hidden problem: they are not *direct* relations, they are *derived* relations. This means that even if the intermediate Data Objects are not shown, they are implicitly assumed to be there. Of course, being intelligent humans, we can step over that problem and just use them as if they were direct Realizations.

A third option is also ArchiMate-compliant. We can directly link the Business Process elements to the Artifacts. We use the generic Association relation to model the 'access' between the two. This is shown in View 328 on page 182. Effectively, we are working around a limitation of ArchiMate.

Question 9. What other relation is allowed between Artifact and Business Object and why is it not appropriate?

Answer 9. A Serving relation is allowed. But what this means is that the Artifact Realizes an Application Component that has a derived Serving relation with the Business Process.

This solution does come with a disadvantage, though. Because, what is not shown is what happens in the 'Create and Send Answer Report' Business Process with regard to the application that is being used. The application layer needs that Data Object and that Data Object can Realize a more appropriate Business Object as in View 327.

Having seen three different options, which is best? Personally, I would prefer to use the solution of View 327 and give the business process modelers freedom to link either Artifacts or Business Objects or both. The ArchiMate model could contain a 'direct' Realization relation between Artifact

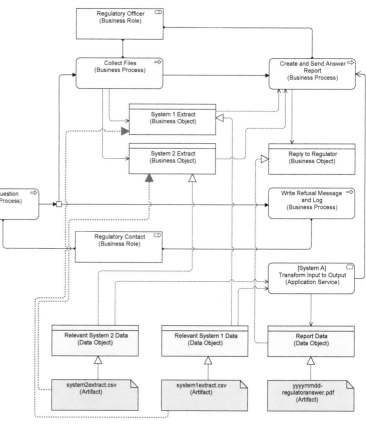

View 327. *Business process of View 324 with files represented as Artifacts as well as Business Objects (ArchiMate 2).*

and Business Object if there are activities in the BPMN model that do not use an application to access the data.

30.8 Processes communicating via an ESB

Earlier, I presented modeling the ESB in Section 25.4 "Routing and Orchestrating Middleware (ESB and APIs)" on page 129. The story there wasn't finished yet.

We need a solution for the ESB that does not depend on (dynamic) flow relations, but that uses the (structural) Access

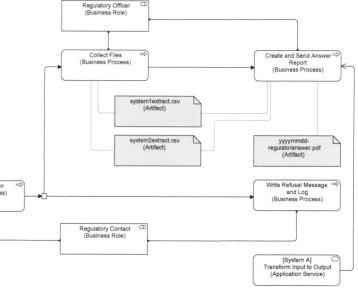

View 328. *Business process of View 324 on page 181 with Associations used to link Business Processes and Artifacts (ArchiMate 2)*

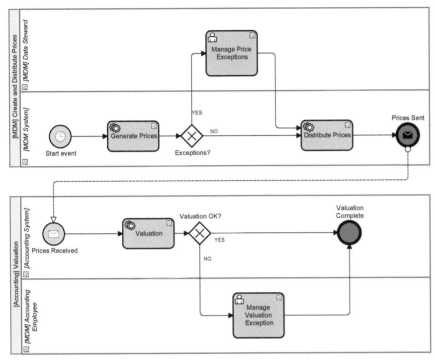

View 329. *Pricing Process delivering Prices to the Valuation Process*

relation and passive structural objects. To illustrate the patterns, I am going to start with the processes. Suppose we have two processes: one is a process that produces price information (e.g. by using data vendors, which we will not show here). This price information is sent (via the ESB) from the Master Data Management system to the Accounting System. To make matters a bit more realistic, both the pricing process and the valuation process are not fully automatic, but they have human exception handling. The setup is seen in View 329 on page 183. At some time of day, the application *[MDM System]* generates the prices. A check follows if there have been exceptions during that automated process. If there haven't been, the prices are distributed and the process ends with a Message End Event. If there have been exceptions, the role [MDM] Data Steward manages the exceptions, after which we end up in the same Message End Event. From this End Event, a BPMN Flow connects the *[MDM] Create and Distribute Prices* process to the *[Accounting] Valuation* process. This, therefore, starts with a Message Start Event and the first Activity is that the [Accounting

System] performs the Valuation automatically. Here too, there is an exception-handling Activity and it all ends in the *Valuation Complete* End Event. Both processes have System Tasks that are performed by a system (shown as label on the lane that contains the System Tasks) and that run automatically. Both have human Tasks that obviously use IT too.

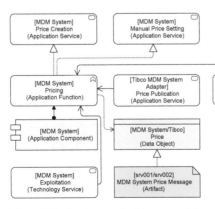

View 330. *Application Architecture of the MDM System that provides the prices.*

Let us first look at the architecture of the Master Data Management System. This is shown in View 330. The MDM System provides two Application Services and uses two. First it uses the *Provide Asset List* Application Service from the Accounting System directly to get a list of assets that need to be priced. Then it creates the prices for those assets, this is the *Price Creation* Application Service that can be used by the Business Process. It also offers a *Manual Price Setting* Application Service that can be used by the business when it manages the exceptions. And finally, it uses the *Price Publication* Application Service of the specific adapter that has been created for our MDM System in the Tibco environment. We publish the prices via Tibco so that every system that has subscribed to them gets them. One of these, we already know, is the Accounting System itself and it is shown in View 331. In both views, we see the Artifact that represents the message that is going from MDM to Accounting. And finally, the Tibco Application Architecture is shown

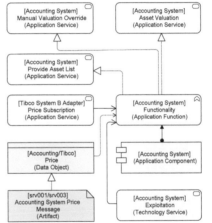

View 331. *Application Architecture of the Accounting System that provides the assets and receives the prices*

in View 332. Tibco is shown, as it was in Section 25.4 on page 129 as a platform in which we have created and deployed three applications: the adapter specific for the MDM System, the Adapter for the Accounting System and the application that represents the internal routing logic. We follow the 'Construction View' approach from Section 31 on page 189 here.

Now, all these applications are used in the Business Process. They either are used by Tasks (actually providing the Task with some sort of Application Service that supports it) or they even perform the Task, if it is fully automated. As we saw before, we may link the ArchiMate elements to a BPMN description. This is shown in View 333 on page 184. The Lanes have been coupled with Business Roles and Application Components imported from the ArchiMate side and they have become 'label links'. To the Tasks the various Application Services are linked (and shown) in popups. And we have added a BPMN Data Input and a BPMN Data Output element, both linked to the message Artifacts and the Price Business Object from Enterprise Architecture. We've selected the Artifacts to be the 'label link'. And, of course, the BPMN Pools themselves have been 'label linked' to the Business Process elements of the ArchiMate model. Following the same 'roll-up' mechanism we described earlier, the business architecture part

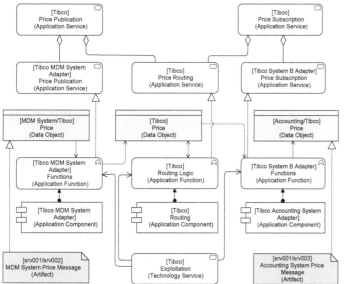

View 332. *Application Architecture of the Tibco ESB connecting Master Data Management and Accounting*

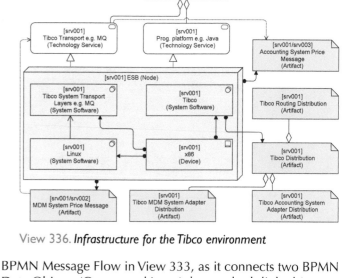

View 336. *Infrastructure for the Tibco environment*

BPMN Message Flow in View 333, as it connects two BPMN Data Objects (Output and Input) that are both linked (not shown) to the Price Business Object, next to being linked to their own specific message Artifact. I would like to be able to connect the

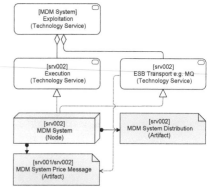

View 335. *Infrastructure for the MDM System*

View 333. *View 329 on page 183 extended with ArchiMate links.*

BPMN Message Flow to the Business Object, but my tool does that allow that (yet), it is, however, the ideal linkage for this scenario.

Of course, we also have infrastructure views on our model. Following the 'construction view' approach, we get View 335 for the MDM System, View 336 for the Tibco environment and View 337 for the Accounting System. A full overview of all layers and relations can be found in View 338 on page 186. Here, you can also see a choice I have made that is an exception

of the ArchiMate model looks like View 334. There are a couple of interesting aspects of this roll-up. The first is that the processes are performed by a collaboration of Business Roles and Application Components, shown as an 'informal collaboration'. This is logical, because both processes are examples of 'exception-based architecture', or in other words: one automates as much as one can. The second is that the part played by the *Price* Business Object can be derived from the

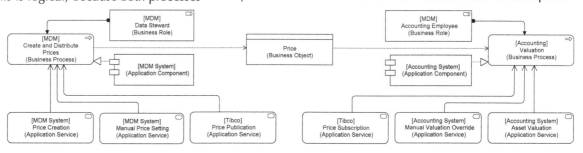

View 334. *Business architecture in ArchiMate, derived from a roll-up of the linkage in the BPMN model.*

to a rule. As a rule, I keep Data Objects specific to applications. But in this case, I make an exception because the Data Objects are so very clearly exactly the same for both. As a result, the flow of information can be easily seen by following the Access to the Business Object in the business layer and the Data Objects in the application layer. We do not have to go to the infrastructure layer to see the shared messages or use Flow relations. Note that Tibco's Price Data Object has no Artifact that Realizes it. It is quite ephemeral

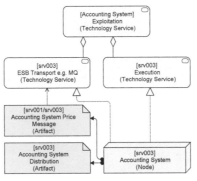

View 337. *Infrastructure for the Accounting System*

and its Realizing Artifact is internal detail that we need not show. It is only there to show the flow as Access relations instead of Flow relations.

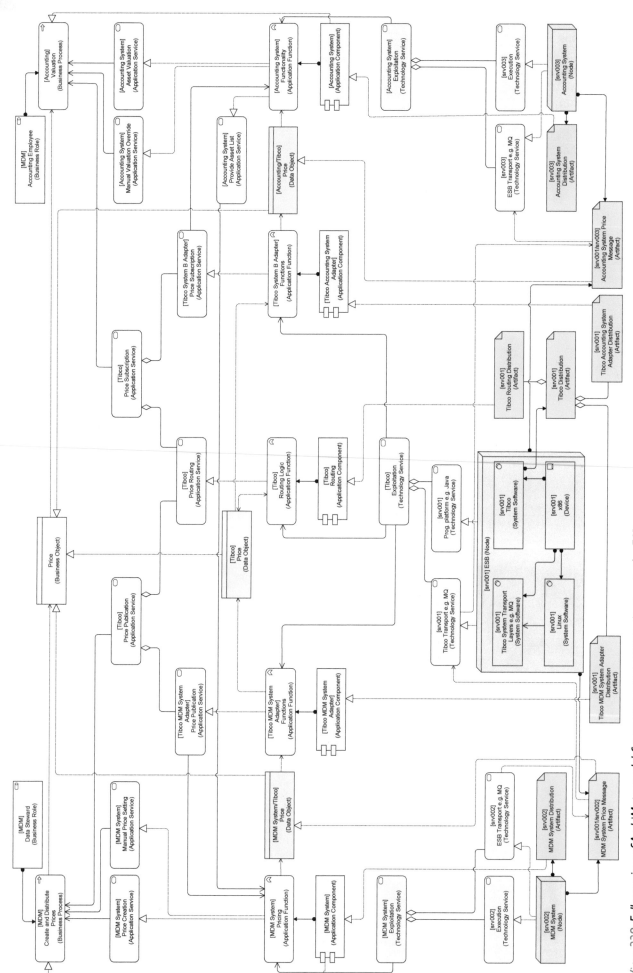

View 338. Full overview of ArchiMate model for two processes communicating via the ESB

This page also intentionally not left blank

Model Use & Maintenance

Model Use & Maintenance

31. Construction & Use Views

When you get *really* serious with ArchiMate, and you for instance model your entire Current State in ArchiMate (partially automatically loaded from other environments), your models will get pretty large. Those that approach modeling 'the enterprise itself' (and I know a few) end up with models that may easily hold 100,000 elements and relations (and

View 339. *Large Model Construction - Business Architecture View*

possibly more in satellite models, see below). This sounds unmanageable, but it isn't if you do it right. From experience: we built & managed the entire current state model with roughly one FTE after doing an initial stint with two FTE. These days, you might even use other sources such as source code control systems, deployment systems and so forth to populate your model and only do some layout work on what has already been entered automatically — provided your tooling landscape supports such an approach. And besides, if you have such a model, it will save a lot of work elsewhere in your organization. Now, apart from the right patterns to which you should stick religiously, you will need a way to model this. One big view of 100,000 elements and relations doesn't cut it.

Before I describe the details, there is one important point and you might to choose differently. We decided *not* to model Interfaces so we could keep our models simpler (they are complex enough as is). My philosophy is that behavior is the core of what happens in the organization and we model around that. This is also the reason we chose the original color setup (with a twist). Basically, it was all about keeping things manageable and communicatable in the light of the huge scale we were planning to do our modeling in.

We decided to use a couple of 'view types' to maintain our current state model (and models for large projects). I think our end result is not yet finished, as we have found that maintaining construction views is not enough to publish the model, so we need other views, specialized for a specific audience. Using the viewpoints mechanism from the ArchiMate standard also didn't cut it for us. So, we created a couple of 'view templates' to divide our landscape in and that we use to model our large environments, especially the current state. Note, these views are not truly ArchiMate 'viewpoints' ('optional' since ArchiMate 3). ArchiMate viewpoints restrict a view to certain element and relation types between them. Our views are not quite like that. For instance, the Application Architecture View does not allow all Business Roles, only explicitly the Change Manager, Application Manager and Application Owner roles. You can see a version of the Construction Views in View 340 on page 190. Here you see three view types:

- The Business Architecture View outlined in red (and seen separately in View 339). This view is for modeling the business architecture, but it also includes Risk, Control Objectives, Counter Measures (Section 20.3 "Modeling Risks and Controls" on page 111) and Secondary Roles (Section 19.9 "Making it Practical: shortcuts" on page 108). Note that for this and the other view types, if an element is not available in the view e.g. Technology Service in the Business Architecture View, any relation to it is also not visible in the view. A special case is the Application Component: only the Application

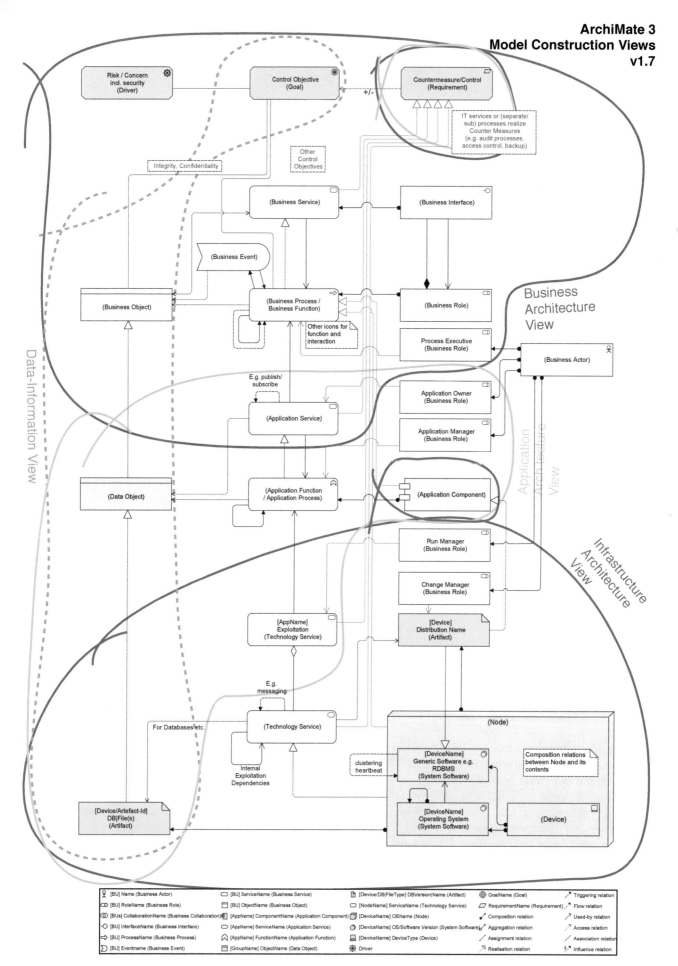

View 340. *ArchiMate 3.0.1 Construction Views (also valid for ArchiMate 2)*

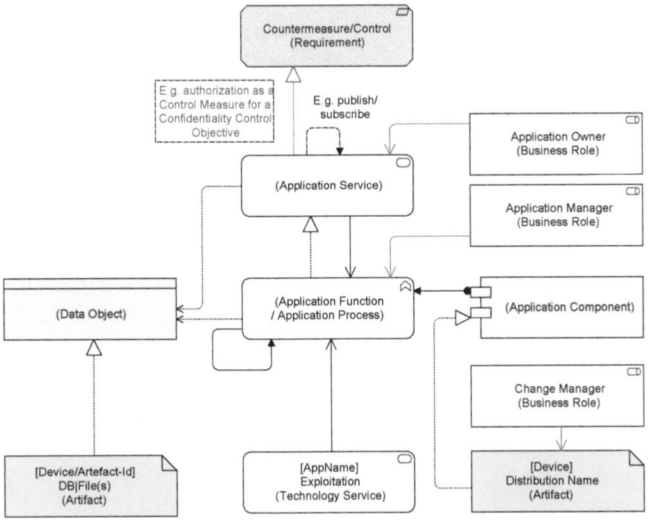

View 341. *Large Model Construction - Application Architecture View*

Components that perform (automated) business behavior are shown.

- The Application Architecture View outlined in yellow (and seen separately in View 341). This view is for modeling the application architecture, but it also includes the 'Exploitation' Technology Service (see Section 15.6 "Infrastructure 'Building Blocks'" on page 69), the 'Application Owner', 'Application Manager' and 'Change Manager' from Section 19.9 "Making it Practical: shortcuts" on page 108) and the Counter Measures (Section 20.3 "Modeling Risks and Controls" on page 111) that the Application Services have to Realize. We have been in discussion about adding the Business Processes that use the Application Services to this view, but you need to keep the number of elements down to keep it manageable. Besides, we had that there because it would make use by the Run Department easier and we decided on a special view for that (see below). Important: we do not use Application Collaboration and Application Interaction.

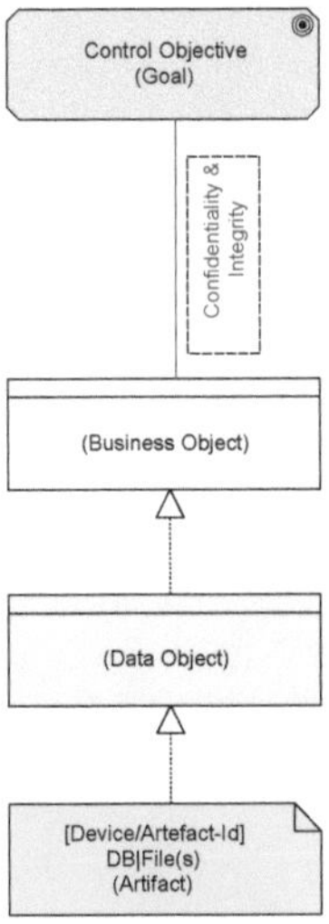

View 343. *Large Model Construction – Data-Information View*

- The Infrastructure Architecture View outlined in brown (and seen separately in View 342). This view contains the infrastructure, the 'Run Manager' from Section 19.9 "Making it Practical: shortcuts" on page 108) and the Counter Measures (Section 20.3 "Modeling Risks and Controls" on page 111) that the Technology Services have to Realize (e.g. Intrusion Detection as a Counter Measure for Control Objective Confidentiality).
- The last view template on View 340 on page 190 is the Data-Information View in green dashed outline (and separately in View 343). This also contains the Confidentiality and Integrity Control Objective for the Business Objects (Section 20.3 "Modeling Risks and Controls" on page 111).

Now, with these views, you can model the entire setup. But that does not mean you have the best views for using the model. As my colleague Jos Knoops experienced, a bit of a specific view about an application helps the IT Service Management department a lot to understand what it is they are actually managing. So he created an application context view for the Run Department which can be seen in View 345 on page 192 as the blue outline (and separately in View 344). I call this the 'Run Manager's Application View'.

Since the 'Run Manager' already knows who he is and what his or her responsibilities are, he or she is not in the view. What is in the view is the basic application setup, which processes it supports and who the most important stakeholders are (Process Executive, Application Owner, Application

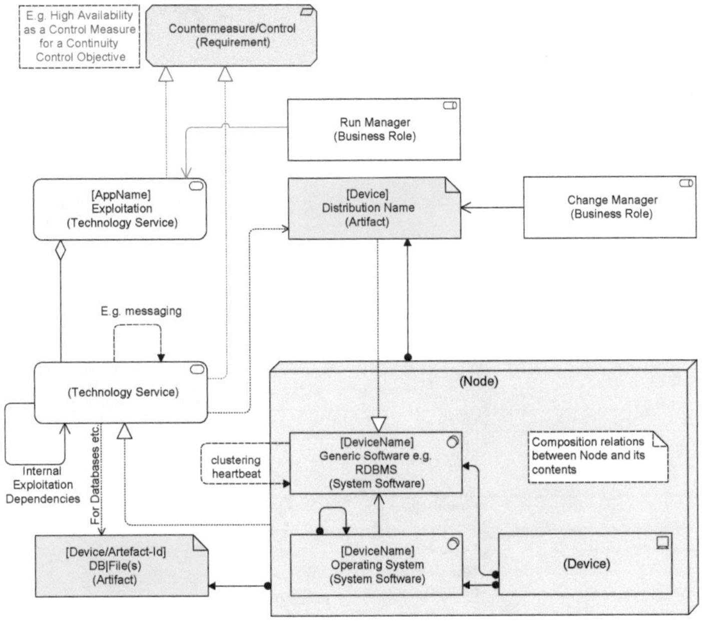

View 342. *Large Model Construction – Infrastructure Architecture View*

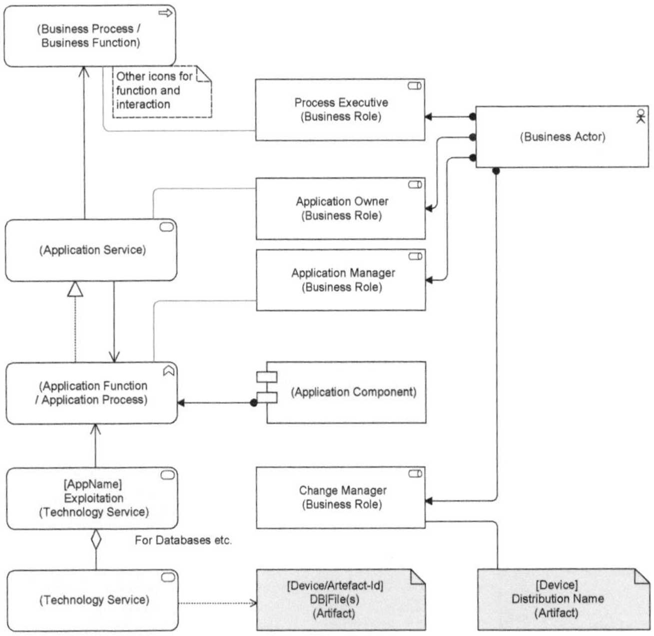

View 344. *Large Model Use – The Run Manager's Application View*

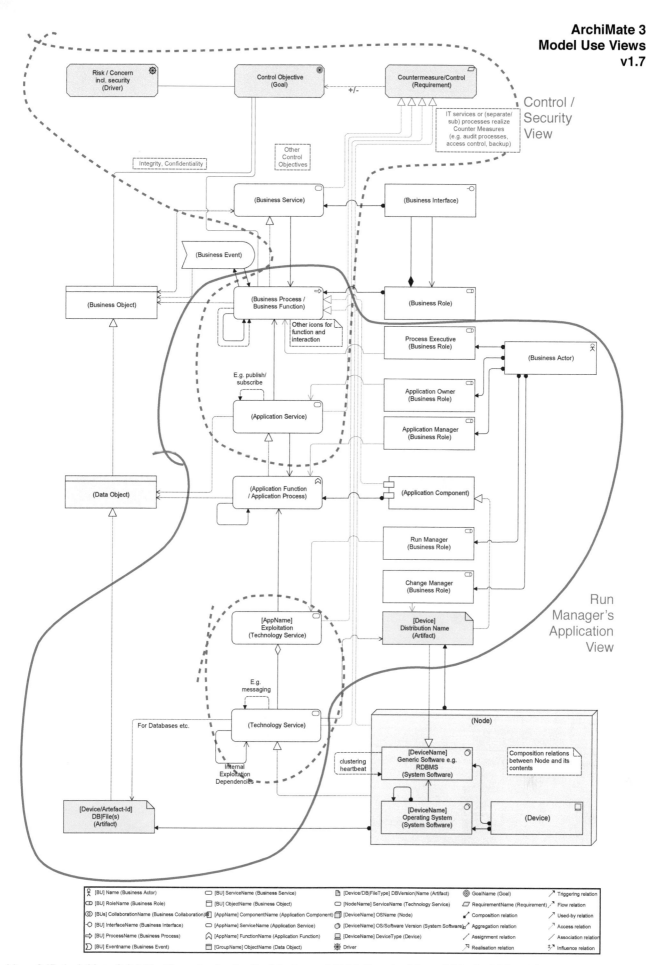

Control /
Security
View

Risk / Concern
incl. security
(Driver)

Control Objective
(Goal)

Countermeasure/Control
(Requirement)

+/-

IT services or (separate/
sub) processes realize
Counter Measures
(e.g. audit processes,
access control, backup)

Integrity, Confidentiality

Other
Control
Objectives

(Business Service)

(Business Interface)

(Business Event)

(Business Object)

(Business Process /
Business Function)

(Business Role)

Other icons for
function and
interaction

Process Executive
(Business Role)

(Business Actor)

E.g. publish/
subscribe

(Application Service)

Application Owner
(Business Role)

Application Manager
(Business Role)

(Data Object)

(Application Function
/ Application Process)

(Application Component)

Run Manager
(Business Role)

Change Manager
(Business Role)

Run
Manager's
Application
View

[AppName]
Exploitation
(Technology Service)

[Device]
Distribution Name
(Artifact)

E.g.
messaging

For Databases etc.

(Technology Service)

(Node)

clustering
heartbeat

[DeviceName]
Generic Software e.g.
RDBMS
(System Software)

Composition relations
between Node and its
contents

Internal
Exploitation
Dependencies

[Device/Artefact-Id]
DB|File(s)
(Artifact)

[DeviceName]
Operating System
(System Software)

(Device)

[BU] Name (Business Actor)	[BU] ServiceName (Business Service)	[Device/DB|FileType] DBVersion|Name (Artifact)	GoalName (Goal)	Triggering relation
[BU] RoleName (Business Role)	[BU] ObjectName (Business Object)	[NodeName] ServiceName (Technology Service)	RequirementName (Requirement)	Flow relation
[BUs] CollaborationName (Business Collaboration)	[AppName] ComponentName (Application Component)	[DeviceName] OSName (Node)	Composition relation	Used-by relation
[BU] InterfaceName (Business Interface)	[AppName] ServiceName (Application Service)	[DeviceName] OS/Software Version (System Software)	Aggregation relation	Access relation
[BU] ProcessName (Business Process)	[AppName] FunctionName (Application Function)	[DeviceName] DeviceType (Device)	Assignment relation	Association relation
[BU] Eventname (Business Event)	[GroupName] ObjectName (Data Object)	Driver	Realisation relation	Influence relation

View 345. *ArchiMate 3.0.1 Use Views: Application Exploitation and Risk& Security (also valid for ArchiMate 2)*

Manager and Change Manager) from Section 19.9 "Making it Practical: shortcuts" on page 108). Here, we do show the actual actors in our model. And we do not show the Counter Measures, because this is in informative contextual view about the application the Run Manager is responsible for keeping running.

Another view type you could add is a view for the Security Officer or the Operational Risk Officer. It is the light purple dashed outline in View 345 on page 192 and it can be seen separately in View 346. A view like this could show the Security or Operational Risk Officer the most important elements related to Risk & Security management from the explanation in View 184 on page 113.

31.1 Exceptional Construction Views

In many cases, the approach with these Construction Views works fine. But in some cases, it is not the best or most pragmatic way. The nice thing about modeling of course is that you can have multiple views with different selections without changing the model (and thus the analyses you can do on the model) at all. I specifically say 'selections', because creating special views with derived relations added to that view adds those relations to the model as well, and as such may damage the usability of the model. But keeping the relations of the patterns exactly the same, different 'cuts' can be made than the Construction Views so far.

One situation where that is very useful is for very large and complex platforms. Such a platform has so many Application Services it provides to the business (and to other systems) that modeling these in single view becomes unwieldy. So, in that case you could separate that single Application Architecture View into multiple Application Architecture Views.

But you can also go outside the standard Construction View setup. Take for instance our ESB. This will often be a very large platform with many, many Application Services. What the ESB does — providing the glue between many systems — leads itself to an alternative approach, an exception.

In the example of View 347 on page 194 (do not worry if it is unreadable because its elements are too small, you're not supposed to be able to read that view), the following was modeled (in ArchiMate 2.1):

- Starting from a Business Process that is executed by a couple of systems and the ESB (top) we created a type of Application Architecture View that contained all the systems that play a role in that process. In this case, on the left a major system, on the right some other systems and external services. This differs from the Application Architecture View, which normally only shows the architecture of a single system;

- Having multiple systems enables us to show how the Data Objects (this example *with* Data Objects differs from the one finally proposed in Section 25.4 "Routing and Orchestrating Middleware (ESB and APIs)" on page 129) and Artifacts play a role in the publications and subscriptions shown.

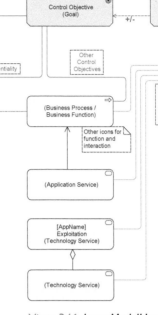

View 346. *LargeModelUse— Risk & Security View*

Such a view might be called an Application Orchestration View. And instead of modeling a pure, but unwieldy, Application Architecture View for the ESB platform, we create an orchestration view for each orchestration, showing multiple applications, but only with the role they play in that orchestration.

One such an orchestration is shown in View 347 on page 194. Maybe 25% may not appear in a normal Application Architecture View. You can imagine that your organization has maybe thirty of these specific orchestrations, or maybe even more and you can immediately recognize that putting the application architecture of the ESB means putting the amount of elements of 25 of these views in a single view. That is way beyond what is reasonable and the standard construction view pattern breaks down.

Our 'ESB Application Construction View', might then be nothing more than links (if your tool supports it) to a series of Application Orchestration Views.

The key thing to remember is that you can design as many types of construction views as you like, but you need to keep an eye on:

- Do the views become unwieldy (too complex for easy maintenance)?

- Can you minimize repetition of model fragments (also an effect on maintenance, change something in one and you have to change all the occurrences of that model fragment wherever it appears)?

- Do not create new model patterns, only view-specific model-fragment selections.

For certain large and/or complex parts of your environment, blindly using the basic construction views may make life unnecessary difficult. One should of course never follow any guideline blindly, certainly not mine anyway...

Be pragmatic.

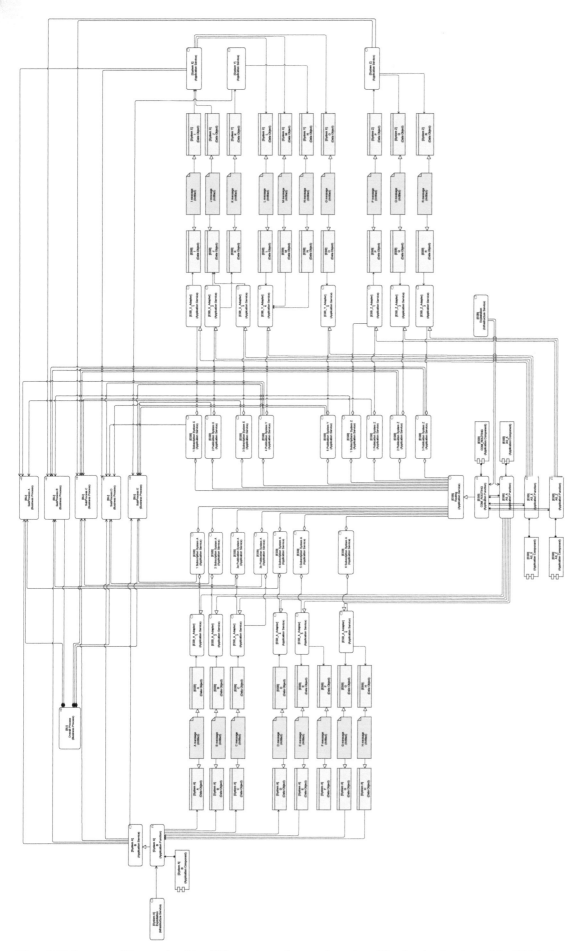

View 347. *Automated Process involving ESB, showing only a small portion of Application Services of the ESB (adapted from a view created by colleague Joost Melsen)*

32. Model Maintenance

A model, especially a large 'current state' model requires proper maintenance. For instance, you need to be kept up to date with changes. In our case, this for instance means that any change that the infrastructure people make in their tool is automatically sent to the Enterprise Architecture department for maintenance. This must be so, because in our case, the CMDB was again fed from our ArchiMate model, so our model *had* to be correct. This feedback loop keeps the basic infrastructure information up to date. Here again, we meet Uncle Ludwig: through the link to the help desk, our Current State model is *used* and therefore acquires *meaning*.

For projects the situation is a bit different. Here the project first should have a project start architecture (PSA) that contains (the most relevant parts of) what the project is going to deliver. When the project finishes (generally, you can start with this when you are at the user acceptance testing phase, you make the model of the PSA complete and when the results of the project go 'live', you include the model of the PSA in your overall current state model.

When things change, you need a basic procedure for change. Here is the one we used when creating our first model of 'the (entire) enterprise itself'.

- Parts of the model, as shown in Construction Views had a state:

  * *Work in Progress;*

  * *Draft;*

  * *Final;*

  * *Erroneous;*

  * *Research.*

Normally, Construction Views progressed in a cycle: they were created by an architect and during that phase they had the *Work in Progress* state. When the modeling was done, the view moved to the *Draft* state and were checked. This validation was done on two aspects:

- Is the view content-wise correct? You check that with people who can vouch for the correctness. E.g. business people for the business architecture, infrastructure managers for the infrastructure architecture, etc.

- Is the view properly modeled according to the chosen patterns and guidelines (e.g. style)? It is generally the lead architect who has to vouch for this.

When the view was checked on both accounts, it moved to the *Final* state. When something had to change again (e.g. an error had been found, a change had to be made), the first thing to do was to move the view again from *Final* to *Work in Progress*.

We also kept some views in an *Erroneous* state. These were known to be wrong but are currently not worked on. And we had some *Research* views, which generally were temporary. Remember; each view here stands for a part of the model.

There is one caveat with all these views, and especially with the Construction & Use Views of the previous section. You can't have too many or maintenance becomes increasingly difficult. Tooling (see Chapter "Tooling" on page 219) generally supports that if you change the label of an element in one view, it gets changed automatically in another (though label layout may suffer). If you remove a relation between elements in one view, you might get warned it appears in other views. But if you add an element or relation that should appear in multiple views, you generally are on your own: the tool will not add the missing relations o other views where both elements appear. Which means that the more views there are where a certain elements must appear, the more work changing a view becomes. Also, keeping a view easy on the eye (HVS, see Section 14 "Aesthetics (Style)" on page 57) sometimes means a lot of work. Add one little element and you sometimes have to layout 20 others and all their relations. Providing good readable views requires hand work (and hard work) and a good eye for layout, so prepare yourself. And don't expect a tool to be able to do this for you. Even the best tools in this area cannot produce the required cleanliness and organization of layout as View 79 on page 58 illustrates (to be fair, the changes in element sizes in that view were added by hand).

Finally: one important suggestion: Clean Up! On a regular basis, check your model for elements that are unused (do not appear in any view and are also not children of elements that are used in a view. We use a script in our tool to do this. And of course, when IT gets decommissioned, make sure you remove it from your model. In our setup that means simply removing the views and then running the unused elements script.

32.1 The Satellite Model Approach

Sometimes, you need certain details for analyses in certain cases, but most of the time those details just get in the way. Take for instance the following situation:

- Your company employs a Scheduler platform in which many activities have been automated. For instance, IT-maintenance jobs, or more to the point: some daily actions on your data like updating from external feeds or creating reports;

- Such schedules generally consist of a main (parent) action (in this example called the 'Flow') which is started at some time of day, and all kind of steps (in this example called the 'Jobs') that are executed in some complicated order when the parent runs;

- A Job is executed on a system (e.g. a server) where it may start an application that actually does something (like creating that report or importing into a system that data another Job has just fetched).

Data-intensive organizations may sometimes have hundreds or thousands of Flows, each consisting of tens of Jobs. Many of these Jobs in turn use several applications that exists in your landscape, the fact of which is sometimes hidden deep in the whole scheduling setup.

Personally, I want my main 'Current State Architecture' (CSA) model to be navigable graphically. That means that my CSA model will have construction views for all applications that are used. If I then publish my model, the organization has access to a usable overview of the whole jungle of dependencies that make up a modern Business-IT landscape. And what is more: I can run analyses when I need to. If I want to replace that large system, an analysis of the CSA will show me where this application or its data is used.

But in the example above, the Jobs are more like application architecture, the inside of the Flow, which is the application, which in turn requires the runtime environment of the scheduling platform. An example can be seen in View 348

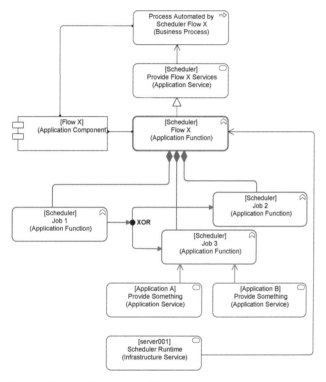

View 348. *Actual structure of Application Services being used by the Jobs of a Scheduler Flow.*

(ignore the colors for now). A very simple Flow is depicted. It contains two Jobs that each use a different application from which only the Application Service is shown here. Note that we have modeled the Scheduler as we did in Section 17 "An Example from the Real World" on page 87. The Scheduler is a *platform*, the Flow is the Application Component that is deployed on that platform. The Jobs are the components that make up the internal structure of the Flow.

If you have hundreds of Flows and you have tens of Jobs on average in each Flow, you are talking about thousands of Application Functions. That could be modeled, of course, if the Flows are not very volatile, but a main issue here is that you are duplicating the maintenance of information. How the Jobs make up the Flows has already been documented in

the Scheduler platform. Keeping those two in sync is problematic.

But if you can export the information from your Scheduler system and import it into your EA modeling tool, you may be able to use the information directly. Adding these thousands of Jobs, however, into your CSA means you have to make them navigable, which is a lot of EA layout work (and re-work if the structure is volatile). Besides, at the EA level, nobody is interested in those details.

Here, the trick of using a Satellite Model comes in. Creating a Satellite Model works like this:

- you clone your main CSA model;

- you import the details of the structure you need. In this case, that would be the whole Flows/Jobs structure. Example: the blue and red items in View 348;

- you add relations (by hand) between the elements that were already in your CSA model and the imported details. Example: the orange Serving relations in View 348;

- you make sure your Flow's and Job's Application Function have an ID that is *unique across models* (e.g. add that to its properties). A possible candidate is the ID it has in the Scheduler system, but watch out for what editing on that side (e.g. modification by delete/add) can break.

There is no need to import the dynamic structure that is available in the Scheduler system (the pink relations) into your Satellite Model.

What you then do is set up a couple of synchronizations:

- From Scheduler system to Satellite Model: import Flows and their Jobs. Name changes can be carried over automatically if there is an independent ID;

- From Satellite Model to CSA Model: roll-up all the relations to the Jobs and turn them into relations to the parent Flow. This can be seen in View 349 where the Serving relations between Application Service and Jobs have been turned into Serving relations between the Application Services and the parent Flow;

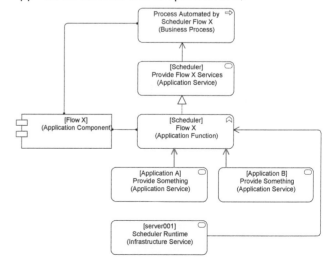

View 349. *Rolled-up view of Application Services Serving the parent Scheduler Flow of View 348*

- From CSA Model to Satellite Model: add/change all non-Scheduler elements.

You also need to set up a reconciliation. Once in a while you produce a report from the Satellite Model that contains the relations between Jobs and applications and this needs to be checked by the Scheduler people for correctness and completeness. Any 'breaks' need to be repaired in the Satellite Model.

Two final remarks. First, the relations used in the roll-up of View 349 on page 196 cannot be derived in the official ArchiMate sense of 'derivation' from the relations in View 348 on page 196. This illustrates a point made in 12.6 "On the limitations of derived relations" on page 51. Second, the relation between the 'model' in the Scheduler system and what you want in your CSA is an example of the fact that you will always have multiple models of the same reality in your organization. More on this issue will be said in section 37 "Multiple Models of a Single Reality" on page 219.

Reflections

Reflections

33. The Role of ArchiMate in Enterprise Architecture

ArchiMate started out as a university/business collaboration with the idea to create a modeling language for the elements that make up an enterprise. This has, in my view, resulted in a very usable and practical Core ArchiMate language which in my experience has been tested to the extreme for that goal and passed with flying colors, resulting in a ~100k elements and relations model/satellite Current State: a true 'model of the enterprise', maintainable with relatively little effort and in sync with other 'models of the enterprise'.

One of the key insights during that development came when we had to address the question "How do we model the owner of an Application?", the answer of which led to the 'Primary/Secondary/Tertiary Architecture' approach in section 19 "Secondary and Tertiary Architecture" on page 104. The main insight behind that approach is that *everything* that happens in your organization is part of the 'enterprise' in Enterprise Architecture. Not just your primary processes, but also HR, finance, IT development, etc.. When you model a business, you may leave some out (it is all a matter of there being a business case to spend the energy on modeling), but even if you do not model them, they remain part of that enterprise. Even your activities in EA are part of the enterprise. There needs to be a business case for them, some advantage they give you or some pressing need. EA then seems special, because when EA is seen as part of the enterprise, you get the situation that EA is the activity that models itself. But take a step back and you will see that this is not such a special situation: the finance department will also handle their own finances, the HR department will also do their HR-work for the people in the HR department, the IT department has its own IT to develop and maintain.

Looking at it that way, it would, in fact, be very strange if a purported EA modeling language like ArchiMate would *not* already be able to capture the secondary, tertiary, etc. activities in an enterprise. Which then begs the question: why were the Motivation aspect and the Implementation & Migration layer added to ArchiMate?

Those extensions seem to stem from a specific — I would say 'classic' — approach to 'doing EA': working with principles and guidelines and working with 'As-Is' and 'Future-State' architectures with 'gaps' that direct your projects and programs intended to change 'As-Is' into 'Future-State'.

There are many definitions of the term 'Enterprise Architecture'. The one I like is:

Enterprise Architecture is about understanding all of the different elements that go to make up the enterprise and how those elements interrelate

from the Institute For Enterprise Architecture Developments. Not that it means I concur with everything of that institute, it is just a definition I encountered and agree with. Many other definitions exist, from MIT, the US Government, etc. The one from the ArchiMate Foundation was: "A coherent whole of principles, methods, and models that are used in the design and realization of an enterprise's organizational structure, business processes, information systems, and infrastructure". Here you see a more detailed role for EA. EA consists of 'models, methods and principles' that are 'being used in the design and realization' of the enterprise. Here EA is not about the 'elements of the enterprise' and their relations (in other words about the 'design (of the enterprise) itself'), but it is something at a more abstract level: EA *steers* 'design (and realization)' (of the enterprise). The ANSI/IEEE Std 1471-2000 standard, which is most often used, combines both in its definition of Enterprise Architecture:

The fundamental organization of a system, embodied in its components, their relationships to each other and the environment, and the principles governing its design and evolution

It says more or less:

- Architecture is the design of 'the thing in itself' as in 'the architecture of a building' or 'the architecture of an enterprise'. This is sometimes called 'operational space';

- Architecture is also the *process* of *creating* the design of the 'thing in itself', as in 'the way a building is designed' or 'the way an enterprise is designed'. This is sometimes called 'architectural space'.

Now, 'architects of the physical' do not confuse the two. If they model, they model 'the thing in itself'. They model buildings, bridges, airports, etc. Their models do not also contain the 'principles' or 'method' of modeling, though they normally will in some way document requirements (what the future owner wants) and constraints (legal, physical) and the like. And of course, the major stakeholder's signature should be on the contract or the architect does not get paid. Enterprise Architects, however, are more often seen to model 'aspects of designing' (principles and such) than the design itself. There is of course a vision behind a design.

Enterprise Architecture has 'fuzzy edges' which are useful to include in your 'models of the enterprise (to be)' such as the risks and control objectives that were modeled in 20.3 "Modeling Risks and Controls" on page 111. These are indeed not 'elements of the enterprise' per se, they are often vague, abstract environmental aspects of the enterprise. But they still are not elements of 'architectural space', they still are elements of design: the 'model of the thing in itself'.

I think modeling 'architectural space', or in other words modeling 'the principles governing its design and evolution' *in combination with* 'the fundamental organization of a system, embodied in its components, their relationships to each other and the environment' ('the thing in itself') often has limited practical value. The relation between the two is far too complex, volatile and fuzzy to be *modeled* adequately and usefully. It works only in 'toy models', little examples often used to explain a method, but it does not scale well. The reasons and intentions for anything as complex as the setup of an enterprise just cannot be modeled with a couple of simple concepts and when you use hundreds it becomes unusable and thus meaningless as well. The assumption that this is useful in practice has a lot in common with the (failed) assumptions behind AI on digital computers. It may be one of the reasons too why EA generally is not seen as very valuable by the business and too detached from reality.

Methods that do not scale well are —sadly enough — a common aspect for methods that result from academic institutions. ArchiMate is an exception (most of it scales rather well), but maybe that is because not just academia designed it, but businesses were closely involved and the result was quite something different than the founders envisioned originally: they were thinking of a language that was also a dynamic system, where you could animate the architecture instead of just draw pictures, hence the name ArchiMate (for Architecture-Animate).

Having said that, one should not be too principled against guidelines. After all, the Enterprise Architect's position differs substantially from that of the architect of physical structures. For one, the physical architecture process is part of an old and well-established and relatively slowly changing human activity with often very clear and concrete goals. The enterprise on the other hand, is confronted with huge amounts of freedom (certainly at the start of change initiatives) and a lot of volatility. This leads to a deeply felt need for stability, in which guidelines may play an essential role. But turning guidelines into principles comes with substantial risks, a subject that is outside of the scope of this book but has been discussed in extenso in my other book *Chess and the Art of Enterprise Architecture*.

34. Why Model? (And for Whom?)

34.1 Two modeling purposes

Though this book has been written mostly from the perspective of large-scale modeling, or modeling that is supposed to be related to large-scale models, there are in fact two purposes for modeling that can be supported with ArchiMate:

1. Modeling so the resulting model can be used for automated analysis;

2. Modeling to explain something to humans.

The first one is the main focus of this book, as it puts the most restrictions on your patterns. You need to use a minimum set or otherwise your automated (algorithmic) analysis becomes unfeasible. The second one gives you more freedom, but it assumes that the person reading your views/diagrams (the actual communication channel) understands ArchiMate well, and not only that, given the vagueness and ambiguity that ArchiMate here and there exhibits (see for instance section 25.2 "Who is Serving Whom Anyway?" on page 128), it requires you to have a common 'style'.

34.2 Better Insight

When I first carefully tried to encourage my organization to use ArchiMate*, instead of the 'free-format MS Visio or — ugh! — MS Powerpoint drawings, I let people free to use either†. At one point, an architect for a project came with his

solution architecture to me for review, and in it, there was a diagram that looked a bit like View 350. The dashed arrows represented data flows.

From an ArchiMate perspective one thing immediately stands out: There is a 'flow' relation between Database

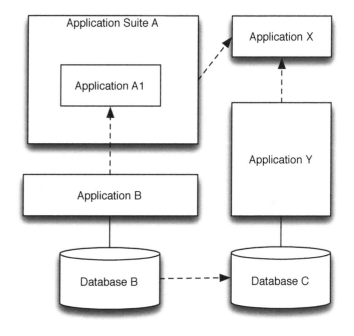

View 350. *How an architect created a diagram without ArchiMate*

---

* Which is funny as they were one of the founding business partners of the ArchiMate language.

† In fact, I have never forced ArchiMate on anyone.

B and Database C, but in ArchiMate, both are probably modeled as passive elements. And you cannot draw such a relation between passive elements in ArchiMate. So, my immediate question was: "What does that arrow between the databases represent?". And he answered: "Well, there is a regular extract from Database B to Database C.". "Ah," I said, "So, who *performs* that extract, then?". And he replied: "Oh, right. The application that performs the extraction is missing." Often, when I try to model something in Archi-Mate and I cannot do it, it means I am forgetting something. Using a stricter grammar helps you in being precise and identifying omissions.

34.3 Overrated and Underrated

Why was ArchiMate invented in the first place? The original research document that defines the ArchiMate language — *Concepts for Architectural Descriptions* — says this about it:

> Because architectures are often complex and hard to understand, architects need ways to express these architectures as clearly as possible: both for their own understanding and for communication with other stakeholders, such as system developers, end-users and managers. To date, there is no standard language for describing architectures; they are often described in informal pictures that lack a well-defined meaning. This leads to misunderstandings, and makes it very difficult to provide tools for visualisation and analysis of these architectures.

Marc Lankhorst also makes it clear in the Preface of *Enterprise Architecture at Work*: Each stakeholder requires specific information presented in an accessible way, hence for both engineers and decision makers. ArchiMate has been designed to fill those gaps. But if you look at actual real-world use of the language, such as presented in white papers, examples (ArchiSurance for instance), conference proceedings and so forth, the attention has been mostly on the gap towards the decision makers. ArchiMate has been sold as the language that makes it easier for decision makers to come to grips with the complexity of the architecture of their enterprise. Also because really large scale complex models are hard to use during simple presentations, the message has often been one with overly simplified examples.

Now, my experience is, this modeling 'language', with its own slightly more strict element and relation forms, does not automatically provide that easy communication at all. I know no enterprise architect who uses a modeling language (UML, ArchiMate, etc.) that really makes communication with the decision makers easier. The only language that comes close is the graphical side of BPMN, as its visual basis can be used in a way (swim lanes with activities) that is pretty intuitive for the non-modellers among us. But, go into BPMN detail with complex exceptions and gateways, and then too everybody but the specialist is lost. The decision makers tend not to agree (not immediately, in any case) with the enthusiast enterprise architects when these tout the superiority of their nice modeling language nor does the rest of the organization when confronted with the architect's love of abstractions.

So, the most effective way of communicating to the decision makers is often still simple graphics with those ambiguous lines and boxes. Adding ArchiMate's structure to simple graphics adds little for management and is capable of complicating a lot. The structure and logic ArchiMate brings adds to the message and it becomes more complex . Yes, some ambiguity is removed and it enables analytical use (except that this requires a modeling rigour that is hardly ever mentioned and tooling that supports it), but at a cost. The decision makers actually don't mind the ambiguity and are not interested in analytical thought. ArchiMate offers them something they neither want nor need. It is here, that in my experience ArchiMate is often overrated.

Now, there is an obvious place where rigor, structure and logic really help: when the situation to model becomes very large and complex and you still want to get to grips with it. Then, using structured approaches (especially if applied in a disciplined fashion) helps. But those are models that are definitely not for management. They are complex instruments that require a high level of 'engineering attitude' to set up and that can be used by those actually working in the detailed reality of those complex domains. This is an approach that is unpopular with many enterprise architects, especially those that constantly search for ways to make their subject matter simpler so it can be managed and communicated more easily. "We're not interested in details", they say, "those are not important for our strategy". Sadly for them, though, details often matter. As Confucius said: "people stumble not over mountains, they stumble over molehills". Just ignoring details often leads to disasters, one needs a way to find and address relevant details. ArchiMate in itself is not going to help you here, as it cannot tell you which details to model and which to ignore. But using ArchiMate, you at least have a language that is actually can be used to model the full enterprise complexity in a powerful way. In the immense complexity of our real enterprises is where a language like ArchiMate actually can really shine, not when communicating rather simple ideas to management. And it is here, that in my experience ArchiMate is often underrated.

Sydney Harris once wrote:

> In every field of inquiry, it is true that all things should be made as simple as possible – but no simpler. (And for every problem that is muddled by over-complexity, a dozen are muddled by over-simplifying).

This is often attributed to Albert Einstein and generally only the first sentence is quoted. I have especially found that seldom mentioned sentence about over-simplification very true in the real life of an Enterprise Architect, especially when you analyse why some projects or programmes fail, go massively over time and budget limits and so forth. ArchiMate — as a way to handle complexity and large scale better that loosely drawn over-simplistic visuals — can really help in fighting that aspect. It is, however, not something you can do by letting a consultant come over for a couple of months, you need to make good modeling part of your foundation of doing Enterprise Architecture.

35. Using Abstractions

35.1 The price one pays

We architects *love* abstraction. Abstraction makes the nitty-gritty and complex details disappear. Abstraction makes the unmanageable manageable. Our business colleagues also love it when we produce abstractions. It makes our end products easier to digest and gives the illusion that the complex is not that complex at all. In ArchiMate, you can do both, which means that — apart from the precision-like modeling that you for instance do when building 'current-state' descriptive models — you can use the ArchiMate language in a more 'loose' setup, e.g. when designing a landscape top-down.

For instance, when designing, if you have a Business Process that requires the services of an application, you generally start with defining that application service in terms of 'what the business needs' and then you design how this service will be realized by one or more applications. Or, to stay completely at the business layer, you define the Business Service you provide to your clients in terms of what your clients' processes need and then move down to define what processes are required to provide that service. A simple example can be seen in View 351. Here, we have recognized that our clients may want to ask us questions. So, we have defined the 'Answering' Business Service that provides these answers. We have decided answers may be asked by phone and by mail and ArchiMate supports that a service is exposed through multiple interfaces, which is useful in a situation like this. In our example, both are Business Interfaces that the client may use if it wants to use the (generic) 'Answering' Business Service.

Having concluded we need an 'answering' Business Service, we turn to the question how this Business Service is to be Realized and we define two Business Processes that are performed by different roles with different skills. The Call Agent performs the 'Answer Client Phone Inquiry' process through the 'Phone' Business Interface. Something like it happens on the mail side. This can be seen in View 352.

So, we have *a single* service that is defined top-down from how it is needed. It could be considered a collection of two services realized by two processes, one for answering by mail and one for answering by phone. (If they were not separable as processes, we would have to use an Interaction instead and a Collaboration to perform it instead). If you look bottom-up, the 'Answer Client Mail Inquiry' Business Process for instance must Realize its own Business Service (Answering by Mail). A process, after all, is a causally related set of behaviors that is intended to produces something. That is true of the process-

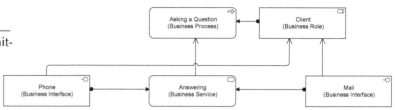

View 351. *Two interfaces for one Business Service*

es in this view too. But we can choose not to model those details, we *abstracted*.

So, ArchiMate's definition of a service allows it to be exposed via multiple interfaces as is shown in View 353.

View 353. *A Business Service exposed via two Business Interfaces*

But its definition of an interface also allows it to expose multiple services. Adding to our example, suppose we have not only an 'Answering' service but also an 'Order Placement' service, which also is available to our customers via mail (we are a mail order company with a phone help desk). This is shown in View 354.

View 354. *A Business Interface exposes two Business Services*

From a management perspective, it is quite a nice simplification, these two Business Services that we provide through that single 'Mail' Business Interface. But a problem lurks here. If we add the processes for both services, we get View 355 on page 203, and if we add the roles we get View 356 on page 203.

As both roles are exposed via the Mail interface, ArchiMate expects the Composition relation between role and the interface. But that leads to something that my tool (and any other as far as I know) accepts, but that is illegal in ArchiMate itself: two Composite relations to the same child. (To be honest, I think there could be reasons to relax this restriction, as I describe in section 36.9 "Allow multiple parents in a Composition" on page 215) in the section where I describe my proposed improvements of ArchiMate.

Now, I do not show this as a critique on ArchiMate. It is to illustrate that as abstraction always leaves

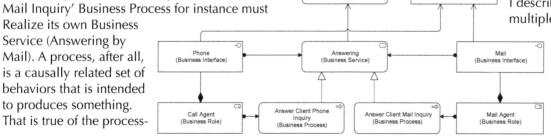

View 352. *The Answering Business Service is Realized by two independent Business Processes, one for answers by mail and one for answers by phone*

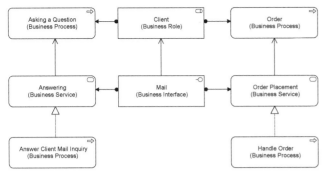

View 355. *Two independent Business Processes, Realizing their Services and exposing them through a single Business Interface*

Technology Service that allows other System Software, such as an FTP-server to run.

I would model the process either as the 'FTP Server (System Software)' element or the 'FTP Server (System Software)' element together with its (possibly Nested) Assigned 'FTP Server Functionality (Technology Function)' element.

something out, it can lead to problems. There are many such potential problems. It depends on your intended use of a model if you run into one of them. For a relatively small Future-State like 'broad strokes' model, it is probably not a problem. For a detailed, used for analyses, Current-State or Project model it is definitely risky. Sooner than later you run into the problem caused by missing information.

I am still leaving out a lot of detail that I could also model (see for instance section 15.2 "A Basic TI Pattern: A Database" on page 63 for a lot of irrelevant detail from an enterprise architecture perspective). So, I would say that it is illustrated that you can go to insane level of details in your ArchiMate modeling. Or in other words: apart from illustrative purposes in a book like this, I guess you would never do this in real life. There is an end to the meaningfulness of 'ever more detail', you can kill your modeling endeavor that way. Choosing the right level of detail/abstraction for the job is one of the main reasons why this is more an art than a science.

This is especially true when you're at the start phase of a project. It is not feasible to design all the details in advance.

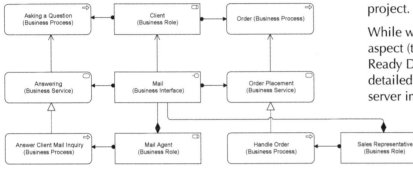

View 356. *Business Roles added to View 355*

While we're on the subject, View 357 also shows another aspect (that briefly was mentioned in Section 28.2 "DevOps Ready Data Center (DRDC)" on page 151): you can model detailed and abstract concurrently. Suppose you have a server image that you can roll out for every FTP Server you need. Some sort of fixed setup. You could model this as the Artifacts in this view. There will be some source image somewhere, the 'FTP Server Software Image Source Instance (Artifact)' that resides somewhere. When a new server is created, this image is used to create a copy on that device. In View 357 this copy is called

ArchiMate has enough freedom to be used to make models with a lot of abstraction, and as such it also supports an approach to Enterprise Architecture design that sees services as abstractions defined top-down (from the needs of those that use the service). In fact, such thinking was an important aspect of the design process of ArchiMate in the first place. But ArchiMate also supports a more specific and precise use that is useful for creating precise 'current-state' models. ArchiMate's power of expression is good for both.

35.2 Too much detail?

If you run the 'ps' command in Unix/Linux or if you look at the processes in Window's TaskManager, you see all these processes that run. How should these be modeled?

Just to show that you can actually do this in ArchiMate: have a look at View 357. Here I made an attempt at modeling the processes that run in an operating system. It shows that the 'Operating System (System Software)' Realizes (indirectly) a

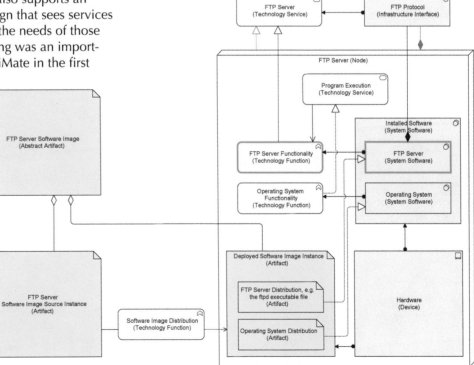

View 357. *An attempt at modeling the processes inside the operating system*

'Deployed Software Image Instance (Artifact)'. Now you can also model an element that stands for all the 'standard FTP server instances. As these are real copies, using Specialization is not proper. But you can put them into a collection which is a sort of abstract Artifact. This is also shown. 'Software Image Distribution (Technology Function)' is of course part of your secondary architecture (see 19.5 "Secondary Architecture: System Exploitation" on page 105).

On the server side, I tend to model the real world, that is, only the elements that we need. That has an underlying reason: servers tend to be pretty specific beasts (unless you are of course in the business of Google, Amazon or any of the infrastructure-in-the-cloud providers). But in *your* business, chances are that your servers all need their own specific setup. I discussed this with ArchiMate modelers from another company once who started out with modeling Server Configurations instead of Server Instances. They ended up with so many different configurations that in the end they would have been better off had they started with instances in the first place.

But for desktops, the situation is different. Generally, organizations use standardized basic desktops, with maybe a limited amount of specific configuration.

In that case, I think it is senseless to keep to the dictum that you want to model as close as possible in the real world, not even in a detailed 'Current State Architecture' model. Here I would suggest only modeling the specific 'configurations', like a 'standard desktop' or 'Trader PC', C# Developer PC, etc.

This page intentionally also not left blank

Discussing ArchiMate

36. Proposed Improvements for ArchiMate 3

I might rightly be called a fanboy of ArchiMate, but that doesn't mean I am without criticism. I had a whole lot of criticism on the ArchiMate 2.1 standard. Much of that has been fixed in ArchiMate 3 (though not always to my exact liking), but in general the ArchiMate 3 standard is much less sloppy and much better put together than any previous version*. It did mean that it was a lot of work coming up with this Edition III, as working around limitations in 2.1 and not having improvements of version 3 turned out to have been influential in the creation of the patterns in Edition II. That experience makes me wary. There is a price to pay when my suggestions are accepted :-).

36.1 Fragmentation of element types

The standard says:

> The most important design restriction on the language is that it has been explicitly designed to be as small as possible

And while the standard has remained economical with relations (only the influence relation has been added since the original report published in 2007, and relations are often coopted for distinct meanings), the same cannot be said about element types. There has been a rather unchecked growth, a doubling in fact, from the original ArchiMate to version 3.0.1 today. Some of this is unavoidable as new aspects and domains have been added, but not all. The new aspects and domains have all brought their own separate world to ArchiMate, and that is *by definition* questionable. After all, all the elements that have been introduced are part of *the* reality of an organization. Hence, in principle they should in one way or another have to be part of what I have called in Section 6 "An ArchiMate Map" on page 17 'the enterprise itself'. Good examples of such disjunctnesses are:

- The Assessment element from the Motivation aspect represents something that has a real counterpart in the organization, e.g. a report or even a mail message. As

such, it is a Business Object that is created (Access) by some sort of business behavior. The same can be said of other elements from Motivation, such as Goal, Requirement/Constraint, Principle, Stakeholder and so forth. They don't exist in a universe outside the organization, they are part and parcel of it;

- The Work Package from the Implementation and Migration layer is almost indistinguishable from a Business Process. But it cannot use applications, nor can it Access data or material;

- Any Business Role is by definition also a Stakeholder. But we cannot model for instance one Business Role Influencing another.

View 358 on page 208 shows a few relations in red that make a lot of sense, but that are not allowed. The blue one is allowed since ArchiMate 3. The situation is actually worse than it looks. The Motivation aspect uses a lot of Associations as formal direct relations. The fact that Association is allowed between all elements hides thus some of the fragmentation because there is a loophole, i.e. I can Associate not just a Stakeholder with a Goal, I can also Associate a Business Role with it, but not because the metamodel is particularly good, but because there is this general rule. This is shown in green.

36.2 Remove historical baggage

Related to this is the growing amount of historical baggage that ArchiMate carries. The designers are apparently very careful to strive for maximum backward compatibility, but the result is a situation that I would label as 'technical debt'.

A good example is the Assignment from Device to System Software. When it was introduced as part of the original ArchiMate, System Software was positioned as the *behavior* of a Device. That made it perfectly logical to use Assignment between the two to model 'performing behaviour' just as

---

* With the exception of the somewhat slipshod version 3.0 which contained the better (though not yet fully complete) foundation, but also many contradictions, omissions and glaring errors, such that it was technically unusable as it forbade even many foundational relations.

between Busi-
ness Role and
Business Process
for example.

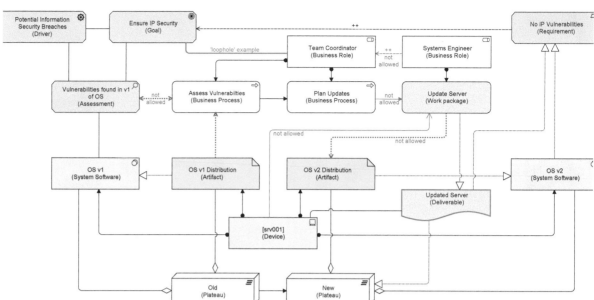

View 358. *Various examples of real relations we cannot do in ArchiMate*

But in ArchiMate 2, inernal Technology behavior (e.g. Technology Function) was introduced to model the infrastructure behavior of infra-structure active elements such as a Device (or any metamod-el-Specialization of Node). The old Assignment was kept and (in part implicitly) redefined as 'deployment'. But not completely. For instance, if I add a special purpose card to a device, isn't that deployment (from Device to Device) too? I can deploy System Software on System Software. Why can't I deploy an Application Component on System Software? Note: if we change something about Realization and/or derivation, this could all be removed and become derivable (see below).

Location was added in ArchiMate 2 as a sort of specialized grouping without the generic Grouping we have now. Then in ArchiMate 3 we got Facility and Grouping as real ele-ments. There is serious overlap between these three. Would we have added Location to ArchiMate 3 if it hadn't been already in ArchiMate 2 (as a 'fix' for not having Grouping)?

Representation has been in ArchiMate from the start, mainly as a means to model printed information (the PDF example has always overlapped with Artifact). Given that we now have Material as well as Artifact, Representation can go.

Path and Communication/Distribution Network may be repositioned in a cleaner way as well. Why aren't they (abstract) Nodes which offer Technology Services through Technology Interfaces? Why do they 'serve' via Associations? Do we really need them? We have Flow!

36.3 Issues with abstractions

There is in my view a many-pronged confusion in ArchiMate over abstraction.

Section 7.17 "Abstractions" on page 31 already gave us an overview of the many ways we can model ab-stractions in ArchiMate. The standard adds to this in Section 3.6, when it (amongst other things) also tells us that we may use behavioral elements as abstractions as they are 'imple-mentation-independent' (which then frankly is ignored in the rest of the standard). Then we have the complicated role of Specialization as described in Section 8.4 "Specialization in the Meta-model" on page 34 and Section 8.5 "The Spe-cialization Relation in an Actual Model" on page 35.

Ignoring the — from the perspective of the rest of the stan-dard — confusing suggestion that the behavior of an active element is an abstraction of the 'implementation' (instead of simply the behavior performed by the 'acting element'), and ignoring the issues surrounding Specialization, we are left with the following abstractions in ArchiMate:

- *Identity*[*]. When one element is an abstraction of anoth-er, the two elements are both a representation of *the same thing* at a different 'level'. We see this in Archi-Mate as the TOGAF logical/physical Realizations within the application and technology layer. We also see this in the Realizations from the passive elements (the Business Object or the Application Component or the System Software represents *the same thing* as the Artifact, just in a different layer or aspect). We also see this in the Realizations of core interfaces and behavioral elements to other layers, and when a Deliverable Realizes a core element;

- *Creation*. When one element is an abstraction of another it means that one element creates another element that does *not represent the same* thing. We see this when internal behavior (function, process) Realizes external behavior (service)[†], when a core element Realizes a Re-quirement, or when a Work Package Realizes a Deliver-able or a core element;

[*]   When multiple elements Realize a single other element, the word 'identity' requires an explanation. All the identities that Realize the target are together the one identity that is Realized. We will not take those subtleties into consideration in the story as they only complicate but not really change this analysis in a fundamental sense.
[†]   Though I know from private communication that seeing service as independent from 'internal' behavior (based on the idea that a service is a sort of 'interaction' that cannot be seen independent from the behavior of the service consumer) was the view of (some of) the original ArchiMate designers, it can nowhere be found in the text of ArchiMate, from the original docment to today. See also Section 36.5.

- *Collection*. The Realization of Strategy elements is harder to pin down. Close to Identity: it can be experienced as collections of a sort of the elements that Realize them. Note: currently, Aggregation is used to create a network or path from underlying infrastructure. It is quite enticing to see Path and Network as abstractions of that underlying infrastructure.

It is confusing that Realization is used for non-Identity abstractions. If something is created, the Access relation is more appropriate. If we are collecting/grouping something, Aggregation is more appropriate.

36.4 Issue with Metamodel-Specialization

Metamodel-Specialization should in my opinion be seen as a strictly one-way relation. If element type System Software is a Specialization of element type Node, then System Software is a Node *but a Node is not (always) a System Software*. Hence, if Node can (as all elements can) Compose or Aggregate itself, it can also Compose or Aggregate System Software. But *as a Node is not a System Software* it is wrong to conclude that System Software can Compose or Aggregate Node. If we want a Specialization of Node to be able to Compose or Aggregate Node, e.g. Facility Composes or Aggregates Node), it must be added specifically to the metamodel. This prevents silly conclusions such as System Software Composes Facility. In other words, in a metamodel-Specialization, you cannot inherit the relations from parent to parent.

36.5 Service as Composite Part of Function/ Process

There are two views of what a service is.

One is that the service is *visible* behavior that is *strongly coupled* to the *invisible* behavior. E.g. if you describe a selling process that creates a service which is used by a buyer, all the behavior that is visible to the buyer is an inseparable part of the process (and its description). It is not only part of the service, it is *at the same time* part of the process and the service is seen as the (visible) Composite part of the process. This, we could call the 'constructionist view' of a service.

The other is that a service provides some value to the environment and that it is an *abstraction* from the nitty-gritty details of the *internal* behavior (e.g. a function). In other words, some people want to see a service as an abstraction that is *weakly coupled* to the (independent) internal behavior. For them, the service is disjunct from and is *independent* behavior, for instance because the actual service delivery requires the behaviour of the service consumer to succeed*. This we could call the 'abstractionist' view of a service.

In the ArchiMate metamodel, the view is mixed: abstractionist on the side of the service and constructionist on the side of the interface, as can also be seen in the basic pattern of View 359.

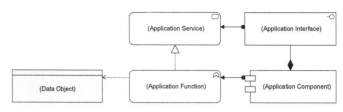

View 359. *The Basic Application Pattern*

The constructionist view fits reality better in my opinion. Suppose, for instance, you have a Business Process that Realizes a Service — say a Sell a Luggage Insurance Business Process that Realizes a Luggage Selling Business Service which Serves a Luggage Insurance Customer — the behavior that the Luggage Insurance Customer actually uses must be part of the Sell a Luggage Insurance Business Process. It cannot be otherwise. *There exists no behavior that Serves the customer that is not performed by the seller as part of a Business Process*. Suppose at some point in the Sell a Luggage Insurance Business Process the contract is presented to the customer. This is definitely part of what the customer experiences, it is 'exposed' behavior, but it is definitely *also* part of the 'internal' behavior, because it is part of the process. Or have a look at View 360, which shows in BPMN how the visible/exposed behavior cannot be anything *but* part of the service provider's process.

In other words: the insurance seller's 'offer the contract for signing' activity is both part of its process but also a part that is externally visible/usable, that is exposed. It is the *same* activity, *not* something independent. Looking at it as something independent introduces an abstraction that makes life more difficult, not easier. After all, we must remember: the best model of the world is the world itself.

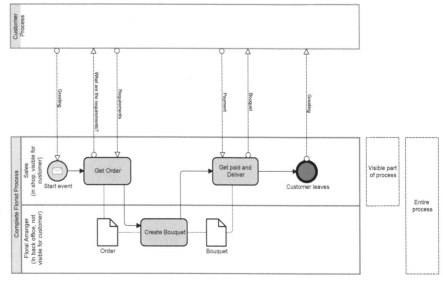

View 360. *Selling Flowers. Exposed behavior is part of the total process.*

---

* A rather transactional view. There are clearly services that can exist without anyone consuming them, such as broadcasts. See also the footnote on page 208

Important to note for this is that I am not talking about modeling the nitty gritty details, even if my argument to make the split different stems from the analysis that the 'external' (detailed) behavior must be part of the 'internal' (detailed) behavior. Both the internal behavior (e.g. process) and the external behavior (service) may be abstract in your model. After all, the fact that, e.g., Business Process and Business Function are hidden from the outside world does not mean they must be detailed. We think in 'hiding the details' but in Enterprise Architecture models you will not want to see something like the process details anyway. For that, we have languages like BPMN. The Business Service is always an abstraction of actual behavior, but so is a Business Process in ArchiMate.

Hence, from a constructionist view, the external behavior must be a *part* of the internal behavior, just as the external interface already is a Composite part of the Node, Business Role or Application Component, offering that interface to the outside world. In other words: from a constructionist view we have 'behavior' and 'external behavior' which is part of 'behavior' and the obvious relation is a Composition.

In the original ArchiMate, there was no Requirement element type. Given the importance of the service consumer, it was logical the requirement side ended up (informally) in the service concept. When thinking along the lines of 'business requirements drive service definition' — hence, outside-in — service also got a role as the 'requirement/value' side, the side that has to do with the consumer. On the interface side, this thinking was mirrored in 'required/provided' interfaces (an aspect already removed from ArchiMate).

But now that ArchiMate has the Motivation Extension to cover the requirement side, I think that we have the means to make a clean cut: the Requirement concept from the Motivation Extension covers the 'requirement/value' side and we can see the service itself — cleanly — as the 'externally usable ('exposed' as ArchiMate itself now puts it) *part*' of the provider's behavior (which has a meaning for the environment). In fact, it has been originally defined that way by the ArchiMate designers. The standard says about the generic 'service' concept:

An external behavior element, called a service, represents an explicitly defined exposed behavior.

The standard explains:

Thus, a service is the externally visible behavior of the providing system, from the perspective of systems that use that service; the environment consists of everything outside this providing system. [...] For the users, only this exposed behavior and value, together with non-functional aspects such as the quality of service,

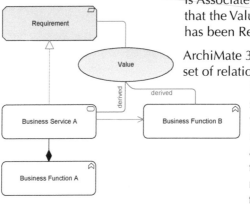

View 361. *Constructionist Interpretation of Service, Combined with Motivation Extension Requirement*

costs, etc., are relevant. These can be specified in a contract or Service Level Agreement (SLA). Services are accessible through interfaces.

The point I am making can be summarized as:

- the service is behavior and *all* behavior of the performer (the process) is an integral whole of which the 'exposed' is a *part*;

- the fact that you can (and probably should) *design* a service independently does not mean it should *exist* independently.

Interestingly. The definitions in ArchiMate 3 have changed from ArchiMate 2 and now support a 'service as exposed *part* of behavior' very well. E.g. for Business Service:

- *ArchiMate 2*: A business service is defined as a service[*] that fulfills a business need for a customer (internal or external to the organization).

- *ArchiMate 3*: A business service represents an explicitly defined exposed business behavior.

Instead of the need and the customer, we now only have the explicit mention that it is 'exposed' behavior Note: 'exposed' does imply that it is behavior solely by the 'exposer'.

The structure surrounding the service concept then becomes like View 361 (example at business layer level), where the service is a Composite part of the function. Using the Motivation Extension, the service Realizes a Requirement which is Associated with a Value. This more or less states that the Value is only there when the Requirement has been Realized, which is kind of nice.

ArchiMate 3 has dropped Association from the set of relations for which derivation rules exist. It would however be nice if some sort of derivation with Association would remain possible as long as the relation also plays a role in the actual metamodel. Hence, I've kept it in the example so show what would be nice derived relations. Together the two orange relations would allow the derivation of the red Association linking Business Service to Value. And as Business Service A can be used by Business Function B, the red Association and the green Serving could be used to derive the blue Association. In other words: Business Function B has an association with the Value (because that Value is there when Business Function B uses Business Service A. I am not yet certain whether I want that derivation both with structural and dependency relations.

I too suspect that in the behavioral column, it has been more natural to talk about a service as being 'created' (the 'second' type of realization in Section 36.3 "Issues with abstractions" on page 208) because the behavioral column is all about 'doing' and 'creating' is a verb. In the active structure column, it could only be sensibly seen as an interface being

---

* Which before haeen defined as: "A service is defined as a unit of functionality that a system exposes to its environment, while hiding internal operations, which provides a certain value (monetary or otherwise)".

'part of' an Application Component or Node or Business Role. But it works as well (even better) if we just see the service as a (usable) part of the function, just like the interface is a (usable) part of the role/component/node. Not external/internal division but exposed/all.

Changing the Realization relation (between function/process and the service it provides) to a Composition relation also removes the unnecessary difference between the behavioral column and the active structure column. The result looks like View 362.

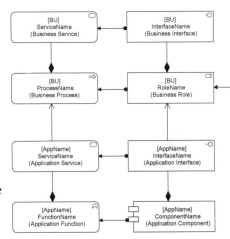

View 362. *Proposal: A service is the Composite usable part of a Function*

This also has the effect that — using the current derivation rules — the derived relation between an active element and its service is always Assigned-To, it no longer depends on the route taken, which is also kind of nice.

36.6 Automated Processes

In Edition II of Mastering ArchiMate, I proposed a few changes. One of these was to use (identity-)Realizations to model automated processes. The idea was that application (and technology) layer would be able to Realize representations of themselves in higher layers. This would make it possible to better combine automated and non-automated elements of your landscape in a single structure. By having an Application Component Realize a (robotic) Business Role, the (robotic) Business Role could be modeled as a full-fledged business entity together with the humans. The proposal can be seen in View 363. This is the 'automated process' version of View 362 on page 211. They are the 'service-is-part-of-behavior' metamodel suggestions of ArchiMate's two ways of looking at layering (See 12.10 "Layering Ambiguity" on page 54).

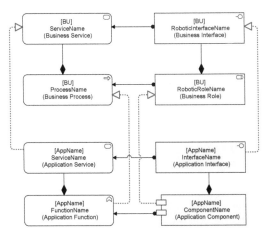

View 363. *Proposed meta-model Realization relations for automated processes*

Now, ArchiMate 3 comes with the three blue Realizations, but not with the red one. It also has added the same pattern to the metamodel between Technology on the one hand and Application and Business layers on the other. Suddenly, the 'identity-Relations' (see Section 12.10 "Layering Ambiguity" on page 54) have become center stage.

I'm not yet quite happy with this. What I like is the flexibility it gives you to have lower layer elements play a first class citizen's role in the business layer. What I don't like is the fact that the derivation of an Assignment (e.g. from Node to Technology Process) followed by an *identity*-Realization (e.g. from Technology Function to Business Function) derives into a Realization. There are two major problems with this.

The first is that the Realization from Node to business behavior misleadingly suggests that the Business Process is an abstraction of the Node. The second is related to this but more practical. Take the semi-automated process in View 364. The

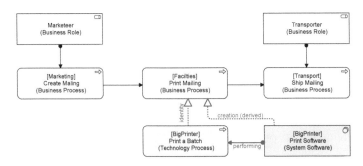

View 364. *Technology performing business behavior*

marketeers prepare a mailing, the big printer system prints it and the transport people ship it. In ArchiMate 3, we can add the Print Mailing (Business Process) and let it be (identity-) Realized by the Technology Process that is performed by BigPrinter's software. Now, you might not want the intermediate clutter and the nice thing is of course that you don't need it. It is perfectly all right to model the System Software to perform that automated business process. The derivation of the (violet) Assignment and the (red) Realization is the (blue) Realization. So, our diagram becomes (View 365):

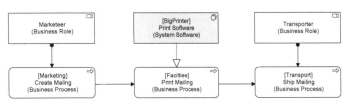

View 365. *View 364 with the technology behavior left out*

So far so good, but these three Business Processes are not full end-to-end processes. They are mere steps, sub-processes, in the whole. If we add the whole we get View 366 on page 212.

Now, suppose we want to get an ever simpler, more abstracted, diagram. We *are* architects, after all. We just want to show the overall Business Process and who performs it. We can do that as shown in View 367:

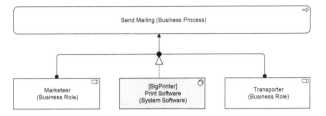

View 367. *Modeling how people and automation together perform the semi-automated process of View 366*

Sadly though, we can't. Because we are not allowed to have different types of relations on a Junction. And that is a wise constraint of ArchiMate because it would be totally undefined what a Junction means if it was allowed.

The problem can be easily solved:

36.7 Changing the Strength of Assignment and Realization

The strength order of structural relations was decided upon, but I have no documentation of why that particular order was chosen and privately I have been told it was more intuitively decided than reasoned. Part of it may have been the result of the 'abstractionist' (weakly coupled) view on the service concept.

What happens if we switch Assignment and Realization in the strength table for deriving structural relations? If we start in the middle of the ArchiMate meta model, the basic Application Pattern (see View 359 on page 209), the *derived* relation of the route from Application Component via Application Function to Application Service changes from Realization to Assignment. Incidentally, that is the same result that we get if we follow the route from Application Component via Application Interface to Application Service.

This is kind of nice in two ways: first, because the derived result does not depend on which route you take. But secondly, because it is kind of nice to have Assignment as the resulting relation between an active component and a behavioral component. It means that you never break the pattern that an active element is Assigned-To a behavioral element. And that is a much more direct statement about your landscape (who does what) than the fuzz that the architect's abstractions bring.

In the real ArchiMate meta-model, the derived relation from Node, via Assigned-To to Artifact, via Realization to Data Object and via Realization to Business Object is Realization. If we switch strengths of Assignment and Realization, the resulting relation would become Assigned-To in its meaning of 'resides on'. In other words the Node is Assigned-To the Business Object, or, the Business Object resides on the Node, which is I think a slightly cleaner way of looking at it than that the Business Object is 'an abstraction' of the Node.

When we change these strengths, the derived relation of "Device Assigned-To Artifact Realizes System Software", be-

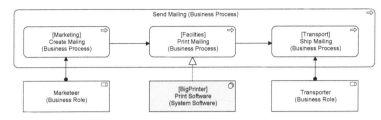

View 366. *The process steps of View 365 Aggregated in an overall parent process*

comes Assignment, which is also the direct relation that still exists in the metamodel, which can than safely be removed cleaning up the baggage of the past.

Another effect is that System Software that is Assigned-To Artifact that Realizes an Application Component becomes a derived Assignment. We nicely get that Application Component — just like System Software — can be deployed on System Software. As is the fact in the real world.

In fact, I would like to see the (identity-)Realization relation become the strongest relation of them all. This makes a lot of sense. After all, what the identity-abstraction says is that both ends of the relation are the same thing, just differently represented. So for me, when someone wants to model TOGAF's logical Architecture Building Block and Solution Building Block, it makes sense that View 368 can turn into View 369.

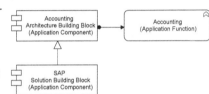

View 368. *TOGAF ABB and SBB*

And finally, I think it makes a lot of sense that the red and blue Access relations in View 370 would be derivable from the others as well. After all: if an Artifact Realizes a Business Object, then the Technology Function does Access the Business Object. But also the other way around: if the Business Process Accesses the Business Object,

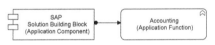

View 369. *Derivation from View 368*

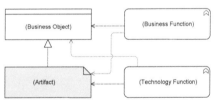

View 370. *Meaningful derivations*

it really does Access the Artifact. They are, after all, the same, but represented differently *in the model*. For that, the (identity-)Realization must not only be the strongest, it must also be bidirectional. Which brings me to some proposals on derivation.

36.8 A better derivation algorithm

One of the main troubles I have with the derivation mechanism is that it turns the proper meaning of derivation via Composition and Aggregation on its head. The funny thing is that ArchiMate already has a better mechanism available: the derivation of the dynamic relations via the structural ones.

What does it actually mean for the children in Compositions and Aggregations if some element has a relationship with their parent? What does it mean for the parent for some element to have a relationship with its children?

ArchiMate has taken the Composition and Aggregation relations from UML. But UML has been designed for software engineering and its idea of Composition and Aggregation has much to do with pointers, memory allocation and deallocation (see below). One can (should) wonder how appropriate their wholesale adoption is in an enterprise architecture setting.

For a look at the meaning of relations with children or their parents and how these are related (or can be derived), I am going to introduce a generic non-IT example: a driver stops his car at a rest area where he can get gas and buy food.

In our example, we have a car with an owner/driver. The simplified car has parts: an engine and a set of wheels, of which one wheel is the spare wheel. The rest stop has a gas station and a market, both owned by different proprietors. To make matters interesting: it is the market that owns the tyre inflating apparatus. Now, the engine needs gas and the wheels need air and the driver needs food. Nested, it looks like View 371:

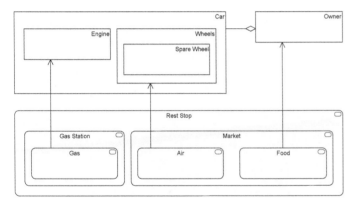

View 371. *The Car and the Rest Stop*

If we unnest this to uncover the hidden relations, we get View 372.

In using Composition and Aggregation I have made a couple of choices, which are of course debatable (otherwise, as Uncle Ludwig explained, they would not be choices, would they?). E.g., I consider both wheels and engine to be inseparable from the car. This is not from all possible perspectives so, e.g. they can be removed or swapped. But here I do subscribe to the definition that a car without engine and wheels is not a car — as you cannot use it as one. In natural language, the meaning of any word, including the word 'car', is not that strictly defined. But bear with me: in our setting: it is not a car if it does not have an engine or wheels. I have made the Spare Wheel something that can be removed from the car without this action rendering the car a non-car, though.

Now, the owner is going in for full service: he fills the car up with gas and air and himself with food.

If we follow ArchiMate's derivation rules from the bottom up, everything seems fine at first. Up to Engine and Wheels of the car. The gas pump Serves the engine, the air pump Serves the wheels (note: I'm using the 'serve' word freely here, this is not important for the argument).

But wait: Starting from Food via Owner, we can, according to ArchiMate derivation rules, deduce *that the engine and the wheels are using Food*. And we *cannot* deduce that the Car is using Gas (or Air). We cannot solve that problem by connecting the Serving from Gas to Car instead of Engine, as this would result in the Wheels using Gas. Hmm, there is trouble in the land of ArchiMate: the derivation rules are not producing sound results.

Now ArchiMate says: if you have a Serving with a parent of a Composition (or Aggregation), you have it with all its children. But that is plain silly. It is as if you say: if you model a Serving relation between the File Sharing Technology Service and the Trading & Reporting application, it is therefore true that both Trading *and* Reporting use File Sharing. But you cannot deduce that in the real world. You cannot even say

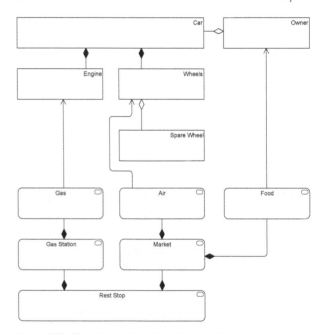

View 372. *The Car and the Rest Stop — Un-Nested*

"either of them does" as there might be a third subcomponent that wasn't modelled. There is, after all, no ArchiMate modeling law that says a model is valid if and only if all (sub-)elements are modeled.

What you *want* to be able to deduce is in fact the other way around: if a child uses something, so does the Composite parent. If the Engine uses Gas, it means that the Car uses Gas because the Engine is part of the Car.

Changing the direction of Composition and Aggregation for derivation would solve that particular problem but it would immediately create the same problem in the lower half of the diagram. There is an alternative that works much better. The rule says:

If there is a structural relation from element B to element A, then you may move the connection of a

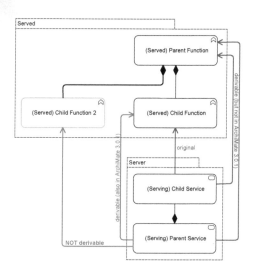

View 373. *Derivation of Composition and Serving. Composite child service Serves Composite child function*

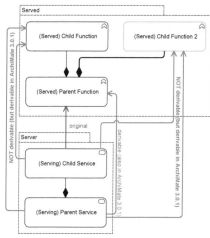

View 374. *Derivation of Composition and Serving. Composite child service Serves Composite parent function*

dependency relation, that starts or ends at element A, to B.

This derivation is *independent* from the direction of the dependency relation. In fact, it resembles what ArchiMate already has for derivation for the dynamic relations, which is also about end points. This solution is thanks to Jean-Baptiste Sarrodie, who thought about if first and put me on this trail by asking me what I thought about derivations (that I had proposed before) in my original Capability proposal and then in the following exchange suggested the use of something akin to what was done with derived dynamic relations: moving endpoints. Honor where honor is due: it is a very smart and elegant proposal.

We take a look at Composition first. Have a look at View 373. In this view, the blue Serving relation and the black Composition relations are what has been modeled. They depict the Composite child of a service Serving the Composite child of a function.

The question is what can be derived. In Current ArchiMate 3.0.1, we can derive the green one, but not the orange and violet ones. It is OK that we cannot derive the orange one (and we also cannot derive it under the new rule, so that is good), but we would like to be able to derive the violet ones. Our new rule exactly does that.

Now have a look at View 374. Again the blue Serving relation and the black Composition relations are what has been

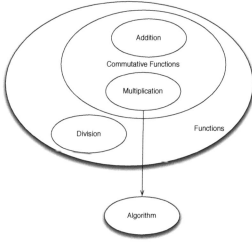

View 375. *A Venn-diagram*

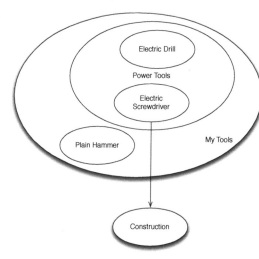

View 376. *My tools in a Venn-diagram*

modeled and the question is what we can derive. Again, the green relation is derivable in ArchiMate 3.0.1 as well as under our new rule. All the orange ones are derivable in ArchiMate 3.0.1 but we do not want them, they are unwarranted conclusions. And our new rule does exactly that: it does not allow them.

The upshot of all this is that if you want to be precise about which Composite children partake in a relation to the parent, you should model them to that child and not to the parent. The relation to the parent should be derivable.

With respect to Realization, If we (cleanly) only use Realization for the 'identity' role, as I would like, it becomes bidirectional and it can be used — instead of Composition — in this approach as well, just in two directions.

What about Aggregation? I have been thinking about this one and my conclusion is yes. The main reason is that — though the existence of the children here is independent from the parent — we might say that that if one child of a collection has a certain relation, then the collection has that relation. Think of it as Venn-diagrams (see View 375).

If we have an algorithm that uses multiplication, it can be said that it uses a commutative function (which is a function where you can safely swap arguments, as in a times b is by definition the same as b times a). We can also safely say that the Algorithm is using a function in general. But we cannot say it is using Division, which is a non-commutative function (a divided by b is not always the same as b divided by a). This is true, even if we have collections that are aggregations instead of compositions. Venn-diagrams don't say anything about this, you can use them for both if you think about it (it has to do with the dynamics of the sets, not any particular point in time), but for a better feel, see View 376).

If I lend my Electric Screwdriver to Jean-Baptiste, the Electric Screwdriver is (temporarily) a member of both 'My Tools' as 'Jean-Baptiste's Tools'. And if he breaks my Electric Screwdriver, this affects both Aggregate sets in their ability to provide the use of an Electric Screwdriver.

The other reason is that it is simpler to let Composition and Aggregation behave the same in derivation. And we like 'simple' don't we? Enterprise architecture modeling is complex enough as it is.

There is a last effect I need to discuss. What if we have Composition and Aggregation (e.g. a Parking Lot Aggregating Cars which Composite Engines)? I would say that any series of Aggregations and Compositions can be replaced by an Aggregation and any series of Composition by a Composition. The old and new rule have the same effect here. That part at least then will be backwards compatible. Always important for people who love 'backwards' ;-).

36.9 Allow multiple parents in a Composition

In ArchiMate, it is stated that an element can only be part of a *single* composition. It has taken that from UML, the modeling language for software engineering.

Now, in software engineering, composition and aggregation are (also) about memory management. Who owns what piece of memory? Who should free the allocated memory? When an element is a composite child of another element, if the parent is deleted, the child should be deleted also. However, when an element is an aggregate child of another element, and the parent is deleted, the child should be left alone. An aggregation only *points* to another element, it does not *own* it. In software engineering, accessing freed objects used (e.g. as a result of 'memory sharing') to be a major source for crashing applications, and not freeing objects used to be a major source for 'memory leaks'. Hence, 'memory sharing' and 'memory leaks' became a sign of bad programming in the early days and a paradigm has stuck, has become a foundational part of OO and UML:

- Composition means that you own the child. That means that if you are removed, you should also remove (free up) your composite parts (the 'children');

- Aggregation means that you do not own the child, you only point to it. That means that if you are removed, you leave the referenced ('child') alone.

This software engineering paradigm has been transported into ArchiMate (see Section 7.7 "Composition and Aggregation" on page 24). But ArchiMate has not transported it in full, it has also added a restrictive paradigm: with a few exceptions in the metamodel: Composition and Aggregation are only allowed between elements of the same (sub)type. This differs from software engineering where elements can both composite and aggregate elements from wildly different types. This is necessary in ArchiMate, because allowing any aggregation and/or composition would play havoc with the ArchiMate metamodel.

But relaxing the multiple-composite-parent restriction for Enterprise Architecture might be very useful as we *do* have real and unavoidable sharing in the real world outside of software engineering (and

with Garbage Collection, Automatic Reference Counting and such, the issue has become less of an issue in software engineering as well, where people now start talking about 'strong' and 'weak' composition). Take the following example. Suppose we model our Technology Services for the exploitation of applications as being composed of several parts, which we name 'infrastructure building blocks' (see 15.6 "Infrastructure 'Building Blocks'" on page 69). For instance, suppose an application requires a file share, a relational database and a system where the application is executed. In a previous chapter, we modeled this by creating a specific abstract Aggregation of Technology Services, that together form the Aggregated 'Exploitation' Technology Service that provides TI-support for the application. An example can be seen in View 377.

This aggregation breaks the possibility of having derived Serving relations between the individual building blocks and the applications that depend on them. Using derived relations, we cannot say, "[rs6sv001/db001] Oracle RDBMS (Technology Service" is Serving "[App Y] Reporting (Application Function)".

But what if we were to release that restriction on multiple parents in a Composition? Suppose we would allow true sharing as in the nasty 'memory sharing' of the early programming years? We could model it like in View 378.

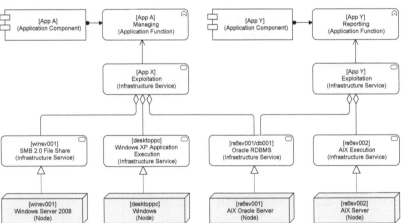

View 377. *Exploitation Technology Services based on Aggregation of (shared) Technology Service Building Blocks*

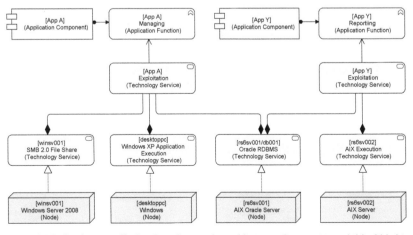

View 378. *Exploitation Technology Service based being a Composition child of Multiple parents*

In the Enterprise, true sharing is not only real, it is often even a desirable state of affairs, e.g. cost-wise. Now, if we would allow multiple parents in a Composition in ArchiMate, we could create real sharing in our models. Remember, if one of the now 'parent' Technology Services breaks, the 'child' Exploitation Technology Service, which in the case of App A in View 378 has three 'parents', breaks too. Which is as it should be. Now we *can* say: "[rs6sv001/db001] Oracle RDBMS (Technology Service" is Serving "[App Y] Reporting (Application Function)". So the advantage for this pattern (apart from enabling modeling true sharing as it is real in the enterprise) is that the official derived relations still can be used. (The proposed new rule of Section 36.8 on page 212) doesn't have that problem, though.) Other advantages are that abstraction less quickly lead to problems (e.g. see View 356 on page 203), enables constructions like several of those in Section 23 "Virtual Machines (Parallelization)" on page 118 (which are technically illegal) and removes the problem that with a Composite of a Composite the derived relation between grandfather and grandchild is formally illegal.

There is however also a disadvantage when used as in View 378. The aggregation version is easier to read for people and the use of the symbol becomes different from UML and that means another addition to the learning curve (this time especially for software architects). Multiple parents confuse. So, personally I can live with the aggregation version (the ArchiMate derived relations are too limited for most analyses anyway) and the fact that it does not clearly shows the real 'make or break' dependency of the abstract 'Exploitation' Technology Service on all its building block components.

We could also let a collaboration element be jointly owned by its parents. This is more realistic also from a derived relations point of view: If two Business Roles together perform an Interaction (or Process, see below) which Realizes a Service, there is currently no derived relation between any of the roles and the service, which we know both roles must be there for the service to exist. But the 'directional' limitation of derivation forbids the derivation. With the new rule for derivation we would get that we conclude from a Collaboration Serving something that all the elements that make up the Collaboration Serving that same something. If that is not true, then you do not have a truely inseperable collaboration, it seems

All in all, relaxing the single-parent limitation makes sense because true 'sharing/co-owning' is both reality and often a desirable state of affairs for the Enterprise (and thus ArchiMate models of that enterprise). It is not necessary to limit our view of the real world by software engineering sensibilities. After all, do we not all state from time to time that it is in the end about the business and not about IT? We are Enterprise Architects, not software engineers after all...

36.10 Make the Access relation multi-directional

ArchiMate 2.0 removed the bidirectionality of the Assignment relation that existed in ArchiMate 1, and that was a good move. That bidirectionality in ArchiMate 1 led to all kinds of senseless derived relations. ArchiMate 2.0 removed all of those and added the ones that were no longer derivable and that made sense explicitly to the core meta-model.

So, why propose now to make another relation bidirectional (after having done the same for (identity-)Realization)? Well, what drives this is a couple of realities, like:

- Some processes are just about Accessing an Artifact. You can imagine Data and Business Objects, but the labels you give these are just representations of the Artifact. They add to the complexity of the model, they do not add to the informational content of the model;

- Behavior may depend on passive elements, not only the other way around. A good example is application maintenance from 19.6 "Secondary Architecture: Application Maintenance" on page 106. Here, the application maintenance process edits a file, say an ini file, that influences an application's functionality. The application's functionality is dependent on the settings in the file (on the 'Settings' Data Object the Artifact realizes). Though the Artifact is shared, the Data Object isn't, which shows up when you make errors in that ini and the application crashes.

Actually, I think it is best to make the direction of the Access relation depend on its 'read/write' status:

- Read Access: direction from passive structure to behavior;

- Write Access (including Create and Delete): direction from behavior to passive structure;

- Both read and write Access, or undefined: bidirectional.

To illustrate what derived relations we can have when Access becomes bidirectional, have a look at View 379.

The violet and blue Access relations are the original ones. Under the ArchiMate 3.0.1 rules, none of the other Access re-

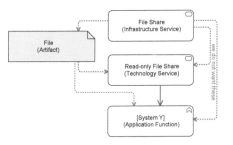

View 379. *Multi-directional Access derivation*

lations are derivable, because the Access relations runs from behavior to passive. However, if we use the multi-directional approach, the green Access relation becomes derivable from the blue Access and Serving relations. But now we also can derive the red Access relations and that is what we do not want. Luckily, the standard limits (in Appendix B) the derivation of Access to end-situations where one side is a passive element. This could be made birirectional. Note that if we limit Realization to the 'identity' role and we start using the

Access relation for the 'creation' role, the situation becomes more complex and the designers need to solve a more complex puzzle.

36.11 Why change ArchiMate?

I think ArchiMate is great. It is the best thing since sliced bread for Enterprise Architecture modeling. The language is not strictly formal, but its concepts and relations have been selected for usability, and as Uncle Ludwig explained to us, that it one of the best tests of meaningfulness.

The world of Enterprise Architecture stretches from the strictly logical world of bits and bytes to the not-always-so-logical world of human behavior. It is unavoidable that such a stretching exercise leaves its marks. So, it is easy to find (logical) fault with the language, as I have shown. But from a business perspective (a human perspective) it is very good at enabling you to model to the extremes of Enterprise Architecture. And the fact that — even without all these improvements — we still were able to use the grammar to the extent we did shows how powerful the language already is.

With the right use of patterns and the right discipline and a good knowledge of the powerful underlying ideas, you can take this language far. Even without the improvements proposed by me in this chapter.

But I do think cleaning a few things up and improving the language here and there would make it greater still. It is up to the — by nature (and rightly so) conservative— standards body to take that step. Standards bodies *should* be conservative and slow, or the standard would be too volatile to be a real standard. On the other hand: when 'backwards compatibility' becomes your main worry, and you cannot innovate, the standard will probably die.

It is up to The Open Group.

Tooling

37. Multiple Models of a Single Reality

You can create your views in a decent drawing tool, like OmniGraffle Professional for the Mac or Visio for Windows. For both applications, so-called 'stencils' are available, and you can use these to create views. In fact, you can use any drawing tool, the stencils and the smart behavior of the graphics only make life a bit easier. But the main problem of tools like these is that they generally are just that: a *drawing* tool, they create views but they do not create a *model*. Some not too complex work can be done that way: restricted to using ArchiMate as a help in explaining (part of) a landscape (See section 34.1 "Two modeling purposes" on page 200). For the rest, what you really need is a good *modeling* tool.

It is important to realize a very important aspect. *There will* by definition *be multiple models of the same reality in your organization.* There is no single model-based tool that supports all uses of any model of your enterprise. The help desk needs a model of all the infrastructure and applications that run on it and if they are professionals, they want to know what business processes are supported. They might want to add aspects like application owners, process owners and such. All this you can do in ArchiMate. But their model needs more: they need to log incidents against applications, they need incident management work flow support and case management, etc.. The operational risk managers on the other hand need a model with risks, control objectives, control measures and also the business processes, functions, roles and actors involved. ArchiMate can do that. But they also need to store the actual assessments, have work flow support for incident management (and reporting on this), require strict access to maintained data, etc. The Business Continuity Managers need Continuity Plans with business processes and the Business Control people need detailed process descriptions with more detail than what is in your ArchiMate Current State model. In section 32.1 "The Satellite Model Approach" on page 195 we required information about the detailed structure of scheduler jobs, something we do not need nor want in our main EA models. The list is long and all these different uses require often subtly or not-so-subtly different IT support and every IT solution has its own model of its part of the organization's reality. And there will not be a single tool that is going to support them all. Your Enterprise Architecture modeling tool is not the tool to log incidents, store improvement plans, etc.

The consequence of this is that it is very important to realize that you will always, *by definition*, have multiple models of your Enterprise reality in your organization. And these different models even need to be used in conjunction sometimes,

for instance when auditors check how well prepared you are for calamities, and they want to look at your Security Architecture, your help desk setup and your Risk Management. If these three systems have an incompatible description of, for instance, your Business Processes, Business Functions, Roles, IT Services, etc., it will be impossible to get a good look. So what generally happens is that the people helping the auditors, create their own 'model' of the organization with everything that specific auditor need. What they create is often incompatible with what has elsewhere in the organization been documented and it will certainly be a duplicate or triplicate effort with another maintenance burden you do not want. You don't want that state of affairs.

Since you have to start from the assumption that it is unavoidable that there will be multiple models needed of your reality, the question does not become: "How do I create *the* best model?", but "How do I make sure the *different* models tell a *single* story?" and "How do I prevent a duplicate of effort?".

There are two ways to make that happen:

- Have one model be the slave of another (master) model. E.g. you export your Enterprise Architecture model from your EA modeling tool and you import it in another tool;

- Make sure all models are compatible enough so they can be translated into each other or reconciled against each other.

Which you use and — in case of the first approach — who is master and who is slave, how does synchronization work, is something that you need to design carefully.

For instance, in one of my previous jobs, we used our EA Current State model effectively as part of our CMDB. Our EA tool had a decent scripting language and import/export facilities. We exported our model (the master) in a way that it could be imported in our IT Service Management (ITSM) system (the slave). Projects that went live were added to our Current State model and thus exported to the ITSM system. But during day-to-day operations, small changes were documented in our ITSM system. The system automatically sent these to a mailbox of Enterprise Architecture and we added the changes to our model. New items got an id in the ITSM system and this id was fed back into our EA model as a property of certain elements. If we changed something in the Current State model and exported to the ITSM system, we could change names of elements, and the id made sure the new names were adopted by the ITSM system. Once in a while, we ran a reconciliation to find any item that had slipped through our net. It was difficult to get this right, but it is doable.

As you have seen in Section 30 "A Possible Linking of BPMN and ArchiMate", we also did link our Process Models with our Enterprise Architecture models. Again, linking these was done with a two-way synchronization, which was slightly more elaborate, but also offers freedom in tool changes.

For other systems (the software engineer's design system, the operational risk manager's risk management system, the process modeler's process modeling tool) we had to make sure that their model was compatible with the Enterprise Architecture model, which played the role of a central core repository.

38. Tool Requirements

Depending on your requirements, different tools may fit your bill. If all you want is directed drawing with not too complex views, many tools will do what you want.

For me, one important point is how the diagrams look. I find it important that the diagrams have a professional high-quality look. It might sound trivial, but if your diagrams look professional, this influences those that see them (even if they do not exactly understand them) and it engenders trust in your own professionalism. Yes, it is crazy, but it really has that effect. Therefore, tools that have poor graphics, that produce 'nerdy' or 'ugly' output (and I'm afraid, this is true for most tools I have seen) are for me not acceptable.

Having said that, the following aspects are important:

- Does the tool support everything in ArchiMate?

- Is the tool not overly restrictive?

- Can the tool handle large complex models and views without crashing, slowing down, etc.?

- Does the tool support a modeling style that is usable for large complex models and views?

- Is it possible to easily configure/use the tool such that it supports your preferred style?

- How good is the support for drawing tricks (e.g. layers, etc.)?

- Is the tool flexible when 'editing'? An example of editing flexibility: Change a Business Function to a Business Process without having to redo all relations (losing them in other diagrams in the process). Can you do 'ad hoc' overrides of visualizations (e.g. how a relation or element looks, changing the icon of an element, etc.)?

- Can you link between different (truly separate) models? Can you set up a good synchronization between different models?

- Can you influence standard layout (colors, standard labels, attachment points for relations, ordering of relations, etc.)?

- Does it have RESTful APIs for integration with the environment?

- Can you add your own metamodels? Easily?

- Does the tool have a good scripting language? Turing-complete, with goodies like regular expressions, object-orientation, and so forth.

- Can elements and relations be augmented with properties?

- Does the tool have good import/export facilities?

- Can the tool produce or make available reports for people that do not use the tool themselves? HTML5/Canvas/Javascript compatible web viewing? Do these reports work when:

    * Views are large and complex (e.g. interactive, or it not scaled such that the contents become unreadable)?

    * Some views should be reported but others not (e.g. do not report 'work in progress' views)?

- Can the tool produce vector-based output of diagrams (e.g. PostScript, SVG or — preferably — PDF), e.g. for large poster prints?

- Is the tool well supported? Is there a good helpdesk or is there an active and experienced user community for the tool?

- Is the tool's file format open for inspection (and emergency repairs)?

- Is it possible to anonymize models? This is useful if you want to send models to tool support or forums without having to disclose company-sensitive information.

- Does the tool have support for managing and reporting the change of architecture over time (other than the Implementation and Migration stuff, which is of limited use by itself)? E.g. can you 'time travel' in your model and have a single model with different elements & relations at different 'times'?

- Does the tool support BPMN and (the setup of) a good linking to BPMN (not any linking will do, simplistic linking generally fails in serious use)

The diagrams in this book have been made with BiZZdesign Enterprise Studio*. I am not affiliated with BiZZdesign.

---

* This statement should not be seen as meaning that it fully conforms to all the requirements in the list preceding it. It does, though, (as you may have noticed) produce very professional looking output.

This page intentionally not also left blank

Index

This page intentionally not left also blank

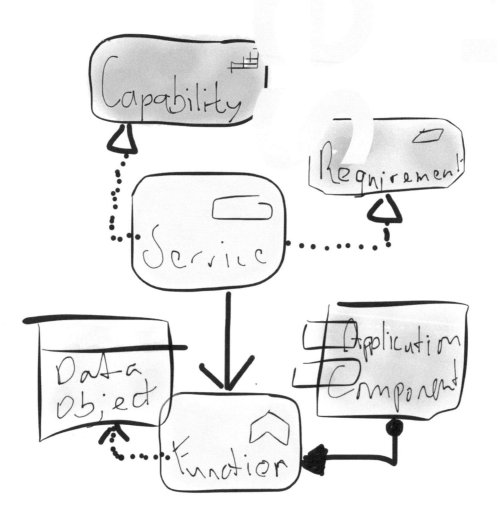

List of Figures

Finger

Finger

This Chapter contains material for easy reference while reading the book You keep one finger between this page and the next, as the next right-hand page has the ArchiMate meta-model.

Additionally: here is the overview of the Style Guide Items:

Style Guidelines

1. Make your relations in general go in vertical and horizontal directions only.

2. Don't let relations overlap

3. Minimize the number of line crossings

4. As far as possible: Group relations according to either source or destination

5. Align relations, even unrelated ones

6. Align elements, even unrelated ones.

7. Use as few as few different element sizes as possible (analogous to not using too many font sizes in a text document).

8. Align elements and attach relations such that relations are as simple as possible and with the least number of line crossings, preferably straight lines from one element to another.

9. If you have a nested element or groupings, align the elements that are on the inside as well.

10. Distribute elements evenly within their `group'.

11. *Make a view as easy on the eye, as 'quiet' as possible without losing essential information.*

One important remark on sizing and arranging: the above guidelines lead to views that are rather 'boring'. For technical views for your fellow architects, that should not be a problem. But when you communicate to non-architects, you will need to take far more freedom to get the message across (technical views do not have a 'message' per se).

Therefore, when I want to commnicate with non-architects (e.g. management or users), I will relax the approach above, or, I will use something else than ArchiMate for that specific message. A message is often only valid at a certain moment in time anyway, so doing a one-off is not really a problem.

This page intentionally not left blank also

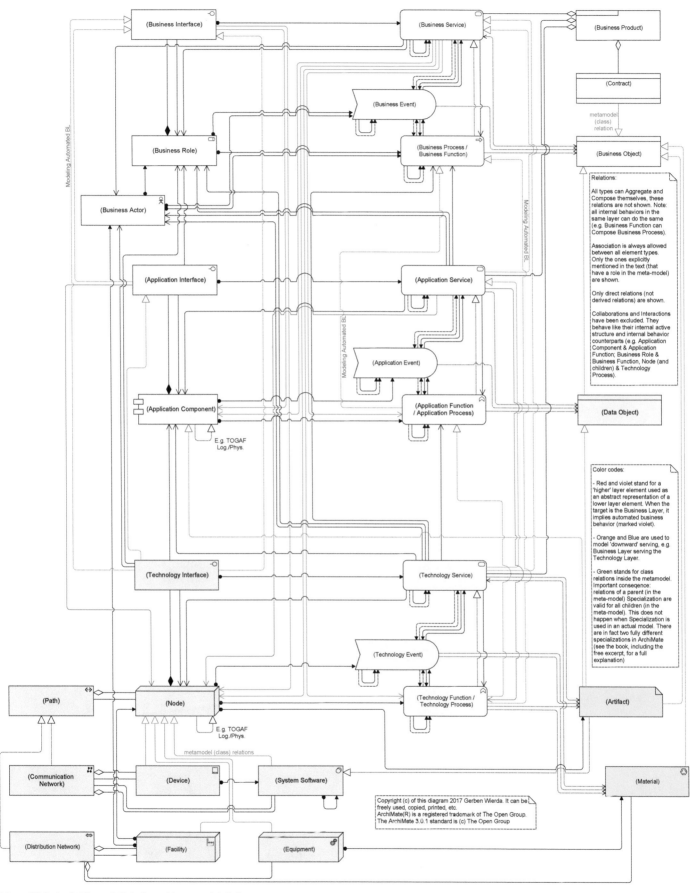

View 380. *ArchiMate 3.0.1 Core Metamodel. Selection*